The Modern Corporation

By the same author:

Public Choice, Cambridge University Press, 1979
Profits in the Long Run, Cambridge University Press, 1986

The Modern Corporation

Profits, Power, Growth and Performance

Dennis C. Mueller

Professor of Economics
University of Maryland

UNIVERSITY OF NEBRASKA PRESS
LINCOLN

658.4
M 946

© Dennis C. Mueller, 1986

Library of Congress Cataloging-in-Publication Data

Mueller, Dennis C.
   The modern corporation.

   Bibliography: p.
   1. Corporations.   2. Executives.   I. Title.
HD2731.M76   1986   658.4   85-20822
ISBN 0-8032-3104-0

Typeset in Times Roman 10 on 12pt
Printed in Great Britain

To Holly and Larry

Contents

An Autobiographical Essay

It requires a certain degree of egoistic courage to write things, say economics, down on paper and presume that others will wish to take the time to read it. It requires courage bordering on audacity to presume that others may wish to read one's autobiographical essay. Since others in the economics profession whom I know and respect have taken the egoistic plunge into autobiography, I have consented to follow in their footsteps. In reflecting upon the major developments of my intellectual life, I have been struck by the important role chance events played at several instances, as I shall make clear below. Here, perhaps, is a lesson worth learning.

My background is decidedly middle-class. My father did not graduate from high school, and worked for more than a quarter of a century as a cab driver. My mother did graduate from high school, and completed a short course at a business professional school that qualified her as a book-keeper. She worked as a bookkeeper both before my parents were married, and again after they were divorced in 1945.

From 1945 until 1957, when my parents remarried, I lived with my grandmother and my mother in the same house on the north side of Milwaukee in which my mother grew up. It was in what used to be a typical, ethnic Milwaukee neighbourhood. The same German and Italian families lived on either side of us when I grew up as when my mother was a child. I went to the same elementary school as she did and had many of the same teachers. Thus, despite my parents' divorce, my elementary and high school years were characterized by a degree of home environment stability that is far rarer today.

My mother was one of seven children and most of my family contacts were with my aunts, uncles, and cousins on her side. Only one of the six brothers and sisters completed college. Although the atmosphere at home was not unintellectual, there was little pressure on me to perform well in school and certainly little pressure to think about going to college as I progressed in the Milwaukee public school system.

Although I was more interested in sports than in studies during my high school years, my grades tended to be mostly As. Thus, it seemed 'natural' that I would go to college upon graduation from high school. Neither of my parents, nor any of my other relatives, gave me much advice, however, as to which college to attend or what to study. Since I was doing well in mathematics and science, engineering seemed the obvious choice for a college major. I had little idea, however, as to what it meant to be an engineer, and was certainly not enthralled by the idea of following this profession. I thus decided to apply to several liberal arts colleges that offered 3-2 engineering programmes. Although I did not much like the idea of having to spend five years to get a four-year degree, or even two four-year degrees, my lack of commitment to engineering as a profession led me to favour the flexibility of a 3-2 programme. Thus, when the time to apply to colleges came around, my applications were directed towards those schools offering the 3-2 programme.

At this juncture, important chance event number one arose. During the autumn of my senior year in high school an interviewer from a prestigious men's liberal arts college visited my high school. Following my interview with him, and on the basis of the advice of the high school counsellor for college studies, I had made up my mind to attend this college should I be awarded a scholarship. The college held an interview weekend in the spring, at which time prospective entrants for the autumn semester visited the college. Interviews with faculty members took place and it was on the basis of these interviews that scholarships were awarded. On the Saturday night of that weekend, a reception was held for the prospective students at the college. I met a couple of members of the college who had formerly been students at my high school. I and a couple of other recruits went off with them to their fraternity house after the reception. We sat around drinking beer and watching 'skin flicks' into the small hours. I am not now and was certainly not at that time prudish. Nevertheless, the thought of spending my weekends sitting around drinking beer and watching 'skin flicks' at an all-boys college near a small town in the middle of nowhere I found extremely unappealing. Upon returning to Milwaukee from the college, I decided I must go somewhere else.

My best friend throughout my youth was my cousin, Tom Dornbach. He was attending Colorado State College in Greeley at the time. He had been through Colorado Springs and was impressed by the town and had heard that the school there was "pretty good". On the basis of this sound advice, I placed an application with Colorado College. I was lucky enough to be awarded a scholarship in chemistry on the basis of my expressed interest in chemical engineering as part of the college's 3-2 engineering programme. The terms of its scholarship award were significantly less attractive than those of the prestigious men's college. Nevertheless, I decided to go to Colorado College, because of its co-educational status, and what seemed to someone who had never been further west than Madison, Wisconsin, its exotic location at the foot of the Rocky Mountains.

My first two years at Colorado College were arduous. My preparation in high school was probably somewhat weaker than those of my classmates, but most importantly being in the pre-engineering programme required that I take extra courses so that I could get in all of the liberal arts and engineering related courses I would need in the three years I was there. In addition, since my scholarship did not cover any of my living costs, I worked in the cafeteria as a waiter's assistant to pay for my meals. During my first two years, therefore, I had little time to pursue intellectual topics beyond those assigned in my science and mathematics-dominated engineering programme, and also little time to pursue anything else, including, ironically, the coeds at the college.

In retrospect, perhaps the most important event which occurred during my first two years at Colorado College was my exposure to one Professor Egbert Miles. Professor Miles had, like several professors at Colorado College at that time, retired from an eastern university, in his case Yale, to live in Colorado Springs and teach one or two courses at the college. Miles was my teacher for calculus over my first two years at Colorado College. He used a quasi-text written by himself. It started with the basic five Peano postulates and proved all of the major theorems in calculus from these postulates upward. Miles was an extraordinarily gifted teacher even then, when he must have been at least seventy-five, (his first position after his retirement from Yale had been at Wesleyan). Yet his enthusiasm for the subject matter was contagious. The first, subconscious inclination to become a teacher was undoubtedly born in Miles's class.

The third year in Colorado College's 3-2 engineering programme was spent catching up on the liberal arts part of the programme. I took psychology, philosophy and economics in that year. What different pictures of man and his behaviour were presented in these courses! For perhaps the first time in my life, I became totally absorbed in my studies. I found each course fascinating and could easily have been convinced to stay on at Colorado College and major in any one of the three, had I not been so far advanced in my study plan. But by the time thoughts such as these began to occur to me, I had already interviewed a representative from Columbia University.

Columbia had a nuclear engineering programme. Athough my original plan was to specialize in chemical engineering, I had found physics more interesting than chemistry and was thus attracted to Columbia's nuclear engineering programme (this was but a few years after Sputnik, and nuclear physics seemed very much the thing). The representative from Columbia thought I would have no trouble getting financial aid and so I applied to that school. It was the only one to which I did apply.

As the spring wore on, I continued to enjoy my chosen electives. The dates for hearing whether I had been awarded financial aid from Columbia passed. I heard nothing. One of my best friends at Colorado College had decided not to go on to an engineering school after his third year, but to stay on and finish a bachelor's degree. He was talking to one of the economics professors about doing graduate work in economics after leaving the college. I made an appointment to see my professor in principles of economics, Kenneth Curran, to discuss the same option. Kenneth Curran was the second, truly great teacher I had encountered at Colorado College, a school with many fine teachers. He had returned in mid-life to Princeton to get a Ph.D., and after a short stint as an assistant profesor at Princeton had gone straight into the chairmanship of Colorado's economics department. Curran thought I would not have difficulty getting into a good graduate programme in economics. During the second semester of principles of economics with Kenneth Curran, I decided to go to graduate school in economics and become a teacher. I never wrote to Columbia to find out definitely whether I had been admitted and received financial aid. The next year, the same representative from Columbia came to the Colorado College campus. He was surprised to find me there. I had been awarded a scholarship the year before. Notification of the award had for some reason not reached me. Had I been notified of the award at the proper time, I would have accepted it, and would have been off to Columbia to study nuclear engineering. What I would be doing today is anyone's guess.

As it was, I was finishing up a major in mathematics at Colorado College (the only subject for which my pre-engineering programme had provided me enough credits to graduate in four years) and thinking about going to graduate school. I approached three of the department's members for advice on which university to attend. Curran recommended Princeton. Al Johnson had studied at Stanford and recommended that school. Ray Werner had a Ph.D. from Nebraska, but had spent a summer at the University of Chicago, and was clearly, I can say today, influenced by the Chicago way of thinking. He recommended Chicago. I applied to these three schools and added MIT on my own initiative. I was applying for an NSF fellowship and thought the National Science Foundation would be more impressed by my application if I stated that I wanted to study at a science-engineering school. Also, I had studies principles from Samuelson's text and thought that a school good enough to have someone who could write such a fine textbook must be pretty good. Such is the sophistication of even a fairly intelligent college senior's thought process in choosing a graduate school.

I received the NSF, but by the time it was awarded my admiration and respect for Curran had grown still further. Moreover, I was taking public finances in the spring, from yet another excellent teacher, Ray Werner, and had decided I wanted to specialize in public finance. Werner touted

Richard Musgrave as the profession's leading authority in public finance, and Musgrave had just joined the Princeton faculty. Thus, Curran and I agreed that I should try to get the NSF fellowship transferred to Princeton. I succeeded and have never regretted the decision. But, a few years later when I became aware of departmental rankings, I realized that with more neutral advice I could easily have gone off to MIT.

But I did not. At the time I attended Princeton, they had a rule that second-year students must submit a Ph.D. proposal halfway through their second year and have it approved prior to May of that year, when one wrote the customary battery of exams which precede the dissertation. I had elected to take public finance in my second year, not knowing that Musgrave would be on leave during the first semester of that year. When the time came to hand in my dissertation proposal, I had not yet seen Musgrave in the classroom and had had no opportunity to work out a topic with him. I had taken industrial organization with Jesse Markham the previous Spring. The study of technological change and research and development was a new hot topic at that time. I did have some ideas for a thesis on R and D, and thus drafted a proposal on that topic. At first, I wanted to remain in the public finance area and formulated my thesis proposal as a cost-benefit study of R and D. It became obvious that this topic was unmanageable and so the cost-benefit part of the proposal was dropped. The thesis evolved as a study of the determinants of R and D, and set me off into the industrial organization field.

I was extremely fortunate that both Markham and Musgrave were at Princeton while I was there (both left for Harvard shortly after my graduate work was completed). I took the second semester of the public finance sequence from Musgrave. This semester dealt with the expenditure side of public finance. I was exposed to the classic works by Wicksell, Samuelson, Arrow and Buchanan, as well as the charismatic Musgrave himself. Ideas were implanted during this semester which would subsequently take root in several pieces of research.

The Ford Foundation had made a large grant to study technological change to a group of economists, which included my thesis advisor, Jesse Markham. Markham helped me tap into those funds and with them I financed my own R and D questionnaire, patterned after the NSF questionnaire. With the data I gathered from this questionnaire, I was able to write my thesis and produce several articles, one of which appears in this volume (chapter 5).

F. M. Scherer was also at Princeton when I was there. Many an afternoon was spent in discussion in his office, despite his not being officially on my dissertation committee and despite the pressures on his time that an assistant professor's appointment carries. Our paths have crossed many times since, to my continual benefit.

I was impatient to cease being a student and went into the job market in my third year. My thesis turned out to be based around empirical tests of two models. Only preliminary results on the first model were available when I 'went on the road' for my job interviews in December and January. My audiences were obviously unimpressed and no offers appeared during the usual time interval. Determined to be done with studenthood, I applied to places as far away as Edinburgh and accepted an offer to teach in Vancouver, Canada, at a school that had not yet opened, from a man I had never seen, Parzival Copes, then in England. My wanderlust had once again surfaced.

I was one of five that made up the department of business and economics at Simon Fraser during its first year. We were expanding by fourteen and recruitment was a major preoccupation. Since both the department and the university were spanking new, constitutions had to be drafted for everything. I was on the department graduate curriculum committee, its representative to the university's graduate curriculum committee, and on, and on. When an offer from the Brookings Institution arrived in March, I was wondering whether I would ever find time to do research at Simon Fraser. I decided to return to the East and do full-time research. Shortly after I accepted Brookings' offer, the rain clouds began to lift in Vancouver and I discovered the magnificent city and environment in which I was living. By the time I left for Washington in August of 1966, it was with great reluctance.

My dissertation had acquainted me with the work of Schumpeter and, like so many others, I was captivated by Schumpeter's description of capitalist development. During my first year at Brookings, I decided to study the growth of corporations, using a sort of Schumpeterian framework in which I analyzed growth by technological innovation, growth by marketing innovation, and growth by organizational innovation. The study was to consist of theoretical discussion illustrated by case studies. As an example of growth through innovation, I chose Xerox. Several trips to Rochester were made and I was fortunate in being able to interview Chester Carlson, Xerography's inventor, Joseph Wilson, the president of Xerox (then Haloid) when it decided to take up the invention, John Dessauer, the vice president in charge of R and D, who first brought the invention to Wilson's attention, and several other key executives. For my marketing innovation, I chose the discount department store, 'invented' by Eugene Ferkauf, the founder of E. J. Korvette's. As an organizational innovation, I decided to look at mergers. Since there were many *different* patterns to growth through merger, I had selected several companies to illustrate this form of growth.

It was through these case studies that the idea of the corporate life cycle impressed itself upon me. Xerox appeared to be going through such a cycle and was still in a fairly early phase of it when I was studying it (1967). Korvette had rocketed through its life cycle and had already been rescued from its creditors in 1966 through an acquisition by Spartan Industries, only eighteen years after Ferkauf opened his first discount store. Many of the companies, which chose to grow by acquisition, seemed to do so because they lacked any other avenue for growth, that is, they were in a mature phase of their corporate life cycle, when internal growth through technological and marketing innovations seemed blocked. This life cycle view of corporate development, gained during my research at Brookings, has influenced the way I look at corporate development ever since. It is apparent in chapters 6, 7, 8 and 9.

As I began to examine more closely each of the companies I had chosen to illustrate growth by merger, I discovered that it was typically not possible to claim that this growth strategy had been successful in the sense of increasing profitability. In some cases, growth-through-mergers had been clearly at the expense of profits and had nearly destroyed the firm. I looked around for a company which would clearly illustrate the positive side of the growth-through-merger strategy. I selected Litton Industries, a company frequently featured in the business press at that time (mid-1967) as the archetype, new-breed corporation that grew through acquisition.

As I was pulling together the various parts of the book, my showpiece example of growth-through-merger, Litton, began to disintegrate. The first articles on its myriad merger troubles began to appear. Litton began to look like the other growth-through-merger companies, successful at growing but not necessarily at generating profits.

It was at this time that I began to marry the idea that managers would pursue growth to satisfy their own interests and the life cycle idea. I had been greatly impressed by Marris's *Managerial Capitalism* and carried along his managers-maximize-growth hypothesis as one to be examined with my case studies. The growth performance of Xerox up through the late sixties had been extraordinary and its management certainly talked as if that was their primary goal. But Xerox's profit and common share performance had been equally spectacular and it was difficult to see any conflict between managerial and shareholder interests here.

The same could have been said of E. J. Korvette's until around 1960. But starting then its share price ceased to rise, and instead bobbed irratically around roughly the same mean value. Ferkauf had announced a policy of not paying dividends and ploughing back all of the earnings to finance the expansion of the firm. He owned enough shares so that takeover attempts could be warded off, and they were until 1966. Litton had the same policy of not paying cash dividends and Litton's managers also owned a substantial fraction of the outstanding shares. E. J. Korvette and Litton seemed to embody the kind of behaviour Marris described. Marris's model of managerial capitalism seemed to fit these and other mature corporations. I revised the book manuscript to include this theme.

Shortly after arriving in Ithaca in the autumn of 1968, the manuscript was finished. I sent it to Joe Pechman, then director of the economics section at Brookings. Pechman read the manuscript and said Brookings would not publish it. It was not the kind of thing Brookings published: case studies of corporations illustrating various arguments in the theory of the firm. I originally intended to submit the book to another publisher, but never did. John Tilton had been working on his book on transistors when I was there and we had written a paper that incorporated some of the insights he had gained from his work on transistors and I on xerography (chapter 6). The *Quarterly Journal of Economics* accepted the theoretical introduction to the mergers' case studies (chapter 9) and I had begun a major empirical study with Henry Grabowski. Although it seemed a waste not to publish all of the case study material I had written, particularly that based on the interviews with the key personnel at Xerox, the two years at Brookings turned out to have had a major impact on my future research. I had gained insights into corporate behaviour and the modern capitalist process that influenced my work for the next two decades.

Besides the two articles just mentioned, one other publication came out of my stay at Brookings, which was to be an important precursor of future research. In 1966, James Coleman published an intriguing article in the *American Economic Review* in which he claimed that 'logrolling' in Congress served to reveal individual preferences and thereby produced a social-welfare-function-like outcome. The paper rekindled my interest in public expenditure issues. I thought Coleman's analysis was incomplete and furiously wrote out a comment in which I proposed the creation of Walrasian-like markets for votes. It became my first *AER* publication and my first contribution to what would become the field of public choice.

I arrived at Cornell just as Alfred Kahn was leaving the economics department to become Dean of the Arts College. I was sorry to learn of this at the time and my disappointment grew as I came to realize just how brilliant a mind Kahn has. But even as Dean, Kahn took the time to read some of my papers and offered many truly insightful comments. I sometimes wonder how much more research I might have done had Kahn been just another colleague down the hall.

As it was, my main collaborator while I was at Cornell turned out to be someone at Yale. Henry Grabowski and I had been graduate students together at Princeton and had both done dissertations on the determinants of R and D using an overlapping data set. We first decided to follow up our dissertation work, which involved cash flow models of R and D, by recasting the simultaneous equations model I had employed in my dissertation in such a way so that we could test a managerial version of the model against a neoclassical one (chapter 5). This paper led to several others (e.g. chapter 8). Certainly one of the luckier things that has happened to me down through the years is to have had Henry as collaborator and friend.

Not too long after I arrived at Cornell, the School of Business and Public Administration hired Bob Tollison and Tom Willett. By then I had found time to scratch my Public Choice itch and had several papers going in this area. The three of us teamed up for a few more. In addition, Bob suggested to James Buchanan that I might be a good candidate for the post-doctoral fellowship the Public Choice Center awarded each year. In the autumn of 1972, I found myself in Blacksburg, Virginia.

It was my first personal contact with both James Buchanan and Gordon Tullock. Buchanan is as impressive in person as he is on paper, one of the truly great intellects of the profession. Tullock dazzles with a stream of facts and questions. In addition to these two giants, the Public Choice Center had several fine younger scholars, and an impressive list of visitors. James Meade spent the spring there. That year in Blacksburg added several strands to my research, particularly in public choice.

In December of 1973 I presented a paper at the AEA meetings in New York, at a session which included papers by John Rawls and James Buchanan. I came across a former Cornell colleague, Paul Hohenberg, in one of the hotel corridors, and we began to exchange greetings. As so often happens in the chaos of an AEA convention, someone else came by, who knew Paul, and I began chatting with the person with whom Paul had originally been talking. It turned out he had the same last name, 'aber mit Umlaut'. Jürgen Müller had studied at Stanford with Paul, and was now at the International Institute of Management in Berlin. Although the institute was only three years old, I had heard of it because Mike Scherer had gone there. But Mike was leaving, I then learned, and they were looking for someone in industrial organization. My 'wanderlust' was again stirred, and come September of 1974 I was in Berlin.

The IIM's research programme was organized around projects. To make sure that what I was doing would be acceptable to the institute's directors, I had proposed, prior to accepting an offer, to conduct an international comparison of merger activity. I had published one paper on mergers in 1969 (chapter 9), but beyond that had done nothing on the topic. Nor had anyone else done much on the 1960s' merger wave at that time, especially in Europe. An international comparison fitted in well with the character of the institute. The idea was to collect data and test a common set of hypotheses across as many countries as possible. The first year was largely spent using the institute's ample travel budget travelling

Europe to find willing and able participants for the project, and working up the set of hypotheses to be tested. I was lucky to find scholars meeting these criteria in six different countries.

To my knowledge, no study exists in economics of precisely the same kind as 'the merger project': seven studies conducted by seven sets of scholars for seven different countries, each testing a common set of hypotheses for nearly the same time periods using a common methodology. Having spent six years acting as entrepreneur, manager, cheerleader, and final product editor, I now know why. But the merger study was in many ways a most rewarding experience. Its main findings are reviewed in chapter 10.

The history and reputation of Berlin are such that many wish to see it. We had no trouble attracting outstanding vistors. Oliver Williamson visited and presented a quasi-critque of Stephen Marglin's 'What do Bosses Do?' About the same time, Michael Jensen came through and presented his paper with William Meckling on agency costs. My colleague Felix Fitz-Roy and I found ourselves in partial disagreement with both papers. The seeds were sewn for what would eventually become chapter 3.

Another visitor was Keith Cowling, who stayed the summer of 1975. I had initiated a brown bag seminar in *IO* shortly after my arrival at the institute. Since our numbers were small, we often discussed work emanating from outside. One such session, while Keith was visiting, was on Comanor and Smiley's *QJE* article on the costs of monopoly. The paper got us thinking about the original social cost of monopoly question Hargerger had posed, and eventually to the paper, which appears as chapter 12.

Indirectly, it also led to chapter 13. In writing chapter 12, Cowling and I had to wrestle with the conceptual issue as to how a world, which was perfectly competitive in all markets, really would look. The answer we gave, although breaking with tradition in some respects, was, like the literature preceding it, a static representation. But, this exercise led me to begin to try and evisage how a world, which was perfectly competitive over time, would look. I can recall quite vividly, barging into John Cable's office one morning to try out on him the methodological ideas that were to underlie chapter 13.

Another visitor to Berlin was Robin Marris. Robin had taken over the chairmanship at the University of Maryland in the autumn of 1976, and came to Berlin to give a seminar that year. Discussions began on what was to become a move back to America, to the city of College Park. Thus, in August of 1977 ended three of the happiest and most productive years of my life. I had arrived in Berlin carrying the scars of a recent divorce. I left with a wife and a new-born son. Such is the attraction of Berlin, and of these memories, that I have returned several times since. Indeed, I write these lines on one of those occasions.

Although Robin Marris's presence at Maryland was one of the attractions in going there, his chairmanship duties kept us from having much intellectual contact during the first couple of years. An invitation to Robin from Mark Perlman, to write an essay on corporate capitalism for the *Journal of Economic Literature* led to lunch to discuss what might go into such a survey. My work on the social costs of monopoly had led me into the rent-seeking and nonprice competition literatures and I thought that that was a dimension of capitalist competition that was underemphasized. Robin agreed, and the capstone essay to this volume was underway.

A few months after my arrival at Maryland, I was asked to give a seminar at the FTC. I was interested in following up my paper on the persistence of profits with a larger study to explain why one observed persistent differences in profits across firms. I had learned that the FTC had collected market share data for 1972 as a follow-up to their 1950 survey. I wished to test for the impact of market share on profitability and inquired about the availability of the 1972 data. Dave Qualls was head of the Industry Analysis section at the time. It turned out that he had recently completed a paper on the profit-stability question, and was interested in the persistence issue. Thus began a research project that was to last too long, and a friendship that was to end too quickly. One meets but a few people in one's life for whom the adjective *good* can be applied to describe every aspect of their personality and character. Dave Qualls was one of these rare individuals.

The persistence of profits project proved to be as ambitious and exhausting as the merger project. But after five years, an FTC report did finally emerge in 1983, and fuller treatment of the issue is contained in a book, which will appear coterminously with this volume.

As the results regarding persistent differences in profits in the US began to take shape, the question naturally arose whether similar patterns could be observed in other countries. During my second sustained stay at the International Institute of Management between 1981 and 1983, I once again found myself contacting scholars from different countries to investigate whether systematic differences in profitability exist across firms in other countries. This study is currently in mid-stream with researchers from eight countries participating.

With this observation we are brought up to the present. My research agenda remains a mix of industrial organization and public choice, my travel horizons remain wide. With luck my sabbatical year 1986-87 will find my family and I in Australia for six months, and Turkey for six months. Perhaps, the next cross-national comparisons study will include these two, rather different countries.

Writing this autobiographical essay has forced me to look backwards, something I seldom do. I was struck, as perhaps the reader was, by how many truly important chance events changed the direction of my career's development. Moreover, in most cases it is difficult to say whether the chance event definitely improved or worsened my subsequent life. I wonder if chance plays as great a role in other lives as it seems to have done in mine. I often meet people at a small, unknown college in the United States or Germany, or outside academia entirely, whose knowledge and insight suggest that they might have led a truly productive research career under somewhat different circumstances. I can think of counter-examples at prestige universities, whom I observe with equal surprise.

On the whole, chance has been kind to me until now. I hope she will continue to smile upon me as the subsequent chapters in my life unfold.

Acknowledgements

Putting together this volume, while a fairly light job for the author, was a miserable job for his secretary. My intense gratitude is extended to Rebecca Flick for her cheerful and expert execution of this task.

The author and publisher would like to thank the following for permission to reprint the essays in this volume:

Kyklos (chapter 2), *The Swedish Journal of Political Science* (chapter 3), *The Quarterly Review of Economics and Business* (chapter 4), *G. DeBoer, North Holland* (chapters 5 and 8), *The Canadian Journal of Economics* (chapter 6), *Basil Blackwell* (chapter 7), *John Wiley and Sons* (chapter 9), *Oelgeschlager, Gunn and Hain* (chapter 10), *Elsevier Science Publishers BV, North Holland* (chapter 11), *Cambridge University Press* (chapter 12), *Tieto Limited* (chapter 13), and the *American Economic Association* (chapter 14).

1 Introduction

Adam Smith's invisible hand theorem remains today one of economics' crowning intellectual achievements. It takes the basic behavioural building block of the discipline, the assumption that rational individuals act to advance their own ends, and combines it with the focal point of much of economic analysis, competitive markets, to produce economics' most powerful normative proposition. The theorem has buttressed arguments for free trade from Adam Smith's day to the present. The movement for deregulation which has swept over the world is but another, recent example of the theorem's force.

The beauty of the theorem stems in large part from the almost magical way in which individual pursuit of own ends leads to the *unintended* aggregate outcome that no one can be made better off without harming someone else. Critics of *laissez faire* have emphasized the other, unintended consequences of market competition as for example on the distribution of income, and on the environment. The solution to problems such as these has seemed to many to replace the semianarchic institution of the market with one in which aggregate outcomes are a more direct consequence of individual intentions. Such an institution, at least as Max Weber (1947) described it, is bureaucracy. Not only are the individuals in Weber's bureaucracy rational, but the institution itself has a rationality, a logic, a set of goals that personify the organization. For at least a century now, bureaucracy has been the logical alternative to the market as a principle for organizing human action.

Both principles come together in the modern corporation, a bureaucracy operating in a market environment. To understand the corporation one must study the interplay of market forces and bureaucratic organizations. There is no better place to begin this study than Ronald Coase's classic paper written almost a half century ago. 'It can, I think, be assumed that the distinguishing mark of the firm is the supersession of the price mechanism' (1937, p. 334). Frederick von Hayek (1945) emphasized the informational role prices play in a market economy. Combining the insights of Coase and Hayek one recognizes the salient feature of the corporation, the supplantion of the price mechanism as a signalling device in favour of bureaucracy's hierarchical communication structure. More generally, one's study of markets and hierarchies is

1

focused on their relative efficiency as information gathering and processing institutions.

Information's value derives from the presence of uncertainty. Frank
Knight (1921) made uncertainty the determinant of profits in the market
economy. Profits accrue to individuals willing to take the plunge, to bear
the uncertainties inherent in economic activity. If they choose the right
industry, the right firm, the right time to enter, they earn positive profits.
Mistakes bring negative rewards. Successful entrepreneurs know when
and where to enter. Thus, knowledge along with the willingness to bear
uncertainty characterize the entrepreneur. Information emerges as the
key determinant of profits. This theme is developed in the essay, which
follows this introduction.

In a profit-oriented organization, successfulness in gathering and processing information leads to profits and those charged with these tasks
play the entrepreneurial role and earn the entrepreneurial reward. But
uncertainty also exists in non-profit-oriented organizations, and information has value here also. What is the reward to the information holder in
a non-profit bureaucracy? Power. In an uncertain environment, the information possessor can induce others to undertake actions they would not
have undertaken had they also been in possession of the same information. The relationship between information and power is developed in
chapter 3.

Possession of information in an uncertain world conveys power. Power
is the ability to induce others to act in your interests but not in theirs. In
an environment in which power can be monetized, power can be converted into profit. Using information to create profits is a special case of
the more general power–information relationship.

Information is the root cause of both power and profits. It plays a central role in explaining the existence and nature of hierarchical organizations. Individuals join together in certain production and consumption
activities to reap the benefits from indivisibilities. Joint supply creates
incentives to free-ride and the contractual arrangements binding in joint
consumption and production must be monitored. Information must be
gathered and those charged with gathering and evaluating information in
joint production and consumption organizations are in potential positions
of power *vis-à-vis* the other members of the organization.

In the modern corporation, the managers are the information
evaluators and decision makers, monitors of other team members'
behaviour. This role puts them in a position of some power, power to shift
the gains from cooperative productive in their favour. Conflict between
managers and other team members over the distribution of the gains from
cooperation is a natural consequence of management's specialized role as
information gatherers and the power asymmetric holdings of information

confer. Two conflicts have figured prominently in the literature of corporate capitalism: the manager–worker, or going back to Marx, capitalist–worker conflict, and the manager–stockholder conflict. Both are discussed in chapter 4 in which the salient characteristics of contractual organizations are described.

Thus, the focal point of Part I is information. Information is viewed as the prime cause of profits and power and its distribution in hierarchical organizations sows the seeds for conflict among the members of the organization. Parts II and III explore different aspects of the manager–stockholder conflict.

Management chooses product prices. It makes the investment decisions, which in the long run define the product mix. It decides what costs to incur. Over time its actions determine both the revenue and cost streams of the company. The decisions of how much of revenues are defined as profit, of how much profit is declared as dividends rest largely with management. To make these decisions, management must be in possession of all sorts of information about demand conditions and costs, investment opportunities and capacity constraints. It is the possession of this information that gives management power over the stockholders. Management knows what revenues and costs could have been, stockholders observe only what managers choose to define them as.

The discretion to define profits by choosing revenues and costs can be utilized to achieve a variety of managerial goals. On the job consumption, excess staff and emoluments (Williamson, 1964), security (Amihud and Lev, 1981; Fisher and Hall, 1969) and a host of other goals one might simply lump together under the X-inefficiency heading (Comanor and Leibenstein, 1969; Leibenstein, 1966). Joseph Schumpeter (1934, p. 93) placed empire building in first place on his list of entrepreneurial goals and noted that the private corporation is one of the few places remaining in society where this urge can be gratified. Behavioural support for the hypothesis that the personal goals of managers are tied closely to the size and growth of their corporation is abundant (Marris, 1964 ch. 2). The same behavioural assumption is typically made to describe bureaucratic performance in non-profit organizations (Niskanen, 1971).

Manager–stockholder conflict over the growth rate of the firm is in essence a conflict over investment policy. A management wishing to maximize growth chooses a short-run price to maximize current profits, because profits are the means to future growth (J. Williamson, 1966), just as a management pursuing excess staff and emoluments chooses quantity to maximize short-run profits (O. Williamson, 1967 ch. 4). Managerial discretion to pursue excessive growth lies in management's power to define investment opportunities and determine the retention ratio. Management is constrained, however, by the sources of investment funds available. While management can issue new debt and equity to finance investment, if the investment is excessive, if the investment promises a return below the owners' opportunity costs, going into the market to raise capital brings attention to management's suboptimal investments in a way reliance on internal fund flows does not. Moreover, external finance cannot be relied upon indefinitely to pursue excessive growth. Assuming that the capital market is governed by rational expectations, at least in the long run, the capital market will deny a firm capital to pursue investments at below market rates of return. In the long run, a management's ability to pursue excessive investment is limited by the available flow of internal funds.

Thus, the theory of the firm in which growth is a primary managerial objective implies a cash flow investment equation. The leading microanalytic theory of investment today is undoubtedly the neoclassical theory as developed by Dale Jorgenson in the late sixties and early seventies. Most directly related to the theory of the firm is Jorgenson and Siebert's (1968) testing of the neoclassical model against the cash flow and other investment models. They found the neoclassical model offered a fit to their time series data on fifteen companies superior to that of other models. J. W. Elliott (1973) retested the various theories using an expanded sample of 184 companies and both cross-section and time series estimation techniques. The cash flow model was superior to the neoclassical model in both the time series and cross-section tests.

In chapter 5, another test of the managerial and neoclassical investment theories is presented. It differs from these other tests in that the investment equation is imbedded in a simultaneous equations structure in which R and D and dividends are also determined. The neoclassical model appears inferior to the managerial model in a number of respects in presenting a complete view of corporate dividends and investment policy.

Marris's (1964) theory of the firm is a steady state theory. Managers pick a growth rate and retention ratio and stick to them. Demand, profits, the size of the firm and all other variables grow indefinitely at a constant rate. But demand does not grow indefinitely at a constant rate. Industries and firms are both subject to life cycle and business cycle effects. Of particular importance to the managerial theory are the life cycle effects. Whether or not and the extent to which a management over-invests relative to the investment that would maximize the firm's market value depends on the extent of its investment opportunities. Firms which are born from a Schumpeterian innovation often find themselves in a competitive-technological struggle for survival in their early years—Schumpeter's gale of creative destruction (see chapters 5, 6 and 7). The potential returns on investment are high and so too are the risks. All of the available cash flows will be reinvested and outside capital sought. Interests of management and ownership are one, raise as much capital as possible and survive. Indeed, managers often hold a large fraction of outstanding ownership claims in a young firm. As the industry matures, many companies fall by the wayside. Those that do not find that the pace of technological competition slackens. Profits growth outstrips investment opportunity growth. The potential for over-investment arises and with it the potential of manager–stockholder conflict over investment policy. Managerial pursuit of growth is a most serious problem with respect to the most mature firms in the economy.

This managerial-life cycle theory of the firm can account for several empirical regularities, which neoclassical theory has had limited success in rationalizing. The first is why it is that rates of return or reinvested cash flows appear to be significantly below the returns on capital obtained from external sources.[1] The second is why it is stockholders seem to possess an irrational preference for dividends over retained earnings—the so-called bird-in-the-hand fallacy. If managers maximize the present value of a firm's shares, they should choose a dividend payout such that at the margin shareholders place the same value on an extra dollar of dividends as they do on an extra dollar of retained earnings. But for many companies and industries shareholders prefer the extra dollar of dividends. A variety of auxiliary hypotheses have been put forward to reconcile shareholder preferences for dividends with managerial maximization of shareholder wealth: announcement effects, clientele effects, and the like (see chapter 7). Almost none of this literature attempts to test the most obvious explanation that shareholders may prefer a dollar of dividends to retained earnings because they can invest that dollar at a higher return than their company's management will.

In chapter 8, we estimate share price and dividends–retentions equations, along with returns on investment. The same companies for which shareholders prefer dividends to retentions are found to be earning significantly lower returns on investment. The irrational preference for dividends appears not to be so irrational. These firms with relatively low returns on invested capital are in mature phases of their life cycle in mature industries. For young firms or those in recently founded industries with high investment opportunities, stockholders do not prefer dividends to retained earnings. But for mature firms, which constitute a majority of the largest companies in the economy, the evidence suggests significant over-investment, as the managerial-life cycle theory predicts.

These results, along with those of others in support of the managerial theory, have important implications that go beyond the theory of the firm. Much has been made of the fact that leading firms in the United States' steel industry continued to invest in out-of-date technologies in the fifties and sixties (Adams and Dirlam, 1966). But this has been regarded as a peculiarity of this industry alone, attributable to its concentrated market structure and high entry barriers. Our results for the two-digit primary metals group indicate a strong preference by shareholders for lower retentions and greater dividends even in the fifties and sixties (chapter 8). Friend and Puckett's (1964) results indicate an even more dramatic preference for greater dividends for a more narrowly defined sample of steel firms in the late fifties. But steel and primary metals are not the only areas in which evidence of investment at rates of return below those available elsewhere is apparent. The steel industry's over-investment in obsolete technologies in the fifties and sixties is just one well-publicized example of the more general phenomenon that managers of mature firms continue to reinvest in their firms at below market rates of return to increase or maintain the size of their companies.

The shift from optimal investment levels to over-investment generally occurs so gradually as to be imperceptible. Investment schedules shift at a glacial pace, dividend payout ratios are adjusted infrequently. Thus, managerial over-investment policies go undetected. On occasion, a sufficiently sudden economic shock occurs to expose the magnitude of the over-investment phenomenon. Such a shock occurred in 1973 when the OPEC cartel significantly raised the price of oil. The immediate impact of the oil price rise would most plausibly be to reduce the returns on investment in existing technologies that were oil or energy intensive, or like autos were complements to oil. Investment in technologies that were substitutes for oil consumption or oil unintensive would be stimulated, but one would not expect a sufficient number of these to be available on the shelf so that technologies efficient at the new price ratios would fully displace those that were not efficient. Thus, a fairly substantial net decline in the aggregate, marginal return on investment schedule seems plausible. Assuming the cost of capital was not immediately altered by the same degree, the immediate effect of the OPEC price increase should have been a substantial decline in the level of investment, little change in the marginal return on investment, and either a build-up of cash reserves or an increase in dividend payments.

But none of this occurred. Instead, investment expenditures maintained a steady growth rate and the marginal return on capital plummeted to near zero.[2] Since profits declined somewhat, it was necessary to cut dividends to maintain investment levels (Hall, 1980, p. 507). Not surprisingly, given the returns these reinvested funds were earning in the seventies, observers of this period find once again a preference by shareholders for greater dividends (Brainard *et al.*, 1980, p. 500). What Part II claims occurs gradually over time as firms mature—over-investment in existing firms and technologies, low marginal returns on investment, stockholder preference for dividends–occurred almost overnight across a wide cross-section of the economy in the wake of the economic shock of the OPEC price increase and its reverberations.

Productivity declined steadily during 1973 and remained at unusually low levels throughout the seventies. Numerous industries in the United States have lost large fractions of their traditional markets to foreign competition. The experience of the steel industry has been generalized to much of the economy. Many explanations have been given for the poor performance of the United States and European economies in the seventies. None seems totally convincing. The theory presented and tested in Part II implies that capital moves slowly across firms and industries in response to changes in marginal returns on investment. Managers reinvest cash flows in their own companies even when more attractive opportunities exist elsewhere in the economy. The sluggish response of managerial capitalism to the oil price rise and other events of the sixties is quite consistent with the managerial theory of the firm.

When Schumpeter wrote *The Theory of Economic Development* at the turn of the century, those interested in founding 'a private kingdom' probably had to create one. Thus, for Schumpeter empire building and entrepreneurial activity went hand in hand. But today one need not build an empire to possess one; private kingdoms can be bought on the New York Stock Exchange.

Were it possible to buy up a company at its current market price in the equity and bond markets, and these markets were efficient, investment in other companies would provide a normal return. Companies could grow indefinitely and still earn the normal return on capital. But the acquisition of other companies typically requires paying a premium for their share, and lawyer, stockbroker and other transaction costs raise the gross price still further. Even at a price 25 per cent or more above their pre-merger market values, however, ongoing companies can provide a quicker and higher return avenue to growth than to reinvest in one's own, possibly declining product lines.

Chapter 9 reviews some of the leading hypotheses to explain conglomerate mergers and suggests a managerial interest in growth as a possible explanation. Chapter 10 reviews results from a seven country, cross-national comparison of the determinants and effects of mergers. Chapter 11 reviews the results from a variety of studies in the United States.

As with investment and dividend policy, the managerial theory is capable of offering explanations for several empirical paradoxes which the neoclassical hypotheses find difficult to explain: (1) why mergers typically come in waves and why these waves have tended to be procyclical; (2) why mergers do not lead to improvements in operating efficiency, profits, sales, or market share; (3) why shareholders of acquiring firms do not benefit from the mergers. The latter two paradoxes are easy to explain, if managers are pursuing growth rather than profits or stockholder welfare. Even losses in internal efficiency and internal growth can be acceptable, if they are compensated for by sufficiently rapid external growth. In an economic upswing, both profits and share prices rise. Thus, both the means for making acquisitions and the discretion to do so increase in an economic upswing. It is not surprising that managers choose to take advantage of these twin developments.

Once again, the hypotheses and literature discussed in Part III have ramifications that go beyond the theory of the firm, or theory of mergers. Since merger activity began its climb in the fifties, the United States' economy has seen over 30,000 mergers take place. The leading, neoclassical hypotheses see mergers as improving the allocation of capital in the economy and/or replacing bad managers with good ones. Yet, the United States' economy went through one of its poorest decades in terms of economic performance, immediately upon the heels of one of its most gigantic merger waves. Could it be that the microevidence, indicating a lack of efficiency gains if not losses resulting from mergers, is linked to the more aggregate economic failures of the United States economy? Hiroyuki Odagiri (1981) argues that Japanese managers, like US managers, are growth maximizers. But, in Japan, institutional differences make mergers a less attractive vehicle for growth. Thus, Japanese managers place a greater emphasis on internal growth than US managers. Could this help explain Japan's more rapid adjustment to the OPEC price increase in the seventies, and superior overall performance over this decade?

The performance of an economy can be measured along many dimensions. A traditional one is to compute the welfare losses from monopoly. In chapter 12, previous approaches to this question are critiqued and new estimates for the UK and US are presented. They suggest that the average welfare loss for a typical, large manufacturing firm is anywhere from four to thirteen per cent of its value added, depending upon how one chooses to measure monopoly welfare losses.

One of the innovations of chapter 12 is to add in rent-seeking outlays to the social costs of monopoly. Implicit in all previous estimates of monopoly welfare losses has been the assumption that all forms of competition are price competition, and thus that all of the social costs of monopoly are consumer surplus losses. But if companies invest resources to sustain or seize existing monopoly rents, these expenditures merely preserve or redistribute existing rents. They do not create new consumer's or producer's surplus. They do not improve the allocation of resources. These expenditures are part of the social costs of monopoly.

Chapter 12 implies that the social costs of monopoly, when measured in a static, partial equilibrium framework, appear to be rather large. The implication that monopoly may be a serious problem cannot be accepted, however, until one examines the impact of dropping both the static and the partial equilibrium restrictions. Unfortunately, empirical estimates of the welfare losses from monopoly using a general equilibrium framework appear to be beyond the current state of the art of empirical work in this area. Bergson (1973) presented some calculations for illustrative purposes a little over a decade ago and the literature has not advanced much beyond that point. The extent to which consumer's surplus losses measured on a firm by firm, or industry by industry, would 'wash out' when measured in a general equilibrium context remains an open question. Two observations on this point are in order. First, for policy purposes, it is not clear that the general equilibrium question is relevant. Most antitrust policies in execution focus on a given firm or industry. Only if one is trying to decide between eliminating all monopolies simultaneously versus repeal of the antitrust laws is the general equilibrium question fully applicable. Second, even if the consumer's surplus measures would largely was out, the wasted outlays on rent seeking, even in a general equilibrium context, would not. Thus, there are annual social costs to creating, maintaining, and transferring control over monopoly rents and these might be made the target of antitrust attack. Whether they should or not depends on what the benefits from the dynamic competition are, which leads directly to the issue of the effect of dropping the static framework when viewing the monopoly problem.

There are basically two criticisms one can make against the static nature of all estimates of the social costs of monopoly. (1) The profits from which the losses are calculated are only short-run, transitory rents. In the long run, they disappear and the long-run social costs of monopoly are much smaller if not zero. (2) Measuring only the social costs of monopoly gives a one-sided picture of monopoly's impact on social welfare. The potential for earning monopoly rents leads to a dynamic competition to create monopolies and society benefits from the innovations this competition produces.[3]

Chapter 13 presents evidence that a substantial share of the differences in profitability observed at one point in time persist indefinitely. Monopoly rents are not merely short-run aberrations on a long-run competitive landscape.

Although the invisible hand theorem underlies most microeconomic policies—deregulation, no price supports, free trade—when it comes to defending capitalism as a system it is Schumpeter's name which is most often invoked (e.g. Kirzner, 1973; Littlechild, 1981). By providing opportunities to earn profits, free-enterprise capitalism encourages innovation and technological change. The West outpaces the East not so much by producing a given array of products more cheaply, but by producing a continually expanding and evolving set of products and processes. Schumpeter's 'perennial gale of creative destruction' is capitalism's driving force.

This view of capitalism as a dynamic competitive process is scrutinized in the final chapter. There it is argued that the benefits dynamic competition yield in the form of new products and processes must be weighed against the wasteful duplication of innovation and marketing investments monopoly induces. Rent producing and rent seeking are not synonymous and the latter's costs must be added up before a full evaluation of the fruits of dynamic competition is possible. To date, economics has failed to produce a dynamic equivalent to the invisible hand theorem. We cannot prove whether the billions spent on advertising cigarettes, or developing drugs, have resulted in social benefits in excess of their costs.

The normative issues are blurred still further when the existence of managerial discretion and managerial motives other than pure profits maximization are admitted. When managers are willing to invest in projects at returns below the opportunity cost of capital, social welfare may decline even when new products ensue. Excessive investment can take place in R and D and advertising as well as capital equipment. Rent seeking's non-productive social costs may be compounded by managerial pursuit of excessive growth. In the case of mergers, the distinction between corporate growth and macro growth drives a further wedge between private success at achieving company growth and the social objectives of real growth in income per capita. A system that allows managers freedom to pursue growth and profits as they choose does not necessarily result in the best set of outcomes that are possible under some form of government-market controlled economy.

The essays in this book reveal and discuss some of the more negative aspects of managerial capitalism. Monopoly rents exist and persist and when not dissipated in unproductive rent seeking, can be misallocated to socially unproductive corporate growth. Contractual cooperation in productive organizations can produce distributional conflicts as well as efficiency gains. Lest my message be missed, let me also add that managerial capitalism does have its virtues—and they are impressive. It does provide opportunities to get ahead by producing new and better products benefiting all. Its superiority in this and other respects to centrally managed economies that do not rely on the price mechanism and profit motive is obvious. What also seems obvious from the economic performance of managerial capitalism over the last ten to fifteen years is that it could do much better than it has. Unfortunately, recognition of why it has performed badly and how it might be improved has been obscured by the litanous repetition of praise its defenders constantly sing. The following essays are offered as a modest counterweight to this chorus in the hopes of stimulating serious dialogue concerning both the vices and virtues of managerial capitalism and possible measures to curb the former.

NOTES

1. *See* the original results of Baumol *et al.* (1970) and subsequent exchange between Friend and Husic (1973) and Baumol *et al.* (1973).
2. *See* the discussion in Mueller (1984) and Brainard *et al.* (1980).
3. *See* Littlechild (1981) and Cowling and Mueller (1981).

Part I
Profits, Contracts and the Theory of the Firm

2 Information, Mobility and Profit*

In a literature starting with Smith (1937) and extending at least through Schumpeter (1934) and Knight (1965, first edn. 1921), the 'profit motive' is a prime mover in the capitalist (free enterprise) system; the impetus behind the invisible hand. In Marx's (1906) critique of capitalism, profit also figures prominently as an unearned 'surplus value' above wages. Somewhat similarly, profits are the focus of attention in much of the literature of industrial organization. The persistence of profits in a firm or industry for a long period is typically interpreted as representing non-competitive market performance and an indication that antitrust intervention is warranted.

Despite the importance of profit as an economic concept, the literature remains somewhat ambiguous as to what it is, how it comes about, how it differs from rent, and how it helps to allocate resources. Indeed, it is not even obvious from the literature, whether profits in any meaningful economic sense still exist. Schumpeter (1950) himself predicted their disappearance through the institutionalization of the innovation process. Somewhat similarly, profit, as an anticipated income capable of affecting decisions, disappears in Weston's (1950) extension of Knight's uncertainty-theory of profit. And, if profits do exist, it is not clear from the literature who receives them. Theories of the capital market seem to assume that they go to the stockholders, while recent contributions of the theory of the firm imply that they are absorbed by the managers. These ambiguities obviously make it difficult to appraise the extent to which recent proposals to redistribute profits and control to the workers would in fact redistribute anything, and if so from whom.

This paper attempts to rehabilitate 'profit' as a useful concept for exploring these and other questions. It develops a theory of profit as both a component of *ex ante* incomes determining each decision to supply or withdraw a factor's service, and as a part of *ex post* incomes assuring that

*Earlier drafts of this chapter were presented at the University of Maryland, VPI & SU, Louvain, and IIM, and numerous helpful comments were made by the participants in these seminars. In addition, special thanks are due to James Buchanan, Thomas Borcherding, Martin McQuire, Roger Sherman, and Oliver Williamson for the suggestions for improvement they offered. Reprinted from *Kyklos*, **29**, 1976.

the sum of total factor incomes equals the total revenue of the firm. Its novelty lies in stressing the importance of information and mobility in the creation of profits, and explaining their role. Section I is devoted to this task. Section II presents the theory directly, while in Section III it is briefly related to other theories of profit. In Section IV the usefulness of the theory is illustrated by applying it to the question of who the modern recipients of profits are. Section V indicates some possible additional applications of the theory.

I.   THE ROLE OF INFORMATION AND MOBILITY IN THE CREATION OF PROFIT

We define profit as the residual over contractual or potentially contractual costs as in (Knight, 1965, ch. 9). If c_i is factor owner i's contractual or potentially contractual income, and R, the firm's total revenue, then profit is

$$II = R - \sum_{i=1}^{n} c_i$$

The total income of i, is his contractual income plus a share, α^i, of the residual,

$$Y_i = c_i + \alpha_i II, \text{ where} \sum_{i=1} \alpha_i = 1$$

A factor owner's income is thus composed of a fixed, known magnitude, c_i, and a potentially variable component,, $\alpha_i II$. Although a contract might be written establishing a factor owner's share of the residual, α_i, we shall refer only to c_i as his *contractual* income, for only it represents a contractually established *magnitude*. A contractually set share of an unknown quantity does not provide the individual with any set amount of income. An $\alpha_i = 0$ implies that the contractual income is guaranteed by the other factor owners. The larger $\alpha_i II$ is as a fraction of i's total income, the more it varies with profits and resembles a simple share of profit.

With perfect certainty, the firm's revenue is known, and each factor owner can be guaranteed his total income ($Y_i = c_i$, and $\alpha_i = 0$, for all i). When R is uncertain, some factor owners can expect or receive incomes different from those for which they nominally contracted. Some α_i's must differ from zero, some factor owners must share in profits.

A number of writers have observed that all factors are affected by uncertainty and receive a share of uncertainty-generated profit (Knight, 1965; Bronfenbrenner, 1960; Weston, 1950). It is often not clear, however, exactly how each participates in the sharing of profit, for most supply their services for what appears to be a contractually fixed remuneration. Nor does this literature contain a discussion of the extent to which factor owners also share in the entrepreneurial decision role, what this role is, and how it is exercised. Most factor owners (e.g. many workers, bond and stockholders) seem to exercise control on the firm only through decisions to supply or withdraw their services (Simon, 1952). Yet this seems far removed from the decisions usually associated with 'entrepreneurship' in the theory of the firm. We first briefly discuss the question of how factors share in the residual profit.

Factor incomes can fluctuate either because the rate at which they are paid, or the length of their contract is variable. Workers might, for example, be hired at a fixed wage, w, on the expectation that total revenue remains at R. If total revenue is actually $R_a < R, F$ workers might be let go (where $R - R_a = wF$) with the remaining workers continuing to receive the contractual wage, w. Alternatively, the contract could specify a fixed number of workers over a period with their wages determined by fluctuations in total revenue. The latter arrangement is clearly a form of 'profit' sharing. The former scheme can also be. If workers know they have a probability of being laid off, they will demand a higher wage than if employment were certain. In this way, workers share in 'profits' during the periods when they are employed in compensation for their losses when unemployed (Smith, 1937, pp. 103-6; Marshall, 1920, pp. 460-2; Nelson, 1961). The difference between the two profit-sharing schemes is entirely one of distribution. In the former profits are shared equally among all workers, in the latter they are assigned to those who are vulnerable to being layed off.

Given knowledge of the rules of compensation each factor can calculate his expected income, given levels of R, and this can be translated into a contractual and residual share. Under the first payment scheme, the worker's income depends on his fixed wage, and the relationship between R and the probability of his being laid off. Were this probability zero, the wage would be of the form of a contractual wage. Under the second scheme, his entire income is of the form of a share of a variable residual. While the actual payment schemes for any firm are likely to be complicated and difficult to interpret as simple contractual and residual share components, it is pedagogically useful to maintain this distinction.

We turn now to a discussion of the entrepreneurial role and its relationship to the creation and distribution of profits.

A. Mobility and Profit
In the Knightian profit theory, the entrepreneur guarantees a fixed remuneration to all other factory owners and receives the residual, i.e. all $\alpha_i = 0$ except for his (Knight, 1965, pp. 271-272). Schumpeter challenged this view, with the plausible argument that 'the one who gives credit comes to grief if the undertaking fails'.[1] In the absence of unlimited liability no set of contracts can make an entrepreneur totally responsible for all losses; the owners of the other factors bear some of the risks of the organization's going under. But why does Schumpeter feel the owners of capital bear the risks? Implicit in his position is the notion that capital is

to some degree fixed, that other factors have prior claims on total revenue, that they can collect their shares leaving capital to assume any residual loss; just as Knight hypothesized that other factors had the prior claims and the entrepreneur received the residual. But, logically, it is no more necessary for capital to be the residual claimant than it is for the entrepreneur or any other factor owner. A set of contracts could be written, providing that the suppliers of capital claim the first share of total revenue, and the other factors share the residual. Schumpeter's idea that the most immobile factor bears the uncertainties of the firm can be generalized to all factor owners.

Since the concept plays an important role in our theory, let us define mobility precisely. A factor owner is perfectly mobile if its income in its present employment equals its income in its next best employment, after deducting the transaction costs of changing employments. The difference between a factor owner's income in its present employment, and in its next best employment, net of transaction costs, measures the degree of its immobility.

When he joins a firm, a factor owner is perfectly mobile. Let us call y_i, the income he can earn in his best alternative employment, and assume for simplicity it is perfectly certain. If a contract can be written guaranteeing him $y_i (c_i = y_i, \ \alpha_i = 0)$, he will accept it. If such a contract cannot be written, he will demand an income *on average* equal to y_i, plus or minus any premium he requires to compensate for the risk involved.

Upon joining a firm, a factor owner may become immobile, either because he agrees to accept a large proportion of his income in the form of a share of the residual, or because transaction costs arise in changing employments after he has joined the firm. In the former case, the factor owner risks becoming immobile, at least for the time horizon upon which his expectations are formed. If the firm initially does worse than he expects in the long run, his income is less than he had anticipated, and the difference between it and the income he could have earned elsewhere measures the extent of his short-run immobility. What is more, if his long-run expectations about the firm have not altered, he can only recoup his losses by staying with the firm, and waiting until a period of above average expected performance occurs. A factor owner, who must incur large transaction costs to change employments, is immobile by definition. And, as Schumpeter stressed, he is *de facto* the bearer of uncertainty and recipient of the residual share. Should the firm begin to do worse than expected, the mobile factor owners will leave, and the immobile are left to assume the residual share. To compensate for these risks, any factor owner who knows *when he joins a firm* that he will become immobile upon joining, will demand a formal share of the profit to ensure that he shares in both the unexpected increases in firm revenues as well as the declines.[2]

The questions then arise as to which factor owners choose to accept the largest residual share; and whether there are differential characteristics of factor owners that make some more immobile after joining a firm than others. A simple answer is to assume that the factor owners with the greatest proclivity for assuming risk accept the residual shares (voluntarily immobilize). With this view, entrepreneurship becomes equated with preferences for risk, or optimism as Knight (1965) thought. While there is undoubtedly something to this view, it seems unsatisfactory to leave the entire theory of profit dependent on subjective differences in tastes. We turn to an alternative explanation.

B. Predictions and Profit

So far we have examined only the impact of stochastic changes in the environment on factor incomes. The theory is now extended to give factor owners a more active role in creating profits.

To begin, assume that information about the determinants of revenue changes can be gathered. Factor owners, who can predict which firms and industries will have higher revenues than generally expected, earn higher incomes. For example, suppose the risk-free interest rate is i. Ignoring any risk aversion on the part of lenders, firm X must pay r_X (where $r_X = i + \gamma r_x$) if the market expexts it to default on its payments γ per cent of the time.[3] An investor, who predicts that the true default rate in coming periods will be less than γ, can earn a surplus (profit) by lending at some effective rate above i, if his prediction is accurate. Similarly workers can earn higher than average incomes if they can correctly predict that the amount of time they will be unemployed in an occupation (industry, firm) will be less than generally expected. Organizers of new firms can earn incomes higher than zero, which the market expects in equilibrium, if they correctly predict a higher demand for the product than is commonly anticipated. More generally, any factor owner possessing information, not fully available to others, on the future demand and supply for his services can earn a surplus over the income expected by the market by joining (immobilizing himself in) a firm or industry (Nelson, 1961). Suppliers and customers can also earn surpluses with information not available to others (Stigler, 1963). Of course, factors, buyers and services with incorrect information will misestimate demand and supply conditions and earn losses.

C. Information and Profit

Information can play an even more central role in creating profits than in simply allowing factor owners to make better predictions in situations of uncertainty. A classic example is Schumpeter's innovator–entrepreneur, who has information on new products, processes, or organizational structures. If demand increases or costs decline as the innovator predicts, he earns a surplus, which lasts as long as others fail to imitate the innovation. The profit he receives can be ascribed to the information he possessed, which others did not have or were deterred from using due to uncertainty.

In some cases, one might prefer to attribute this profit to intuition or pure luck rather than to information. Although some successful innovations are undoubtedly a result of luck, I prefer a more deterministic theory in which the profit is imputed to something at least as tangible as information or, perhaps, articulateable intuition.

Coase (1952) described the entrepreneurial function as one of internalizing activities that can be coordinated more efficiently via a command system within a firm than through the market. The relevant information here is the entrepreneur's knowledge of the transactions for which contracts can be more cheaply written and enforced within the firm. Malmgren (1961) extended this argument focusing on the reduction in uncertainty of factor supplies that follows their being hired for sustained periods, as opposed to being purchased each time period in the market.

More recently, Alchian and Demsetz (1972) depict the entrepreneur as a monitor of worker effort (see also Crew, Jones-Lee and Rowley, 1971). In their theory, the key characteristic of the firm's production process is the inseparability of the contributions of the individual factors.[4] The firm operates as a team whose total output is greater than the sum of the allocable contributions of the members. As in any teamwork situation, the opportunity exists for free-riding or *shirking* as they call it. Any member who conceals his shirking can experience a non-pecuniary gain, since shirking provides positive utility. The possession and concealment of information about one's shirking becomes, therefore, a method for increasing one's share of total product. Conversely, anyone who discovers a way to monitor and control shirking can earn a surplus equal to the difference between the efficiency gains from reduced shirking and costs of monitoring. Information on shirking and methods to police it thus become a potential source of profit in their theory, with the entrepreneur–manager emerging as the recipient of these residual rewards.

The existence of information of these types need not lead to the creation of profits as we have defined them. It will only if its possessors must bear the uncertainties surrounding its value, must to some extent become or remain immobile, to obtain this value. If information can be bought and sold like other commodities, and the ability to gather it hired like other services, all changes in revenues or costs it produces can be predicted and contractually guaranteed. The compensation for search can be a functional return like any other time consuming activity. The acquirer or holder of information need bear no uncertainty over information's eventual value or his ability to realize it. Uncertainty and therefore profit need not be present. Weston's (1950) arguments against an *ex ante* concept of profits rest on the assumption that managerial abilities, including those of gathering and evaluating information, can be objectively appraised and purchased in the market. *Ex ante* total contractual costs always add to equal expected revenues and no profits need exist, *ex ante*. They appear only *ex post*, as the difference between expected and actual incomes. Schumpeter's (1950) belief that capitalism could give way to socialism without a loss in efficiency came from a view that the innovation (new information) process could be routinized.

Certainly some information can be bought and sold at prices accurately reflecting its value, and the ability to gather information, exert extra effort and care, and so on, routinely appraised. But when uncertainty in the Knightian sense (Knight, 1965, pp. 19-20) is present, the past is not a sufficiently accurate guide to the future to allow one to make accurate predictions on the basis of past experience or performance, and profits can be earned by acquiring additional information or exerting extra effort. Views that such profits do not exist ignore the essential properties of both uncertainty and information. As Arrow (1962) pointed out, the important attribute of information is its non-appropriability. Its holder often cannot sell it without revealing its content and thereby effectively giving it away. To recoup information's potential value, its possessor usually has to undertake an entrepreneurial role directly. A young man, with information that the future demand for electrical engineers will be higher than generally expected, may occasionally be able to sell this information, often not. Indeed, the very act of revealing it eliminates its value as other young men switch into this profession. He may only be able to gain from it by becoming an electrical engineer himself, that is, by voluntarily immobilizing himself in this profession. Similarly, one can often benefit from information that a specific firm will do better than others expect, only by investing in or working for this firm. The knowledge (belief) that one's own talents or skills are worth more than others will contractually agree to pay for them can yield an additional reward only, if the individual obtains a claim on the residual income the application of these skills will create. And, the holder of information on an innovation is typically thrust into the entrepreneurial role.

Thus, the non-appropriability of information's full value forces its holder to accept a claim on the residual to secure this value. In this way, the holder becomes immobile, tied to the firm or occupation in which he chooses to supply his information or extra effort. If the information he has on the demand for the product, the innovation, or his own skills is incorrect, his income will be lower than he expects, and he will incur the loss that follows. While, within the firm, some factor owners can have more profitable information than others (see below), everyone can possess information on the future demand for his services, and on his own skills and capacity for extra effort. Everyone is thus a potential recipient of profits.

II.   STATEMENT OF THE THEORY

Having discussed the role of immobility and information in the creation of profits, the theory can be presented directly. Consider first a world of perfect information (certainty), and resource mobility and divisibility. Factor owners provide their services to the occupations, industries and firms making the highest bids. Firms appear whenever opportunities exist for teams of factor owners to supply a product at a cost less than its market price. Entry continues until product price has fallen and/or factor prices risen to where total revenue equals total factor costs. Perfect mobility and divisibility imply either a linear homogeneous world from the start, or in equilibrium with each firm at the bottom of a U-shaped cost curve. The income of a factor owner equals both his marginal revenue product in his present employment, and the income he could earn in his next most attractive opportunity ($c_i = y_i$). It is the amount he must be paid to induce him to supply his services to the firm.

Now relax the assumption of perfect mobility, but retain perfect information. Immobility is present whenever a difference exists, in equilibrium, between a factor owner's income and its opportunity costs. A factor owner's marginal revenue product might be higher in one firm or occupation due to some special skill that other factor owners either do not possess, or are barred from using. Their effective immobility prevents them from competing with the factor owner and bidding his income down. He, too, is effectively immobilized in that he cannot leave the firm or occupation without sacrificing the economic advantage he possesses due to his special skills or position. An immobile factor may earn an income below its opportunity cost, whenever the costs of changing employments exceed the difference in the two incomes. Similarly, total revenue of the firm may exceed or fall short of the sum of the opportunity costs of its factors, due to some barriers to mobility which either prohibit other firms from entering into competition with it, or some members of the firm from leaving.

Let us define the difference between a factor owner's perfectly certain income in one firm and its perfectly certain opportunity cost as its economic rent.[5] If opportunity costs are defined net of the transactions costs of switching employments, then this definition of rent makes it a quantification of the degree of immobility defined in Section I-A. With perfect information, these economic rents must be ascribable to natural scarcities, and the other identifiable impediments to mobility which cause them. It is, therefore, conceptually possible to write contracts assigning them to the specific impediments that cause them and allocate the rents among the factor owners.[6] Total revenue is still equal to the sum of contractual and potentially contractual costs, the latter redefined to include both the fully certain opportunity costs of the factor owners, and their economic rents.

Uncertainty may also deter factor owners from entering an occupation, creating a positive gap between the incomes earned by those who did enter and the incomes they would have earned had they not. Uncertainty can deter firms from entering an industry, producing a positive residual between revenues and costs for those who do. Thus, uncertainty, lack of information, can effectively immobilize other factor owners and firms creating profits for those who do choose to accept the risks in a given occupation of industry. Uncertainty may also lead to excessive entry (insufficient exit) and negative profits.

Uncertainty can also create additional income for factor owners who exert additional effort or apply (acquire) extra skills. To the degree a factor owner's efforts can be monitored, the payment for his skills and knowledge can be contractualized. But no monitoring system is likely to be perfect, and an employee always retains some information of value (be it only his potential for secret carelessness and sabotage), and some contributions to firm success are not fully measurable. Therefore, a potential element of profit is likely to be present in every employee's income.

Three forms of factor income are thus distinguished: (1) the highest perfectly certain contractual payment a factor owner can earn in another firm or by being self employed—its opportunity cost; (2) the contractualizeable difference between this payment and its present income attributable to some identifiable impediment to mobility—its economic rent; and (3) the non-contractualizeable difference between its income and opportunity cost, due to the lack of perfect information, to uncertainty—its profit. The profits of the firm are defined as the sum of the profits of the individual factor owners.

Since the first two incomes are perfectly certain, they obviously can exist as both *ex ante* and *ex post* concepts, and as such are always equal. Profit can also exist *ex ante* and *ex post*. The uncertain difference between the income a factor owner anticipates from joining a given firm or exerting additional effort, and his opportunity costs is his *ex ante* profit. Anticipated profits are a subjective, personal magnitude, which can differ from one factor owner to the next. These differences in *ex ante* profits will help to determine which firm (occupation) a factor owner joins, how much extra effort he contributes. The actual difference between a factor owner's total income and his contractual income is his *ex post* profits. The existence of these *ex post* profits ensures that total realized factor incomes equal total realized revenues. Profit is the only income that differs from *ex ante* to *ex post* (see also Machlup, 1952, pp. 211-269).

Both profit and rent have been defined as a difference between a factor owner's income and his opportunity cost. Both are, therefore, linked to the idea of immobility. Immobility's link to economic rent is obvious, and is related to some generally recognizable impediment to mobility, a scarce skill or resource. With respect to profit, the link arises because of uncertainty and the non-appropriability of the value of information. Uncertainty immobilizes those who do not have information, and keeps them from seizing the opportunities to earn extra income which exist. The non-appropriability property of information forces those who do have information to earn the income it can provide by voluntarily assuming claims to a share of the residual in any firm or occupation they join. The possessor of a not widely held piece of information of value within a given firm is as tied to that firm for compensation for this information, as is the possessor of a generally recognized special skill of value only to a given firm. They differ only in so far as compensation for the latter can be contractualized, for the former it cannot.

The similarities between profit and rent, and the distinction based on the non-contractual nature of profit, explains the view of many, most notably Schumpeter (1934), that profits are transitory, disequilibrium phenomena, temporary quasi-rents. Much managerial activity is bent upon eliminating uncertainty, gathering information, measuring and monitoring skills and effort (Knight, 1965; Alchian and Demsetz, 1972). Any advantage from owning information is likely to be short lived. The application of an idea or a special skill places it in the public domain and leads to the subsequent imitation Schumpeter described as the perennial gale destroying monopoly profits. Knowledge that these profits are vulnerable to destruction leads in turn to a further storm of activity, however, to protect these transitory surpluses by erecting impediments to the entry of competitors. Patents, trademarks and institutional barriers to entering jobs and occupations are examples of these impediments. What would otherwise be transitory increases in factor incomes arising and disappearing with uncertainty, can become permanent differences (economic rents) attributable to institutional barriers barring the use of information once it has become generally available. Although analytically distinguishable, profits and rents are thus likely to be intertemporarily related, and any empirical separation of them may be difficult.

Since the potential discretionary contributions of information and effort of each factor owner cannot be fully known (for then they could be contractualized), one may wonder how a set of shares to the residual can be assigned, corresponding to the potential discretionary contributions of each individual or group. Again we deal with a piece of information, the optimal distribution of the residual, and an extra reward is to be earned by those who have the information or intuition to select superior matchings of residual shares and factor owners. One can envisage the contracts being chosen by an individual (entrepreneur), a team (the managers), or perhaps an assembly of the entire membership of the firm. In a competitive environment, the ultimate choice of contractual relationships is dictated by conditions in the market. A firm which offers a low share of the residual to a factor group capable of making large positive or negative[7] discretionary contributions will either not attract members of the group at all (or at least the most capable members), or will not be able to elicit sufficient discretionary effort from those present to compete in the product markets. The largest shares of profit must go to those capable of making the largest *unmeasurable* contributions to total revenue (Cheung, 1969). The *effective* choice of contracts is made by the decisions of consumers to buy or not to buy, by firms to enter and exit markets, by factor owners to offer and withdraw their services and discretionary effort. Control is by exit, to use Hirschman's term (Hirschman, 1970). The same contractual relations would emerge over time if each firm initially picked a set at random (Alchian, 1950; Winter 1971).

The less competitive the firm's environment, the greater is the number of possible sets of contractual relationships consistent with the firm's survival. Slack is introduced, and the process determining the contractual relationships becomes a blend of the external forces of the market, and the internal goals and bargaining strengths of the factor groups (Simon, 1952). At the opposite pole from the totally competitive environment, one can envisage a centralized economy in which neither consumers nor factor owners can exercise any control via voluntary exit and entry. Selection of the rules for determining the fixed or variable portions of each individual's income, for sharing the uncertainties (profits) of the economy, are now made entirely through the bureaucratic and/or democratic procedures governing the state—by Hirschman's voice (Hirschman, 1970). The rules determining factor incomes now reflect the relative political and social bargaining strengths of the factor groups.

III.   A CLASSIFICATION OF DIFFERENT PROFIT THEORIES

The present theory draws upon and includes elements of a number of other profit theories, and is perhaps useful to illustrate its relationships to them before going on to apply the theory. No effort is made to 'survey' the literature. Instead, we simply try to indicate the common threads running through previous work and the present approach.

A number of theories have argued that uncertainty creates profits for those factor owners who choose to become immobile and accept a residual share. In the classical theory, the costs of labour and materials were typically thought to be advanced by the organizer of economic activity, so that, as Adam Smith put it, 'something must be given for the profits of the undertaker of the work who hazards his stock in this adventure' (Smith, A., 1937, p. 48). In agriculture, this would be the farmer, in manufacturing the capitalist (Ricardo, 1911, pp. 70-1). Smith also mentions the possible transitory gains and losses of labour from unpredictable changes in product prices (Smith, A., 1937, p. 58).[8]

Marx depicted the capitalist as the buyer and seller of labour and materials, of course (Marx, 1906, pp. 186, 395). Stochastic changes in product prices would raise and lower the surplus value (profit) going to the capitalists, labour continuing to get its subsistence wage.[9] In traditional neoclassical theory, the entrepreneur hired mobile labour, land and capital at fixed, guaranteed fees and received any residual profit. In the modern neoclassical theories, stochastic changes in profit produce immediate changes in the present value of the firm's stock, so that it is the stockholders who receive the profits from their decisions to become immobile, in the face of these stochastic changes, by purchasing a company's stock. Note that the speed with which stockholders can dispose of their shares does not spare them from being the immobile factor and recipient of profits under the assumptions of the neoclassical theory. Since stock prices adjust instantaneously in response to changes in earnings, a wedge is instantaneously driven between the value of an owner's shares, and the value he could have secured had he invested in another firm, thus making the stockholder effectively immobile in the face of these stochastic changes. In the managerial theories of Baumol (1967), Marris (1964), and Williamson (1964) managers are viewed as identifying with their company, as receiving psychic income from managing it, as engaging in on the job consumption, etc. They are thus relatively immobile and receive at least a large share of the impact of exogenous changes. Theories of profit sharing among all the workers generally stress their heavy involvement in the fortunes of the firm and their potential for voluntary contributions of information and effort; while the generalized theories recognize the potential immobility of all factor owners and even of outside groups. These various theories are listed in Table 2.1, with some representative names of various proponents.

On the right hand side of Table 2.1, those theories which stress the importance of judgment or information are listed both with regard to the nature of the information and the identity of the gatherers (some theories are not explicit on both points). Since we have discussed a number of

Table 2.1: *Classification of profit theories*

Immobility Related Profits		Information Related Profits		
Immobile Factor	Theory	Type of Information	Gatherer of Information	Theory
Capitalist	Classical Marxian (Ricardo, Marx)[9]	Unspecified	Managers	Baumol, Marris, Williamson
Entrepreneur	Traditional Neoclassical (Knight)	Managerial ability	Stockholders, take-over raiders	Knight, Manne
Equityholders	Modern Neoclassical (Modigliani and Miller)	Innovations	Entrepreneur	Schumpeter
Managers	Managerial theories (Baumol, Marris and Williamson)	Inefficient market transactions	Entrepreneur	Coase, Malmgren
Workers	Socialist theories (Vanek)	Shirking by workers	Managers Workers	Alchian and Demsetz
All factors and outside groups	General theories of profit (Weston, Bronfenbrenner)	All facets of firm, plus the individual's own effort and skills	Workers	Vanek

theories in Section I, we shall not review them here. Although no claim is made that the list is exhaustive, it is broad enough to reveal the importance of information, and mobility as underlying factors in the theories of profit, and the firm.

IV. THE RECIPIENTS OF PROFIT

In this section, we discuss the distribution of profits among various groups in society. Since the essential characteristic of profits is its non-contractual nature, it is difficult to 'test' one theory against another. For if it were possible to measure profits and relate them to a set of variables, it would also be possible to contractualize the magnitude of their payment, in which case they would no longer be profits.

One can, however, attempt to determine the *ex post* recipients of profits by looking for the recipients of the most variable incomes. The causal link between profits and uncertainty makes them a volatile component of factor incomes. If the predictions of the present theory accord with the actual recipients of profit, it can serve to explain the *ex post* distribution of profit. Since the emphasis in the present theory is on the importance of information in the creation of profit, we expect to find those factor owners with the greatest access to non-generally-held information, or with the greatest potential for discretionary contributions of information and effort to be the major recipients of profit. In this regard, the theory leads to different predictions than those theories, which argue that payment for these services can be routinely contractualized (e.g. as in Weston, 1950).

Let us begin by considering an average worker. He is at his maximum mobility at the time he enters the work force. He then has the most incentive to gather information on alternative jobs. Over time a worker's mobility decreases, because he acquires 'consumption capital' in the community or neighbourhood (home, friends, schools for his children), because he acquires skills specific to the firm, and because the costs of acquiring information about other jobs increases (Alchian in Phelps, 1970; Bodenhöfer, 1967; Doeringer and Piore, 1971; Gallaway, 1969). At the same time, he acquires information and skills that may increase his ability to affect the performance of the firm through discretionary effort, that is, to share in profits. In general, however, the average worker's incentive and ability to make discretionary contributions is likely to be quite restricted. The size of his factor group makes it difficult to distinguish his contribution to total product from that of his fellow workers, and provides strong incentives to free-ride (Alchian and Demsetz, 1972). The bulk of his acquired skills can probably be accurately evaluated and contractualized through reclassification and promotion. We thus expect a greater percentage of the income of young workers to be profits than of senior workers. And this seems to be the case. Turnover and income variability are highest among teenagers and new entrants into the labour force, and this turnover appears to be voluntary and independent of both the worker's socio-economic background, job level, or wage (see Doeringer and Piore, 1971, pp. 184-8, and references on p. 187).

It is also interesting to note how the form of control a worker exercises varies with his mobility. At the point of entry, his control is almost entirely via exit, and his wages tend to conform to market conditions. Entry into the higher skilled positions is more often through internal advancement of older workers. The salary levels for these positions are more dependent on the bargained contracts between management and unions, and show a greater disparity across firms (Doeringer and Piore, 1971). Thus, the worker's ability to influence decisions via voice (backed up by the threat of collective exit in the form of an organized strike) is greater for the less mobile older workers.

Managerial mobility and accumulation of skills (information) follow much the same pattern of other workers. For managers, however, the acquisition of skills and knowledge specific to the company is likely to be far more important than for lower level workers, for much of the job of managing is concerned with the gathering and accumulation of information. Managerial ability to make discretionary contributions and share profits should, therefore, increase with their tenure and advancement in a company. The smallness of their numbers makes it easier to isolate the individual contributions of a manager, and gives them an incentive to make discretionary contributions, an incentive which increases the higher up they are in the organization.

Managerial income may be both pecuniary and non-pecuniary. A large literature now exists on the various forms of non-pecuniary incomes managers earn (Alchian, 1965; Baumol, 1967; Marris, 1964; Williamson, 1964; Williamson, 1970). The ability of managers to secure non-pecuniary rewards varies directly with the actual or potential size of the residual profit. Williamson, for example, found managerial hiring of extra staff and other emoluments varied directly with the business cycle (Williamson, 1964, pp. 134-9). Comanor found discriminatory hiring practices positively associated with accounting profitability (Comanor, 1973). Grabowski and Mueller found a positive relationship between past profits and investment and R and D, and argued that the profits were used to increase firm growth excessively to gain its non-pecuniary advantages (Grabowski and Mueller, 1972). Edwards and Heggestad observed an inverse relationship between reported profits and their variability and argued that managers used profits to purchase security (Edwards and Heggestad, 1973). Leibenstein has made the more general claim that managers pursue a combination of security and leisure (Leibenstein, 1969), ad perhaps most closely related to the present paper, McCain has linked Leibenstein's notion of X-efficiency to the information environment of the firm (McCain, 1975).

In higher ranks, managerial income is directly related to the success of the firm via various bonus and stock option plans. Particularly pertinent to the theory is the option to earn additional income by engaging in insider trading. Here a manager may effectively profit from the firm-specific information and effort he possesses and can, at his discretion, contribute (Manne, 1966). A comparison of Lewellen's data with the business cycle indicates that executive compensation varies directly with the cycle, as do company profits (Lewellen, 1968, pp. 128-31; McCain, 1975). More importantly, executive compensation exhibits much more variability than the incomes of either production workers or new *MBA*s (pp. 174-80). Taking into account both the pecuniary and non-pecuniary components of managerial compensation, these studies suggest that a substantial component of managerial income varies with the performance of the company, with the discretionary contributions of information and effort managers make.[10]

A manager's ability to employ exit as a means of control decreases over time due to his accumulation of company-specific knowledge and skills and/or skills not evaluable from outside. These same skills and knowledge, however, coupled with the capacity to withdraw them voluntarily even without leaving, increase his authority and ability to participate directly in the control of the company. Since the survival of the firm depends on the quality of the decisions and skills of its managers and other factor owners, their power of control via voice is still constrained ultimately, however, by the market.

Although a manager usually does not possess information of importance to a specific firm when he joins it, and thus is not expected to receive a large share of profits initially, there is one important exception: a manager (entrepreneur) starting a new firm. He typically has ideas about a new product, production technique, marketing strategies, demand conditions, etc. which others do not share. It is this information that leads him to envisage earning a profit and induces him to start the company. Investors possessing the knowledge (intuition, or perhaps luck) to purchase stock in a new venture that succeeds may receive a substantial return on their investments. The portion of this return above what the market expects can be regarded as profit attributable to the information that led them to buy stock in this particular company. This information usually comes from the entrepreneurial founder who must reveal part of his innovative ideas to raise capital. Thus, the founder and the initial suppliers of capital (perhaps one in the same) both possess relevant information and share the risks and profits of the new enterprise. Both share in control as well. The entrepreneur does this directly by taking a top managerial position. The suppliers of capital acquire control through any conditions they set on the use of their funds and, if the amount of capital they supply is large, by holding a large block of voting stock and perhaps seats on the board of directors.

As the company grows and matures, the concentrations of stock holdings by the initial suppliers of capital are typically dissipated. Control passes to the officers and board of directors.[11] Information about the future profitability of a mature firm, whose stock is traded on a major exchange, is sufficiently widespread so that the typical stockholder's potential earnings from gathering information about the company are quite small. He neither exercises control over the company nor can much of his earnings be regarded as a share of its profit. The bulk of earnings on stock of a large mature corporation probably constitute a simple return on capital.[12]

The potential profit for a bondholder, from gathering information to avoid defaults on interest payments, is even smaller. Indeed, the major difference between a bond and a stock holder is probably the former's greater unwillingness to research the companies in which he invests, the key piece of information on a bond being the readily available investment service rating.[13] Stockholders of large corporations *can* make substantial profits, if they have information not generally available. These 'insiders' are usually managers, however, and these earnings are best regarded as part of their compensation as managers as discussed by Manne (1966) and above.

If stock and bond holders do not receive a large share of profits and managers do, the income from stocks and bonds should be relatively stable compared to profits or total (pecuniary and non-pecuniary) managerial incomes. The returns on corporate bonds are fairly stable. Indeed, much of their variation comes from changes in bond prices, which are probably more dependent on expectations about inflation rates and other general market phenomena, than on the company's performance and changes in expectations about the company defaulting.

The wide variability in the returns on a common stock may suggest that stockholders do receive a substantial share of profits, and may explain why many observers still feel that the stockholders are the true residual claimants and not the managers. Although there are 'profits' to be made in the wide purchase and sale of stock, they have little to do with the profits of the companies being traded. For a stockholder really engages in two activities when he purchases a share of common stock. One is to become a factor owner in the firm. If he buys a new issue he contributes capital directly to the firm. If he buys outstanding shares, he helps raise the share price and provides managers with cheaper capital and/or more freedom from take-over and thereby freedom to use internal fund flows as they choose (Marris, 1964; Grabowski, 1972). In general, he does not affect the firm's profitability, however, by contributing additional information or effort or exerting direct control by voting his shares. The second activity a stockholder engages in is that of entering or leaving the market—of playing the market. An individual or institution that buys and sells stocks can be regarded as a firm in the business of buying and selling stocks. The entrepreneurial activity in this business is one of gathering and evaluating information about a company *vis-à-vis* other companies, and about the ups and downs of the market itself. Firms, be they individuals or institutions, which gather accurate information not widely held about a company or market movements can earn a profit from this information, just as in any other industry. It is a profit they themselves earn through their decisions to buy or sell, however, and has only a tangential effect via the cost of capital on the performance of the company being traded. Since entrepreneurial activity (information gathering, intuition, luck, risk taking) is a large component of the inputs to stock trading, profits should make up a large percentage of the returns. It must be stressed, however, that these are profits stockholders receive in their role as entrepreneurs 'playing the market', and not profits from participating in the running of 'their' companies. The distinction is similar to that made by Hirshleifer (1971).

Under normal conditions stock and bond holders remain extremely mobile, and exercise control through exit and its impact on stock and bond prices. Should stock prices fall precipitously, however, say following disclosure of a serious error in managerial judgment or a decision to reduce dividends drastically, stockholders become *effectively* immobilized. Their ability to sell quickly does not allow them to avoid sharing in this loss or to exercise control and reverse the managerial decision. Voice *may* become an effective means of control under these circumstances. If the managerial decision is sufficiently egregious, stockholders may be able to either reverse the decision or replace the managers by voting their shares. Thus, under extreme conditions, when stockholders become immobile, they may be forced to gather information and be thrust into assuming an entrepreneurial role in the company and receiving a share in its profits.[14]

The analysis could be extended to the independent professions, in which the variability in incomes, and widespread use of direct profit sharing and democratic control procedures can undoubtedly be related to the large potential for discretionary contributions of effort and skill which exists in these occupations. But, hopefully, the examples presented so far suffice to illustrate the usefulness of the present approach.

V. FURTHER APPLICATIONS

Previous theories of profit depict entrepreneurship as a proclivity for risk taking, daring, ingenuity and other similarly randomly distributed characteristics. In contrast, the present theory stresses the role of the more tangible, information and mobility. Information and mobility play a central role in recent theories of both the internal and external labour markets. 'Job search' (Phelps, 1970), 'signalling' (Spence, 1973), 'shirking' (Alchian and Demsetz 1972; Crew, Jones-Lee and Rowley, 1971), and 'X-efficiency' (Leibenstein, 1969; McCain, 1975) can all be related to a concept of profit emphasizing information and mobility. Similarly proposals to introduce worker participation in profit and control sharing (e.g. Vanek, 1970) should be analysed, in the light of the present theory, in terms of the types of information the different members of the firm possess, their potential for discretionary contributions of information and effort, and so on.

More broadly, the theory of profit can be fruitfully employed to analyse the differences between capitalist and socialist economies. A free enterprise economy copes with uncertainty through the decentralized decisions of individuals and firms to gather information, contribute effort and skills, and voluntarily accept responsibility for these decisions (become immobile). Profit provides the incentive to undertake these decisions; exit the means of control. The bankrupt firm, unpaid dividend, and unemployed worker are the logical casualties of the operation of this process. From Marx to the present day, a central focus in the socialist critique of capitalism has been on its distribution of the uncertainties of the market, particularly as they affect workers. The lack of visible unemployment, and other casualties of uncertainty, are among the more conspicuous characteristics of soviet-style socialist economies; and even in the West much of the thrust of social welfare programmes has been in the direction of reducing the effects of market uncertainty.

Uncertainty does not disappear under socialism, of course, it simply is handled in a different way. If the uncertainties accompanying voluntary decisions to offer and withdraw services are to be eliminated, so too must either the opportunities or incentives to do so. Restrictions on the foundation of new firms or on entry and exit from occupations, become natural complements to the elimination of bankruptcies and unemployment[15] (as do, on a more limited basis, unemployment insurance and guaranteed annual incomes). The frustrated worker seeking in vain a change of job or occupation, and the frustrated innovator–entrepreneur are the socialist counterparts to the unemployed worker and bankrupt firm. Exit is replaced by voice as the means of control: voice being some combination of the forces of party democracy and bureaucratic hierarchy.

None of these questions *has* to be analysed using the theory of profit. 'Profit' is, after all, just a concept, a definition. One can employ other definitions and concepts if one chooses. But, given its venerable history, it seems a pity not to employ the concept of profits, if this term can be used in such a way as to provide insight into the problems being analysed, as it can.

NOTES

1. Schumpeter, 1934, p. 137. Schumpeter's criticism was of an earlier uncertainty-profit theory of J. B. Clark, but is equally valid with respect to Knight's theory.

2.   A factor owner, who does not know when he joins a firm the extent of his future immobility, may not secure a contract which allows him to share in both the above and below average revenues of the company, that is, he is vulnerable to exploitation by the other factor owners. Marx's concept of exploitation rested, in part, on his view that the initial labour contract was asymmetric to the worker's later disadvantage (*see* p. 196 and note 9 below). It should also be noted that the factor owners are not the only ones who can suffer losses following a decline in a company's revenues. Businesses in some way dependent on the company for sales may suffer. These could be suppliers who cannot readily find other buyers due to technical or locational specialization, or local retailers catering to the company's employees. Again, these businesses should charge higher prices to the company and its employees to compensate for these risks, and thereby essentially capture a share of profits. Small retailers will move into a one-company town, for example, only if they anticipate charging higher prices (than they would in a city, perhaps) to compensate for the risk that the company may reduce employment and lower the retailer's sales. The company's employees demand higher wages, both to compensate for the risks of job loss and to pay the anticipated higher prices for local services. In this way some of the profits generated by the uncertainties facing the firm are passed on to those outside of it, and the theory is capable of being generalized to include all individuals in some way dependent on the company.
3.   None of this discussion depends on risk attitudes.
4.   If output, z, is a function of factors x and y, then Alchian and Demsetz (1972) assume

$$\frac{\partial^2 z}{\partial x\, \partial y} > 0.$$

5.   The amount of economic rent a factor earns will differ depending upon whether one measures opportunity costs from the point of view of the firm, the industry, or society. A piece of land may earn zero economic rent from the perspective of a firm bidding it away from another firm. Yet, for a society all of the income going to land may be an economic rent. The focus here is on the firm or the self-employed individual. We follow Worcester (1946) and define these contractual surpluses over opportunity costs within the firm as economic rents, leaving the more general term 'rent' to be used for the total income of land. For further elaboration of the economic rent concept *see* Robinson, 1933 ch. 8.
6.   The factor owners that 'produce' the surpluses need not receive them, of course. Owner A may have a special skill which produces x dollars in additional revenue above his opportunity cost, but B may receive it due to, perhaps, his special bargaining skill.
7.   Managerial concern over worker morale and fear of sabotage suggests the existence of some *negative* discretionary effort. The existence of sabotage illustrates the problems of monitoring all factor owner efforts, and is consistent with the receipt of a small percentage of profits by workers.
8.   Not surprisingly, I suppose, the potential role of information is also touched upon. Smith mentions the potential for prolonging a rise in profits by concealing its cause (Smith, A., 1937, p. 60); Ricardo the profits from discovering or first employing a machine, profits which would disappear as it came into general use (Ricardo, 1911, p. 263).
9.   Wages might rise or fall in response to cyclic changes, but these would not be

profits by our definition, since in Marx's description of the process there is nothing voluntary in the individual worker's decision to become employed. The workers are inherently immobile due to the class structure of society. Any rise in wages during a boom would, from the point of view of the capitalist class but not from the individual firm, be an economic rent arising from the workers' temporary scarcity. Just as a fall in wages below subsistence becomes a sort of negative rent stemming from the workers' temporary overabundance. Interestingly enough Marx remarks that under capitalism intelligence in production (profitable information?) resides with the capitalist; the labourer being 'stripped of the power to think' (Marx, 1906, pp. 396–7).

10. In the *M*-form structures of the modern diversified firm, the traditionally entrepreneurial functions, *à la* Schumpeter (1934) and Coase (1937), are undertaken by division heads and their subordinates. Top managers serve chiefly as monitors of 'shirking' by lower managers (Williamson, 1970, ch. 6). It is interesting to speculate whether these managerial-monitors receive the bulk of firm profits, or whether they too are monitored, by potential take-over raiders. Again the issue hinges on the importance of information and uncertainty. If 'inside' monitors can be easily monitored from outside, their incomes can be contractualized by the market, and the residual claimants become the raiders. If the information on managers is widely disseminated, the market for take-overs is perfect, take-overs are routinized and potential profits from monitoring disappear. An interesting exercise would be to compare the variability of incomes of division heads (including the periods following their removal by top managers), top managers (including the periods following their removal via take-over), and take-over raiders.

11. Berle and Means, 1932. Even the board of directors usually does not possess sufficient information to exercise much control. Note the following observation of Chandler (1962) on a statement by the Board of Directors of the Pennsylvania Railroad made in 1874 more than fifty years *before* Berle and Means.

'"The present form of organisation (part-time directors and full-time officers) makes practical ciphers of the Directors, and this is from no deliberate intention, but from the very necessities of the case." Once a large business has reached a size that required the services of several full-time administrators, the board and the stockholders had only a negative or *veto* power on the government of their enterprise and on the allocation of its resources. They could say no, but they had neither the information nor the awareness of the company's situation to propose realistic alternative courses of action' (Chandler, 1962, p. 313).

12. This fact is recognized by managers, who accordingly do not treat stockholders as the sole residual claimants. Instead, they treat them more like suppliers of capital entitled to a stable stream of income. At least this is suggested by Lintner's (1956) well-supported hypothesis that each quarter's dividend payment is largely determined by the previous quarter's payment. And the long-run payout ratio is chosen to avoid outside take-overs (Marris, 1964; Singh, 1971).

13. Alchian and Demsetz distinguished between bond and stockholders on the basis of the latter's greater optimism over the company (Alchian and Demsetz, 1972, p. 789, n. 14). Going a step further, this greater optimism can be attributed to a greater amount of information about the company held by the stockholder.

14. We thus disagree with Manne (1966), and Alchian and Demsetz (1972, p. 789) about the unimportance of the voting right attached to a share of stock. It is true that under 'normal' circumstances the voting right is of no importance and

the manager is free to run his company, and the stockholder to run his, i.e. to buy and sell, without the one having much affect on the other. But it is the voting right that helps preserve this, by giving managers an incentive to run the firm so as to sustain these 'normal' circumstances. Note managers will bear the brunt of their past errors if a take-over is attempted for they find themselves either severely constrained or out of a job following such an attempt.

15.   When these restrictions do not appear in a socialist economy, as in Yugoslavia, the problems of bankruptcies and unemployment reappear.

3 Power and Profit in Hierarchical Organizations*

The development of economics as a social science has rested on two postulates concerning human behaviour: individuals act out of self interest, and are rational. Thus, consumers are assured to maximize their utility; entrepreneurs maximize profit. The economy is driven by self interest, the corporation by the profit motive.

Recently the postulates of rationality and self interest have been extended to the study of political science through the development of the public choice area. In one of the pioneering works in this area Anthony Downs (1957) postulated that candidates pursued their self interest by trying to maximize the number of votes they obtained. Although vote maximization has proven to be a plausible and useful assumption to explain candidate behaviour, it clearly cannot explain all political behaviour, since many politicians are not elected and/or cannot be re-elected. In particular, this postulate cannot explain bureaucratic behaviour.

The classic analysis of bureaucracy is, of course, Max Weber's (1947) and the natural objective for the bureaucrat, following Weber, would be power. The large corporation is run by managers seeking profit; the public bureaucracies by individuals hunting for power. Economic man pursues profit; political man power.

In the pages which follow I attempt to develop an analogy between power and profit, and use it to analyse the objectives and conflicts that arise in hierarchical organizations. Since the literatures on both of these subjects are long and tortuous, I make only selective reference to each. Let us begin with power.

I. THE CONCEPT OF POWER

At the most intuitive level the word 'power' connotes the ability or capacity to do something, see Wagner (1969, pp. 3-4). But 'something' can

*Reprinted from *The Swedish Journal of Political Science*, 5, 1980.

stand for a variety of objects, each of which leads to a different concept of power. Physical power is the ability to apply force. Economic power is the capacity to purchase goods, and so on. Political power must be defined as the ability to achieve certain ends through a political process. In this essay we shall take a rather broad view of the latter, considering virtually any collective decision-making body or organization from a committee to a bureaucracy as being governed by some form of political process. To observe the exertion of political power it is necessary that at least some participants in the political process have conflicting goals. If all members of a committee favour the same alternative as *A* and this is chosen we cannot say that *A* has exercised power. If only *A* favours an alternative and it is chosen, *A* has political power.

Political power can arise directly from the rules by which the political process operates. These rules might simply grant *A* a dictatorial right. Under most rules, the committee chairman has more capacity to influence the outcome than other members, yet he need not be the most powerful member of the committee. What interests us here is not the direct capacity to influence an outcome granted by the rules, but the differing capacities individuals have to influence a collective decision, independent of the set of rules.

Bertrand Russell (1938) listed three ways in which an individual can exert influence in a political context (1) by direct physical power, for example imprisonment or death, (2) by offering rewards and punishments, and (3) by exerting influence on opinion through the use of education and propaganda. The first two are obviously closely related to procedural power. The dictator may have authority to imprison or execute subordinates, they most certainly will not have similar legal authority over him. As Cartwright (1965, p. 139) has observed, 'Of the many possible means of influence, persuasion is commonly advocated as most suited to a democratic, or rational, social system'! Thus, the third of Russell's sources of influence is of most interest to us here. On the surface, it also seems to come closest to our description of power. For education, propaganda, and persuasion are all forms of information. As we shall attempt to demonstrate, political power, other than of a procedural kind, is possessed by those who have information. Uncertainty creates the potential to exercise power, information provides the capacity to do so.

Although information will provide the most power in a political process governed by persuasion, it is not limited to these most democratic forms of political interaction. To illustrate the generality of the uncertainty–information–power nexus we first examine a situation that seems to come closest to Russell's first source of influence, pure physical power. Consider the classic power struggle encapsulated by the demand 'your money or your life'. *G* has a loaded gun which he aims at *W* and demands that *W* give his loaded wallet over to G. Here we have what appears to be the simplest case of power by force with information playing no visible role. Let us examine more closely. W must choose whether to hand over his wallet or not. He must, therefore, predict what G will do should he not hand it over and if he does. Suppose W knows that G will not shoot in either event, G is then without any power. W keeps his wallet and G does not shoot. Suppose W knows G will shoot in either event. Again G is without power, that is the ability to command, since W knows the wallet now belongs to G, and it is simply up to W to decide whether he wants to give it to G and then be shot, or let him take it after W is dead. The same holds true for the case when G will shoot if he does not get the wallet, but will not shoot if he gets it. If W knows that with certainty, suppose G is a programmed robot, G is without any real power to command. The choice is W's whether to live without his wallet or die with it, and G merely carries out his programmed action following the real decision by W. The only situation in which G can actually command W to do something against his will, is when W does not know what G will do following W's action. W might then give G the wallet when G would not have shot him anyway.

It is in this situation, and really only in this situation, that G can be said to be exercising political power over W, as political power is typically defined, see Dahl (1957, p. 80), Simon (1953). If G would not shoot W if W failed to give him the wallet, and yet he can get W to give him the wallet, he has succeeded to get W to do something he would not otherwise have done. G has done so, however, not solely because he has a gun, but because W is uncertain about what G will do with the gun. It is not the presence of the gun *per se,* but the uncertainty that accompanies it that gives G power. In the absence of the gun, G does not have power over W because W is not worried that G will kill him. If G gets a gun, he will have power over W, because, or more precisely if and only if, W is uncertain about what G will do with it. G has power because he has the information about what he will do and W does not.

In this example, the gun plays the role of procedural power and clearly it places G in a better position to achieve his goals than W. But it alone does not determine the outcome so long as there is uncertainty on the part of the individual of the other's reactions. It is this uncertainty that gives G power over W, and can give W some power over G.

The importance of uncertainty and information can be further demonstrated by slightly changing the example. Suppose that W has buried the wallet some place in his yard and only he knows the location. Now there is considerable uncertainty on both sides: W not knowing whether he will get shot, G not knowing the location of the wallet. Given the increase in uncertainty and relevant information in the hands of W his power should be enhanced. He can now quite possibly force G to unload or throw away his gun in exchange for information on the wallet's location. Indeed, he might get off with both his life and his wallet. Even though the advantage of force still lies on the side of *G,* the increase in *W*'s possession of relevant information gives him the potential for exercising considerably more power over *G.*

As a final extreme example, assume *G* and *W* both have wallets and known programmed response patterns in the event that one has a gun. A gun is given to one on a flip of a coin. Given the programmed reactions of each, no real power is meted out via the coin flip, although the flip will affect the lives and/or wealth of *W* and *G.* What power that exists in the situation is with the coin flipper, or a fate which knows the outcome of the flip.

Returning to Russell's list of sources of power, we can see that it is the uncertainty that surrounds a dictator's use of physical power, or a supervisor's issuance of rewards and punishments that allows them to control their subordinates. If *B* knows with certainty that *A* will give him a reward if *B* does *X*, the rules require it, then *B* in carrying out *X* exercises as much power over *A* as *A* does over *B*. In a bureaucracy in which no uncertainty existed, lines of authority might exist, but no real power would accompany authority. All employees would know all of the possible events that might occur and all could predict the eventual outcomes or decisions that would follow each. Employee grievance procedures would be completely codified and both the supervisor's and the employee's reaction to any situation would be perfectly predictable. In a world of complete certainty, all individuals are essentially acting out a part, 'going by the rules', and those at the top of the bureaucracies are as devoid of discretionary power as those at the bottom. All power is purely procedural, see Simon (1953, p. 72).

This type of situation comes close to the conditions existing in the French Monopoly Michel Crozier (1964) described in *The Bureaucratic Pheonomenon.* As Crozier depicts it the monopoly does operate in a world of certainty—with one exception—the machines sometimes break down. This places the women operating the machines completely under the power of the mechanics responsible for repairing them, since the women have a quota of output for each day and must work harder to make up for any down time. More interesting, the supervisors who nominally have more authority also have less power than the mechanics. Since the mechanics know how to repair the machines, and the supervisors do not, the supervisors are unable to exert any real control over the mechanics, see Crozier (1964, pp. 98-111).

It is instructive to note the tactics used by the mechanics to preserve their power. The operators were severely scolded for 'tinkering' with their machines in an effort to keep them going or repair them. Only the mechanics knew how to repair the machines; each machine was different and just how it needed to be fixed was known only to the mechanics; repairing them was an art not a science. When clashes arose between the mechanics and the supervisors it was over whether the latter could, on occasion, work at repairing the machines. The supervisors were further hampered in this endeavour by the continual 'mysterious' disappearance of machine blueprints from the factory. The mechanics always worked without the aid of blueprints.

It is easy to extend Crozier's description of the tactics employed by the mechanics to maintain their control of information and power to other groups of experts. One of the first things any group does to protect its position is to develop a set of terms or jargon that makes much of what it does inaccessible to outsiders. This can be further buttressed by perfecting techniques of analysis so complicated that outsiders cannot follow them. This done it becomes extremely difficult for those outside groups to take away or evaluate the information possessed by the expert. Examples of this behaviour are obvious. Scientists and engineers perhaps come first to mind. In these professions the non-specialist is clearly at a loss to understand and exercise effective control over the professions. Even within the disciplines the tendency is for information boundaries to arise giving groups power *vis-à-vis* their colleagues. Thus, the inability of one branch of physics to evaluate the work of another strengthens the position of the inaccessible branch in gathering R and D funds, grants, department positions, or what have you on the basis of its own criteria. The 'pecking order' both across and within disciplines tends to be from 'hard' to 'soft' science on the grounds that the more theoretical or mathematically oriented hard scientists can or could always understand and evaluate the 'soft stuff', while the reverse is not necessarily true. The counter argument by the more applied is a rather weak claim of expertise because the theorists are not really familiar with the data or the institutions.

Other professions attempt to create and maintain power in the same way. Consider law. Here is a profession whose language could be, and once was, accessible to the average citizen. Over time, however, the profession has so complicated the language and procedures used in the judicial system that it is nearly impossible for an outsider to participate without hiring a lawyer. The medical profession follows a similar strategy, with the practice of writing prescriptions in Latin being an interesting illustration.

Lacking Latin or mathematics to conceal information and preserve their power, individuals typically resort to the more blatant device of secrecy. Examples ranging from the fraternal 'secret handshake' to the classification procedures of the Pentagon and CIA come easily to mind. In each case the purpose is the same, to protect the insider's position by keeping relevant information from the outsider. Although the purported purpose for classifying many documents is to preserve national security by keeping them out of the hands of the nation's enemies, the true, intended 'outsiders' often appear to be our own citizens, and the 'insiders' whose security is being protected, government bureaucrats.[1]

Crozier further buttresses the hypothesis that uncertainty is the source of power by examining the seemingly anomalous preference for technological change by the director of the Industrial Monopoly and the resistance to this change by the technical engineers. On the basis of social background and status the technical engineers should be more liberal and promote technological change, while the more conservative backgrounds of the directors should lead them to resist it. Decisions to institute changes in technique are made by the directors, however. In the absence of these changes, decisions are sufficiently routine that effective control lies with the engineers. Thus, the only time that the directors can effectively demonstrate their authority is when they initiate changes in plant technique. Uncertainty is then introduced, with the top directors in possession of the relevant information on the new technique. Following the change, uncertainty gradually diminishes, routine returns, and power passes down to the lower levels, until the directors are forced to introduce another change in technique, see Crozier (1964, pp. 155-5).

Again, one can easily think of additional illustrations of the importance of information in establishing a group's power. Perhaps, the best one is that of the military. Here one has a situation in which uncertainty over a weapon's effectiveness, levels of preparation, offensive and defensive strategies, etc. is endemic to the activity. This gives the military a strong advantage over other federal bureaucracies in obtaining funds from both Congress and the Executive Branch. The development of an impenetrable jargon, classification of data and so forth, all serve to maintain this uncertainty and strengthen the power of the leadership of the military hierarchy who have or claim to have the relevant information. The otherwise surprising preference of one of the oldest and most conservative bureaucracies, the military, for new and more sophisticated weapons systems, becomes understandable by analogy with the case studied by Crozier.[2]

These examples hopefully illustrate the role uncertainty and information play in creating and distributing power in bureaucracy. We shall return to an examination of bureaucratic power, after investigating the role information and uncertainty play in generating economic profit.

II. PROFIT

Consider a world of perfect certainty. All tastes and technologies are known. Labour, land and capital are combined to produce goods and services. Competition ensures that the prices of all goods and services are driven to the point where they just cover factor input costs. There is no residual left for the entrepreneur (other than a normal compensation for whatever labour services he provided), since there is nothing that requires entrepreneurial skill in a world of perfect certainty.

When uncertainty exists revenues and costs are not always equal. Unexpected changes in tastes, weather, competing technologies and so on produce changes in demand and cost schedules that leave positive or negative 'residuals' between total revenues and costs. These revenues accrue to those who assume the responsibility for organizing the company, the entrepreneurs, and are defined as the profits of the firm.[3]

With uncertainty present, the possibility of 'making' profits by correctly anticipating or inducing changes in tastes and technologies arises. The entrepreneur, who knows what style of shoes will sell next spring, who knows that a certain technology will reduce costs, and so on, earns profits. Those who do not know these things or makes mistakes earn losses. Entrepreneurial activity thus consists of gathering and evaluating information on what will sell, and what will reduce costs. As long as one entrepreneur has information on what will sell, and others do not (are uncertain) he can earn a profit. Information on consumer tastes and innovations thus provides a firm with the ability to earn more than other firms in the market—with power over the market. This power dissipates as others acquire information about consumer tastes and imitate the innovations. As uncertainty vanishes so do profits. The 'perennial gale of destruction' described by Joseph Schumpeter thus consists of a process of gathering or creating new information which produces surpluses for those who have it, but soon is obtained by all, eliminating profits and setting the stage for a new finding, a new wave of profits and imitation, and so on.[4]

While Knight, Schumpeter and Coase stressed the importance of information not held by 'outsiders' to the firm in generating profit residuals, more recently Alchian and Demsetz (1972) and Oliver Williamson (1975) have emphasized the importance of the distribution of information inside the firm to the generation and sharing of the residual. Alchian and Demsetz emphasize the team aspects of production within a firm. These can perhaps be best illustrated by considering production a positive sum game of a prisoner's dilemma variety. The cooperative strategy can be interpreted as carrying out some previously agreed set of tasks at a given level of care and effort. The non-cooperative strategy is 'shirking' on some of these tasks. All members of the team are better off if all adopt the cooperative strategy than if all do not, but some may still be tempted into shirking if they think they can do so without affecting the choice of strategy by other members of the team. In a small, productive team each member may be able to observe and monitor the behaviour of the other members. In a large team this will be inefficient, however. A specialist at monitoring must be chosen. To ensure that this monitor does not, in turn, shirk he must be given the claim to the residual profit of the firm. Thus, in the Alchian–Demsetz theory, profit is also information-uncertainty related. The potential for profit exists in the behavioural uncertainties surrounding the prisoner's dilemma–teamwork production relationship. The profits accrue to the manager-monitors who gather information on other members of the team and ensure that they do not engage in shirking.

III. POWER, PROFIT AND THE GOALS OF THE ORGANIZATION

Uncertainty creates the potential for gains and losses, for correct decisions and mistakes. He who has the knowledge or information or intuition to make the correct decisions obtains power. This is true both within and outside of organizations. The individual who chooses the 'right' career, buys the 'right' piece of property, backs the 'right' candidate, plants at the 'right' time of year, and so on is ahead of those making the wrong choices. The general principle, then, is that uncertainty creates power for those having the information to make correct decisions in the face of the uncertainty. In the corporation, where the pursuit of profit is an accepted goal, this power is frequently monetarized in the form of high salaries, stock options, insider trading gains by the managers and so on.[5] In the non-profit organization or the public buraucracy power must more often be used to obtain non-pecuniary goals: security, leisure, status and prestige.[6]

The contrast should not be overdrawn, however. Corporate managers are interested in prestige, security and other non-pecuniary goals. And a number of writers have argued that the corporate manager's objectives are a package of pecuniary and non-pecuniary goals rather than the maximization of profits.[7] Indeed, since reported profits are by custom and, to some extent, by law the property of the stockholders, managers must exercise their claim on the firm's residual in such a way so that it appears as a legitimate operating cost. Their options for doing so in a way that produces direct pecuniary benefits are limited, so that managers are almost forced to accept part of their share of profits in a non-pecuniary form. On the other side, there are a variety of possibilities by which public officials can gain financially from their position including the use of insider information, the receipt of gifts, bribes, kickbacks, etc.

The analogous role information and uncertainty play in the profit-oriented corporation and the non-profit bureaucracy suggests that the behaviour of individuals in these organizations, managers and bureaucrats, should in many ways be similar.[8] Both will seek to acquire information–power. Where they will differ, if at all, will be in how they utilize whatever power they possess to achieve their own personal pecuniary and non-pecuniary goals. We can thus expect managers and workers in industrial enterprises to adopt strategems similar to those Crozier describes in the two French bureaucracies of creating self-serving uncertainty, maintaining secrecy regarding information in one's possession, and so on.

The monitoring function managers serve in a teamwork organization suggests another strategy they might employ to increase their power. Recall that the need for monitor-specialists arises essentially because of the free-rider problem created by the prisoner's dilemma nature of teamwork production. The free-rider problem is worse, the larger the team. Thus, the need for monitor-managers and the importance of the information they possess will increase, the larger the size of their organization.

Several writers have posited size or growth in size as goals of corporate managers, see Baumol (1967) and Marris (1964). The reasons given are typically the correlation between organizational size and managerial salaries, and the non-pecuniary rewards from managing a large, growing company. Our analysis suggests an additional reason why managers pursue size and growth. Growth can be expected to create uncertainty about the size of the residual profit and, thus, increase the value of the information managers gather. Increasing size worsens the free-rider problem, again increasing the value of the monitor-managers' information. In short, the power of managers within the corporation should increase with size and growth. Managers should favour size and growth as corporate objectives, since they increase their power to achieve any other more direct personal goal the managers have.

The major constraint on management's claims on the profit residual is the threat of outside take-over, see Marris (1964), Manne (1966) and Alchian and Demsetz (1972). The free-rider problem keeps the average stockholder from carefully monitoring managers, but the voting rights which accompany common shares provide incentives for outside entrepreneurs to buy out large blocks of shares and take over the company transferring the incumbent management's share of profit to itself. To do so, however, the potential take-over raider needs to have information on the profit he can earn from a successful take-over. This is information that is possessed and for obvious reasons guarded by the incumbent managers. Here again size and, more specifically, diversification can increase the power of managers *vis-à-vis* potential take-over raiders by increasing the volume and complexity of the information required to evaluate the potential gains from a take-over raid. Ajit Singh (1971) has presented empirical evidence that the probability of a company's being taken over, given its profitability, does decrease significantly with its size.[9] Now size should not be an impediment to a take-over in a perfect capital market. But the capital market cannot operate perfectly if there are asymmetries in the distribution of the relevant information, see Stigler (1967). Such asymmetries are precisely what we can expect managers to seek and create to protect their positions, and these would appear to correlate positively with size and growth.

Jensen and Meckling (1976) have developed a model of the managerial firm in which managers do have some discretion to pursue their own goals, but are induced to reveal information about their company's performance to raise capital. The predictions of their model would, thus, seem to be at odds with ours, and also, fortunately, with reality. The Securities and Exchange Commission was founded following the Great Crash of 1929, which revealed that many corporate managers had concealed information from investors, which furthered managerial interests at the expense of bond and stockholders. Since its inception the SEC has fought an on-and-off battle with corporations to induce their managers to reveal more information to which they are privy. The most recent round of this battle has been over the reporting by large diversified corporations of sales, profit and similar operating data by corporate division. This is precisely the kind of information one would not expect managers to reveal if they feared a take-over attempt, of course. Indeed, the reason why the company has diversified may be to conceal it. The situation in Europe is, if anything, worse.

The reason why corporations do not have to reveal information of this type to raise capital, as Jensen and Meckling predict, is that most corporations are not heavily dependent on the external capital market for investment funds. This is particularly true of large, mature companies. Thus, reliance on internal fund flows as a source of investment capital is complementary to a management's goals of preserving its power *vis-à-vis* the other factor owners.[10]

Once again, analogous arguments can be extended to regulated firms, non-profit organizations, and government bureaucracies. William Niskanen (1971) develops his model of bureaucracy on the assumption that bureaucrats are self-interested individuals, who maximize the size of their budget. Niskanen gives little justification for the latter behavioural assumption. The theory presented here helps to explain why this is a plausible goal and in so doing links Niskanen's theory to the traditional literature on bureaucracy extending back to Weber. Increasing the size and complexity of a bureaucracy should increase the insider-bureaucrat's control over information relative to that of its monitors, thus increasing the bureaucrat's power to achieve his personal goals, whatever they might be.

IV. HIERARCHY, POWER AND THE DISTRIBUTION OF PROFITS[11]

The traditional way of dealing with situations of uncertainty, in which one party may be able to take advantage of another, is for the parties to form a contract specifying the rights and obligations of each under the various contingencies that may arise as time unfolds and the uncertanties disappear. Should conflicts arise at some point, the parties to the contract can then appeal to an impartial third party to arbitrate their claims as established and guaranteed under the contract. Given the uncertainties and potential for conflict over the distribution of residual share that exist in the firm, one would naturally expect the members of this team to resort to the use of contract to protect their claims to the residual share. The major factor owners òf the firm are, of course, joined in a form of contractual relationship. Let us see therefore how information and uncertainty are handled under these contracts.

The contract between the common shareholders and the corporation is decidedly open ended. Although the profits of the company figuratively belong to stockholders, the determination of what gets reported as profits is made by the management, and the determination of what fraction of those profits that are reported gets paid as dividends is made by the board of directors. In principle, this latter body is supposed to serve as an impartial third party between management and stockholders to ensure that management does not abuse its insider's position at the expense of the stockholders. In practice it is typically under management control with management occupying several positions on the board, and undoubtedly wielding more power than its numbers suggest due to the greater amount of information its representatives possess about company operations. Indeed, since the board is heavily dependent on the management for information it must be largely under management's control. This fact is revealed in the following quote from the Board of Directors of the Pennsylvania Railroad made more than 100 years ago, and some fifty years before Berle and Means (1932). 'The present form of organization (part-time directors and full-time officers) makes practical ciphers of the Directors, and this is from no deliberate intention, but from the very necessities of the case.' After presenting this quote, Alfred Chandler (1962, p. 313) went on to observe that, 'Once a large business has reached a size that required the services of several full-time administrators, the board and the stockholders had only a negative or *veto* power on the government of their enterprise and on the allocation of its resources. They could say no, but they had neither the information nor the awareness of the company's situation to propose realistic alternative courses of action.'

Thus, the stockholder's contract with corporate management does not offer much protection against the management's power to claim a larger fraction of profits than was understood at the time both became parties to the contract. The stockholder's major means of controlling management remains his right to sell his shares, or refuse to buy. We are thus back to the threat of take-over, and the discipline of the capital market. It should be stressed that either of these would suffice if the management could not withhold information from the market. Solow (1971) has shown that the capital market can discipline a growth-maximizing management to maximize stockholder welfare by withholding capital from the company at the time of its inception. To do this, however, the market must know at the time the company is born what its growth and investment pattern will be throughout its entire life. Armed with this amount of information, the capital market has full control (power) over management. But obviously the uncertainties which surround a company's future at its birth allow no such discipline. As time passes, and the future becomes the present, information on how the various uncertainties facing the company are being resolved accrues asymmetrically to management and the stockholders. This unbalanced accumulation of information shifts the balance of power in favour of management and allows it to interpret the terms of the stockholder–management contract in a way which is most favourable to the latter.

As John Commons (1924, p. 285) once observed, the wage contract typically 'is not a contract, it is a continuing implied *renewal* of contracts at every minute and hour based on the continuance of . . . satisfactory service . . . and compensation'. The chief, and often only, explicit stipulation of the contract is that the employee agrees to accept authority within some limits for a certain wage. See Simon (1957). Thus, the labour contract is open ended with respect to both time and duties. Given that labour and management participate in a teamwork activity, the fruits of participation will appear as a joint product the division of which is in part arbitrary. The potential thus exists for conflict between worker and management over how the jointly produced residual is divided (wages), and how the vague limits to managerial authority are determined in practice.

The nature and complexity of the employment relationship requires that the bulk of the terms of this contract remain vague and implicit. Indeed, as Williamson (1975) has emphasized, implicit contracts are the distinguishing feature of hierarchical organizations. But with the bulk of the terms of the contract implicit, they cannot be arbitrated by impartial third parties. Instead, one of the parties to the contract must itself arbitrate the contract, and this task naturally falls to management given its role of information gatherer and monitor. But, this also gives management great latitude to interpret (arbitrate) the contract in ways most advantageous to itself.

The worker's ability to ensure his share of the company's joint product comes not from his ability to enforce the terms of contract on an ongoing basis, but, in much the same way as with stockholders, in his right to quit or not join the company. Economists often assume this right suffices. Alchian and Demsetz (1972), for example, compare the worker–manager relationship to the customer–grocer relationship. But labour is seldom as mobile as this analogy suggests. Softness in the labour market, the accumulation of industry or firm-specific skills, or merely the inertia residence in a given community builds up over time produce rents that can be appropriated by management. The only way for labour to protect itself from this form of exploitation is to demand more explicit contracts amenable to third-party arbitration.

It is interesting to note in this regard that employment contracts in the public sector have typically been much more specific and protective of employee rights than they have been in the private sector. Why this should be so is not clear. Public sector employees would not appear to be inherently less mobile, as a group, than private sector employees, although in some areas the government is in a monopsonist position, and conceivably could exploit exployees with 'firm' specific human capital. Whatever the explanation, it is interesting to observe the extension of civil service-type rules from the public to the private sector, a trend more pronounced in Europe than America but nevertheless observable there also. The growth of labour unions and the strengthening of the labour contract is also in part a method for increasing the worker's capacity to monitor managers, in part a formalization of the worker–management contract to allow third-party arbitration. Finally, experiments in worker participation are efforts to involve workers directly in information gathering and the mutual monitoring of managers. Not surprisingly these have met with the greatest resistance from management.

V. CONCLUSIONS

Since the end of World War II both governments and business have grown tremendously in size. What is more, in most countries this appears to be a continuation of a secular process rather than the outgrowth of a cycle. In the United States at least, the growth of the former has recently been treated with some alarm. Social scientists from a variety of disciplines and ideological persuasions have begun to explore models of budget-maximizing bureaucrats and vote-maximizing legislators. Somewhat surprisingly, the growth in business size has not met with a similar reaction. Economists, in particular, to the extent that they notice it at all, appear to treat it as the natural consequence of the Darwinian forces of the market seeking out more efficient organizational forms.

The arguments of this paper suggest that the two phenomena may be more closely related than generally believed. The differences between profit and non-profit institutions may be far less than seems to be implied by the economics literature, at least. All organizations must deal with uncertainty, all must gather and process information to do so. In the process, certain individuals within the organizations will be vested with the power to advance their own goals to the disadvantage of other members of the organization, and can be expected to exercise that power. These characteristics all organizations have in common, and they can be expected to produce important similarities in their performances. Rather than continually stressing the difference between profit-oriented and non-profit-oriented bureaucracies, we might begin now to explore some of their similarities.

NOTES

1.   The importance of secrecy to creating and preserving political power has been emphasized by Francis E. Rourke (1961, 1969). *See also* Mills (1956) and Weber (1947).
2.   *See* Amacher *et. al.* (1976) and Rourke (1969, pp. 55-8). The military is one of the three major groups making up Mills' (1956) power elite. Mills also lays great emphasis on the importance of secrecy in maintaining power.
3.   The most extensive development of the uncertainty-based theory of profit is by Knight (1965, first edn. 1921).
4.   Schumpeter did not speak of information but of innovations. They amount to the same thing, however. For an innovation is nothing more than an idea that a new product (invention), or process, or organizational structure will produce a profit. And it is successful only to the extent that the idea (information) is a good one. Schumpeter's theory is best developed in *The Theory of Economic Development* (1934).

Other important theories of the firm and of profit can also be related to information of a specific kind. Thus, Ronald Coase stresses information about what kinds of activities are more efficiently handled within the firm than in the market (1937). For further discussion *see* Mueller (1976).
5.   On the link between managerial salaries and profits. *see* Lewellan and Huntsman (1970) and Masson (1971). On insider trading *see* Manne (1966).
6.   *See* e.g. Downs (1967).

7. *See* e.g. Baumol (1967), Marris (1964), Williamson (1964) and Galbraith (1967a).
8. Several writers have sought an analogue for power in the economic sphere. Peter Blau (1964) compares the Knightian entrepreneur's receipt of profit to the political leader's receipt of power as reward for making risky decisions, but does not develop the analogy. Talcott Parsons (1963) compares power to money.
9. Kuehn (1975) and Smiley (1976) present additional evidence regarding the slack in the take-over mechanism. Smiley's results are particularly interesting. He found that a successfully taken-over firm had fallen to 50 per cent of its potential value by the time of its take-over, but that only 30 per cent of this loss appeared to be recoverable following the take-over. Thus, as one might expect, the managers exercised their claim on the company's profits in such a way as to limit the gains from successful take-over to a fraction of their potential magnitude.
10. For further discussion of the relation between the managerial theory of the firm and internal investment theories *see* Grabowski and Mueller (1972). On the importance of firm maturity to the stockholder/manager conflict *see* Mueller (1972) and Grabowski and Mueller (1975).
11. This section draws in part on FitzRoy and Mueller (1984).

4 Cooperation and Conflict in Contractual Organizations*

Some fifty years ago Berle and Means (1932) called to the attention of economists the separation of ownership from control in the modern corporation, an economic fact at odds with the usual assumption made in the theory of the firm. The overwhelming response of the profession was to continue to ignore this fact.[1] A reason for this not so benign neglect is easy to imagine. Berle and Means had delivered a message the profession did not want to hear. Not only was something wrong with the assumptions economists were making about the corporate firm, something was wrong with the corporate sector of the economy. Concentration was increasing, ownership had lost control of the corporation, and those in control, the managers, seemed not to be pursuing ends in the interests of either ownership or society.

Although Berle and Means's message fell on deaf economic ears, it was in tune with the popular concerns of the time. Stigler and Friedland (1983) may be right that the publication of *Private Property and the Modern Corporation* came too late to be an important factor in the passage of the legislation of 1933 and 1934 to regulate corporate managers and securities markets, but the book certainly provided a justification for this legislation, and has continued to do so ever since. The book was accepted by non-economist students of the corporation almost as uncritically as it was dismissed by economists.

So things stood, more or less, for at least a quarter of a century. Thus, in 1958 Modigliani and Miller could develop a theory of corporate investment that would influence the development of the corporate finance literature for the next twenty years, blithely assuming managers maximize the value of the firm, that is, ownership wealth, without even expressing a caveat. About the same time, however, a literature was beginning to evolve that did, for the first time, build on the Berle and Means insight into corporate structure. Starting with Baumol's sales maximization hypothesis in 1959, a series of papers and books appeared exploring the implication that managers had discretion to pursue objectives in conflict with ownership interests, and used it.[2] Although this literature was

*Reprinted from, *Quarterly Review of Economics and Business*, 24(4), Winter 1984. Felix R. FitzRoy and Dennis C. Mueller.

orthodox in its basic assumptions and methodology, managers maximize utility subject to constraints, it, like the Berle and Means book, raised implicitly and sometimes explicitly as in the work of Leibenstein (1966, 1969) questions about the overall efficiency of a corporate sector in which corporate managers pursued their goals with seemingly wide discretionary latitude. Again, the response, or lack thereof, by the profession was predictable. Most economists ignored the challenge of the traditional neoclassical assumptions. Those who took it up dismissed the arguments of the managerialists as theoretically unsound and/or quantitatively insignificant (Alchian, 1965; Baldwin, 1964; Machlup, 1967).

Then, in the 1970s an interesting development took place. The separation of ownership from control problem was rechristened the principal–agent problem, and became the focal point of analysis for a large and rapidly growing number of neoclassical economists, as part of a new, *generalized* neoclasical economics that emphasizes transactions costs.[3] Why the need for a new name, given that 'separation of ownership and control' had been around for forty years and was well known if seldom used by economists? Our guess is that the term 'separation of ownership and control' was discarded precisely because it was so well known and so closely associated with Berle and Means, and thus carried with it the connotation that all was not right in the corporate sector. For indeed, within the new, generalized neoclassical economics, it turns out that the principal–agent problem is really not much of a problem after all. Just as we have learned to expect from old, traditional neoclassical economics that all will be well if markets are allowed to function freely, agency costs too are minimized by market forces. All that appears at issue is which market it is that assures these efficient outcomes. For Jensen and Meckling (1976) it is a capital market governed by rational expectations, for Fama (1980) the market for managers; for most, it is the market for corporate control.

The position of Oliver Williamson's work in this evolution of economic theory is interesting. On the one hand, his first publications were seminal contributions to the managerial theory of the firm (1963, 1964), on the other hand, his writings on transactions costs form the theoretical foundation for the new, generalized neoclassical theory, most especially, of course, *Markets and Hierarchies*, 1975. Despite the latter, Williamson himself has been unwilling to conclude that existing markets and institutions resolve all normative issues raised by agency cost problems.[4] Nevertheless, he does stress the importance of the evolution of the M-form organization in mitigating if not eliminating control-loss problems, while at the same time assuming that top management in the M-form organization maximizes shareholder welfare. Thus, Williamson effectively assumes away a separation of ownership from control problem for the large, diversified M-form corporation. The normative implications Alfred Chandler wished to convey about the evolution of corporate structures through the title of his justly famous book, *The Visible Hand* (1977), could be drawn by a not scrupulously careful reader of a number of recent Williamson works (1975, 1980, 1981, 1984).

This view of corporate capitalism is too sanguine. Its saccharine flavour arises because most of the transactions-costs, agency-costs literature focuses only on the effects of organizational form on allocative efficiency, that is, on how the hierarchy or the market minimizes these costs. But the separation of principal of agent, of ownership from control, raises distributional as well as efficiency issues. It is from the distributional consequences of hierarchy that the conflicts between one factor group and another stem, and it is these distributional conflicts that often lead to the demands for state intervention in corporate governance. A full understanding of the growth and evolution of hierarchical structures requires that one looks at both the efficiency and distributional implications of organizational form.

In this paper we employ Williamson's transaction costs approach to examine the distributional conflicts that inevitably arise in a hierarchical organization. We first review the salient characteristics of contracts to achieve allocative efficiency gains. We then employ these concepts to describe the entrepreneur, manager and firm. In Section III we take up explicitly the issue of how conflict arises in a contractual economic organization. Positive and normative implications are then drawn.

I.   CONTRACTS TO ENSURE COOPERATION

Economists have traditionally viewed social cooperation as division of labour and market exchange of resources by egoistic individuals. Repeated exchange reduces or spreads the cost of acquiring the information necessary for rational decision making, and increasingly many participants avoid bargaining costs by generating competitive prices as the core shrinks down to the set of competitive equilibria (Arrow and Hahn, 1971). However, such market exchange actually represents only the tip of the iceberg of economic activity or exchange in general. For most people, most of their working time, cooperation consists of communication or other interaction with coworkers in some joint productive endeavour. Informational, material, and social exchange *without* the help of prices dominates, and trips to the market, though essential complements to the process of production, represent only interludes in an economic actor's allocation of time.

Non-market cooperation through face-to-face, personal interaction generally takes place in expectation of a share in the gains from joint activity. Agreement in some sense on the distribution of these benefits is thus a prerequisite for cooperation. But these benefits in turn depend upon the detailed activity of the participants, and hence agreement over the latter is required before estimates of the gains to be shared can be formed. But now egoistic individuals have an incentive to improve their bargaining position by misrepresenting future intentions or deceiving their partners 'opportunistically' (Williamson, 1975). For when agreement has been reached, the interdependence of cooperative action means that individuals may not bear all the costs of reneging or reducing their efforts, while gains therefrom such as leisure are individually appropriated. Given the externalities in this situation, individual optimizing *ex post* reduces the potential gain from cooperative behaviour and leads to the familiar prisoners' dilemma game.

The essential features of this game are: first, benefits from cooperation do exist. Any production activity with increasing returns to scale or gains from cooperation is of this type. This feature of cooperative contracts is emphasized by Alchian and Demsetz (1972). Second, the advantages available through cooperation cannot be achieved as cheaply via market transactions, the point raised by Coase (1937). Third, the possibility exists for one individual to become better off by not conforming to the behaviour required for the cooperative solution to the prisoners' dilemma.

When individually beneficial shirking, carelessness, and on-the-job consumption can take place, one must assume that it will (Alchian and Demsetz, 1972; Williamson, 1964). To encourage honesty and attain efficient cooperation rewards must be tied to performance to penalize shirking or free-riding (Olson, 1965, pp. 50-1, 132-5). When promises exchanged in contract can be profitably broken, monitoring is necessary to sanction breach of promise. Monitoring is costly, so it is of interest to investigate how this cost varies with the nature of the contract, and the conditions under which it is carried out.

We take it to be axiomatic that all members of a cooperative agreement are mobile at the time they join in the agreement, that is, all have other options in the market they could pursue. Often members of a cooperative agreement become immobile upon joining or over time due to the transaction costs of exit and entry, or the accumulation of non-transferable human capital.[5] Thus, a prospective entrant incurs considerable risk unless he holds firm expectations that *other* members will adhere to the terms, implicit or explicit, of an initially attractive agreement. Such expectations can be created through the writing of a formal contract or guarantee enforceable in the courts. Alternatively, informal assurances may suffice, when the prospective entrant holds a degree of trust in the good faith of other participants. Trust is likely to be reinforced by successful cooperation and the establishment of personal ties and empathy, aided by the absence of intensive monitoring or close supervision. One way of reducing uncertainty before entry is for the organization to develop customary or traditional modes of cooperative behaviour. Long-term attachment and a stable environment foster such a pattern, and then the inertia of tradition, the costs of abandoning a transactionally economic system of well-tried informal incentives toward efficient cooperation, offer an implicit guarantee for continuity and insurance against tyrannization of the newcomer. Indeed, an organization which depends for survival upon attracting new entrants willing to immobilize themselves needs to demonstrate a stable history of equitable distribution of the gains from cooperation.

The definition of mobility employed here is more general than the word's usual connotation so we shall define the term precisely. An individual is perfectly mobile if his present income equals his income in his next best employment, net of any transaction costs of changing employment. It follows then, that any individual who cannot receive an income in an alternative occupation equal to his marginal revenue product *plus* his share of the gains from cooperation is immobile. This definition allows us to quantify immobility as the difference between present and net opportunity income.[6]

Consider first the situation in which all parties to a cooperative agreement become immobile over time. Each can withdraw from the cooperative arrangement and this threat of withdrawal remains the ultimate sanction by which each can enforce an equitable sharing of the gains from cooperation. But the cost of withdrawal, loss of the gains from cooperation, is high and one expects less drastic sanctions to be used more often. When the players are immobile, the same prisoners' dilemma game is effectively repeated over and over. Uncertainty over individual behaviour declines as knowledge accumulates. The necessary contractual agreement needed to solve the prisoners' dilemma is reached over time through the development of trust and mutual understanding, enforced in extreme cases by the threat of unilateral termination of the cooperative agreement.[7] With large groups, the withdrawal of a single member may not force the dissolution of the cooperative group. Nevertheless, exit may impose costs on the other members, and the threat of expulsion remains an effective deterrent to free-riding if the members have inferior alternatives outside the group, that is, they are immobile.

With exit a measure of last resort, 'voice' plays the major role in adapting organization to a member's needs and external constraints (Hirschman, 1970). Homogeneity and small numbers are clearly the most favourable conditions for informal communication and peer-group pressures to maintain cohesion and effectivity under the 'high-trust' relationship immobility fosters (Fox, 1974). The closer decision making is to the rule of consensus the stronger is the reinforcement of this relationship, with consequent saving of monitoring costs, minimization of shirking and propagation of 'consummate cooperation' (Williamson, 1975, p. 69).

Now consider what happens when one of the members of a cooperative agreement remains mobile after the agreement is formed. The mobile member need no longer police the behaviour of the other members. So long as he continues to receive an income equal to his opportunity costs he is indifferent to the shirking or non-shirking of the others. At the same time, his incentives to shirk are greatly increased. The threat of dissolution of the group, or expulsion from it, is no longer menacing. Thus, he can be expected to 'take more chances' in engaging in deceptive shirking, since the full cost of any reduction in revenue is now borne by the immobile members.

Even when the mobile members of a cooperative group remain in it for long periods of time, their capacity to leave the group quickly on favourable terms makes them appear mobile in the eyes of the other members. When shirking *is* profitable, low trust on the part of others is prudent, and informal communication channels are likely to be distorted by opportunistic deception (or suspicions thereof). The immobile member of the team can be expected to demand a more explicit statement of the duties to be performed by the mobile member(s) to facilitate monitoring. For all policing is now shifted to the immobile member, who has no choice but to remain in the cooperative agreement. All of the residual gains from enforcing the level of effort required for the cooperative solution to the prisoners' dilemma now fall to him. His own extra effort is ensured by his full claim on the residual; the extra effort of the other member(s) must be ensured by intensive policing. Bounded rationality imposes limits, however, on the specificity of contracts, and the effectiveness with which they can be enforced. Simplification of the tasks of the mobile team members is thus encouraged.

The mobile member of a cooperative agreement exercises *control* on other members via exit or the threat thereof. Whenever he does not receive rewards, pecuniary or otherwise, in accord with opportunities elsewhere, he can force an increase in his share of the gains from cooperation by threatening to leave. The immobile member must rely on voice, however. Specialized policing of performance requires authority to dispense formal rewards and penalties, while discretionary decision-making power must be vested with authority to direct activity and sanction disobedience. Thus, while groups in which all members are immobile, and information and control equally shared, should be characterized by high trust and consensual decision making, asymmetries in mobility lead to informational asymmetries, concentrated authority, and low-trust relationships. Those in authority, the immobile, suspect the mobile of shirking within whatever limits bounded rationality places on the specificity of the contract, and their ability to police it. The mobile do not necessarily distrust the other members, but there is no reason to expect them to trust them either. The mobile can afford to be indifferent to the other members' behaviour.

Indifference reaches the extreme when all members of the cooperative group are fully mobile. The division of the gains from cooperation is then fully determined by conditions in the market. All team members enforce the agreement by the threat of exit.

Specialization in monitoring and the concomitant concentration of authority can be brought about by the existence of economies of scale, or specialized talent at monitoring, however, even when all members of the team are equally mobile or immobile (Arrow, 1974; Williamson, 1975). When authority and information asymmetries are not matched by asymmetric mobility, low-trust syndromes are reinforced. When those lacking authority are mobile, their trust or distrust of other members is immaterial, since they can exercise effective control via the threat of exit. When absence of authority is combined with immobility, however, these members must to some extent trust those in authority to give them their 'rightful' share of the collective gains from cooperation. But their combined lack of mobility and authority places them in a vulnerable position. The asymmetric distribution of information which led to the asymmetry in authority reinforces suspicions that those in authority may abuse their position and take an excessive share of the surplus.

In such an environment those entering a cooperative association demand, to the extent their initial mobility allows them, specific guarantees to protect their position after they become members of the group and immobile. Thus, while demands for specific contracts come from those in authority when authority is based on immobility, demands for specific contracts will come from those without authority when authority and immobility are not matched, and authority is derived from concentrated possession of information. In the limit with highly specific contracts, outside arbitration of disputes is feasible. The potential advantage of arbitration is impartiality; the opportunism which led to conflict can be set aside and distributional questions settled by a disinterested third party. But then the incentive to invest the necessary time for effective arbitration may be lacking (Williamson, 1975, p. 101). Impartiality gives way to indifference. The costs of writing contracts rises with the specificity and complexity of the cooperation covered. Simplification of tasks is thereby further encouraged, like a completely specific contract under the uncertanties of continuing productive cooperation (Williamson *et al.*, 1975). Thus, transaction cost considerations suggest that outside arbitration of contracts will play a limited role in settling the conflicts inherent in asymmetric allocation of authority unmatched by mobility asymmetries. But then the potential for conflict in an atmosphere of distrust must remain.

Between the polar cases of concentrated unilateral authority, and evenly distributed control are a variety of control structures. There are well-known limits to the potential of peer-group pressure and informal consensual rules for reaching decisions (Williamson, 1975, pp. 45-9). When formal voting procedures are employed, something less than a full unanimity rule is usually optimal, to eliminate incentives for strategic behaviour and inordinate delays. In general, the smaller the majority required to reach a group decision, the quicker this decision can be reached. But, the smaller the required majority is, the more likely an individual is to be excluded from the winning majority, and, given opportunism, the more likely he is to be 'tyrannized' by the winning majority (Buchanan and Tullock, 1962). Thus, even in cooperative groups in which democratic decision procedures are employed, there are pressures to demand more explicit initial contracts specifying the rights and duties of individual members, and/or greater resort to exit, as authority becomes concentrated in the majority, a body of representatives, or the executive. These demands are most intense when all authority is concentrated in a hierarchical organization structure. The various possibilities are illustrated in Table 4.1. The rows differentiate between alternatives for gathering information, the columns differentiate according to the distribution of mobility. Entries in the table depict the form of control mechanism, and the expected characteristics of the cooperative agreement. It should be noted that 'authoritarian' control structures can include tyrannical autarchies, benevolent dictatorships and majority rule democracies, tyrannous or otherwise.

Table 4.1: *Mobility, information, and the control structure in the organization*

Information	Mobility		
	Uniform Low Mobility	Asymmetric Mobility	Uniform High Mobility
No Economies of Information Gathering	Consensual high trust	Authoritarian exit	Anarchic exit impersonal
Economies of Scale and Specialization	Authoritarian low trust	Authoritarian exit low trust	Authoritarian exit impersonal

When information is evenly distributed and all participants equally mobile, we have essentially the conditions of market exchange. Social interchange is impersonal. The gains from cooperation (trade) and specialization are achieved through the working of the price system, and distribution of these gains is effected impersonally by the market. On the other extreme, uniform low mobility isolates the participants from the market and requires a determination of the distribution of the gains from cooperation by some bargaining or collective choice process. With a symmetric distribution of information, uniform low mobility should produce consensual, high-trust cooperation, and a mutually acceptable distribution of gains. Low mobility and an asymmetric distribution of information, however, produce the lowest trust, most conflict prone of the possibilities. All of the distributional issues must be decided collectively, but bargaining positions are unequal due to the asymmetric distribution of information. As one moves rightward across the bottom row, tensions inherent in the asymmetric distribution of authority ease, as those lacking authority become capable of policing the contract by exit. The distribution of the benefits becomes increasingly determined by the market, as each mobile participant claims a share at least equal to what he can earn elsewhere. The range for bargaining shrinks and is left to the immobile members. An exception occurs only when the most mobile also have the most information due to some advantage of skill or position in the organization. Such an individual has all of the bargaining advantages and can exploit these to obtain all of the benefits from cooperative action. In the bottom right-hand corner is the organizational equivalent to the market, a cooperative arrangement in which all members are equally mobile, but some are charged with authority for directing the activities of others. All, including the monitor, then receive an essentially market-determined income, and the sharing decision is made impersonally without conflict.

II. THE CONCEPTS ILLUSTRATED

In this section, we use the features of cooperative contracts to describe the economic functions of the entrepreneur, the manager, and the firm.

A. The Entrepreneur

One's intuitive notion of a contract is a pact among (legal) equals. At first such a view seems incompatible with the usual description of the entrepreneur, which places him somehow above the other parties to the contract. But, even a pact among equals must be initiated. It is unlikely that all potential signatories to a mutually beneficial agreement simultaneously realize the desirability of such a pact and propose it. A potential definition of the entrepreneur is the initiator of contracts, which *ex ante* are beneficial to all parties.

Consider a contract to share risk. Such contracts have the salient features of the prisoners' dilemma. All can achieve superior risk/return positions *ex ante* by joining the contract, some can typically experience further *ex post* gains by opportunistic behaviour, which in the context of an insurance contract is usually called 'moral hazard' (Pauly, 1968). A risk-spreading contract is the exchange of a claim to the return from a risky asset (say, a share of common stock) for a safe one (money). An innovative idea is a risky asset. Its very newness creates uncertainty, and the incentive to spread its risks by bringing in other individuals. Even if the entrepreneur possesses sufficient capital to finance the innovation's introduction himself, the risky innovation is likely to assume a large portion of his portfolio, and create pressure, if he is risk averse, to exchange some claims against it for safer assets. By definition the innovator knows about the innovation (or more about it), and others do not. Thus, the entrepreneurial role of *initiating* a contract to share risk is a natural one for a Schumpeterian innovator to play.

It would seem that the role of initiating contracts to share risks ought also to be compatible with the Knightian definition of the entrepreneur as the bearer of uncertainty. But it is not. In Knight's theory, the entrepreneur provides no capital, guarantees all factor owners a certain income, and receives the uncertain residual. He is willing to do so because he is 'confident and venturesome', while other factor owners are 'timid and doubtful' (Knight, 1921, p. 269). But more than asymmetric attitudes towards risk are necessary to get all parties to join such a contract. In particular, the capitalist's loan b is really *safe* only if the contractual repayment, say, rb, is less than the sum of random net income (y_s), liquidation value of the firm's assets (k), and whatever private assets of the entrepreneur are appropriable in case of bankruptcy A_e, or

$$rb \leq \min_s y_s + k + A_e \qquad (1)$$

If (1) does not hold, the capitalist has made a *quasi*-loan and assumed a *quasi*-profit-sharing role. The exact nature of the profit-sharing component of the contract depends on the specifications of what takes place if (1) is not satisfied. That (1) would be satisfied without a fairly large A_e, seems unlikely in any activity involving significant risks. If (1) is satisfied by the presence of a large A_e, then the entrepreneur's relative willingness to bear risks is explained, but it is also obvious that he is bringing more to the firm than a penchant for risk taking. He is in part playing the role of a capitalist assuming the risks of default in exchange for a share in the returns of the risky asset.

At one point Knight notes that wealth may be a necessary prerequisite for the entrepreneur as he defines him, but Knight immediately places it in a secondary role.

In actual society, freedom of choice between employer and employee status depends normally on the possession of a minimum amount of capital. However, *demonstrated* ability can always get funds for business operations. A property-less employer can make the contractual payments secure by insurance even when they may involve loss... (p. 274, emphasis added).

From elsewhere in the text, it is clear that this demonstrated ability consists in a talent or judgment for making decisions in the presence of uncertainty (e.g. pp. 270-1). But, unless this ability has been demonstrated to such a degree that uncertainty has completely disappeared, the supplier of capital or seller of insurance must also bear some risk that the ability demonstrated in the past will not continue into the future, and we are back to a risk-sharing contract.

The ability to make decisions in the presence of uncertainty Knight identifies with entrepreneurship is quite compatible with the role of the entrepreneur as initiator of contracts. Indeed, in some ways the Knightian entrepreneur is a generalization of the Schumpeterian entrepreneur. In an uncertain environment, some have a greater capacity to see profitable opportunities (including innovations) than others, and they become the initiators of the contracts required to realize these profits. But, the nature of the contracts is not as Knight describes it. In general, all participants (capital, labour and land) bear some of the uncertainties surrounding the activity, and, for that matter, assume a *quasi*-entrepreneurial role in exercising judgment as to whether the terms of the contract they sign are to their maximum advantage (Mueller, 1976).

Knight further argues that the entrepreneur, as guarantor of a contractual wage, must direct the activity of the worker, for the latter '. . . party would not place himself under the direction of the first without such a guaranty', (Knight, 1921, p. 270). But, Knight is then casting the entrepreneur in the dual role of internal monitor or functional authority for efficient contract enforcement, as well as uncertainty bearer (residual claimant).

Two problems arise. When capitalist and entrepreneur are separated, the former is guarantor if anyone is, and the latter as initiator or innovator may, himself, be monitored and even directed by the ultimate insurer whose funds are at stake. That is, the sharing of the revenues of the firm and the monitoring task can be divided in a number of different ways as described above, and neither the initiator of the original contract, nor the supplier of capital, nor any other single party to the contract need assume either sole claim to the residual, or the entire monitoring role. Secondly, in the absence of long-term wage contracts, it is only income until dismissal which is guaranteed, so the existence of search and mobility costs for the worker imposes risks upon him which weaken Knight's rationale for the worker's acceptance of entrepreneurial direction. As we noted above, the acceptance of a single internal member of a cooperative agreement as sole arbitrator of this agreement is directly related to the mobility of the other participants. But neither the capitalist nor the workers can necessarily be assumed to be fully mobile as is implicit in Knight's view of the firm. When they are not, all may have, or wish to have, a share in monitoring activity.[8]

All members of the firm can also share in the entrepreneurial role. A worker, say, who chooses appropriate training and/or just initiates a contract to sell his labour-power on most advantageous terms is an entrepreneur *in this capacity*. Indeed, any self-employed activity which culminates in beneficial contracts or transactions can be entrepreneurial within our definition, irrespective of the particular nature of the contract which emerges. In a world of uncertainty, all market exchange and cooperative interaction are predicted upon *some* prior entrepreneurial activity. A pure entrepreneurial *profit* can then be naturally defined as the (pecuniary or psychic) return to the essentially information-gathering or disseminating task of initiating mutually 'profitable' contracts (Johnson, 1973; Mueller, 1976). As we shall see, enforcement activity may be necessary to appropriate this return, but it is the initiating activity *prior* to whatever is laid down formally or informally in the contract to which 'pure' profit is imputed.[9]

One of the most important classes of contracts it is profitable to initiate is that joining individuals in a productive activity characterized by a prisoners' dilemma. An important entrepreneurial role is to recognize such situations, and to propose contracts for realizing the gains from cooperation. This definition of the entrepreneurial role comes close to that described by Coase (1937). The firm includes, by Coase's definition, activities conducted more efficiently via a hierarchical control system than by the market; the entrepreneur sees which activities are more efficiently conducted within the firm than in the market. Thus, a Coasian entrepreneur initiates contracts to achieve the gains from cooperation in prisoners' dilemma situations.

Coase also describes the entrepreneur as a 'coordinator' of the activities of the firm, a definition already encountered here and employed by many other writers. The idea of a coordinator of economic activity comes close to what we describe as the manager, however, and so, we turn to him now.

B. The Manager

Once initiated, a contract must be enforced. Alchian and Demsetz (1972) assign this role to the manager. They recognize the incentive problems inherent in sharing contracts, and argue that the manager should receive all of the residual. They thus cast the manager in the same role as Knight places the entrepreneur: the guarantor of other factor incomes, and sole recipient of the residual share. This argument is subject to the same criticism levelled against Knight's description of the entrepreneur; if the only thing the manager brings to the firm is a talent for monitoring, he cannot guarantee a fixed income to all other factor owners. Some sharing of the residual in times of depression must take place; managerial shirking may hurt the other factor owners, so the manager must be monitored. Alternatively, if the manager has sufficient capital invested in the firm, or available to cover its liabilities, he might be able to guarantee other factor income. But then it is in part as capitalist that the manager receives the residual share, not simply due to his monitoring function.

The prisoners' dilemma nature of joint production makes it particularly vulnerable to free-riding by those who have short-run horizons or are highly mobile. This consideration suggests that monitoring be done by the least mobile, that is, by those who have the most to lose from free-riding. We have already noted the converse, that only those who are fairly mobile should be willing to place themselves under the monitoring authoritative control of other members of the team.

An important way free-riding can occur in a productive association is through carelessness with the capital equipment. Here, the initial effect of free-riding on revenues might be small and go undetected. Thus, when capital is supplied by a few individuals, and the income from this capital constitutes a large fraction of the income of its suppliers, the monitoring function (or a large portion thereof) logically goes to the capitalists. Klein *et al.* (1978) use this point to develop a rationale for vertical integration.

But, to the extent the innovator-entrepreneur accepts a share of revenue as payment for his innovation, he too has 'invested capital' subject to erosion through free-riding by other factor owners. Thus, the innovator-entrepreneur may be forced to assume a managerial-monitor role to recoup the potential gains from his innovative idea. This is most clearly evident when the innovative idea is a joint production process itself, capable of producing a surplus for all participants. If the innovator only initiates the contract, and then leaves the other 'productive' members to carry it out and pay him his share, he exposes his share to erosion through the free-riding of the 'active' members of the contract.

Workers can also have 'invested capital' that is subject to erosion, and therefore, an interest in monitoring the other participants in the contract. The more skilled the worker, and the more specialized his skills are to the activities of the particular cooperative, the more interest he has in the other members' actions. Those charged with planning and coordinating activities, marketing, raising capital, and other 'managerial' tasks a productive group requires may have particularly heavy investments in group-specific human capital. They are thus, 'natural' candidates for assuming the monitoring role in many cooperative productive groups.

If all team members were fully mobile, one could be chosen by lot, or on the basis of his talent for monitoring, and assigned the monitoring task. The others could receive fixed payments guaranteed by their perfect mobility. This view of cooperative agreement is taken by Alchian and

Demsetz (1972), who then define the monitor as the manager. If all factor owners are not fully mobile, however, those with the greatest sunk costs (the least mobile) are the *de facto* bearers of risk, the residual recipients. Out of self interest, they will demand a proportionate share of the monitoring authority. If we equate monitoring to managing, the manager-monitor role is likely to be divided among several members of the cooperative agreement. If the innovator-entrepreneur is still around, he is likely to assume a large role; if capital ownership is concentrated, the capitalists are likely monitors; the workers, including those at the top of the hierarchical pyramid, may be the most immobile and hence also be monitors, and so on. How the monitoring is divided up depends on the mobility and informational asymmetries of a particular membership. To assert more a priori does not seem possible.

It is clear from this discussion that the manager in Fama's theory (1980) cannot be the residual claimant-monitor of contracts. Fama argues that the agency cost problem is attenuated by the manager's concern for his market value upon leaving the firm. But this implies that managers enforce their part of the contract by remaining mobile. Someone else must then be the residual claimant and thus effectively immobile. The most obvious candidate for this is capital. Thus, Fama's view of the firm is essentially the same as Knight's in which stockholders hire and fire managers from a competitive manager market. But, then 'ultimate authority' (that is, the power to dismiss management) rests with the stockholders as does the claim to the residual. Fama's model of the firm denies the existence of the very agency cost problem it purports to solve—a separation between ownership and control.

C.   The Firm

It can, I think, be assumed that the distinguishing mark of the firm is the supersession of the price mechanism (Coase, 1937, p. 334).

While the supersession of the price mechanism is *a* characteristic of the firm, it is not *the* characteristic that distinguishes it from other cooperative institutions. One could, for example, replace 'the firm' in Coase's definition with 'the state' and have an equally valid statement, although 'the distinguishing' would now certainly be in doubt.

The inability of the price system to allocate resources efficiently in certain situations creates a potential gain from cooperative behaviour. As Coase himself showed in 1960, however, the potential for mutually beneficial cooperative behaviour creates a *prima facie* case only for the appearance of voluntary contracts among individuals, not necessarily for the state or, for that matter, the firm.

   The state appears whenever the transaction costs of writing contracts to engage in collective consumption due to the number of individuals involved, the policing costs, etc. become so large that formal written contracts become impractical and the implicit social contract or constitution underlying the state is required.

   The following analogous definition seems appropriate for the firm. The firm is a cooperative production agreement in which the number of individuals involved, nature of activities to be specified, and costs of policing the agreement are such that formal written contracts specifying the actions of all individuals are inefficient, and implicit contracts, enforced by members of the cooperative itself, are mainly used to coordinate and monitor the activities of its members.

   The definition of the firm is, thus, made to rest on the *form* of contractual relationships among the participants in a productive activity, not the *existence* of a cooperative contract *per se*. The importance of this distinction to the concept of the firm has been stressed by Williamson (1975, pp. 49-56, 67-72) in critique of Alchian and Demsetz (1972). The existence of joint production (teamwork) activities creates the need for a cooperative contract to avoid the prisoners' dilemma problem, but this contract does not necessarily have to take the form of a firm. A series of specific, perhaps fairly complicated, contracts among owners of capital, land, and labour services could be envisaged in which each maintained his autonomy to a sufficient degree so that the existence of a 'firm' as it is typically thought of would not be present. Such a set of cooperative agreements characterized the much discussed 'putting out' system of the eighteenth century (Nutzinger, 1976). Interestingly enough, the putting out system disappeared in part because of the complexity and transaction costs involved in implementing it. It is these transaction costs that require an 'informal' set of contracts, but these in turn raise the potential for additional free-riding, and the question of how the informal contract is to be enforced. This latter question is crucial to the notion of the firm suggested here. A formal, specific, exhaustive contract between two parties can be fairly easily enforced by disinterested third parties, if they can obtain access to the necessary information. If the information required to enforce the contracts can be concealed by the individuals involved, if they have too much autonomy, if the contracts must be too complicated, and so on, other procedures are required. The two main features of the firm are the informal, non-specific nature of the contracts, and the consequent necessity for enforcing them *internally* by the exercise of authority by some of the parties to the contracts themselves. Thus, in contrast to Alchian and Demsetz (1972, p. 777), it *is* 'the power to settle issues by fiat, by authority, or by disciplinary action superior to that available in the conventional market', *vested in some participants in the teamwork activity,* and not the presence of teamwork *per se,* that is the distinguishing characteristic of the firm. The distinction between 1960-Coase and 1937-Coase is fundamental here. Only when contracts become too expensive to write and enforce by third-party arbitrators does the firm appear.[10]

It should be emphasized that this definition of the firm based on the internal enforcement of the contract leaves open the question of who enforces the contract. It could be enforced by all members sharing equal authority, as under some form of consensual voting rule, by a qualified majority, or a single authoritarian figure, the manager-monitor.

There is a continuum of arrangements from market to formal contract and firm organization. Drawing a line between any of these is somewhat arbitrary. For example, some 'market' transactions are accompanied by formal contracts specifying future services (e.g. maintenance). Others may have a guarantee of certain quality or durability characteristics. Others contain implicit guarantees (contracts, trust relationships) regarding quality. The problem of delineating 'the firm' from other contractual, productive relationships is difficult. The putting out system typically had its entrepreneurial founder who brought the members together, and provided contract policing services. The system of 'inside contracting' was even more of a combination of an arms length, formal contract system, and the informal contracts of the firm.[11] Even within what is generally agreed to be a firm, the degree of formality of the contracts, method of enforcement, and so on, may differ sufficiently so that some factor owners are not really 'members of the firm', while others are.

III. CONFLICT AND COOPERATION

The firm appears to solve the same types of collective choice problems that confront the state. All of the conflicts and paradoxes which characterize collective choices within a polity exist within the firm. The preceding sections imply that the optimal set of outcomes from this collective choice process is a sharing of insurable risks, the gains from cooperation, entrepreneurship, and the control functions by all members of the team depending on their relative mobilities and capacities to gather information. With many 'provisions' of the contract left informal, and monitoring by the participants themselves, the stage is set for conflict and distrust. Thus, it is natural to expect the cooperative production agreements which characterize the firm to result in occasional conflict. And these conflicts have occupied much of the critical literature on the capitalist firm. To illustrate this point, we shall apply these concepts to two much-discussed conflicts between different members of the firm.

A. The Manager–Stockholder Conflict

Consider again the contract between an innovator-entrepreneur and a supplier of capital. These are essentially insurance contracts for spreading the risks inherent in the innovation. As such, they are subject to moral hazard. If full authority for the enterprise is lodged with the entrepreneur, he can be expected to take greater risks, enjoy more leisure, be less careful, and perhaps undertake other activities, which he would not undertake if he alone bore their full cost, (Jensen and Meckling, 1976, pp. 316-19).

Given this potential for moral hazard, we can immediately predict that if the contract binding the capitalist and entrepreneur is internally arbitrated, the capitalist will either demand a monitoring role or remain highly mobile. Alternatively, the capitalist may demand a highly detailed contract requiring easily obtainable information concerning the entrepreneur's behaviour, and amenable to outside arbitration. We next relate these predictions to but two of the many capital-transfer instruments that exist: common stock and corporate bonds.

The corporate bond is a highly detailed contract between a capital supplier and firm specifying the precise amount to be paid per time period, conditions under which it will not be paid, and so on, (Jensen and Meckling, 1976, pp. 331-7). In case of conflict, the bondholder typically resorts to third-party arbitration.

In contrast, the contract binding the stockholder to the firm is much more informal. It specifies nothing about how much the stockholder is paid or under what conditions. It makes no provision for repurchase of the stock. Arbitration of most disputes takes place inside the group of owners and managers through the annual stockholders' meeting, and by appeal to the board of directors, a mixture of inside and outside monitors. Under these conditions, we predict that the capital supplier either demands a direct monitoring role over the entrepreneur-manager, or remains highly mobile. A stockholder who owns a large fraction of a firm's stock, can claim representation on the board of directors and exercise a direct monitoring and control function. He cannot, in general, quickly liquidate his holdings without suffering some loss. A stockholder with a fractional holding is more mobile, but exercises less control. His voting right still allows him, in principle, some control over the management, but, more important, serves as a partial guarantee of his mobility. We emphasize this point, since some recent discussions of the stockholder–manager relationship assume that the shareholder's voting right is an incidental and irrelevant aspect of the stockholder–manager contract. This is false, if we think of the rest of the provisions of the contract remaining unchanged. Given the unspecified nature of the obligations placed on the managers inherent in the present contractual relationship, there is nothing to stop the managers from reducing the dividends paid to zero, and allowing the stock's price to fall accordingly. The voting rights attached to shares prevent this by allowing some stockholders to seize control and exercise a monitoring function, if management does not meet its *implicit* obligations to the stockholders.

The vulnerability of a share of non-voting stock to the adverse exercise of managerial discretion (moral hazard), would make these securities far less marketable than common shares today are, if the other provisions of the contract remained unchanged. The ability to sell a share quickly *after* its price has plunged to zero does not provide its holder with much effective mobility. One thus predicts that, if non-voting shares of common stock did exist, the contractual stipulations on management would be quite different from those of a share of common stock today. And, those who have discussed non-voting shares may have had this in mind. Jensen and Meckling (1976), for example, develop their theory of the firm by hypothesizing non-voting shares entitling holders to a *pre-specified* fraction of the firm's reported profits. This instrument differs from a share of present-day corporate stock *both* with respect to the non-voting property, and the pre-specification of a proportional dividend payment. If voting rights were removed from common shares, stockholders would demand a more explicit contractual statement of the conditions and amounts under which dividends would be paid. Denied the potential for direct, internal control through the exercise of concentrated voting rights, and the indirect control through the threat of take-over this right implies, stockholders would require more formal statement of their claims on the profits of the company written into the initial contract. In cases of conflict, (e.g. were all the deductions from revenue in arriving at reported profits legitimate under the terms of the contract?), the stockholder's appeal would now be to outside, impartial arbitration. His contractual linkage to the firm would be much like that of the bondholder, except that his return would be proportional to profits, as contractually defined, while the bondholder's is fixed.[12]

One reason the voting right for common shares has seemed unimportant to some observers is that they have assumed that the managers are heavily dependent on the equity market for capital. Jensen and Meckling assume a single capital financing decision with an eventual full payout of profits (1976). When they discuss an extension of their model to the multiperiod case, they assume the managers remain continually dependent on the equity market for capital (p. 349). It is clear, that if the entrepreneur-manager is continually dependent on the equity market for capital, he is involved in a form of infinite supergame with its suppliers which disciplines his behaviour. But many corporations make little use of the equity market for capital. The moral hazard or 'agency' problem inherent in the non-specific obligations managers have towards stockholders then becomes particularly important, and makes the voting right a crucial safeguard of stockholders' interests. Jensen and Meckling's assumptions that the firm is continually dependent on the external capital market, and that management owns a large fraction of outstanding shares make their theory inapplicable to the agency cost problem as it exists in the modern corporation, a fact which they seem to acknowledge (p. 354).

The Great Crash of 1929 proved that stockholder exit was not a fully effective means for monitoring managers. Stock prices could still fall faster than people could sell their stock. In the aftermath of 1929, enough managerial indiscretions during the 1920s were exposed to suggest that some managers were exploiting their positions as contract monitors at the stockholders' expense (Galbraith, 1972). Legislation followed. The activities managers could and could not undertake were more precisely delineated, additional requirements for supplying stockholders information were created and, most important, the procedures for outside monitoring and arbitrating of the manager–stockholder contract were strengthened. The Securities Acts of the 1930s govern in part how the gains from cooperation are divided between management and stockholders. Their passage was a natural response to the recognition than management is both party to and arbitrator of the manager–stockholder contract, and to the perception that management had abused its arbitrator role. An understanding of why such legislation comes about and its possible benefits as well as costs is impossible, if one does not recognize the distributional as well as allocative consequences of the informal contractual relationships compromising the modern corporation.

B.   The Capitalist–Worker Conflict

The capitalist brings his capital into a cooperative production agreement, the landowner his land, the entrepreneur his innovative ideas, and the worker brings his labour, something which, to many, has seemed less tangible than the services brought into the agreement by the other participants, (Coase, 1937; Simon, 1957; Williamson *et al.,* 1975). The intangibility of the worker's contribution makes *both* specification *and* enforcement of his *quid pro quo* of the contract necessarily imprecise. This imprecision necessitates internal monitoring of the labour contract. It follows from the analysis already developed, that workers either remain highly mobile to ensure efficient control over the terms of the contract, or demand a direct input into the internal monitoring and control structure of the firm.

Several writers have stressed the inherently short-run nature of the worker's explicit contractual tie to the firm. As John Commons observed sixty years ago, the wage contract typically 'is not a contract, it is a continuing implied *renewal* of contracts at every minute and hour, based on the continuance of . . . satisfactory service . . . and compensation', (1924, p. 285).

Alchian and Demsetz share this view:

Telling an employee to type this letter rather than to file that document is like my telling a grocer to sell me this brand of tuna rather than that brand of bread. I have no contract to continue to purchase from the grocer and neither the employee nor the employer is bound by any contractual obligations to continue their relationships. Long-term contracts between employer and employee are not the essence of the organization we call a firm (1972, p. 777).

Implicit in this view of the firm is obviously an assumption of high labour mobility. The worker can quit his job and find another paying roughly the same wages for the same services, as easily as a customer can find another grocer offering a similar kind of bread. Similarly, the employer can find an employee with the same typing and filing skills in as little time as a grocer must wait for another tuna customer to come into his store.

Other writers have taken a different view of labour's mobility. Knight argues, for example, that

The pecuniaries of labour in relation to readjustments form one of the main sources of injustice and hardship in an individualist economy. The risk of loss in the value of acquired knowledge and training means a constantly impending threat of indigence. Labourers are attached to their homes and even to their work by sentimental ties to which market facts are ruthless (1921, p. 346).

A few pages later, Knight adds the risk of loss of life or limb to the 'hazard of loss of specialised skill and training'; and observes that '. . . these "risks", seemingly so much greater than those incurred by the property owner do not carry with them control of the business . . . and . . . the actuarial value of the workers' risks depends quite as much on the quality of the management as in the case with those of the owner of material property' (p. 356). As with stockholders, one expects workers to react by demanding either a share in internal monitoring or more explicit contracts that can be arbitrated by outsiders. Knight does discuss the first possibility in a footnote (p. 350), but the main thrust of his argument is that the entrepreneurial rights of enterprise control devolve naturally upon the property–owner as uncertainty bearer. Knight accounts for this by:

an appeal to a 'fact of human psychology' that the owners of 'things' are less willing to trust those 'things' to the control of others without an adequate guarantee in kind than are men who own only themselves to hazard such outside control without even the poor safeguard of a guarantee against economic loss (1921, p. 356).

The theory developed here allows us to explain the widely observed identification of 'ultimate' managerial-monitoring authority with the ownership of material capital in another way. As was noted, physical capital can be easily eroded or even destroyed in the short run by free-riding by *short-term* workers, who are not contractually liable for future losses or bound to future service. The benefits to such a worker from continuing the employment relationship are of a very long-run nature and uncertain in any case, and in appropriate circumstances, may be plausibly outweighed by the immediate gains from free-riding. This, we suggest, is the basic economic justification for the capitalists' demand to monitor the employment contract, and stems directly from the inherently short-run nature of these contracts as described in the quote from Commons above. The prevalence of job- or firm-specific human capital does, of course, frequently create strong incentives for both employers and employees to maintain a long-term employment relationship, (Thurow, 1975; Williamson, 1975). When this relationship is mutually expected (and beneficial) it is often referred to as an 'implicit' labour contract, or an 'invisible handshake' (Okun, 1981). But these implicit contracts are vulnerable to all of the tensions and suspicions on the part of labour, due to the asymmetric authority and information under which they are typically monitored.

The organized labour movement can, in large part, be interpreted as an effort to replace these implicit contracts and the series of short contracts described by Commons, with a formal written contract subject to the internal monitoring of both management and labour representatives, and in cases of conflict, to outside monitoring. Predictably, the labour movement has had its greatest success in recruiting membership, and winning legislative support during periods of high unemployment, when labour mobility is at its lowest point. The most dramatic example is the Great Depression when outside monitoring of the 'labour contract' became in the United States a fact of life.

Economists have traditionally viewed unionization as simply an attempt by labour to monopolize a basically competitive market (Johnson, 1973). Without denying the importance of monopoly power to the union movement, this view of unionization cannot explain the movement's heavy emphasis, at least in Europe, on more direct participation in decision making. For example, codetermination and particularly works councils in West Germany have arguably helped to harmonize industrial relations and moderate inflation (McCallum, 1983). An interesting alternative to the formalization and monitoring of employment relations via unions is represented by modern Japanese practice (Ouchi, 1981). There low mobility and high trust are accompanied by widespread residual sharing, little overt conflict, and consummate cooperation. As our theory predicts, consensual decision making and informal pressures provide efficient communication and incentives in these circumstances, and have contributed to Japan's remarkable economic performance (Reich, 1983).

Stimulated in part by Japanese success, increasing concern with the costs of capitalist–and manager–worker conflict in adversarial industrial relations has arisen in the West (*Business Week*, 1981). Informal worker participation in relevant areas of decision making, profit sharing and job enlargement are increasingly seen as alternatives to formalized and hence rigid union agreements in an environment of rapid change and innovation, and as steps toward reducing the conflict potential inherent in the traditional employment relationship under collective bargaining. Indeed, a 'fair' share in enterprise surplus can motivate worker cooperation for efficiency rather than a recurrent redistributive struggle over relative shares in the surplus, and generate effective social sanctions, against shirkers which complement managerial supervision (Bradley and Gelb, 1983; FitzRoy and Wilson, 1984). The 'loyalty and team spirit' which Alchian and Demsetz (1972) relegated to a footnote in their theory of the firm appear to be major elements in the success of Japanese firms and participative management styles elsewhere (Ouchi, 1981; Reich, 1983). We take up the distributional consequences of participation in the next section.

IV. IMPLICATIONS

Recognition of the informal contractual structure of the large corporation with its heavy reliance on internal arbitration of disputes has important implications for both positive and normative analysis. Turning first to the positive side, several dimensions of corporate behaviour can be better understood by taking into account the distributional aspects of the corporate contract.

Example. The separation-of-principal-from-agent problem is in essence a free-rider problem. Like all free-rider problems, the existence and extent of the problem is dependent on the *number* of riders, that is, the number of principals relative to the agent. Given that the agent arbitrates the contract, he has an incentive, *ceteris paribus,* to increase the number of principals, to reduce the incentive of each principal to gather information and police the agent. Thus agents (managers) have an incentive to expand and diversify the firm beyond any efficiency gains from expansion. This incentive to grow may explain why reinvested cash flows in large corporations earn returns far below stockholder opportunity costs (Baumol *et al.,* 1970; Grabowski and Mueller, 1975; Hiller, 1978), and why corporations continue to make large, risky acquisitions in the face of

considerable evidence of modest if not negative returns from these investments (Mueller, 1977, 1980, 1981).[13]

Similarly, management's penchant to subdivide and routinize the tasks
of labour over the course of the last two centuries takes on a different
light. The standard explanation for this development from Adam Smith
to the present is that specialization increases efficiency, and so it does in
some cases. But, it is also more difficult for a divided and ignorant labour
force to evaluate whether management has arbitrated fairly the implicit
contract binding labour to the firm. Only the Marxists have stressed the
distributional advantages for management of a 'divide and conquer'
strategy (D. Gordon *et al.*, 1982; Marglin, 1974).

The distributional conflict between management and the other factor
owners is likely to be most apparent following large and unanticipated
changes in corporate revenues. Another of the empirical regularities of
corporate mergers, which the prevailing neoclassical theory is unable to
explain, is their occurrence following large run-ups in the acquiring
companies' share prices. Several studies have observed that acquiring
companies experience large increases in the returns on their common
shares, presumably due to increases in actual or anticipated profits, com-
mencing as early as forty-three months prior to a merger's announcement
(see e.g. Dodd and Ruback, 1977; Langetieg, 1978; Mandelker, 1974).
The relationship between these run-ups and the subsequent mergers is
inexplicable by the prevailing explanation for mergers, the market for
corporate control hypothesis, since it focuses on the characteristics of the
acquired firms, and presumes the mergers occur because the acquired
firms are badly managed. But a run-up in stock price or a large increase
in profitability gives management an opportunity to engage in mergers it
might not have undertaken, had the corporate pie not expanded. The
most dramatic, recent evidence of this behaviour was the flurry of large
acquisitions by major oil firms following the OPEC price hikes in the
seventies. Oil companies suddenly found themselves in possession of
huge windfall increases in revenues, revenues that could have been distributed to shareholders by increased dividend payments or, to avoid the
dividends tax, through the purchase of outstanding shares. But, these
uses of funds provide little advantage for management, and should management repurchase its own company's shares might actually reduce ownership's costs of policing management. The oil companies' response of
acquiring other firms, at premia over market value in some cases of more
than 100 per cent, seems best understood as a decision by management to
distribute these windfall gains in a manner largely beneficial to management, and management only. To rationalize this distribution of funds as
being to the stockholders' benefit, one must argue that the assets acquired
were worth in the hands of oil company managements as much as double

their pre-merger market value, *and* that this fact became apparent to oil company managers only after OPEC raised the price of oil.[14]

Tension over how corporate revenues are distributed are even more likely to rise following their sudden decline. The demands for outside monitoring of the implicit contracts of the firm in the 1930s already discussed can be viewed in a different light, when one recognizes management's discretion to arbitrate distributional issues to its advantage.

Recognition that management controls both the size of corporate revenue and its distribution, immediately suggests that management may allow some reduction in total revenues to take place in exchange for an increase in their share of the total. Efficiency may be sacrificed for distributional gains, and positive economic insights give rise to normative economic questions. Interference with management's discretion to arbitrate its contracts with capital and labour may improve economic efficiency as well as alter the distribution of wealth. How else can one explain why unionization, a most significant form of constraint on managerial prerogative, can actually *increase* productivity as well as wages (Clark, 1980; Freeman and Medoff, 1979)? Similarly, there is a wealth of evidence on the productivity-enhancing effects of participative management and profit sharing in Japan and in many firms elsewhere.[15] On the other hand, decentralization of decision making involves an explicit shift of information rights and authority away from the traditional supervisory hierarchy, and this redistribution will inevitably lead to a downgrading of certain managerial functions in the long run. For example, both the ratio of supervisory to production workers and salary–wage differentials are much smaller in Japan than in the US (Bowles *et al.*, 1983; R. J. Gordon, 1982). These redistributive consequences of organizational changes, which actually increase efficiency, can thus explain traditional managerial opposition to proposals from labour to share in decision-making authority.[16]

When Berle and Means documented the separation of ownership from control, it would seem that they wished to raise a distributional issue, a question about the distribution of power within the corporation, a question about the distribution of corporate income. After largely ignoring the consequences of the separation of ownership from control for forty years neoclassical economists have taken up examining the consequences of the separation of ownership from control on allocative efficiency. Not surprisingly, if one assumes sufficiently competitive markets they are benign. The distributional consequences of the separation of ownership from control, the conflicts they precipitate, and the side effects of these struggles on allocative efficiency have yet to be fully explored. This chapter attempts to pick up the challenge laid down by Berle and Means.

NOTES

1.   For a discussion of the profession's reaction to Berle and Means *see* Stigler and Friedland (1983).
2.   Baumol (1959), Marris (1963, 1964), Williamson (1963, 1964).
3.   The term 'generalized neoclassical economics' is taken from De Alessi (1983).
4.   *See* e.g. his critique of Alchian and Demsetz (1972) in *Markets and Hierarchies* (1975, pp. 49-56, 67-72) and (1983, 1984).
5.   Alternatively, artificial immobility can be established by posting bond *in order* to minimize the incentives to free-ride and the costs of policing (Becker and Stigler, 1974).
6.   For further discussion of this definition of mobility and its relationship to the concepts of profit and rent, *see* Mueller (1976).
7.   For a discussion of different supergame strategies for eliciting the cooperative outcome to prisoner's dilemma games, *see* Taylor (1976, pp. 28-68).
8.   Knight clearly recognized this point, and we return to it later.
9.   Compare Kirzner's (1973) notion of profit as reward for 'alertness', which is, however, marred by his failure to recognize the activity involved and hence to claim that profit is 'something for nothing'.
10.   Although Coase does not define the firm in these terms, he does stress the importance of these transaction costs as *one* of the causes for 'market failure' and the creation of a firm (1937, p. 336-7).
11.   *See* Buttrick (1952), Stone (1974), Nutzinger (1976) and Williamson (1980).
12.   Alchian and Demsetz (1972) also look with some favour on the days when non-voting shares existed. 'The entrepreneur in those days could hold voting shares while investors held non-voting shares, which in every other respect were identical' (p. 789, no. 14). The last condition is essential because it ties the entrepreneur's interests directly to the stockholders' and thus *helps* to police his behaviour. Nevertheless, a dollar declared as dividend would still provide the entrepreneur with less income than an extra dollar of salary, or, perhaps non-pecuniary emoluments. Thus, one would predict that even non-voting shares of this type would involve heavy third-party policing costs to ensure that the entrepreneur did not use his voting rights to advance his salary and expenses *qua* manager. We further expect that the reason these non-voting shares are not allowed on listed exchanges is that much of the transaction costs of policing these contracts would fall on these third parties themselves. But, as Alchian and Demsetz note, this is a ripe area for further research.
13.   Much of the claim that the market for corporate control improves economic efficiency rests on the large percentage gains to acquired firm shareholders that occur at time of take-over (Jensen and Ruback, 1983). But this evidence leaves unanswered the question of why acquiring firm managements participate so vigorously in a market with such high risks and low returns as the market for corporate control?
14.   As these examples indicate, many dimensions of corporate behaviour are affected beyond simply profitability and managerial income as most tests of the 'managerial theories' postulate. Most of these tests use share ownership concentration to measure managerial discretion. But size and diversification can also provide considerable freedom to management by concealing the details of the company's performance and hampering effective action even when managerial indiscretion is observed. Since most samples are drawn from the lists of largest

companies, these firms are all to a large degree managerial controlled, despite modest differences in ownership concentration.

A second shortcoming in this literature is the failure to distinguish between management's shareholdings and outsiders' shareholdings (but *see* McEachern, 1975, who also reviews this whole literature).

Of particular relevance to our argument are Firth's (1980) findings of a positive relationship between growth through merger and managerial income, despite a negative return on the acquisitions.

15.   *See* all the references at the end of the foregoing Section III-B.

16.   More recently, informal participation in decisions and profits to foster cooperation and flexibility has been increasingly recognized as an alternative to the rigid work rules and job classifications associated with formal, low-trust collective bargaining. Union leaders in turn correctly perceive this development as a threat to their own influence, and have generally strongly opposed such schemes, which are often explicitly designed to avoid union influence (*Business Week,* 1983; Reich, 1983).

Part II
The Firm's Decision Process and Long-run Development

5 Managerial and Stockholder Welfare Models of Firm Expenditures*

This study investigates within a common analytical framework the determinants of firm expenditures on capital investment, research and development and dividends. Its two basic objectives relative to past work are: first, to probe more deeply into the forces determining these outlays by taking into account the interdependencies among them,[1] and second, to provide a framework for evaluating alternative assumptions regarding firm motivation. A firm maximizing stockholder objectives will exhibit different behaviour in its expenditure decisions from one pursuing managerial goals. Consequently, two main variants of a model of firm expenditures, based on these rival concepts of motivation, are developed and tested.

I. DEVELOPMENT OF THE MODELS

One has reason for expecting on theoretical grounds that a general interdependence exists between the various alternative uses of investment funds. Whether managers maximize stockholder or their own personal objectives, they must weigh the expected marginal returns from any activity relative to competing and complementary uses of funds both within and outside the firm. These basic tradeoffs, adapted to alternative goal structures, underlie the analysis of the interactions among the three key decision variables — R and D, capital investment, and dividends. In principle, one also expects some interdependence between these activities and other investment-type outlays, for example, advertising and external acquisitions. The latter investment activities are ignored largely because of data insufficiencies. Since these activities are quantitatively of less importance for our sample of firms than the outlays actually studied, their omission is mitigated.[2]

Empirically testable models of firm expenditures are constructed in the following section alternatively based on managerial and stockholder objectives.

*A first draft of this chapter was presented at the Economic Society Meetings in December 1969. Thanks are due to Robert Eisner and Guy V. G. Stevens for their very helpful suggestions. Burton Malkiel provided us with some data on corporate risks. Research was supported by National Science Foundation Grants GS-2677 and GS-2678. Reprinted from *The Review of Economics and Statistics*, **54** (1), February 1972. Henry G. Grabowski and Dennis C. Mueller.

A. The Managerial Model

Of the many managerial theories that have appeared in recent years, we employ one that focuses on investment and dividend decisions. It draws most directly from the work of Robin Marris (1964). The hypothesis that a manager's pecuniary and non-pecuniary compensation is more closely tied to firm size than profitability is central to this and most previous managerial models. Consequently, managers are envisaged as pushing investment programmes to a point where their marginal rate of return is below the level which would maximize stockholder welfare. While external capital sources can be used, internal funds are expected to be particularly favoured because they are the most accessible part of the capital market and most malleable to managerial desires for growth. Thus, a major component to the managerial theory is the hypothesis that a greater percentage of internal funds are retained and invested than are warranted to maximize stockholder welfare.[3]

Nevertheless, a growth-oriented management cannot be totally insensitive to the capital market's reaction to its investment policies. At the point where the marginal returns on investment fall below the stockholder's opportunity cost, the firm's stock price starts to fall.[4] The firm becomes more vulnerable to a take-over from outsiders as its market valuation falls increasingly below its potential value, thereby tempering the managers' use of internal funds. In effect, some dividends will probably be paid because they yield utility to the managers by increasing their security against a take-over.[5]

Taking this desire for security into account, the managers' objective function becomes a blend of managerial (growth) and stockholder (valuation) goals. In terms of the three expenditures under study, this implies a utility tradeoff between more growth producing R and D and investment, on the one hand, and more security producing dividend payments on the other. A dominant weight on security will produce policies approximating those that maximize stockholder welfare, while an aggressively growth-oriented management completely unconcerned about a take-over will reinvest nearly all earnings and pay little or no dividends. Our model implicitly assumes managers are somewhere between these two extremes.[6]

In equilibrium, the managers should equate the marginal returns from the three expenditures expressed in units of utility, to the marginal cost or disutility of financing an additional outlay on any of them. The managerial firm's equilibrium conditions then can be written as

$$mrr_R = mrr_I = mrr_D = mcf, \tag{1}$$

where

$R = R$ and D expenditures
$I = $ Fixed capital investment expenditures
$D = $ Cash dividend payments.

We postulate further that

$$mrr_R = a_r + b_R I + c_R R + e_R X_R, \qquad (2)$$
$$mrr_I = a_I + b_I I + c_I R + e_I X_I,$$
$$mrr_D = a_D + b_D I + c_D R + d_D D + e_D X_D,$$
$$mcf = g\ (R+I+D) + hZ.$$

ιwhere each X is a set of exogenous variables peculiar to the given invest-ment activity and Z is a single set of exogenous variables which deter-mines the marginal cost of capital.

A linear formulation for the marginal rate of return and cost of finance functions can be shown to follow exactly from a quadratic utility function or alternatively may be regarded as an approximation to more complex functional forms. Moreover, it facilitates the econometric estimation of our models by allowing the use of standard linear simultaneous equation estimation techniques.

Many of the signs on the coefficients in (2) can be predicted from the underlying theory. The c_R and b_I coefficients in the mrr_R and mrr_I equa-tions are expected to be negative owing to the law of diminishing returns. The more R and D undertaken the lower the expected returns from the marginal R and D project are likely to be. The impact of the alternative investment programmes on the marginal returns in each activity are more difficult to predict. On the one hand an expansion of the R and D pro-gramme may draw scarce managerial talent away from the firm's capital investment programmes and thereby lower the expected returns from capital investment. More directly, it may speed up the obsolescence of the capital equipment currently installed also lowering mrr_I. Alternatively current R and D may lead to product improvements which increase the firm's image, expand the demand for its product(s) and raise the expected returns on some of its current investments in plant and equipment. Thus, b_B and c_I can be of either sign and could easily be of opposite signs.

The positive utility managers get from dividends can be expected to diminish rapidly after some point. Therefore, d_D is assumed negative and large. Conceivably one could expect the coefficients of I and R to be of either sign in the mrr_D equation. If stockholders have optimistic expectations concerning a firm's internal investment opportunities an increase in I or R could increase the price of the outstanding shares and reduce the necessity to pay dividends. This would imply that b_D and c_D are negative. However, the main premise of our managerial theory is that managers push the rate of return on investment outlays below the rate that maximizes stockholders' welfare thereby lowering the price of the firm's stock. This suggests that over the relevant range additional outlays on R and D and capital equipment will raise the managerial returns to paying dividends. Hence, we predict that if the managerial theory is to be supported, both b_D and c_D should be positive.

The marginal cost of capital is frequently assumed to be lower for internally raised funds than for external capital (Duesenberry, 1958; Kuh and Meyer, 1957, pp. 87-97). While in the context of a stockholder welfare maximizing model a sharp rise in the cost of capital function, at the point where it crosses over to outside funds, seems to impart a degree of irrationality to the managers, such a rapid increase is quite consistent with a managerial theory of motivation. The cost of using internal funds for management-oriented firms is not the rate of return the stockholders can earn in the market, but some much lower totally subjective value set by the managers. On the other hand, the subjective costs associated with external funds cause the managerial firm's cost of capital to increase over this portion of its marginal cost of finance (mcf) schedule. When it issues new stocks or bonds or increases bank borrowings, greater attention from the financial community is drawn to its investment and dividend policies. More importantly, the potential for a loss of control through financial insolvency increases when new bonds are issued or additional bank borrowing occurs. These subjective costs, reinforced by any capital market imperfections causing interest and transaction costs to increase with additional external funding, eventually must result in a rapidly rising cost of capital over this segment of the managerial firm's mcf schedule.

In the long run, a management is almost certain to adopt investment, R and D, and dividend policies which use up all internal fund flows and bring the firm to some point on the rising stretch of the curve. Therefore, over the relevant range, any increase in expenditures will cause the cost of capital to increase. For this reason, the amounts of *R, I,* and *D* have been included as shift parameters each getting equal weight (since they are measured in the same money units) in the mcf equation. The shift parameter, *g,* will have a positive sign.

Normally, the marginal rate of return and marginal cost of finance schedules as set forth in equational set (2) cannot be directly observed. However, given the equilibrium conditions in (1), this system may be solved in a variety of ways which are empirically tractable. We regard it as most informative to do so by equating each of the marginal return functions in turn with the cost of finance function. Substituting from (2) into (1) and solving in this way we obtain

$$R = \frac{a_R}{g-c_R} + \frac{b_R-g}{g-c_R} I - \frac{g}{g-c_R} D + \frac{e_R}{g-c_R} X_R - \frac{h}{g-c_R} Z,$$

$$I = \frac{a_I}{g-b_I} + \frac{c_I-g}{g-b_I} R - \frac{g}{g-b_I} D + \frac{e_I}{g-b_I} X_I - \frac{h}{g-b_I} Z, \ (3)$$

$$D = \frac{a_D}{g-d_D} + \frac{c_D-g}{g-d_d} R + \frac{b_D-g}{g-d_d} I + \frac{e_D}{g-d_D} X_D - \frac{h}{g-d_D} Z.$$

In this case each endogenous variable becomes a function of the other endogenous variables in the model, the set of exogenous variables which determines its marginal returns, and the set of exogenous variables which determines the cost of capital and is common to all equations. This finding is completely general, of course, and is not dependent upon the particular linear formulation employed here.

Given the specific form of our model, and the a priori predictions made concerning the parameters in (2), predictions about the signs of many of the variables in (3) can be made. Since g is assumed to be positive, and c_R, b_I and d_D are all assumed negative, the denominators of all the coefficients in (3) have positive signs. This allows us to predict the signs of the coefficients of all of the exogenous variables unambiguously. It also allows us to predict the signs of two of the codetermined variables. Dividends should have a negative coefficient in both the R and D and capital investment equations. Since c_D and b_D are both assumed to be positive, the signs of the R and I coefficients are ambiguous in the dividends equation, as are the coefficients of R in the investment equation and I in the R and D equation. If the substitute aspects of the investment activities dominate ($b_R < 0$ and $c_I < 0$) then their respective coefficients in (3) are definitely negative. If the complementary aspects are most important, their coefficients will be positive or negative depending on whether b_R and c_I are greater than g. While we expect that the likelihood is that these coefficients will be negative, we cannot rule out the alternative possibility in either case.

An alternative to estimating (3) is to resolve it and completely eliminate R, I and D from the right-hand sides of the equations. This makes each dependent variable a function of *all* of the exogenous variables in the model and none of the other codetermined variables. Unbiased estimates of the parameters of this system can be obtained by using direct least squares. It is not possible, however, to make unambiguous predictions about the signs of these parameters based upon the predictions made regarding (2). For this reason, an algebraically simpler version of the model like (3) is preferred, even though unbiased estimates of (3) can only be obtained using one of the simultaneous equation techniques. Two-stage least squares has been employed here.

B. The Stockholder Welfare Maximization Model

A firm maximizing stockholder welfare or market valuation should equate the marginal rate of return on each investment activity to its marginal cost of finance. The cost of internal funds is the stockholder's opportunity cost (i.e. the rate of return he could earn on another stock of comparable risk), and the cost of external funds is the market rate on debt and new equity. If capital markets were perfect, which is assumed in the strictest neoclassical formulations of this model, Jorgensen and Siebert (1968), Modigliani and Miller (1958), the costs of capital on both external and internal sources are constant and equal. In this market situation, decisions regarding the optimal levels of investment are fully dichotomized from those regarding sources of finance. All investment activities should be undertaken to the point where their expected return equals the constant cost of capital. Since the cost of capital is invariant to the source of finance, the resulting level of investment may be financed by any combination of earnings ploughback, debt or new equity without effecting market valuation.

A number of important implications for the structure of an expenditure model follow from the neoclassical theory. First, dividends are no longer codetermined with the other expenditure variables as in our managerial model, but rather are decided on some subsidiary or residual basis. Second, the level of cash flow, which is expected to be a major variable influencing the position of the managerial firm's mcf schedule and hence its investment expenditures, is irrelevant for the neoclassical firm's investment decisions. These are very strong hypotheses distinguishing the two approaches.

Because this neoclassical variant of the stockholder welfare model has received a great deal of prominence recently, both theoretically and empirically, and also because it offers the greatest differentiability from the managerial model, it will be the focus of our attention here. If the neoclassical model with its exclusion of all finance-related variables except stockholder opportunity cost, statistically outperforms the managerial model, this may be viewed as strong evidence against the managerial approach. Since a case can be made for introducing some of these variables into a stockholder welfare model by relaxing the extreme assumption about a perfect capital market,[7] a strong performance of these variables is not necessarily incompatible with a stockholder welfare orientation of managers. Thus, a full discrimination between stockholder welfare theory with capital market imperfections and the managerial models depends on isolating other differences in behaviour or other independent evidence. After fully specifying and comparing the statistical performance of the managerial model with the strict neoclassical variant, the results will be evaluated from this wider perspective.

With dividends omitted as a codetermined variable and a constant cost of capital, we have as the equilibrium condition on the R and D and investment decisions for the neoclassical variant of the model

$$mmr_R = mrr_I = r \qquad (4)$$

where r = *neoclassical firm's cost of capital*. Linearizing the mrr_R and mrr_I equations as in equational system (3) above (of course the values of the coefficients and sets of exogenous variables may differ), and equating each of the marginal rates of return schedules in turn to the cost of capital, the following structural model is obtained

$$R = \frac{a_R}{c_R} - \frac{b_R}{c_R} I - \frac{e_R}{c_R} X_R + \frac{r}{c_R} \qquad (5)$$

$$I = \frac{a_I}{b_I} - \frac{c_I}{b_I} R - \frac{e_I}{b_I} X_I + \frac{r}{b_I}.$$

The signs of all of the coefficients can be predicted except for the codetermined I and R variables. Equation (5) will be estimated using two different measures of r to be discussed below.

II. THE EXOGENOUS VARIABLES OF THE MANAGERIAL MODEL

In constructing the sets of exogenous variables, we follow an eclectic approach, borrowing freely from formulations of variables in past studies which have been primarily single equation in nature. Where problems of data availability and suitability arise, we tend to use an imperfect measure of a particular effect rather than discard it entirely.

A. The Rate of Return to Capital Investment Equation (the X_I set)
The capital investment decision has been the most exhaustively examined firm expenditure of those investigated here. On the marginal rate of return side, past studies have emphasized demand pull considerations in the form of various accelerator variables (Eisner, 1967). Accordingly we incorporate changes in sales in the current and previous two periods as part of X_I in equation (3). No particular lag structure is imposed but rather the regression coefficients are allowed to specify the appropriate structure. Moreover, since the focus is on cross-sectional variations, these sales-change terms are weighted by each firm's average capital to sales ratio over the eight-year period under study, 1958–66. This particular weighting scheme is based on the assumption that the firms on average

were producing at or near full capacity over this period.

Because the level of *gross* investment is being investigated, another component of investment demand arises from the need to replace a depreciating capital stock. Depreciation and depletion flows, calculated on an accounting basis, are used as an imperfect proxy for replacement demand.

A third component of investment demand which has received much less attention in the literature is the induced demand generated from successful R and D of each firm. This is because the output from R and D, technological change in the form of new products and process, has been difficult to quantify in any meaningful way. One measure of the output from R and D which is admittedly imperfect, but has been used by Schmookler and others, is the number of patents granted over a particular period (Grabowski, 1968; Scherer, 1965; Schmookler, 1966). The advantages and limitations of patent statistics have been amply discussed elsewhere (Schmookler, 1966, ch. 2). Without going into the details of the discussion, we feel that patents can be a useful albeit partial measure of technological output, as long as any cross-section uses of it are confined to firms with similar product structure and technologies (Comanor and Scherer, 1969; Mueller, 1966). Therefore, a moving average of patent grants is included among the X_I set of variables.

B. The Rate of Return to R and D Equation (the X_R set)

The determinants of R and D have received far less attention in the literature. Work done to date suggests that R and D activity like other investment decisions is influenced by rate of return and cost of capital considerations, (Grabowski, 1968; Mansfield, 1968; Mueller, 1967; Schmookler, 1966). In a prior single-equation study, one of the authors found that past research productivity, as measured by the size of patented output per professional R and D employee, is a significant explanatory variable of current research intensity (Grabowski, 1968). Because of its success in this prior analysis and the absence of any better measures of technological output we continue to use this past productivity measure as an index of the firm's capacity to do successful R and D.

While our whole model is, in a fundamental sense, a test of the managerial theory of the firm, it also seems plausible that the *degree* of management control would have a discernible impact on the investment and growth policies of the firm.[8] This hypothesis has been tested with respect to capital investment and advertising in previous studies by Williamson (1964) and Kamerschen (1970), with conflicting results. Hence, it seemed useful to place a measure of management control somewhere among our exogenous factors in the managerial model.

For both theoretical and statistical reasons, our index of management control is included in the mrr_R equation. In technologically progressive industries R and D is likely to be the investment activity having the greatest long-run effect on growth, and hence can be expected to be particularly favoured by management-controlled firms. In addition, technological leadership has become a prestige symbol in some management circles and may be a recipient of some of the cash over which managers have discretionary control (Brittain, 1966). Hence, we predict the greatest positive impact for the management control variable will be in the R and D equation.

An analogous, although theoretically somewhat weaker case, can be made for including management control in the capital investment equation. Unfortunately if we include this variable in both the investment and R and D equations, the number of variables left to identify the capital investment equation is reduced sufficiently to introduce instability into the two-stage estimates for this equation. Therefore, we have had to be satisfied with an attempt to isolate the impact of this variable on the extreme growth-producing end of the investment spectrum.

As a measure of the degree of management control, we follow Williamson and employ the percentage of the board of directors who are also executives of the firm (Williamson, 1966). While it differs somewhat from Kamerschen's measure relating to the dissemination of stock ownership, both are positively and significantly correlated for the subset of our sample for which both measures are available.[9]

C. The Rate of Return to Dividends (the X_D set)

Most attempts to explain dividend payments adopt some variant of Lintner's basic model (Lintner, 1956) and employ profits or total cash flow and lagged dividends as explanatory variables (Brittain, 1966). This approach is not used here. While cash flow is an explanatory variable in our system through cost of capital factors, lagged dividends are not included in the model. Since the focus is on cross-sectional variations, the analysis must essentially center on the long-run management decision of the optimal dividend payout ratio. In this regard, to say that this year's payments are determined in a large measure by last year's dividends, with a slight adjustment towards an unaccounted for long-run payout ratio, is not very enlightening.

In his original work, Lintner suggests as determinants of the payout ratio — the growth rate of the firm, the variability of its profits, and the payout ratio of its competitors in the capital market (Lintner, 1956). Some of the considerations expressed by these variables are captured directly in our model through the endogenous variables whose levels reflect alternative profit opportunities of investment within the firms rather than paying dividends. Following Lintner's hypothesis, however, we include as exogenous variables influencing inter-firm differences in dividend payouts, the firm's long-run growth in earnings per share over the eight-year period spanned by our samples, and its variability in earnings to net worth over this period.

It may be noted with Lintner's scheme, both of these variables are expected to have a negative effect on dividend outlays. While we definitely expect this to be the case for the growth rate variable, for a management-oriented model one would tend to expect higher variability in earnings to result in greater rather than less dividends. If dividends provide utility to the managers primarily by giving some security against the threat of loss of control, then higher variability in earnings will increase this threat if it produces lower stock prices and *ceteris paribus,* the managers should try to offset this with higher dividend payments. We thus predict a positive coefficient for this variable in the dividends' equation, and the accuracy of this prediction becomes another test of the managerial theory of the firm.

D. The Marginal Cost of Finance Equation (the Z set)

From the discussion of Section I it is clear that the main exogenous variables determining the position of the vertical stretch of the cost of finance schedule are the components of its internal cash flows — after tax profits and depreciation and depletion charges. In addition to the theoretical justifications for including these cash flow variables, numerous studies have found them to be effective predictors of firm outlays. Following Kuh and Meyer (1957) a number of studies have appeared that include some measure of cash flow as an explanatory variable (Duesenberry, 1958; Kuh, 1963; Meyer and Glauber, 1964; Mueller, 1967). Previous work on our part has indicated that these revenue flows are important determinants of expenditures on R and D (Grabowski, 1968; Mueller, 1967) and advertising (Grabowski and Mueller, 1971). John Brittain's work also indicates that Lintner's results on dividends can be improved by a consideration of both profits and depreciation.

Managers are assumed to require some interval to process and evaluate information on cash flow, so these variables are included with a one-year lag. Furthermore, because after-tax profits are assumed to index funds available for R and D, investment and dividends *before* these decisions are made, 50 per cent of current R and D outlays are added to the reported profits figures. The United States tax provisions allowing R and D to be totally expensed produce an understatement of pre-R and D profits by roughly this amount.

Variables influencing the actual terms of external finance (the firm's level of indebtedness, the state of the capital markets, etc.) are not included. If, as suggested above, the managerial firm's mcf schedule exhibits a sharp upward discontinuity at the point where it obtains funds externally, these variables can be expected to have secondary and somewhat irregular impacts on firm decisions. Moreover, previous attempts to incorporate them into cross-section type studies have not met with encouraging results (Meyer and Glauber, 1964).

E. The Managerial Variant in Operational Form

All the exogenous variables to be used in the managerial model have now been specified. In symbolic notation, they are

1. X_I set
    ΔS_t, ΔS_{t-1}, ΔS_{t-2} — lagged and unlagged sales changes
    DP_{t-1} — depreciation and depletion charges in period $t-1$
    P_t — average number of patents awarded over a previous three-year period.
2. X_R set
    $(P/W)_t$ — the number of patents per professional scientific employee over a prior three-year period.
    MC_t — percentage of a firm's directors who are also full-time managers in period t.
3. X_D set
    g — the growth in earnings per share over the period 1958–1966
    σ_r — the standard deviation in earnings to net worth over the period 1958–1966.
4. Z set
    π_{t-1} — profits after tax in period $t-1$
    DP_{t-1} — depreciation and depletion changes in period $t-1$.

Before doing any empirical estimation, it is desirable to normalize many of the above variables with respect to some index of firm size. Failure to do so is likely to result in heteroscedasticity in the residuals as well as simple scale factors dominating the explanation of the cross-sectional variation in the endogenous variables (Kuh, 1963, pp. 91-6; Mueller, 1967, p. 63). Accordingly, all size-related variables both endogenous and exogenous, are deflated by sales and expressed as intensities (i.e. percentage of sales) rather than absolute quantities. While we have some a priori reasons for choosing sales as the deflator,[10] this particular choice is not critical from an empirical standpoint. We ran all the equations using assets as a deflator and the results change only slightly.

A few of the variables (P/W and MC in the R and D equation and g and σ in the dividends equation) are not deflated by sales because they are already in ratio form and are in effect deflated by size-related measures.

The managerial model previously set forth in equational system (3), may be expressed now in operational form as

$$\frac{R_t}{S_t} = m_0 + m_1 \frac{I_t}{S_t} + m_2 \frac{D_t}{S_t} + m_3 \left(\frac{P}{W}\right)_t \tag{6}$$

$$+ m_4 MC_t + m_5 \frac{\pi_{t-1}}{S_t} + m_6 \frac{DP_{t-1}}{S_t} + \mu_{Rt}$$

$$\frac{I_t}{S_t} = k_0 + k_1 \frac{R_t}{S_t} + k_2 \frac{D_t}{S_t} + k_3 \frac{\Delta S_t}{S_t}$$

$$+ k_4 \frac{\Delta S_{t-1}}{S_t} + k_5 \frac{\Delta S_{t-2}}{S_t} + k_6 \frac{P_t}{S_t}$$

$$+ k_7 \frac{\pi_{t-1}}{S_t} + k_8 \frac{DP_{t-1}}{S_t} + \mu_{It}$$

$$\frac{D_t}{S_t} = n_0 + n_1 \frac{R_t}{S_t} + n_2 \frac{I_t}{S_t} + n_3 g + n_4 \sigma_r$$

$$+ n_5 \frac{\pi_{t-1}}{S_t} + n_6 \frac{DP_{t-1}}{S_t} + \mu_{Dt}$$

where μ_{Rt}, μ_{It}, and μ_{Dt} are statistical error terms.

Collectively there are twenty coefficients to be estimated for the managerial model. We can predict the signs of sixteen of these, exempting only k_1, m_1, n_1, and n_2 which depend on whether substitutability or complementarity is dominant between the respective pairs of endogenous variables. For the other coefficients, our hypotheses suggest three will be negative (k_2, m_2 and n_3) with all the others positive.

III. THE EXOGENOUS VARIABLES: STOCKHOLDER WELFARE MAXIMIZATION

All the exogenous variables previously specified for the mrr_I and mrr_R equations (the X_I and X_R sets) are retained for our stockholder welfare maximization model, with the exception of the management control variable. Moreover, all the hypotheses concerning the direction of impact of these variables on the two investment decisions are also unaltered, although the expected magnitudes of the coefficients can be expected to differ under alternative motivational assumptions.

With dividends omitted as a codetermined variable in the neoclassical model, the X_D set of exogenous variables are dropped from the equational system.

The most fundamental difference between the two models, of course, is the replacement of the cash flow variables in the mcf equation by the neoclassical cost of capital variable, the stockholders opportunity cost. Jorgenson has used as a proxy for the stockholder opportunity cost variable, a measure based on the earnings to price ratio of the firm. This seems to us more a measure of stockholder expectations about future earnings than of outside investment opportunities (Eisner and Nadiri, 1968). Consequently, it is desirable to devise a measure of stockholder investment opportunity which tries to get directly at the alternative investment choices.

The basis for constructing an externally derived cost of capital depends on one's characterization of the risks involved in holding an asset. We shall develop two concepts of stockholder opportunity cost that are tied to alternative views of risk. One is based on the variance of the stock's rate of return. The other is a covariance measure of risk designed to reflect how the security contributes to the overall variability in a diversified portfolio.

First, related to a variance concept of risk, an opportunity cost variable is constructed based on the rate of return realized by holding stock in firms in a comparable risk class. In order to construct such a rate of return variable, we made use of a study by Nerlove investigating the rates of return to stockholders (for a large sample of firms on the Compustat tape over the period 1950-64 (Nerlove, 1968)). Nerlove's data were used to compute the annual rates of return freom holding each stock (based on cash dividends and capital gains) on the assumption that the stockholder went in and out of the market each year, alternatively at the high and low price for the stock.[11] The greater the variance in these annual rates of return from holding the stock, the greater the likelihood a stockholder forced to sell might realize a return below a given percentage of the market average.

The 369 firms from Nerlove's sample for which data were available were then ranked according to this variance measure of risk, and grouped into risk classes consisting of the thirty firms in Nerlove's sample with realized rates of return closest to its own. The average rate of return of the thirty stocks in each firm's risk class is used as our estimate of the firm's neoclassical cost of capital, that is, as the average return a stockholder could expect from investing in stocks of comparable risk. In our empirical work, this variable is denoted as r_1. In contrast to our second measure, it is a time invariant measure for each form over the eight-year period under study. Since the behavioural composition of a firm's shareholders changes only slowly, the assumed constancy over time of this variable probably does not introduce any large errors.[12]

The alternative measure is based on a concept of portfolio risk, in accordance with a Markowitz-type portfolio selection model. This approach argues that the rational investor neutralizes most of the variance risk through diversification leaving only a covariance component. The recent work of Sharpe and others generalizing this approach to a full theory of equilibrium in the capital markets provides a basis for empirical measurement of portfolio risk (Sharpe, 1964). Using Sharpe's analytical framework, one can regress each firm's rate of return, r_f, on some overall market average, r_m,

$$r_f = \alpha + \beta r_m.$$

The slope of this equation, β, then gives one an approximate measure of the risk associated with an incremental increase in the holding of the f firm's shares in a diversified portfolio. Since the theory suggests a linear relationship between realized rates of returns in each period and the degree of portfolio risk, β, we can substitute the calculated measures of β directly into the mcf equation, rather than constructing stepwise risk classes to get at the rate of return-risk tradeoff curve as we did in the variance cases.[13] *Ceteris paribus* we predict a negative relationship between this β variable and investment as our second test of the stockholder welfare maximization model.

To construct the β's for each firm, we regressed annual rates of return (based on year-end stock prices and dividends) on the annual return for the Standard and Poor's composite 500 average over successive seven-year intervals.[14] The β_t measure used in the empirical analysis is the one obtained from the regression based on the immediately preceding seven-year period. It was felt that seven years provided a long enough interval to capture the relevant historical information relating to the market's current evaluation of a firm's future returns.

Our simultaneous equation system for the stockholder variant of the model can now be fully specified.

$$\frac{R_t}{S_t} = V_0 + V_1 \frac{I_t}{S_t} + V_2 \left(\frac{P}{W}\right)_t + V_3 r_i + \mu'_{Rt}$$

$$\frac{I_t}{S_t} = W_0 + W_1 \frac{R_t}{S_t} + W_2 \frac{\Delta S_t}{S_t}$$

$$+ W_3 \frac{\Delta S_{t-1}}{S_t} + W_4 \frac{\Delta S_{t-2}}{S_t} + W_5 \frac{P_t}{S_t}$$

$$+ W_6 \frac{DP_{t-1}}{S_t} + W_7 r_i + \mu'_{It}$$

with $V_2, W_2, W_3, W_4, W_5, W_6, > 0$

$V_3, W_7 < 0$

where r_i is the neoclassical cost of capital under the variance or covariance method of calculation.

IV. THE NATURE OF THE DATA SAMPLES AND ANALYSIS

Both simultaneous equation systems are estimated on data spanning the eight-year period 1959–66, for sixty-six firms from seven separate industries—chemicals, drugs, petroleum refining, paper, agricultural and construction machinery, machine tools and ferrous metals.[15] The basis of this sample is a questionnaire survey in which R and D data corresponding to the National Science Foundation definition were solicited from approximately 120 firms in ten separate industries. The industries selected for this questionnaire survey were those for which R and D was primarily company financed. Within each industry data were solicited from the top dozen or so firms ranked by sales. The industries in the current group represent those for which at least a 75 per cent response rate was achieved, thereby giving a representative sample of the large R and D performers in the industry. The sixty-six firms in the sample account for roughly one-third of all company-financed R and D in the country.

These data can be used in a number of ways to analyse the models presented above. It is, therefore, worth discussing some methodological considerations before proceeding to the empirical work.

three decision variables by equating their respective *mrr*'s to the mcf function. If a cross-sectional analysis is employed, deviations from ultimate equilibrium values are likely to be a minor component of the overall variation. The model can be estimated in its present form and the coefficients interpreted as estimates of the long-run parameters (Kuh, 1963, p. 182). On the other hand, if we were to adopt a time-series approach, the adjustment mechanism to the desired values would become a central component of the period-to-period variations in the observations. In a time-series analysis, therefore, further specification of a dynamic adjustment process—preferably also simultaneously determined—would be required. Rather than further complicate the model at this stage, we instead focus on the cross-sectional component of variation that corresponds best to the equilibrium values specified by our analysis.

On the basis of these considerations one might choose to estimate annual cross-sections from our sixty-six firm sample, perhaps allowing for inter-industry effects by means of dummy variables. However, a number of advantages can be obtained by pooling all the data into one grand sample, and then taking deviations around industry-year means. This procedure is equivalent to dealing with the variation which remains after performing a regression on fifty-six industry-year dummies (seven industries times eight years) and then using the remaining residual

Table 5.1: *Estimation of the managerial variant of the model*
(*TSLS estimators with all variables computed as deviations from industry-year means*)

Dependent Variable	$\dfrac{R_t}{S_t}$	$\dfrac{I_t}{S_t}$	$\dfrac{D_t}{S_t}$	$\left(\dfrac{P}{W}\right)_t$	MC_t	$\dfrac{\Delta S_t}{S_t}$	$\dfrac{\Delta S_{t-1}}{S_t}$	$\dfrac{\Delta S_{t-2}}{S_t}$	$\dfrac{P_t}{S_t}$	g	σ_r	$\dfrac{DP_{t-1}}{S_t}$	$\dfrac{\pi_{t-1}}{S_t}$	$\bar{R}^2/F$
$\dfrac{R_t}{S_t}$		-0.087 (1.69)	-0.023 (0.28)	0.011 (2.21)[a]	0.007 (2.63)[b]							0.202 (3.63)[b]	0.245 (3.50)[b]	0.37/45.11
$\dfrac{I_t}{S_t}$	-0.462 (0.59)		-0.217 (0.45)			0.111 (3.85)[b]	0.039 (1.49)	0.031 (1.07)	0.017 (0.29)			+0.916 (5.57)[b]	0.417 (1.22)	0.26/17.86
$\dfrac{D_t}{S_t}$	-0.552 (2.39)[a]	-0.132 (1.15)								-0.081 (3.72)[b]	0.479 (3.55)[b]	0.000 (0.000)	0.870 (13.83)[b]	0.62/125.3

Notes: Total number of observations — 441.
Numbers in parentheses are t values.
[a] Significance at 5 per cent level for a two-tailed test.
[b] Significance at 1 per cent level for a two-tailed test.
(If standard t tests are applied — small sample properties in a simultaneous equational system are not known.)

variance to estimate the parameters of the model. In effect, it 'sweeps out' the time series and inter-industry component and leaves only the intra-industry component of variation for which the present formulation appears most applicable. Compared to the annual cross-section approach, this technique results in both a substantial increase in the number of degrees of freedom available and a reduction in the instability of the parameter estimates that arise from year-to-year cyclic variations in the data.

Two-stage least squares is used to estimate the model. There are, of course, well-known difficulties in interpreting the results of all simultaneous equation estimators because of the lack of knowledge about their small sample properties. Nevertheless, we calculate and report the *t*, *R* and *F* statistics in all cases and treat them as useful information bearing on the validity of the hypotheses incorporated in our model. Partial justification for this is provided by John Cragg's work with Monte Carlo experiments on various simultaneous equation techniques (Cragg, 1967).

V. THE EMPIRICAL RESULTS

A. The Managerial Goals Maximization Model
Table 5.1 represents the coefficient estimates for the managerial model using TSLS and computing all variables as deviations from the appropriate industry-year means. Considering first the interdependence between the endogenous variables, all six coefficients take on a negative sign. This implies that substitutive interactions are outweighing any complementarity between these variables. Thus, factors positively influencing the return to one of these codetermined variables will ultimately have a negative effect on the other two. However, since only one of these coefficients has a *t* value above two, many of these substitutive effects may not be very pronounced in character.

Turning to a consideration of the exogenous variables, their performance on the basis of correspondence to expected sign is excellent with all the coefficients exhibiting the predicted sign. Moreover ten of the fourteen coefficients are statistically significant at the 5 per cent level or better. While it is not surprising that the variables take on the expected signs, since most have been successfully employed elsewhere in single-equation studies, it is reassuring that they can be incorporated directly into this simultaneous framework and not exhibit any unusual properties.

For the R and D equation, the most significant of the exogenous factors are the two cash flow terms. Their coefficients are quite similar in magnitude and possess almost identical and highly significant *t* values. On the other hand, the patent per worker variable, reflecting the productivity of past R and D, and the percentage of managers on the board of directors, have somewhat smaller, but nevertheless significant t statistics. In their present form, both of these variables introduced via the mrr_R side have some measurement problems and are at best proxies for factors which are not easily put into quantifiable form. Nevertheless, their significance in the present situation is encouraging and the performance of the management control variable in particular provides a separate strand of support for the managerial model.

For the capital investment equation, the exogenous variables exhibiting the best performance are the unlagged accelerator term, indexing demand pull effects, and the level of depreciation which was included both as a measure of replacement need and as a component of cash flow. Both are highly significant. The two lagged accelerator terms and profits take on the postulated signs with t values above 1.0, but not at statistically significant levels (5 per cent test). The lagged patents variable has the worst performance with a t value well below 1.0.

The investment equation, while highly significant, exhibits the poorest explanatory power of the above system with an $\bar{R}^2$ of 0.26. This relatively weak performance can be attributed to two factors. First, since capital investment is more sensitive to business cycle and other volatile factors than the other variables, the adjustment process may be quite important even in a cross-section analysis. That is, the variation between actual and desired levels for each firm may not be insignificant compared to the cross-section variation in desired levels across firms. Thus, the specification of a dynamic adjustment mechanism could significantly reduce the amount of unexplained variance observed here. Second, the intra-industry component of variation for variables, such as the accelerator and cash flow terms, might be viewed as less 'permanent' than their corresponding inter-industry component. Eisner has made such an interpretation and showed that the explanatory power of the accelerator variables, in particular, improves when performing an inter-industry analysis in comparison to an intra-industry approach (Eisner, 1967).

The dividend equation has the highest F and $\bar{R}^2$ statistics of the three equations. The profit component of cash flow has a very dramatic impact with a t value of 13.8. The strong showing of profit is in accordance with Lintner's basic finding regarding dividend payments of individual firms over time. The very high t value also tends to suggest that over a cross-section of similar firms, payout ratios tend to converge somewhat to a common value in accordance with his hypothesis of an imitative reaction among rivals in their long-run payout policies. On the other hand, depreciation has little explanatory power. Since profits are the most visible cash flow element to the shareholders, one can interpret these

Table 5.2: *Estimation of the stockholder welfare variant of the model*
(TSLS estimators with all variables computed as deviations from industry-year means)

Dependent Variable	$\frac{R_t}{S_t}$	$\frac{I_t}{S_t}$	$\left(\frac{P}{W}\right)_t$	$\frac{\Delta S_t}{S_t}$	$\frac{\Delta S_{t-1}}{S_t}$	$\frac{\Delta S_{t-2}}{S_t}$	$\frac{P_t}{S_t}$	$\frac{DP}{S_t}$	r_1	B_t	$\bar{R}^2/F$
$\frac{R_t}{S_t}$		0.095 (3.13)[b]	0.023 (3.80)						-0.0227 (4.79)[b]		0.025/5.90
$\frac{I_t}{S_t}$	1.15 (0.63)			0.110 (3.27)[b]	0.052 (2.01)[a]	0.053 (2.00)[a]	-0.065 (0.56)	0.899 (5.04)[b]	0.610 (1.74)		0.17/13.6
$\frac{R_t}{S_t}$		0.103 (2.33)[a]	0.013 (2.19)[a]							-0.0032 (2.33)[a]	≈0/≈0
$\frac{I_t}{S_t}$	-3.24 (0.30)			0.101 (3.26)[b]	0.051 (2.06)[a]	0.052 (2.04)[a]	0.034 (0.52)	0.065 (6.43)[b]		0.0019 (0.39)	0.23/18.7

Notes: See Table 5.1.

results as indicating that managers only use this more commonly followed component to arrive at dividends and essentially keep the 'hidden' depreciation charges to finance investments. The latter does perform strongly in both the R and D and investment equations.

The two variables introduced via the mrr_D equation, the g and σ_r variables, are also highly significant. The observed results for these variables imply the higher growth in earnings per share, *ceteris paribus*, the lower dividend payouts will be, whereas the greater the variability in earnings to net worth of the firm, the greater dividend payouts. These results correspond to the predictions for the managerial model. Dividends are paid essentially to obtain security from take-over and similar external pressures, and any factors which diminish this likelihood, like vigorous growth in earnings per share, diminish dividends, whereas factors like high instability of earnings increase the take-over threat and thereby produce higher dividends.

The coupling of dividends with these exogenous factors in precisely the manner predicted by the managerial theory lends considerable support to this theory of motivation. The result concerning the earnings variability coefficient, in particular, is quite inconsistent with a stockholder welfare theory where, if anything, the opposite sign might be expected.[16]

B. The Stockholder Welfare Maximization Model

Table 5.2 presents the corresponding estimates of the stockholder welfare model using TSLS with all variables computed as deviations around the appropriate industry-year mean. The first half of Table 5.2 gives the estimates for the system in which the stockholder opportunity cost variable is based on a variance concept of risk, whereas the lower half presents the corresponding results using the covariance related concept. In the two R and D equations, the cost of capital variables perform in accordance with the predictions of the stockholder welfare model, both being negative and significant. However, in the capital investment equations the reverse is true, with their signs being positive in both instances (significant in the case of r_1). Therefore, at best, the estimates on these variables give mixed support for a stockholder welfare model.

All the other exogenous variables for the stockholder welfare model, with the exception of the sum of patents, take on the postulated signs and many are significant. However, with the omission of cash flow terms, dividends, the dividend related exogenous variables (σ_r and g), and the management control variable, a drastic decline in the $\bar{R}^2$ values for the stockholder welfare model occurs. Compared to the $\bar{R}^2$ of 0.37 in the managerial model, the R and D equations in Table 5.2 have $\bar{R}^2$'s of 0.025 and a slightly negative value.[17] The investment equations exhibit a less dramatic decrease in $\bar{R}^2$, but a decrease nonetheless.

By relaxing some of the assumptions of the strict neoclassical stockholder welfare model, one could reintroduce some of the variables present in the managerial model and narrow the differences in performance between the two. Capital market imperfections could be hypothesized to justify including profits and depreciation. Profits could be included as a measure of expectations. A stockholder preference for some dividends over capital gains would rationalize introducing a dividends equation, and so on. All of these 'real world' modifications should improve the performance of the stockholder welfare model by moving it closer to the managerial version. We have no objections in principle to attempting to rationalize the stockholder welfare hypothesis by making these modifications. Indeed, it is precisely such real world considerations as the separation of ownership and control, the resulting managerial discretion, and its likely effect on investment behaviour, that causes us to develop this managerial model of the firm.

The behaviour of two variables in the managerial model cannot be reconciled with a stockholder welfare approach, no matter how liberal the formulation. The significant positive effects of earnings variability on dividends (see note 16) and the management control index on R and D are in clear conflict with the stockholder welfare theory. Thus, in the two extreme instances where the theories unquestionably diverge, the results favour the managerial theory. This suggests that the strong performance of the cash flow terms is probably not just an indication of capital market imperfections, but a reflection of the effects of managerial discretionary behaviour.

The interpretation of our findings as support for the managerial approach receives considerable reinforcement from a recent study by Baumol *et al.*, investigating the returns to alternative sources of finance for investment expenditures (Baumol *et al.*, 1970). Using a multiple regression analysis, they find a significantly lower return on internally generated funds (3.0 to 4.6 per cent) in comparison to that for external funds (4.2 to 14 per cent for debt financing and 14.5 to 20.8 on equity capital). Their samples are quite large and the findings quite robust to alternative specifications. Discrepancies of this magnitude are difficult to rationalize by a hypothesis that managers are maximizing stockholder objectives, even if there are capital market imperfections. Rather, these results seem best explained in accordance with a managerial model like that employed here, that is, the lower returns on internal funds results from the conscious policies of managers that have considerable discretionary power over their cash flow and use this power to pursue objectives like growth beyond the point beneficial to shareholders.[18]

In summation, the managerial model is statistically superior to a neoclassical version of the stockholder welfare approach. Moreover, the results for the managerial model exhibit a strong pattern of overall consistency which cannot be fully rationalized even in terms of a less extreme formulation of the stockholder welfare model. Coupled with evidence from other sources, these results provide a considerable measure of support for a managerial theory of motivation.

C. Reduced Form Equivalents of the Model

Table 5.3a presents the directional effects of the exogenous variables in the managerial model on R and D, capital investment and dividends as implied by the estimates from Table 5.1, omitting the sum of patents variable because of its low t value. These directional effects represent the net impacts of each exogenous variable after allowing for all of the interactions in the model.[19] Thus, they provide the most useful information for the policy maker interested in affecting any of the three decision variables (Mueller, 1967, pp. 81–4).

In addition the estimated impact multipliers of Table 5.3a can be used to provide another test of the validity and consistency of our simultaneous equation approach. This can be accomplished by comparing the derived reduced form with one estimated directly using ordinary least squares. If the present approach is appropriate, a substantial number of variables entering a reduced form equation from the other two equations in the system should be of the postulated signs and as a group they should provide a statistically significant increment in explanatory power. The statistical performance of the simultaneous model was not of a high enough quality to expect *all* of the variables to perform as predicted, however.

Table 5.3b presents the signs and t value ranges for the reduced form estimated by direct least squares, again employing deviations around industry-year means. One may note first that all the exogenous variables directly influencing the return to a particular activity have the correct sign and are significant. Likewise, the cost of capital variables in each equation exhibit this property.

Of the thirteen coefficients associated with variables introduced into the reduced form equations because they affect the returns to a substitute decision, four have t values above 2.0 and another five have t values above 1.0. Of these nine coefficients, seven have the sign postulated in Table 5.3a. Thus, several of the exogenous variables introduced from other equations are significant or near significant and consistent with the predictions of Table 5.3a based on our simultaneous equation estimates. While the performance of these variables as a group is not statistically overwhelming, they do provide additional support for the hypothesis of substitutive interactions as predicted from the structural estimates.

The current analysis underscores our previous point about the

Table 5.3a and 5.3b: *Directional impacts associated with the managerial model as derived from the simultaneous equation estimates (Table 5.3a) and from estimation directly by ordinary least squares (Table 5.3b)*

Dependent Variable	$\left(\dfrac{P}{W}\right)_t$	MC_t	$\dfrac{\Delta S_t}{S_t}$	$\dfrac{\Delta S_{t-1}}{S_t}$	$\dfrac{\Delta S_{t-2}}{S_t}$	g	σ_r	$\dfrac{DP_{t-1}}{S_t}$	$\dfrac{\pi_{t-1}}{S_t}$
$\dfrac{R_t}{S_t}$	+	+	−	−	−	+	−	+	+
$\dfrac{I_t}{S_t}$	−	−	+	+	+	+	−	+	+
$\dfrac{D_t}{S_t}$	−	−	−	−	−	−	+	−	+

Dependent Variable	$\left(\dfrac{P}{W}\right)_t$	MC_t	$\dfrac{\Delta S_t}{S_t}$	$\dfrac{\Delta S_{t-1}}{S_t}$	$\dfrac{\Delta S_{t-2}}{S_t}$	g	σ_r	$\dfrac{DP_{t-1}}{S_t}$	$\dfrac{\pi_{t-1}}{S_t}$
$\dfrac{R_t}{S_t}$	+ (a)	+ (a)	+ (c)	− (b)	− (a)	− (a)	+ (b)	+ (a)	+ (a)
$\dfrac{I_t}{S_t}$	+ (c)	− (b)	+ (a)	+ (a)	+ (a)	− (b)	− (a)	+ (a)	+ (a)
$\dfrac{D_t}{S_t}$	− (b)	− (c)	+ (c)	− (b)	− (a)	− (a)	+ (a)	− (a)	+ (a)

Notes: (a) *t* value greater than 2.0.
(b) *t* value greater than 1.0, but less than 2.0.
(c) *t* value less than 1.0.

desirability of first specifying and estimating the full simultaneous equation system rather than proceeding directly to the reduced form. From a hypothesis testing standpoint, it is easier to make accurate predictions about the signs of the coefficients of the structural variant of the simultaneous equation model and the resulting estimates are less plagued by the statistical problem of multicollinearity.[20] Moreover, by obtaining the reduced form coefficients both directly and indirectly from the structural estimates, one has a further check on the consistency of the model.

VI.   SUMMARY AND CONCLUSIONS

We may briefly review our findings in terms of our two initially stated objectives. First, the current simultaneous equation approach demonstrates the basic interdependence between decision variables that can be postulated on theoretical grounds, whatever the motives of the firm's decision makers. For the most part, the results tend to substantiate the findings of single equation studies of these decision variables. However, they suggest a set of interactions often overlooked in such work. From a policy standpoint, a recognition of these interactions is clearly important in formulating and assessing measures to influence firm expenditure behaviour.

The second basic conclusion emerging concerns the motives of corporate managers. The managerial variant of our model has proved both conceptually and statistically superior to the pure stockholder welfare maximization version. Its theoretical advantage derives from its much broader scope which allows stockholder welfare to be *one* of the factors affecting investment and dividends decisions, but also provides for the impact of variables that are solely related to managerial welfare. We feel that investigations of the kind presented here, that explicitly derive the relationships between the dividends and investment decisions one expects under different motivational assumptions, and then test and compare these predictions, provide one of the most promising means of discriminating between modern and more traditional theories of the firm. Further analysis along these lines, perhaps expanded to include other investment decisions, like advertising and mergers, should provide important insights into this central issue of microeconomics.

NOTES

1. There have been to date a handful of studies attempting to look at these types of decisions in a simultaneous decision-making framework (Anderson, 1964; Dhrymes and Kurz, 1967; Mueller, 1967). In particular our analysis extends both theoretically and empirically a previous study by one of the authors (Mueller, 1967).
2. Data are available for some expenditure decisions—e.g. investment in liquid capital assets—which are not included as interdependent activities but rather treated as having lower priority in the hierarchy of firm decisions.
3. Investment opportunities may be so promising that all internal funds can be exhausted without pushing the marginal rate of return below the stockholders' opportunity cost. No conflict between the managerial and stockholder-oriented firm regarding retention policies then exists. Elsewhere one of the authors has argued that this is most characteristic of firms in the early stages of their life cycle and is likely to pass with time (Mueller, 1972).
4. This relationship has been well observed in the literature and runs counter to the stockholder welfare predictions of the Miller and Modigliani hypothesis. For a discussion of the importance of this finding for the managerial theories *see* Mueller.
5. Marris puts the most emphasis on the threat of take-over as the chief deterrent to managerial pursuit of growth through investment (Marris, 1964). Other variants of a managerial theory of the firm which stress a manager–stockholder conflict, and thus implicitly contain a managerial utility functional for paying dividends as a means of placating stockholders are developed in Baumol (1967), Mueller (1969), J. Williamson (1966) and O. Williamson (1964).
6. Lintner's famous discovery that managers tend to decide this year's dividend payment by slightly adjusting last year's payment, depending on current profits, is fully consistent with a managerial theory (Lintner, 1956). Once the stockholders get used to a given dividend payment they are not likely to challenge management's policies providing this payment is not dramatically curtailed and that it tends to move with profits. In the short run, therefore, managers essentially may determine dividends prior to investment, as a number of previous studies have implicitly assumed by regressing investment on cash flow net of dividends (Grabowski and Mueller, 1971; Kuh, 1963; Kuh and Meyer, 1957; Marris, 1964). Over the long run, an interdepence between dividends and investment can be expected, however.
7. The nature of the expected relationships will depend on the shapes and positions of the firm's internal and external funds portions of its mcf curve. If the cost of capital on internal sources remains constant and is always below that on external funds (because of transactions costs), dividends will still be residually determined. Moreover, the total amount of cash flow will have an impact on the cost of capital only when investment opportunities are so promising as to completely exhaust internal funds and force a resort outside capital. On the other hand, if both the internal and external segments exhibit an increasing slope and overlap over the relevant range of investment expenditures, a general interdependence will occur as in the managerial case.

8.   Although an absence of any relationship between the degree of management control and growth is not necessarily inconsistent with the growth hypothesis. For an elaboration of this point *see* Mueller (1970).

9.   The percentage of directors is more readily available and exhibits more variability than the conceptually somewhat more satisfying measure based on stock ownership. When one classifies the firms in our sample in a polar manner using stock ownership data, most fall into the management-controlled rather than stockholder-controlled categories. This will be true of any representative sample of large firms in the manufacturing sector.

10.   Essentially we prefer sales to assets as a deflator in a cross-section analysis because it is a more 'neutral' size measure. Since a significant positive relation between the capital intensity of the firm's production process and overall size has been observed, deflating by assets may introduce a definite bias. Nevertheless, our results tended to exhibit great similarity, irrespective of the size deflator, with slightly higher $\bar{R}^2$ and t values on most variables occurring in the sales-deflated case.

11.   This somewhat unusual assumption on the shareholders entry and exit price was made to get at the *maximum* risk that owning a particular stock could impart to a shareholder. We also computed a measure based on entry and exit at the annual mid-point prices for the stock, but the alternative measure based on high–low sequence always performed better in the regressions (from the standpoint of the neoclassical theory). Hence, we used the latter measure.

12.   Of course, the rate of return is influenced by general economy-wide factors and shifts cyclically over time. However, since we primarily deal with a cross-sectional analysis here, it is the rate of return relative to that of other firms which is most important for the current analysis. The above measure should capture this component.

13.   Recent work of Friend and Blume (1970) suggests that the relationship between the *realized* rates of return and β had a systematic non-linear character over most of this period, exhibiting a declining slope with increasing risk. For this reason we included non-linear terms in β in our formulation. These exhibited signs consistent with the finding of Friend and Blume but were not statistically significant in any of the models.

14.   The rates of return for both variables were computed using end of year prices and annual dividend payments, rather than market highs and lows as with r_1. Since we wanted to have a measure of the covariance between the firm and market returns, we wished to use prices that are synchronized in time, and a high–low measure would not have this property.

15.   R and D data were not available for all eight years for some of the firms. In addition, we omitted some observations because of large-scale mergers. In all, a total of 441 observations was available.

16.   In the perfect capital market case, no particular relation between these variables need be expected. On the other hand, with imperfect capital markets a *negative* relation between dividends and earnings, reflecting a substitution effect away from external to internal sources because of an increased risk of insolvency associated with the increased earnings variability, would be predicted by the stockholder welfare theory. Such an effect also can exist for the managerially oriented firm. However, the observed positive sign on σ_r suggests that the fear of take-over from dissident shareholders is outweighing any fear of loss of control through

insolvency. This is the prediction in Marris's formulation of the managerial model (Marris, 1964).

17. Since the $\bar{R}^2$ for TSLS estimation is computed after substituting the actual values of the jointly determined endogenous variables for the corresponding instrumental values used in the second stage, the $\bar{R}^2$ statistics are not constrained to be positive. A negative $\bar{R}^2$ indicates that the estimated equation is inferior, in terms of the percentage variation explained, to a set of equation estimates equal to the appropriate dependent variable mean values.

18. The low estimates of output/capital elasticities obtained by Jorgenson and Siebert (1968) are also consistent with a growth-oriented managerial theory.

19. Since all the interactions between the endogenous variables are negative (i.e. substitutive relationships) the impact coefficients have a straightforward interpretation. The only variable for which relative magnitudes are important is depreciation, which influences the dependent variable through both the mrr and mcf equations. The calculated signs are positive in the investment and R and D equations (the cash flow effect of depreciation dominating in the latter), and negative in the dividends equation where the non-existent direct cash flow effect of depreciation is swamped by its replacement pull on investment.

20. In general, multicollinearity is a more severe problem in estimating the reduced form, because every exogenous variable is present in all three equations. This factor may be influencing some of the reduced form estimates since significant, although not excessively high, correlations exist between many of the independent variables.

6 Research and Development Costs as a Barrier to Entry*

The view that large firms are responsible for a relatively greater amount of inventive activity, and introduce proportionately more innovations, than small firms has, for some time now, appeared under various guises in the economic literature. The classic statement of the hypothesis that of Joseph Schumpter, argues that relative (rather than absolute) size or market power is the key stimulus to entrepreneurial innovative activity (Schumpeter, 1950). Recent variants of the Schumpeterian hypothesis have stressed size alone, (Lilienthal, 1952; Galbraith, 1952) diversification, (Nelson, 1959) or size combined with oligopolistic rivalry (Villard, 1958) as the key determinants of innovations.

While space considerations do not permit a complete review of this literature, one important distinction between Schumpeter's hypothesis and those of the neo-Schumpeterians must be noted. Schumpeter argued that the entrepreneur whose firm possessed some market power would lead in undertaking innovations, because he would be sufficiently free from the day-to-day struggle for survival which competition imposes to devote his energy to introducing innovations (Schumpeter, 1950). This freedom to innovate, combined with the financial capacity to innovate which stems from the flow of monopoly profits to the entrepreneur, makes him the prime instrument of development. In contrast, the neo-Schumpeterian hypotheses all seem to rely on some form of economies-of-scale argument. Only the large company, they argue, can undertake the great fixed costs of a modern research laboratory, achieve the degree of specialization necessary for adequate team work, benefit from risk-pooling by undertaking a number of R and D projects simultaneously, and sponsor basic

*William M. Capron, Merton J. Peck and an anonymous referee for the *Canadian Journal of Economics* made many helpful comments on an earlier draft of this chapter. Mrs Barbara Fechter aided in gathering the case study material. The Brookings Institution supported this work with the assistance of grants provided by the Alfred P. Sloan and Ford Foundations. The views presented here, however, do not necessarily represent those of the trustees, officers or staffs of these organizations. Reprinted from *Canadian Journal of Economics*, November 1969. John E. Tilton and Dennis C. Mueller.

research with reasonable expectations that the results will have commercial applications in areas of interest to the firm.

This chapter contends that the validity of these hypotheses varies depending on the age or state of development of an industry. A new industry is created by a *major* process or product innovation and develops technologically as less radical, follow-on innovations are introduced. In the following discussion, an industry is regarded as passing through four separate stages of technological growth: innovation, imitation; technological competition, and standardization. Any breakdown of this nature is, of course, somewhat arbitrary and unrealistic. Technological development, like other growth processes, is continuous. Yet, we feel that this breakdown has sufficient pedagogic value to warrant its introduction in this chapter, which proposes to examine at each of these four stages of technological development the magnitude of entry barriers and economies of scale attributable to R and D.

I. THE INNOVATION STAGE

A new product or production process is invented, developed, and introduced into the market during the innovation stage. At this stage its technical and market potential is most uncertain. For, until the invention is converted into an economically viable product or process, the innovator can have only very crude estimates of the returns he will reap from its introduction.

It is at this stage that Schumpeter's hypothesis should be most applicable. The 'process of creative destruction' consists of introducing products and processes so radically new that even the monopolist cannot rest easy for fear of being wiped out by some innovating entrepreneur outside his industry.

Schumpeter's hypothesis has never truly been tested for this stage of the technological development process. Indeed, by focusing upon the most important technological innovations, it eliminates the possibility of testing by means of traditional statistical techniques, since, to ensure that they are sufficiently important to classify as Schumpeterian innovations, the researcher is forced to be selective, and hence non-random, in his choice of innovations. The researcher is thus limited to analysing a series of case studies which are always subject to question and refutation by counter example. Still, the existence of a reasonably large number of examples which do not fit the hypothesis must be considered as fairly strong evidence against its general applicability.

In discussing the Schumpeterian and neo-Schumpeterian hypotheses, we shall make frequent references to case study evidence to support our arguments. It will be helpful in examining the plausibility of these hypotheses at this first stage if we further break the process down into the invention and development phases.

A. Invention

The bulk of the empirical evidence on the origin of major inventions suggests that the R and D laboratories of large corporations have not been an important source of major inventions. This is the conclusion Daniel Hamberg reaches after a rather extensive search of the case study literature.[1] Hamberg presents a number of plausible explanations for this finding: (i) large corporations generally prefer R and D projects promising short payoff periods rather than the lengthy projects usually necessary for major innovations; (ii) large firms frequently have a vested interest in the present technology and may hesitate to pursue major innovations which would displace currently profitable products; and (iii) highly creative scientists and inventors often find the team-work atmosphere of many large corporate laboratories unattractive. This list can be further buttressed by the addition of what we shall call the communication and incentive problem in the large corporation.

The technical and scientific competence to judge the feasibility of a specific invention or perceive the inventive potential inherent in a given scientific advance normally lies with those working *in* a company's laboratory. A decision to fund an R and D proposal which, if successful, promises to produce a major invention must be made by someone fairly high up in the corporate structure. This individual is often too far removed from the laboratory to judge the technical merits of the proposal and, given the great risks involved and inadequate financial incentives, is likely to reject it. The problem of communications and incentives is much simpler in the small firm. Managers are only once removed from the R and D laboratory and reap a large portion of the benefits that any major innovation produces. In the large corporation, managers once removed from the R and D laboratories seldom have the authority or the personal incentives to initiate a development programme on an important and radically new invention.

B. Development

The same communication gap which may keep large firms from financing R and D activity directed toward major inventions may inhibit them from funding the development needed to convert a major invention into a commercially successful product or process innovation. This is particularly likely when the invention is made by small firms or individuals outside the company. The not-invented-here bias which at times causes corporate R and D directors to look askance at ideas not originating in their own laboratories may impede the adoption of outside inventions by large corporations.[2] This prejudice combined with the heavy financial risks and lengthy payoff period normally associated with developing and marketing any radically new invention often keeps big companies from acquiring the major inventions made available to them.

We have already noted the case of xerography, an innovation which a very small photopaper company developed after numerous industry giants had turned the inventor down. In investigating the forty-two innovations attributed to small firms and individuals in the Jewkes, Sawyers, and Stillerman study, (Jewkes *et al.*, 1959) we found six were developed with substantial government assistance because of their military and strategic importance. Small firms (with annual sales of under $50 million) developed over half of the remaining inventions at least to the point where their commercial potential was clearly visible.

Relative size does not appear essential either. Enos' study of major petroleum innovations notes that the smaller petroleum firms developed those innovations based on inventions made outside the industry after the giants had turned them down.[3] The Dirlam–Adams study of the diffusion of the oxygen-injection process for making steel documents the leadership position taken by the smaller firms in adopting this innovation in the United States.[4] And so it goes. Despite some well-known exceptions, like nylon, the magnitude of R and D expenditures necessary to develop most innovations is not beyond the financial capacity of small and medium-sized firms. Neither large absolute size nor market power appears to be a necessary condition for successful development of most major innovations.

This is a remarkable conclusion, when one considers that the Schumpeterian hypothesis should have its greatest applicability at the development phase of the innovation process. The heavy capital investments required to develop and market major innovations would seem to make the large corporation with its large capital flows the natural home for developing major inventions. However, it is the large capital requirements combined with the still substantial technical and marketing uncertainties that frequently keep these companies from underwriting the development programmes. Here again we have the communication and incentive problem in the large corporation. The decision to go ahead with a major development project is made at the very top of the company because of the magnitude of the outlays involved. The chief proponents of the development effort, usually the inventor and some of his close associates, are people further down the corporate hierarchy who may not have the incentive or the ability to instil in top management the vision and enthusiasm that they have over the potential of the invention.[5]

II.   THE IMITATION STAGE

Once a major innovation is successfully introduced, much of the uncertainty disappears. Other firms can judge the innovating firm's success in overcoming the technical obstacles and also gauge the likely commercial potential of the innovation on the basis of the initial market reaction.[6] Occasionally the innovating firm has an airtight patent position and prevents other firms from entering the industry or adopting the process.[7] Generally, however, this is not the case. Even firms which can establish an exclusive position often choose to license new entrants and avoid a conspicuous monopoly.[8] Hence, one usually expects a rush of firms entering a newly formed industry or adopting a new process innovation shortly after it is introduced.

Follower firms first set up R and D programmes to obtain a familiarity with the technology and science underlying the new innovation. They then attempt to develop their own variants of the innovation. Although we have called this stage in the development cycle the imitation stage, in fact, the firms which enter after the innovator do not attempt to reproduce the innovator's achievement exactly. Instead, they try to develop a version of the product or process which is as different or superior to the innovator's as possible.[9]

During the early period of entry and experimentation immediately following a major innovation, the science and technology upon which it depends are often still only crudely understood. The rudimentary state of knowledge about the relevant scientific principles can easily be comprehended by someone familiar with the area. R and D work undertaken to increase the stock of scientific knowledge may by necessity follow a trial-and-error or empirical approach. Typically, research is less amenable to the team work and highly specialized approaches of the modern large industrial research laboratories. Because of the newness of the area, the R and D worker often must devise his own experimental apparatus which tends to be rather crude and makeshift in nature.

All of this suggests that the large firm may not have an advantage over the small firm in undertaking R and D at this stage in the technological growth of an industry. The small firm can hire a few capable scientists and engineers and equip them to work as efficiently as their counterparts in the larger firms. The cost of conducting technically efficient R and D at this stage may be low enough to allow all but the very smallest firms to enter. The one major advantage the large firm conceivably might possess comes from its ability to pool risks. A large firm can finance a number of parallel R and D projects to improve on a major innovation, while a small firm can sponsor only one or two. The large firm can thereby reduce the risk that it will come up with no significant improvements. This advantage, however, must be weighted against the numerous disadvantages of the large corporate laboratory listed above.

The manager of the small firm entering a recently opened industry in response to a major technological innovation, knows that if his firm can successfully establish a place for itself, the rewards will be substantial. These small firms are usually technically oriented. Their managers are likely to have scientific or engineering backgrounds and may even participate in some of the R and D work in the laboratory. They certainly keep in close touch with developments in the laboratory, participate heavily in major decisions connected with the R and D programme, and are rewarded in direct proportion to the success of the company. This situation must be contrasted with the decision-making process in the large firm where, as noted above, the responsibility for moving into new areas is separated from the technical competence to judge the potential in these areas.

While a fair amount of case study material has been gathered regarding the performance of large and small firms at the innovation stage, very little has been done on the history of an innovation immediately following its introduction. Research we are currently conducting on the semiconductor and photocopying industries does provide some evidence. Bell Laboratories, which developed and patented the original semiconductor technology necessary for transistor production, followed by a very liberal licensing policy and made the technology available for a minimal fee to all interested firms. Both large firms like RCA, General Electric, and Westinghouse, and firms that were initially small like Texas Instruments, Transitron, and Fairchild, entered the industry. The latter contributed substantially to the technology of the industry[10] and in the process grew rapidly. Their ability to compete successfully with the large firms is demonstrated by the magnitude of their industry sales.

Despite the strong patent position of the Xerox Corporation, more than forty firms have entered the photocopying industry since the development of xerography. Most of these new entrants like Xerox itself were originally very small firms, although a number of them were later absorbed by much larger companies.

This limited empirical support and the a priori reasoning above lead us tentatively to conclude that technological barriers to entry and economies of scale in R and D are still comparatively small at this stage of an industry's technical growth. Small firms can be expected to enter and in a fair number of cases do reasonably well in advancing the industry's technology.

III. THE TECHNOLOGICAL COMPETITION STAGE

As the number of firms entering the industry increases and more and more R and D is undertaken on the innovation, the scientific and technological frontiers of the new technology expand rapidly. Research becomes increasingly specialized and sophisticated, and the technology is broken down into its component parts with individual investigations focusing on improvements in small elements of the technology.

Many of these developments work to the advantage of the large research laboratory. The popular conception of the modern industrial research laboratory as a well-equipped technology factory where R and D problems are subdivided into small projects and farmed out to teams of specialized scientists is a fair representation of R and D *at this stage of an industry's technical maturity*. Once a good understanding of the basic science underlying the process is achieved, this subdivision and specialization becomes feasible and often technically advantageous.

Since most firms in the industry are by this stage carrying on extensive R and D programmes, small firms outside the industry find it difficult to enter and establish small R and D efforts which compete efficiently with the established firms. Added to the economy of scale problem that the small firm now faces is the heavy initial investment in R and D typically necessary to bring the small firm up to date technologically in the industry. The amount of unpublished knowledge—production techniques, characteristics of the materials used, reliability of various components of the innovation—the existing firms in the industry have acquired, often through production experience,[11] may be substantial. The ante for entering is further raised if the early entrants established strong, overlapping patent positions. This forecloses many otherwise potential avenues open to the firm[12] and forces it to invent around existing patents, adding further delays and expenses to the necessary R and D efforts.[13] Hence, we conclude that the barrier to entry in the form of required initial R and D outlays at this stage in an industry's technical development generally is quite high and discourages small firms from entering. Where economies of scale in on-going R and D activity exist, this conclusion is reinforced.

Small firms already in the industry may continue to do fairly well even with economies of scale in R and D if they have carved a niche for themselves (often producing a specialty product) and have protected it with some patents. A small firm considering entering the industry, however, must invest considerably more in R and D than the small firm already in the industry, since it has both to catch up in knowhow and establish a protective patent position to guard its own chosen interstice.

Frequently, especially in the case of product innovations, demand for the product (at prices that allow producers to prosper) greatly exceeds supply during the early growth period, and the many new entrants into the industry during the imitation stage do fairly well. Later, as production catches up with demand, however, competition eliminates the weaker newcomers. In particular, those firms falter which do not succeed in making significant improvements in the innovator's product or production process and cannot, therefore, attract customers either on the basis of quality or price. Their growth slows and eventually declines. Finally, they are forced to drop out of the industry. This whole process is accelerated by economies of scale in R and D, for then the stagnant firm tends to fall further and further behind its growing competitors technologically.

IV. THE STANDARDIZATION STAGE

Eventually, technological progress in the industry slows down and the production techniques become quite standardized. The necessary scientific knowledge for production is of the textbook variety. Many important patents of the innovation and imitation stages expire and in general barriers to entry based on initial R and D requirements fall. Barriers that remain depend on the capital requirements necessary to establish efficient production and marketing organizations. Competition has shifted from technological to price competition.

V. ENTRY OVER THE DEVELOPMENT CYCLE

The discussion of this paper is summarized in Figure 6.1 The solid line depicts the weight of the entry barrier represented by the expected R and D costs for successful entry. The chief component of these barriers generally is the extent of economies of scale in the R and D process. These economies are relatively low in the innovation stage, increase gradually during the imitation stage, reach a peak in the technological competition stage, and then taper off as the industry's technology becomes standardized.

The second major factor contributing to R and D entry barriers is the accumulation of patents and knowhow on the part of incumbent firms. Even if there were no economies of scale in R and D, a late entrant would have to undertake more R and D than an average firm of its size in order to acquire information about the technology and to invent around existing patents.

The dotted line in Figure 6.1 reflects the uncertainty of payoff to R and D expenditures. While the absolute height of this curve is arbitrary, it does illustrate how uncertainty varies over the four stages of the

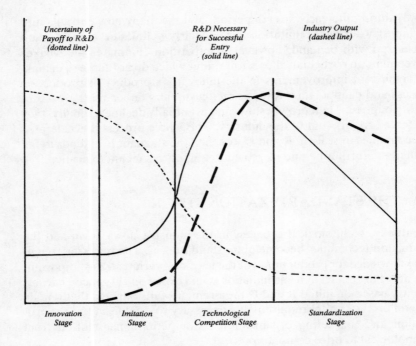

Figure 6.1: *Entry and the technological development cycle*

development cycle. The greatest uncertainty exists at the beginning of the innovation stage when the pioneering firm or individual has very limited information about the innovation's potential. Uncertainty decreases as knowledge concerning technological and commercial aspects of the innovation accumulates.

A firm's decision to enter an industry is a function of all barriers to entry and the expected profits following entry. (The reader is reminded that we consider only R and D costs and uncertainty entry barriers here.) Future profits should be a function of industry output, which is depicted by the dashed curve in the figure. Again, the absolute height of this curve is arbitrary, the purpose of the curve is merely to show how output varies over the development cycle. In actual practice, its peak is substantially higher than that for the curve reflecting R and D entry costs.

In the innovation stage, the major deterrent to entry is uncertainty. The chief inducement is the potentially very profitable position a firm can establish as an industry leader should the innovation be successful and the industry move up along the dashed curve. Indeed a successful innovator's profits might well be regarded as his reward for having had the insight, daring or luck to have crossed the uncertainty barrier. Entry is generally most rapid during the imitation stage. Here the potential profits from establishing an early proprietary position are still fairly high, the uncertainty barrier is rapidly declining as outsiders are able to evaluate the technological and economic potential of a marketed innovation , and the R and D costs of entry are still rather low. During the last two stages, which normally are longer than the first two, entry is much slower. The R and D costs for successful entry act as a major barrier in the technological competition stage. In the standardization stage, declining sales and falling expected profits deter firms from entering.

NOTES

1. Illuminating insights into the problems large firms encounter in producing and developing major inventions are also found in P.E. Haggerty (1969).
2. This bias against outside inventions often is so pervasive that even companies which adopt policies of actively searching for inventions from non-company sources apparently cannot overcome it. The Xerox Corporation has yet to come up with an important outside patent after over three years of searching, and other companies have had similar experiences with outside patent departments. Yet, Xerox is particularly sensitive to the potential of such patents since it obtained the basic patents on xerography from Chester Carlson (after many large firms turned him down). Xerox was a very small chemical firm (named Haloid) at the time it acquired these patents. The decision was made by the president of the company and the vice president for R and D. The latter had happened upon an article describing the invention while searching for literature for something new for the company.
3. Enos (1962) on the other hand Edwin Mansfield found that the percentage of innovations introduced by the four largest petroleum firms exceeded their share of industry capacity. See Mansfield (1968).
4. This study has stirred up a bit of controversy—chiefly regarding the performance of the US steel industry *vis-à-vis* the European and Japanese industries. The authors' conclusion that the laggard performance of the industry giants in contrast with their smaller rivals tends to refute the Schumpeterian hypothesis seems to us on a solid ground, however (Adams and Dirlam, 1964; Slesinger, 1966; McAdams, 1967; Maddala and Knight, 1967).
5. The outside inventor has an even more difficult task trying to get a company's management to listen to him and carefully consider his proposals. This problem of communication is the chief obstacle the outside inventor faces in trying to sell his inventions to corporations.
6. The problem of estimating the market potential is obviously much more acute in the case of new products than of new processes.
7. Polaroid has had such a patent position.
8. The chief impetus for generous licensing policies in the United States is the antitrust statutes. Large firms in particular hesitate not to license other firms for fear that a judge or jury will later construe such behaviour as a predisposition to monopolize.
9. In the drug industry, for example, most innovations are followed by a large

number of imitations which differ from the original innovations in a number of important respects. Imitators are motivated to differentiate their products to attract customers and to avoid infringing on the innovator's patents. *See* Comanor (1965).

10. Lists of important semiconductor innovations and the firms responsible are found in: U.S. Department of Commerce, (September 1963); Freeman, (November 1965).

11. For a survey of the learning-by-doing literature, *see* Nelson *et al.*, (1967).

12. If the firm chooses to obtain licenses from some of the other firms in the industry, then its entry expenses are effectively raised by the capitalized value of its royalty payments.

13. A number of synthetic fabrics have been developed to get around basic patents held by pioneers in this industry. The extent to which these patents can act as a barrier to entry is illustrated by the experience of the rayon industry where a flood of new entrants followed the expiration of American Viscose's basic patents. *See* Markham (June 1950).

7 A Life Cycle Theory of the Firm*

Profit maximization is one of the most frequently attacked and commonly used hypotheses in economics. During the last thirty years the number of its critics has grown considerably and with it the list of competing hypotheses of business motivation.[1] The most formidable of these appears to be the hypothesis that managers maximize the growth in absolute size of the firm (Baumol, 1967; Galbraith, 1967; Meyer, 1967; Mueller, 1969; Penrose, 1959; Williamson, 1966). It compares favourably to profit maximization in terms of simplicity and lends itself well to inclusion in formal models—a disadvantage of other attractive hypotheses. The amount of support for it based on psychological and behavioural considerations is formidable and dispels much of the intuitive appeal of the profit motive (Galbraith, 1967; Marris, 1964, chs. 1 and 2). The chief obstacle to its gaining widespread acceptance among economists has been the inability of its proponents to produce empirical evidence that allows one to discriminate between the growth and profit motives of managers (Marris, 1964, ch. 7; Meyer, 1967).

One reason for the lack of success in testing the growth hypothesis has been the failure of both its defenders and its critics to recognize that its validity probably varies depending on the age of the firm and its investment opportunities. This paper attempts to fill this void by developing a life cycle theory in which the tendency of managers to pursue growth, rather than stockholder welfare, increases as the firm grows and matures. Once this is accomplished it will be seen that the competing theories can be tested, and that the available evidence indicates that many managers do pursue growth at the expense of stockholder welfare.

The life cycle theory of a profit-maximizing firm is developed in Sections I and III with consideration of the rate of managerial economies in this cycle given in Section II. The growth hypothesis is presented in Section IV and the contrasting development of a growth-maximizing firm is presented in Section V. The relevant empirical evidence for testing the

*Alfred E. Kahn and a referee of the *Journal of Industrial Economics* made many helpful comments on an earlier draft, although they bear no responsibility for the resulting conclusions. Reprinted from *Journal of Industrial Economics*, **20**, June 1972.

two hypotheses is reviewed in Section VI, and the implications of the paper are drawn in Section VII.[2]

I.   THE LIFE CYCLE OF A ONE-PRODUCT PROFIT-MAXIMIZING FIRM

Uncertainty is a major deterrent to a new firm's creation or an existing one's entry into another industry. This barrier is removed when some entrepreneur believes he possesses special insight or knowledge that allows him to penetrate the surrounding uncertainties. Frequently, the insight takes the form of an idea for developing a new invention, a new marketing technique or a more efficient organizational structure for the firm.[3] Thus, profits accrue to those entrepreneurs who possess the information, intuition, courage or luck to make correct investment decisions in the face of uncertainty.

The innovating entrepreneur has to promise the suppliers of the initial capital a payment equal to the market rate of interest plus some allowance for the uncertainty surrounding the new venture and the possibility of default. In the case of a new stock issue this is true, because implicit in the minds of the stockholders is probably the view that they have become partners with the entrepreneur, and will share with him any profits earned in proportion to the new venture's success.

If the innovating idea is a good one, the firm will expand. This expansion follows the familiar S-shaped growth pattern (Burns, 1934; Mueller and Tilton, 1969). The expected return on investment discounted for uncertainty rises greatly during the early stage of rapid growth as the initial uncertainties surrounding the new idea are reduced. During this period the stockholders will want all of the capital consumption allowances reinvested and probably all of the profits, too, in order to take advantage of the now easily apparent profit opportunities inherent in the new idea. It also may be desirable to raise additional outside capital during this period. As competition develops and other firms begin to adopt and improve upon the innovating entrepreneur's new idea, the profit opportunities begin to decline. This process is helped along by the saturation of the market which eventually takes place. During this period it is generally not to the stockholders' advantage to have all of the profits reinvested, and so a stockholder-welfare maximizing manager begins paying dividends. As the market potential of the innovation further declines due to changing tastes and technologies, an ever-increasing share of profits goes into dividends. Eventually, the depreciation flows begin to be paid out also, until all of the capital stock has been consumed. On the last day of the firm's existence, the entrepreneur gives the last revenue flow over contractual costs to the stockholders as dividends. Following this, the value of the outstanding stock falls to zero and at that point equals the book value of assets. The firm, which came into existence to exploit the profit potential in a given idea, expires once all of that potential has been exhausted.[4]

II. MANAGERIAL ECONOMIES AND DISECONOMIES

Innovation in the modern firm consists of more than the exploitation of a single idea. Indeed, chief among the manager-entrepreneur's duties today is the creation of an organization and environment in which innovations and new ideas spring forth. This requires the establishment of an R and D programme, incentive system for lower management, etc., that stimulate innovative thought and 'risk taking'. There are sufficient indivisibilities and economies of scale in establishing these programmes and organizational units that it may not be to the advantage of the stockholder for the firm to disband once the profit opportunities of its first product have been exhausted. Instead, his welfare is maximized if the firm moves into as many new areas as it has a cost advantage (Coase, 1937).

Given the importance of penetrating uncertainty to create profit and the crucial role of information in removing uncertainty, a firm will have this kind of a cost advantage chiefly in those areas where it has more information. Hence, the ability to process and evaluate information becomes a key determinant of the direction and size of diversification and expansion.[5]

The major advantage of size in this process is that it tends to eliminate the impediment to the transmission of information created by information's non-appropriability characteristic. By not having to go into the capital market, the gatherers of information on profitable investment opportunities can give the information to the managers in charge of supplying capital without the firm's losing possession of it. Hence, the obstacle to the flow of information that exists when entrepreneurs are separated from the sources of capital is removed. This should produce an improved flow of information and capital within the large firm over what exists when entrepreneurs must resort to outside sources of capital.

The information needed to make investment decisions is obtained from the R and D laboratories, marketing and sales departments, and other units at the bottom of the corporation's organizational pyramid. Responsibility for supplying these units with capital rests with the officers at the top. The flow of information upward through the hierarchical tiers results in a loss in both the quality and quantity of information reaching the top. Similarly a certain amount of distortion of orders takes place by the time they reach the individuals who must execute them. All of this combines to produce a discrepancy between the work done by lower rank members of a corporation and the objectives of their superiors (Monsen, 1965; Williamson, 1967).

In an attempt to reduce this discrepancy, the typical growing corporation is continually decentralizing its decision-making apparatus to ensure that decisions involving uncertainty are made by those with adequate information and incentives.[6] This decentralization process results in a continual downward shifting of authority, with the key decisions involving information gathering and evaluation being made by lower and lower ranking managers. This process can continue within the confines of a single organizational structure until one of two extremes is reached. All of the authority for making decisions has been passed down to lower level managers, in which case the chief executives are managers in name only, serving as a perfunctory appendage whose operating expenses constitute a dead-weight loss to the company.[7] Alternatively, they may still exercise some authority in determining policies, in which case their lack of adequate information to undertake these actions can be expected to result in an eventual reduction in profitability.

The case study literature of corporations is replete with situations in which the chief executives of a large diversified firm find themselves one day in a 'crisis of control' (Burch, 1967; McDonald, 1967; Rukeyser, 1968; Smith, 1963; chs. 1, 5, 6, 9, 10). Frequently, these crises have been brewing for some time, but, owing to the lack of information about the division or individuals involved, the leaders of the firm are not aware that any problem exists until calamity strikes. What is more, these losses of control are not endemic solely to business corporations. The crises that have befallen large universities, branches of the government, the church and other large bureaucratic organizations in recent years are typically attributed to the lack of adequate information by those at the top of the difficulties being encountered by people further down in the hierarchy.

Thus, while information can be transmitted within the large corporation without loss of ownership (by the organization), it must undergo a loss of content in the process. The availability of capital is greater in the large firm, but the quality of information used to allocate it is less than for the small firm. What is more, the R and D director who has a worthy project proposal turned down has no alternative sources of capital available to him. An entrepreneur for a small firm with the same R and D proposal may face an audience that is *on average* more hostile, when he is in search of capital. But the probability that he will find at least one source of capital open to him may actually be much greater than for the R and D director, as a result of the large number and variety of sources available to the entrepreneur.

The relative advantage of large size in transmitting information should decline as the corporation grows, since there is a floor below which the cost of capital cannot fall as uncertainty is reduced—the expected return on a riskless security. On the other hand, the loss of information through repeated transmissions can go on indefinitely. Hence, after some point the latter phenomenon should begin to dominate the former, and we expect the socially optimum size of the corporation to be reached.

Oliver Williamson has developed a static model in which he demonstrates that the loss of information and control places a limitation on the optimal size of the firm (Williamson, 1967). The importance of these losses is likely to be even greater when dynamic factors are taken into account (Williamson, 1967, pp. 136-7). Change produces uncertainty. The more uncertainty there is, the greater the need for information. Any deterioration in the information flow to the top decision makers reduces long-run profitability. Therefore, even if there were no increase in the costs of producing the present product line with existing techniques, there would be a limit to the optimal size of the firm beyond which further expansion would reduce its ability to introduce new products and techniques and thereby effectively lower its profitability.[8]

Dynamic diseconomies are likely to be less amenable to the improvements in organizational techniques that are often said to compensate for whatever tendencies toward managerial diseconomies of scale exist (Williamson, 1967, pp. 136-7). Most of these techniques involve some combination of two elements: a method of collecting and compiling data, and a set of steps or programmes for evaluating them and issuing orders. The decisions regarding what data are to be collected and what rules of thumb are to be employed to formulate the orders must be based on the past experience of the firm. But it is precisely in situations in which change plays a significant role that past experience is an inadequate guide to the future and rules of thumb frequently break down.

What empirical evidence there is on the matter confirms the hypothesis that managerial diseconomies are more pronounced in the dynamic decisions of the firm. Most statistical analyses of production cost have failed to uncover any tendency for unit costs to rise after a certain size (Johnston, 1960, ch. 5). On the other hand, the various studies of the determinants of inventive activity have found generally that at best large firms come up with proportionally the same number of inventions, and in a number of industries actually do relatively fewer, than the medium-size firm (Mansfield, 1962, chs. 2, 5; Scherer, 1965).[9] This despite the fact that the larger sales and cash flow of the biggest firms should make inventive activity more profitable for them.

Of even more interest are the case studies of the sources of major inventions. Here the performance of the large corporations has been surprisingly poor.[10] One observer has concluded that the small firm and lone inventor have a comparative advantage in producing the major invention, while the large company's comparative advantage lies in developing these inventions and adding more routine follow-up improvements to them (Hamburg, 1963). This is, of course, what one expects if there are significant managerial diseconomies in the invention process. Major inventions involve a great deal of uncertainty (Nelson, 1959). Often the inventors have only intuitive reasons for recommending research into certain areas. This kind of information is very difficult to transmit and interpret. Therefore, if final authority to pursue research in directions leading to major inventions rests with managers distantly removed from the sources of information, it is unlikely that sound decisions will be made. Conversely, it is much easier to adopt rule of thumb procedures based on past experience in directing R and D activity on run-of-the-mill inventions. Here the potential for avoiding information loss by adopting new managerial techniques is much greater.

III.   THE LIFE CYCLE OF A MULTIPRODUCT FIRM

Taking into account the foregoing managerial economies and diseconomies of scale, the scenario for the modern stockholder- welfare-maximizing firm might go something like the following: It comes into existence to exploit an innovative idea of its creator. In doing so it develops a capability to innovate that leads it into new areas—most likely closely related to its initial product line at first. From here it moves into still newer areas related to the second set of products. This expansion and diversification continues to take place in radial directions moving ever further away from the position from which the firm started. All along the firm continues to decentralize its organizational structure. At some point it is a loosely tied collection of nearly autonomous divisions. Any further expansion can only reduce its internal efficiency. If the divisions are still capable of generating innovations, it is in the stockholders' interest for the firm to dissolve, leaving in its place a group of much smaller firms consisting of the previous divisions of the company. Alternatively, one can envisage a sequence in which a division or groups of divisions are continually spun off over time with the parent unit remaining at roughly the optimal size for managerial efficiency.

IV.   THE GROWTH-MAXIMIZATION HYPOTHESIS

Neither of the two scenarios from Sections I and III corresponds very well to the histories of most mature corporations today. It is an hypothesis of this paper that a major reason for this is that the mature corporation is operated with the intention of maximizing managerial, not stockholder, welfare.

The managers of the large mature firm generally do not own enough of its stock to induce them to identify with the stockholder. If they are among the founders of the firm or their descendants, they probably have diluted their interests in it, in order to raise capital, sufficiently to force a loss of control.[11] More typically in the mature corporation, the managers are distantly removed from the entrepreneurial originator and have even less incentive to identify with the owners.

Although there is some disagreement regarding whether managerial incomes are more closely related to the size, growth in size, or profitability of a firm, it seems reasonable to argue that their non-pecuniary rewards (e.g. status, power, etc.) are directly associated with size and growth, and not with profitability.[12] Given the relatively high income and wealth positions of most top managers, it is also quite likely that non-pecuniary factors receive a fairly heavy weight in managerial utility functions *vis-à-vis* purely pecuniary ones. Thus, pending additional evidence linking managerial *utility* to profitability and growth, we shall assume that a manager's primary objective is to expand or maintain the size of the company and not necessarily to maximize stockholder welfare.

If the marginal returns from investment decline after a point, either because of the applicability of the law of diminishing returns to investment in a single activity, or through the impact of managerial diseconomies from expansion into different activities, then eventually a tradeoff point will be reached between additional investment and growth, and stockholder welfare. Since more investment can be expected to produce faster growth *ad infinitum*, management's pursuit of growth is presumably limited only by the availability of investment funds, the threat of take-over by an outside stockholder group should the market price of the firm fall very low, and compassion for the stockholders. For a large, mature firm, its internal fund flows are likely to be so large as to make the first constraint inoperative. Although the latter two factors should restrain the managers from pursuing unlimited growth, there is no reason to suspect that they will be held back to the point where stockholder welfare is maximized.

We thus expect the growth-maximizing management to undertake more investment than a stockholder-welfare maximizer, pay equivalently smaller dividends, grow at a faster rate, and have a lower market value for its firm.

Before closing this section, it may pay us to refute the often heard argument that stockholders prefer to have the earnings of the company reinvested, *even if they must be invested in submarginal investment opportunities*, because of the differential tax treatment accorded dividends and capital gains income. This argument would have merit were it not that I dollars of earnings can be distributed as I dollars of capital gains, by using the funds to buy the firm's stock; whereas, reinvestment of I dollars at a rate below the cost of capital produces *less* than I dollars in capital gains.

To see this let[13]

i = the cost of capital,

r = the marginal return on investment (we include R and D, advertising, mergers, etc. in investment),

S_t = the value of the outstanding stock in period t,

X_0 = the expected returns from current assets assuming no additional investment takes place, and

N = the number of shares outstanding at time 0.

If the firm has no outstanding obligations other than its stock, then its initial value is

$$S_0 = \frac{X_0}{i} = P_0 N. \tag{1}$$

As soon as it is announced that I will be used to purchase the firm's own stock, its price rises to its new equilibrium value, P_1, at which the firm purchases M shares

$$I = P_1 M \tag{2}$$

Since the expected returns of the firm have not changed, its new market value must still be equal to the original capitalized value of the firm

$$S_1 = \frac{X_0}{i} = S_0 \tag{3}$$

By definition

$$S_1 = P_1(N-M). \tag{4}$$

Substituting equations (4) and (1) into (3) we get

$$P_1(N-M) = P_0 N \tag{5}$$

And substituting for M from equation (2) and rearranging gives us

$$P_1 - P_0 = \frac{I}{N}. \tag{6}$$

That is, if I dollars are used to purchase the company's own stock, each stockholder (including both those who sell their shares and those who continue to hold them) receives a capital gain per share equal to the dividend payment per share he would receive if the I dollars were distributed directly as dividends.[14]

Thus the preferential tax treatment of capital gains does not alter the rule for dividing the internal flow-of-funds between investment and stockholder payments so as to maximize stockholder welfare, but only the optimal way for making these payments to the stockholders. Namely, the excess cash flow should be returned to the stockholder in the form of a capital gain by purchasing the firm's stock.[15]

V.   THE LIFE CYCLE OF A GROWTH-MAXIMIZING FIRM

To pursue growth at the stockholder's expense, managers must be relatively free from stockholder control. This freedom typically appears as the holdings of stock are diffused among more and more individuals reducing the power any single stockholder has to control the management with his votes (Berle and Means, 1932; Knight, 1921; Modigliani and Miller, 1958). It may also occur, however, when a single group of stockholders holds a controlling interest in the firm, but refuses to exercise this control and block the management's growth aspirations. This might occur, for example, if the controlling stockholder group contained the top managers and their managerial motives for growth outweighed their purely pecuniary interests as stockholders.[16]

The point to be stressed here is that this freedom to pursue growth, and the management–stockholder conflict that accompanies it, appear only over time as the firm expands and matures. At the firm's creation the stockholders have complete control over the amount of investment undertaken, since they supply all of the initial capital (Marris, 1964, pp. 23-4). If they were able to predict with perfect certainty their future dividend stream, the stockholders would adjust their offer for the initial stock issue to the amount that equated their return on this investment with the market rate. A management that promised low future dividend payouts would receive a low price for its initial stock offering and would have little money to invest in the early years. It could pursue later growth through high retentions only by forgoing early growth by lowering its ability to raise capital. Assuming the managers have roughly the same inter-temporal desires for growth as stockholders have for dividends, there should be little incentive for them to do this.

Of course, neither the stockholders nor the managers are able to perceive the future with much accuracy. Indeed, the great degree of uncertainty which surrounds the early years of most firms' lives makes it difficult to raise outside capital, and the firm can be viewed as facing a very steeply rising cost of capital schedule (Mueller, 1969, Figure 1). At this time the managers' and stockholder's interests coincide; they are both intent on raising sufficient capital to exploit the available investment and innovation opportunities.

If the innovative idea which started it is a good one, and/or it is followed by other innovations, the firm moves up along its S-shaped growth curve and its capital shortage disappears; first because its internal fund flows eventually outpace its new investment opportunities, and secondly because the reduction in uncertainty regarding the future following its early success lowers the cost of outside capital. It is at this point that the possibility for a gradual shifting of policies away from stockholder welfare-maximization arises. The stockholders will want to see an ever-larger proportion of the profit and depreciation flow returned to them (or continual spin-offs with the proceeds going to the stockholders) as the investment opportunities decline and managerial diseconomies set in. With the interests of management tied to the firm's existence and expansion, it is implausible to assume they will encourage this withdrawal and perhaps oversee the company's eventual dismemberment and demise.

If the shift to growth maximization is gradual, it is likely to go unnoticed. The typical stockholder's fortunes are tied more closely to short-run events than to long-run dividend policies and he is more concerned with the company's performance during this period. Then too, it may be that no visible *change* in dividend policy takes place. The management may simply set a dividend payout ratio and fail to raise it as the firm's investment opportunities decline.

The stockholder is generally powerless to prevent this. The company's internal cash flows are probably sufficient to allow a substantial over-investment without resorting to outside capital. Even when new stock is issued, the number of shares is usually too small to result in a noticeable dilution of existing stockholder interests, and hence does not precipitate a sufficient decline in stock price to elicit any attempt to control management.

It should further be noted, somewhat ironically, that it is in general probably not the fastest-growing firms in the economy that are growing at a rate greater than that which maximizes stockholder welfare, for the fastest-growing firms are typically the young firms exploiting the innovative ideas that created them. Instead, it is the large sluggish firms that are investing too much in growth, for in many cases they should not be growing at all.

VI.   EMPIRICAL SUPPORT FOR THE GROWTH HYPOTHESIS

To date, only two studies have attempted to test the growth hypothesis directly, and they have produced rather inconclusive results (Marris, 1964, ch. 7; Meyer, 1967). Unfortunately, the recent studies by Kamerschen (1968) and Monsen *et al.* (1968), which examine the relationship between control and *average* profit rates, do not shed much light on the validity of the hypothesis either. The stockholder–management conflict depicted in the growth hypothesis is over the marginal returns of corporate investment not the average returns. While the two are likely to be correlated, the correlation may not be strong enough to allow one to accept or reject the growth hypothesis solely on the basis of the results for studies of this type. In addition, the two studies arrive at opposite conclusions regarding the relationship between management control and firm profitability, indicating a need for further empirical work in this area.[17]

A similar set of offsetting results has been obtained in studies relating the degree of management control to dividend policies. Oliver Williamson found that management-controlled firms reinvested a significantly higher proportion of their internal fund flows than stockholder-controlled firms do (Williamson, 1964), while David Kamerschen using a different sample and statistical technique found that the reverse was true (1970). A further difficulty with studies of this type occurs in that they do not present any evidence on the key question from our point of view—the amount of investment each firm undertook *vis-à-vis* the amount that would maximize stockholder welfare—but instead only compare the investment rates of the two types of firms (Mueller, 1970).

Some support for our life cycle view of the firm is contained in Fizaine's recent study using data on 1183 establishments in the French economy (Fizaine, 1968). He found that age is a better explanatory variable than size in determining growth. In fact the latter loses all of its explanatory power when age is included with it in an equation having growth as a dependent variable. If these results also apply to firms, they indicate that young firms grow faster than old ones regardless of their size, and that large and small firms of the same age have the same growth rate.

One direct test of our version of the hypothesis is simply to examine stockholder attitudes toward corporate dividend policies. If the marginal return on internal investment exceeds the return a stockholder can earn outside of the firm, he will prefer to have an extra dollar of internal funds reinvested. If the internal return is less than the stockholder discount rate, he prefers to see the dollar paid as a dividend. If the two rates are equal, he is indifferent to how the funds are used (Modigliani and Miller, 1958). Hence, if all managements maximized stockholder welfare, we would expect to find that stockholders either favour internal investment over dividends or are indifferent between them. On the other hand, a stockholder preference for dividends is consistent with the hypothesis that management ignores the outside investment opportunities and pushes investment beyond the point that maximizes stockholder welfare, in an effort to obtain growth.

Virtually every study that has examined the question has found that stockholders place a higher value on a dollar of dividends than on a dollar of retained earnings.[18] Sometimes the tradeoff has been put at as high as four-to-one.

In an important re-examination of the whole question of dividends versus retentions Irwin Friend and Marshall Puckett attempt to vindicate the stockholder-welfare maximization hypothesis by putting forward various econometric alternatives to the model usually used to test it (Friend and Puckett, 1964). They reject outright as 'highly suspect' the hypothesis that investors view the marginal returns on internal investment for their company as less than the returns they can earn elsewhere (Friend and Puckett, 1964, p. 659). Their reasons for this rejection are based on the casual observation that 'marginal profit rates in a substantial number of industries appear to be quite high' (although no proof is presented for this assertion), and on 'a generally favourable market reaction to new public stock offerings in recent years'. Actually both these observations might be true, in part, and the growth hypothesis still be valid. The hypothesis is that *mature* firms over-invest in growth and as a result that *their* stockholders prefer dividends to retained earnings. It is the fast-growing, often relatively young, firms that typically resort to the equity market to raise capital. These firms have relatively high internal rates of return. Indeed, the very fact that they are forced to go to the capital market makes them conform to some extent to the discipline of the market and follow an investment policy in which their internal rate of return remains above the market discount rate. The key question from our point of view concerns how stockholders feel about investment policies of firms that do not have to go to the capital market, that is, would stockholders prefer more dividends from them?

Friend and Puckett attempt to answer the question of dividends versus retained earnings by making a number of econometric refinements on the basic model employed in previous studies, a regression of stock prices on dividends and retained earnings. Their results for this simple model are presented in Table 7.1. If stockholders are indifferent between dividends and retentions, then the coefficients of these two variables will be equal. If stockholders prefer dividends to retentions, $b>c$, etc. In

Table 7.1 *Regression equation:* $P_t=a+bD_t+cR_t$

Industry (Size Sample)	Regression coefficients (Standard Errors)				
	t	a	b	c	R^2
Chemicals ($n=20$)	1956	−0,86	+29.94 (3.00)	+2.91 (4.98)	0.868
	1958	−5.29	+27.72 (2.22)	+13.15 (5.65)	0.910
Electronics ($n=20$)	1956	+7.32	+7.27 (9.77)	+17.87 (6.60)	0.410
	1958	+8.53	+13.56 (12.80)	+26.85 (6.57)	0.524
Electric Utilities ($n=25$)	1956	+0.85	+13.86 (2.35)	+14.91 (3.42)	0.842
	1958	+1.11	+14.29 (3.36)	+18.54 (5.22)	0.772
Foods ($n=25$)	1956	+0.78	+15.56 (1.70)	+5.23 (1.30)	0.834
	1958	+1.50	+17.73 (2.10)	+4.35 (1.56)	0.805
Steels ($n=20$)	1956	−2.28	+17.60 (2.65)	+2.45 (1.42)	0.869
	1958	+8.55	+15.23 (1.63)	+5.98 (2.08)	0.881

Note: Per-share price (average for year), dividends, and retained earnings are represented by P, D and R, respectively; t designates year; n, size of sample; R^2, coefficient of determination adjusted for degrees of freedom; and standard errors of regression coefficients are indicated under coefficients in parentheses.
Source: (Friend and Puckett, 1964, p. 671).

three of the five industries the familiar finding that stockholders prefer dividends is repeated. Not only are the dividends coefficients higher in these three industries, they are of much higher statistical significance. In the electric utilities industry the Miller–Modigliani hypothesis of stockholder indifference between dividends and retained earnings is supported, since the dividends and retained earnings coefficients are roughly equal. In the electronics industry retentions are clearly preferred to dividends. While these results are obviously not very comforting to adherents of the stockholder-welfare maximization hypothesis, they correspond identically to what one would expect to find if managers maximize growth. The chemicals, foods and steel industries are all mature industries composed of firms with large enough internal cash flows to keep them relatively isolated from the influences of the capital market. We suspect that many of the firms in these three industries have expanded to a point where their internal rates of return are below their stockholder discount rates, and that stockholders would favour increased dividends. Interestingly enough, the relative magnitude of the two coefficients indicates that over-investment was greatest in the steel industry; a fact not inconsistent with the maturity and technical stagnation that characterized this industry during the period. On the other extreme, the electronics industry is a young, rapidly growing industry whose firms have had to make frequent use of new stock issues to raise capital. We expect, therefore, that the return on investment in this industry was in the late 1950s still equal to or greater than the stockholder discount rate.

At first glance, the results for the electric utilities might appear to be inconsistent with what our hypothesis would predict, for electric utilities is certainly a mature industry. The difference between it and the other three mature industries in Table 7.1 is that it is regulated. By allowing the utilities to raise prices whenever their average return on capital falls much below the regulated maximum, the regulating agencies effectively assure the utilities of a constant average return on capital (Averch and Johnson, 1962). Thus, regardless of what their internal returns would be if they were unregulated, the electric utilities will have a constant marginal return on capital that is approximately equal to the maximum rate of return on capital allowed by the regulatory agency.[19]

In closing, Friend and Puckett conclude that 'there is some indication that in non-growth industries as a whole a somewhat (but only moderately) higher investor valuation may be placed on dividends than on retained earnings within the range of payout experienced, but that the opposite may be true in growth industries' (Friend and Puckett, 1964, p. 680). If all growth industries were composed of young capital-hungry firms and all non-growth industries were made up of mature firms isolated from the capital market, then this would be precisely what our theory would predict. While these relations generally hold, there is the occasional exception, like the mature high-growth chemical industry. The difficulty Friend and Puckett have fitting this industry into their scheme suggests that the relevant considerations are not growth and non-growth, but age and reliance on the capital market as put forward in this study.[20]

The recent study by Baumol *et al.* (1970) provides a second, fairly direct test of the life cycle hypothesis. They estimate, using samples of from 434 to 651 companies covering various time periods in the 1950s, returns on investment from three sources of funds: plough-backs of internal cash flows, new debt, and new equity. Most managers, be they stockholder-welfare or growth-maximizers, can be expected to exhaust their internal fund flows before incurring the added transaction costs of externally raised capital. Since only the young firms have investment opportunities sufficiently attractive to warrant their issuing new debt and equity, the Baumol *et al.* estimates of returns on these sources of capital provide a reasonable estimate of the marginal return on investment for a young firm. Conversely, since the mature firms frequently finance all of their investment out of plough-backs, the Baumol *et al.* estimates of returns on this source provide an approximate measure of the marginal returns on investment for a mature firm.

The test of the life cycle hypothesis rests on the estimated marginal returns on investment for mature firms. If managers of mature companies maximize stockholder welfare their marginal returns on investment will equal the return a stockholder could earn in the market. If managers pursue growth instead, their marginal return on investment will be below the market rate. The return on plough-back is estimated at from 3.0 to 4.6 per cent (Baumol, Heim, Malkiel and Quandt, 1970, p. 353). This is considerably beneath Nerlove's averages of returns on holding a stock between 1950 and 1964, which ranged from 12.8 to 13.8 per cent (Nerlove, 1968). Thus, the returns mature firms earned by reinvesting their internal cash flows appear to be substantially below their stockholders' outside investment opportunities, further supporting the life cycle hypothesis.

The estimates of investment returns from new debt ranged from 4.2 to 14.0 per cent, and from new equity from 14.5 to 20.8 per cent (Baumol, Heim, Malkiel and Quandt, 1970, p. 353). These are closer to Nerlove's average return figures and indicate that companies that did resort to outside sources of funds were forced to earn returns more nearly in line with those stockholders could earn elsewhere.[21]

VII. CONCLUSIONS AND IMPLICATIONS

If there were no managerial diseconomies of scale, it would be possible for a firm to expand and diversify indefinitely without undertaking investments promising a return below the market (stockholder) discount rate. With the marginal return on investment equal to the cost of capital, the firm is in a Miller and Modigliani world and the stockholders are indifferent to its investment and dividend policies. The Baumol *et al.* study indicates that the marginal return on investment for a mature firm is substantially below the market discount rate, and thereby helps explain the otherwise seemingly irrational preference for dividends over retentions by the stockholders of mature firms, observed by Friend and Puckett, and others. Together, these findings refute both the hypotheses that there are no managerial diseconomies and that managers maximize stockholder welfare. Instead, we conclude that managers pursue a growth maximization policy.

The implications of this finding are too broad to be dealt with in detail in this paper. Two ramifications should be at least touched upon, however. First, the life cycle theory has important implications regarding the efficiency of the operation of the capital market. If large mature firms are investing *too much*, then someone in the economy must be spending too little. Two possibilities exist. The stockholders may consume less due to the reduction in their dividend income. Thus, the mature firms would bring about a forced saving, which would increase the saving and investment in the economy and thereby the macro growth rate. Stockholders would be left worse off, since they would be consuming less and not receiving an adequate reward for the additional saving. More plausibly, stockholders will take into account the forced saving induced by mature firms and cut back on their other saving activities so as to keep their consumption at the desired level. If this adjustment is complete, and total saving and investment are unchanged by mature corporations' investment policies, then the additional investment by mature corporations will come entirely at the expense of investment by other users of stockholder savings. In particular, young firms making new stock issues will find a lower demand for their issues as stockholders cut back on their purchases of these stocks to compensate for the reduction in their dividend income. Thus, if total saving and investment are unchanged, investments by mature firms at rates of return below the market discount rate will displace investments by young firms at or above the market discount rate, with a resulting lowering of the average return on investment for the economy and a reduction in the macro growth rate. In either case, therefore, it would appear that social welfare is reduced through managerial pursuit of growth.

The second major issue raised by the pursuit of growth by managers concerns the increase in overall concentration (the control of economic activity by the largest 200 firms, say) that results from it. If the interpretation of this paper is sound, these increases in economic concentration have even less justification on grounds of economic efficiency than could reasonably be assumed if the managers of the largest firms were stockholder-welfare maximizers. And should these increases in concentration carry with them an increase in political power (Galbraith, 1967), then the potential for further social losses without any offsetting economic benefits would exist as a result of managerial pursuit of growth.

NOTES

1. The recent wave of criticisms can be traced to Hall and Hitch, 1939. For surveys of this literature *see* Machlup, 1967; Williamson, 1964, chs. 1 and 2.
2. Marris makes an early attempt in this direction (Marris, 1964, ch. 8). Our work differs from his in that we stress the greater applicability of the growth hypothesis to the large mature corporation. This difference in perspective produces the capital market and managerial diseconomies problems discussed below and eventually leads us to different conclusions.
3. We thus combine the theories of Knight (1921) and Schumpeter (1934) by emphasizing the uncertainties surrounding innovations as the chief determinants of profit and entry.
4. Alternatively the entrepreneur can choose to buy up the outstanding stock rather than pay dividends. The firm's final hour then sees the last dollars of revenue used to purchase the remaining shares. When its book value reaches zero there will be no common shares outstanding.
5. Monopoly power can also serve as a base for launching expansions into new areas. We ignore the traditional market power questions throughout the paper, since our conclusions in no way conflict with the standard conclusions and policy recommendations on this point.
6. In 1963 *Dun's Review* published the results from a survey of a group of 300 top corporate executives on the ten 'best-managed' companies. One of the six traits the ten companies were found to have in common was 'a truly decentralized corporate structure'. The article went on to observe that 'One fact about the ten best-managed is inescapable: they are decentralized to a far greater degree than industry in general' (Weiner, 1963). *See also* the statement of the President of General Electric, 'The more decentralized we are, the more growth there will be' (Weiner, 1963, p. 42).
7. Some indication that this is in fact the case is apparent in the description of their jobs offered by top managers. For the most part they view themselves as offering public relations, legal, financial, and industrial relations advice, which is either far removed from the key information evaluating roles entrepreneurs typically play and/or readily obtainable from outside consulting firms. *See* Burch, 1967, p. 135; Weiner, 1963, p. 42; *Business Week*, Apr. 16, 1966, p. 176.
8. Monsen and Downs argue that the distortions in information and message flows in the large corporation are sufficient to lower its rate of growth below its potential maximum. They do not link top management's goals to the firm's growth rate, however, and therefore ignore the incentives managers have to over-invest in the company (Monsen and Downs, 1965).
9. When differences in cash flow are taken into account, there appears to be a significantly negative relationship between R and D and firm size, as measured by sales (Mueller, 1967, pp. 72-3).
10. This literature is surveyed in Hamburg, 1963; Mueller and Tilton, 1969; and Nelson, 1959.
11. Here the size distinction is important. The small mature firm's demands for capital may not have been great enough to dilute the original entrepreneur's control, and it may still be profit or owner-welfare maximizing. Accordingly the scenario of Section 1 should *and does* fit the case history evidence for the small 'family' firm.

12. In contrast with earlier studies Lewellen and Huntsman recently found that managerial incomes are more closely linked to profit or stock price than to sales (*see* Lewellen and Huntsman, 1970, and works cited there). Unfortunately they do not test for a relationship between managerial incomes and growth, and use sales rather than a measure of *total* firm size, e.g. assets, employment or value added. Indeed, they deflate their equations by assets. For a survey of the literature supporting the positive tie between managerial utility broadly defined and growth, *see* Marris, 1964, ch. 2.

13. The proof follows those of Modigliani and Miller, 1958.

14. Note that $(P_1 - P_0) < (I/N)$, if I is invested internally at an $r < i$.

15. The use of profits to purchase a company's own shares has typically been frowned upon by the American Securities and Exchange Commission, because these purchases have usually been undertaken surreptitiously as a means of triggering a short-run spurt in the stock's price and a quick capital gain for the managers. A long-run policy of announcing on a quarterly basis that I dollars of outstanding stock will be purchased over the next Y months should be far less subject to abuse, however.

16. *See* my discussion of this in Mueller, 1970.

17. For a detailed comparison of these two studies, largely critical of Kamerschen's approach, *see* Boudreaux, Chiu and Monsen, 1970.

18. Clendewin and Van Cleave, 1954; Durand, 1959; Gordon, 1959; Graham and Dodd, 1951. One apparent exception to this general pattern is contained in the recent findings of Marc Nerlove (1968). Unlike the above studies, however, Nerlove regresses realized rate of return from holding a stock on retentions and dividends, instead of using share price as the dependent variable. His measure of the rate of return from holding a share is the annual capital gain plus dividend per share divided by share price. His results are thus biased away from showing a high rate of return from buying dividends, since the dividend income is not compounded over the period the stock is held, while the reinvested earnings implicitly are.

   A second problem in using Nerlove's results to test the life cycle hypothesis comes about through the nature of the sample he employs. Since young firms and mature firms are all lumped together, there is no way to tell whether *within the sample of mature firms*, greater dividend payouts yielded higher returns to stockholders. Indeed, to the extent that young firms have higher retention ratios than mature ones, Nerlove's results are consistent with what the life cycle theory predicts.

19. Fred P. Morrissey has shown that there was a gradual shift in stockholder preferences in the 1950s away from favouring dividends toward favouring retained earnings (Morrissey, 1958). Friend and Puckett caught this trend at about its turning point, where stockholders were roughly indifferent between the two (note, however, that the difference between c and b is greater in 1958 than in 1956). This trend, combined with the upward movement in the profit to equity ratios for electric utilities in the 1950s and 1960s, suggests that utility managers have been successful at playing the Averch and Johnson game, for both themselves and their stockholders (Kahn, 1970, ch. 2), and that stockholders were relatively slow to realize this.

20. Five alternatives to the model in Table 7.1 are also presented. Although the dominance of dividends over retentions in the three mature industries is

generally reduced in these models, in only one instance is it completely eliminated, when the lagged price variable is added to the equation in Table 7.1. The addition of a lagged dependent variable is a popular device for improving $\bar{R}^2$. It raises serious problems of interpretation, however (Mueller, 1967, pp. 67-8). It is impossible to determine in this model, for example, the extent to which the lagged price variable merely captures the influence of dividends on present price, as Friend and Puckett note (Friend and Puckett, 1964, p. 675). The negative dividends coefficients in some of their equations clearly suggest an uncomfortable degree of multicollinearity (Friend and Puckett, 1964, Table 4).

21. Some observers argue that new debt can be issued without lowering the common stock price up to the point where the debt to capital stock ratio (i.e. the gearing or leverage ratio) reaches a generally accepted 'normal' level (Marris, 1964, pp. 7-8, 107). If this is true, a growing firm can raise some capital each year at a cost below the market discount rate by issuing new debt. The estimates of returns from new debt at the lower end of the range may be explained by this argument, as might the somewhat surprising practice of many mature firms of issuing new debt and paying dividends at the same time.

8 Life Cycle Effects on Corporate Returns on Retentions

In a recent paper investigating the efficiency of earnings retentions, Baumol, Heim, Malkiel and Quandt (1970) (hereafter BHMQ) estimate the rate of return on earnings retentions, debt and new equity for a large cross section of firms. They find new equity earns considerably higher returns than the plough-back of profit and depreciation, with the returns on new debt falling between. BHMQ do not explain these striking results, beyond suggesting a lack of market discipline on the reinvestment of internal funds.

In their concluding remarks, they pose a number of open questions for future research and analysis.

All of this raises serious questions about the workings of the economy and the efficiency of the investment process. Is it really true that earnings retention serves the interests of the stockholder? Are managements relatively careless in the use of funds that are not subject to the strictest sort of market discipline? Do managements retain earnings first and then look for something to do with them afterwards? None of these is intended as a rhetorical question, for none of them has an obvious answer. Certainly our figures do not provide the answers—they merely indicate strongly that the queries are by no means idle.

While the BHMQ findings have been criticized (Friend and Husic, 1973; Racette, 1973 and Whittington, 1972), the ensuing exchange serves only to heighten the importance of investigating the questions posed above. This study explores these issues and argues that it is for 'older' firms with products in the mature parts of the life cycle where over-investment via retained earnings is most prevalent.

* An earlier draft of this chapter was presented as a contributed paper to the European Meetings of the Econometric Society, Oslo, Norway, August 1973. Some of the research on this chapter was supported by a National Science Foundation grant to the National Bureau of Economic Research. Helpful comments were received from Michael Gort, Thomas F. Hogarty, Alfred E. Kahn, Oliver E. Williamson, and participants in the Industrial Organization Workshop at the University of Pennsylvania. Special thanks are due to David Downs who wrote the computer programs to access the Compustat Tape, and to Barbara White, who gathered the age of firm information. Reprinted from *Review of Economics and Statistics*, 57(4), November 1975. Henry G. Grabowski and Dennis C. Mueller.

I. THE LIFE CYCLE HYPOTHESIS

The central point of the life cycle hypothesis is that the opportunities for over-investment via plough-back increase and the sanctions against such behaviour decrease as a firm and its product structure mature.[1]

Many firms, and sometimes whole industries, come into existence to exploit a Schumpeterian innovation involving a new product, process, marketing or organizational technique. In the initial stages of growth, all or most investment funds typically must be raised externally. Consequently, over-investment via plough-back is unlikely and some checks on investment activity are provided by outside suppliers of capital. Over time, firms that manage to innovate successfully begin to accumulate profits. As long as above average growth expectations hold, managerial and shareholder objectives both encourage full plough-back of cash flows. The favoured tax treatment of capital gains over dividends reinforces this policy.

As a corporation and its product structure matures, however, a number of factors tend to alter its situation. The profitability of further investment to exploit the original innovation declines. The market of new customers becomes saturated; the imitative behaviour of other firms drives profits down. To persist in earning profits above the norm, managers must continually generate innovative ideas and process information in new areas (Schumpeter, 1934).

While some firms have repeatedly innovated, this capacity often becomes limited for a number of reasons. Successive generations of managers frequently are unable to duplicate the innovative performance of the corporation's founders. Several studies in the organizational literature also postulate that with growth and diversification, the corporation tends to become less efficient at handling information. Monsen and Downs (1965) have stressed the incentives for distorting information in a hierarchical organization; Williamson (1967) points to the information and control loss as messages pass between levels. Top managers also lose some control to middle managers because of the same type of information and policing costs which gives them discretionary power *vis-à-vis* stockholders (Alchian and Demsetz, 1972). Middle managers can then engage in risk avoidance, additional staff and emolument purchases, discriminatory hiring, and other activities which lower innovativeness and efficiency (Comanor, 1973; Mueller and Tilton, 1969 and Williamson, 1970).

As the maturing firm shifts to internal funds as the primary means of financing investment, capital market discipline also tends to weaken. The possibility of loss of control through a take-over becomes the main check on a firm's investment activity (Marris, 1971). That is, if managers plough back funds at below market yields, the firm's market valuation will decline, increasing the probability of a take-over. However, the threat of loss of control to outside groups would seem to operate with diminishing force over the life cycle. As the firm grows and diversifies, it becomes more costly for outsiders to gather information. Individual holdings of common stock are more dispersed, further lowering stockholder incentives to police managerial spending. Moreover, the cost of a successful take-over increases with the target firm's size (Singh, 1971).

Hence, because of life cycle factors, managers often reach a point where they are unable to reinvest profitability a good fraction of their cash flows while retaining substantial control over their allocation. Although all surplus internal funds could be transferred to shareholders through dividend payouts or stock repurchases,[2] managerial discretion over these funds may instead result in plough-back at below market yields. A number of writers have hypothesized managerial utility from investment in discretionary activities, although they differ on the form it takes (e.g. Baumol, 1967; Comanor, 1973; Leibenstein, 1969; Marris, 1964; Penrose, 1959 and Williamson, 1964). Alternatively, plough-back at below market yields could result from a divergence of managerial and stockholder expectations, rather than from differences in objectives. That is, managers in a declining market situation might generate unrealistically high expectations and be insensitive to the external opportunities of shareholders.

The life cycle hypothesis thus provides a framework for re-examining the results on investment returns observed by BHMQ. In particular, it suggests that low yields on plough-back will be a phenomenon primarily associated with relatively mature firms. Such firms combine declining profit opportunities with considerable discretionary control over internal funds. While over-investment through plough-back tends to have a self-correcting quality over the long run, in that future earnings decline as a result of lower yields on current investment, substantial losses in efficiency can still occur as this adjustment process takes its course.

In the empirical sections which follow, an operational definition of maturity is developed in order to test the life cycle hypothesis.

II.   TESTING THE LIFE CYCLE HYPOTHESIS: SAMPLES AND CLASSIFICATIONS

The sample is drawn from the 900 or so firms on the 1968 version of the Compustat tape. As indicated above, the concept of maturity is related both to the character of the firm's product structure and its chronological age. One can think of four possible categories:

		Product Technology	
		New	Mature
Age of Firm	Young	1	3
	Mature	2	4

Firms were classified as mature only if they were both chronologically old and made products with mature technologies, that is, were in Category 4. Categories 1, 2 and 3 were included in the 'non-mature' group for two reasons. First, significant over-investment is likely only when both of these criteria are satisfied.[3] Second, with a sample of established firms (all are on either the New York or American stock exchanges), the vast majority are classed as mature even under this strict definition.

Having adopted this concept of maturity, the problem remains of identifying the time point when a firm or industry passes from youth to maturity. Rather than risk getting into arbitrary personal judgments, the following rule was adopted—a firm is labelled mature if it was in existence prior to the end of World War II and 50 per cent or more of its sales are in industries or products existing prior to that time. Using these criteria, 142 companies were classified as non-mature, 617 as mature.[4]

It should be emphasized that the classifications are not just a simple proxy for past success or profitability of the firms. Many of the non-mature firms are in industries not particularly noted for their success (e.g. airlines, defence) and many mature firms were among the glamour stocks of the period (Kodak, Walt Disney). It is not the performance of particular firms or industries that is being analysed, but rather the efficiency with which capital is transferred from mature to young technologies, and the relative performance of mature firms as a group.

III. THE LIFE CYCLE HYPOTHESIS AND THE BHMQ MODEL

BHMQ assume that the existing capital stock produces a profits stream in perpetuity equal to the level of current profits. All increases in profits can then be attributed to increases in capital stock. One has

$$\triangle \pi_{t+1} = r \triangle K_t$$
$$\triangle \pi_{t+2} = r(\triangle K_{t+1} + \triangle K_t)$$

$$\therefore \sum_{i=1}^{n} \triangle \pi_{t+i} = r \sum_{i=0}^{n-1} (n-i) \triangle K_{t+i} \qquad (1)$$

where $\triangle \pi_{t+i} = \pi_{t+i} - \pi_t$ of the change in earnings between period $t+i$ and some base period t; and $\triangle K_{t+i}$ is defined similarly for the firm's capital stock.

The return on investment, r, can be estimated by regressing increases in profits on increases in capital stock appropriately lagged and weighted. The advantage of summing changes over a number of periods is that it removes transitory fluctuations in these variables.

If the increases in capital stock in equation (1) are broken down into the three principal sources of finance, plough-back, new long-term debt, and new equity, these components may be considered as separate independent variables. Their coefficients then become estimates of the returns on three sources of capital. Upon estimating this model for a number of different cross-section samples, BHMQ found the returns on plough-back ranged between 3 per cent and 6 per cent while the returns on new equity exceeded 20 per cent.

Friend and Husic (1973) have questioned whether the true differences in returns are as big as BHMQ claim. They found that: (i) much of the disparity in returns from alternative sources is removed when a correction for heteroscedasticity is made; and more significantly, (ii) when regressions are run *only* on the subsample of firms that have employed new equity at some time during the base period, there is no significant difference in returns on earnings retention and equity. In responding to these criticisms, BHMQ (1973) reestimate their model adjusting for heteroscedasticity and also estimate the returns on investment for those companies that did not issue any new equity. They found the returns on plough-back for companies not issuing new equity to be substantially below (indeed typically negative) the returns for companies issuing equity.

One emerges from the BHMQ-Friend and Husic exchange with the impression that there are really two types of firms in their samples: those that issue a non-negligible amount of equity and those that do not. The former earn substantially higher returns. Viewed from the perspective of the life cycle hypothesis, this is plausible. Firms that issue new equity are likely to be younger or have high investment opportunities relative to cash flow. In effect, the relative characteristic for distinguishing between the two types of companies may not be whether they have issued new equity or not, but rather the levels of their investment opportunities. A mature/non-mature classification is likely to be a better proxy for the level of investment opportunity than one based on new equity issues.

With the focus shifted from the source of capital to the level of investment opportunities, it also becomes clear that one should not estimate separate rates of return for the various sources of capital. On the margin a firm earns the same return on a dollar whether that dollar comes from new equity, new debt, or out of plough-back. Differences in these returns can exist only *across* companies not within them. Hence, it seems more reasonable to assume that a single firm earns the same return on each source of finance, but that different companies earn different rates of return.

We therefore estimate the following variant of the BHMQ model

$$\sum_{i=1}^{n} \Delta \pi_{t+i}$$

$$= r_m \sum_{i=0}^{n-1} (n-i) TFM_{t-\lambda+4}$$

$$+ r_n \sum_{i=0}^{n-1} (n-i) TFN_{t-\lambda+4} \qquad (2)$$

where *TFM* and TFN are the total funds (i.e. the sum of plough-back, new long-term debt, and new equity) invested in period *t* by firms classified as mature and non-mature, respectively; λ is the time lag in the effect of capital investment on earnings.

In Table 8.1 estimates for (2) are presented for three different time periods. Since neither the BHMQ nor the Friend–Husic results seemed to be very sensitive to the choice of lag structure, the same time lag was used in each time period. The dependent variable corresponds to changes in cash flow and the basic independent variable measures the total funds available for investment.[5] All variables are deflated by the square root of sales to eliminate heteroscedasticity.[6]

The first equation for each period gives the returns on total invested funds for the largest samples available in each period. The second equation uses dummy variables to estimate separate returns for mature and non-mature firms (i.e. equation (2)). Looking first at the r_m coefficients, one sees that the rates of return earned by mature companies are comparable to those found by Friend and Husic, ranging from 9 per cent to 12½ per cent. In all three periods the non-mature firms earned higher rates of return on invested capital than did the mature ones, by amounts ranging from 4 per cent to 17 per cent. The range is quite large and is undoubtedly sensitive to differences in sample composition.[7]

The difference in returns between the two classes of firms is largest in the earliest period. The relative decline in differentials that occurs over the later periods is consistent with the notion that any investment advantages of non-mature firms should gradually erode over time due to

Table 8.1 *Rates of return on invested capital for mature and non-mature firms*
$$\Sigma\Delta\pi_{t+i}=r_m\Sigma(n-i)TFM_{t-\lambda+i}+r_n\Sigma(n-i)TFN_{t-\lambda+4}$$

Sample	Equation	r	r_m	r_n	$\bar{R}^2$
(1)					
Dependent Variable Span, 1966–70	(1)	0.144 $(37.41)^a$	—	—	0.52
Independent Variable Span, 1962–66	(2)	—	0.125 $(32.68)^a$	0.235 $(27.53)^a$	0.61
OBS=660					
(2)					
Dependent Variable Span, 1962–66	(1)	0.101 $(28.97)^a$	—	—	0.47
Independent Variable Span, 1958–62	(2)	—	0.095 $(25.51)^a$	0.137 $(15.30)^a$	0.49
OBS=595					
(3)					
Dependent Variable Span, 1957–61	(1)	0.108 $(28.73)^a$	—	—	0.45
Independent Variable Span, 1953–7	(2)	—	0.092 $(23.42)^a$	0.263 $(20.88)^a$	0.49
OBS=498					

OBS Total Number of Observations
[a] Statistically significant at 1% level (2-tail test).

life cycle forces. However, the fact that the smallest difference is observed in the middle cross-section is somewhat puzzling. This period was characterized by more cyclical instability in investment flows than the other two and perhaps this had a more adverse influence on non-mature firms. In any event, whether these inter-temporal differences reflect compositional changes or cyclical phenomena, the returns earned in each period by non-mature firms are always significantly higher at confidence levels well beyond the 1 per cent level. This seems to provide substantial support for the life cycle hypothesis.

Although non-mature companies did resort to outside sources of capital to a greater extent, dummy variables based on the dependence on outside financing either were insignificant or far inferior to the age variable. This lends credence to our hypothesis that the important distinction is the height of investment opportunities, not the source of finance.

The large differences in estimated returns between mature and non-mature firms raise the question of whether large differentials in risk exist between them. With regard to the risk of excessive fluctuations in earnings and the rate of return over time, this is almost certainly not the case. This type of risk variable proved quite insignificant when included in both our model and almost all prior tests. On the other hand, another type of risk, the risk associated with bankruptcy and total default, could be significantly higher for young firms than for old. Since it has not been possible for us to measure this factor empirically, it is possible that some part of the lower returns of mature firms is compensated for by lower bankruptcy risk.

It should be kept in mind, however, that even the non-mature firms in our sample are relatively well established. It would be interesting to expand the sample further by including very young companies. Some would be in their early, spectacular days of growth and profitability, while others would be headed for failure. The net impact of broadening the sample to include this group of successful and unsuccessful young firms cannot be predicted. Nevertheless, our results indicate that within a sample of the very largest corporations, a fairly simple classification of maturity yields quite strong explanatory power of the investment returns pattern observed by BHMQ.

The life cycle hypothesis can also provide insights to two other paradoxical findings in the literature. Radice (1971) compared the growth and profit rates of managerial and owner-controlled firms. His prediction was that owner-controlled firms have higher profits and slower growth than managerial firms. Somewhat to his surprise Radice found the owner-controlled companies had *both* higher profits and higher growth rates. This result is less surprising if one views it in a life cycle context. Many firms come into existence to exploit an innovative idea of an owner-entrepreneur. In the early years control often has to be diluted to raise capital, but the founder and his family usually maintain a substantial interest. Eventually, however, this interest may be sufficiently diluted so that effective control passes to the management. A sample of owner-controlled and management-controlled firms will differ significantly in the age of the firms and their investment opportunities. The owner-controlled firms will on average be younger and have more profitable investment opportunities. Therefore, it is not surprising to find they have higher growth and profit rates than the more mature management-controlled companies. Whether the latter group is growing too fast, over-investing relative to its opportunities, remains unanswered, however, by this sort of comparison.[8]

We now turn to the second paradox.

IV. THE LIFE CYCLE HYPOTHESIS AND THE IMPACT OF DIVIDENDS AND RETENTION ON STOCK PRICE

A number of studies of the stock market's valuation of corporate retention and dividend policies have examined variants of the regression equation

$$P_t = a + bD_t + cR_t + u_t \qquad (3)$$

where the price variable, P_t, is defined as an average price per share for the year (e.g. one half high and low values); D_t is common dividends per share; and R_t is after tax profits less dividends per share.

Equation (3) has been applied to cross-section samples typically grouped by industry categories. Somewhat surprisingly in several sectors the coefficient on dividends, b, has been significantly higher than the one on retentions, c, implying an apparent shareholder preference for more dividends and less retentions.[9]

From a theoretical perspective, Modigliani and Miller (1958) have shown that in perfect capital markets, where there are no taxes, shareholders should be indifferent to any combination of dividends, earnings retentions and other means of finance. Their basic hypothesis is that the firm's total market value (equity plus debt) equals its long-run profit divided by the return for its risk class. If we use the above notation and express all variables in per share terms, this implies

$$P_t + DB_t = \frac{\pi_t}{r} = \frac{D_t + R_t}{r} \qquad \text{or}$$

$$P_t = \frac{1}{r} D_t + \frac{1}{r} R_t - DB_t. \qquad (4)$$

This is essentially equation (3) with the coefficients on dividends and retentions both postulated equal to the inverse of the return for the risk class and the inclusion of debt per share (DB) variables with a postulated coefficient of minus one.

When one introduces the preferential treatment of capital gains over dividends into this theoretical framework, one might expect a shareholder preference for earnings retentions, rather than the contrary results actually observed in a number of studies. The observed findings can be plausibly explained, however, by the life cycle hypothesis. If mature firms do plough-back funds at yields *significantly* below shareholder opportunity costs, an investor preference for dividends for this class of firms would not be surprising, even if tax considerations work in the opposite direction.

To examine this question further, we estimated the following variant of equation (4)

$$P = aD_m + bR_m + cD_n + \qquad dR_n + eDP_m + fDP_n + gDB_m + hDB_n, \qquad (5)$$

where the subscripts m and n refer to mature and non-mature firms, respectively. The life cycle hypothesis would essentially predict that dividends are preferred to retentions for mature firms $(a>b)$, but not for non-mature firms $(c \leqslant d)$.

We have also included in our regression equation, a separate variable for depreciation and depletion charges, DP (measured in per share terms as in the case of all other variables).

If reported depreciation charges accurately measured the deterioration and obsolescence of plant and equipment, this variable would have a predicted coefficient of zero in a stock price equation. However, the accelerated depreciation provisions of the tax laws make it likely that reported depreciation contains an element of 'hidden' profits. This suggests a positive coefficient for depreciation in a price valuation equation. Moreover, if mature companies are over-investing as postulated by the life cycle hypothesis, one would expect any 'hidden profits' to have a stronger impact on the stock price of non-mature firms. Hence, in terms of equation (5), we predict $(e<f)$.

In addition, we include the debt variable in our regression equation, given its presence in the Modigliani–Miller model. While their theoretical framework implies a coefficient of minus one for this variable, at least in a perfect capital market situation, we make no predictions on the relative size of the coefficients on this variable between mature and non-mature firms.

Following previous studies, the companies were assigned to industries and separate regressions run on each group. A cross-section spanning all industries, like that employed in Section III, is too heterogeneous. Market valuation is influenced by industry-related variables. This was confirmed by the dramatic improvement in the overall performance and character of the results as the sample was subdivided into more homogeneous groups. To achieve sufficiently narrow industry classifications and still have enough non-mature observations, the cross-sections were pooled over the eighteen years of data available. We could form twelve industry groups at roughly the two-digit SIC level.

Equation (5) was estimated with the addition of separate year intercepts to account for time-specific factors affecting stock price. The results of this estimation are presented in Table 8.2. The time intercepts are omitted to preserve space and clarity although the majority were statistically significant.

Comparing first the dividends and retention coefficients for mature firms, one finds the life cycle hypothesis that dividends will be preferred to retentions supported in 10 of the 12 industries (the inequalities between coefficients indicate statistical significance at the 5 per cent level). Not surprisingly the two exceptions occur in the technologically progressive scientific instruments and industrial chemicals industries, where even mature firms appear to have attractive investment opportunities.

In marked contrast to the results for mature firms, in only 1 of the 12 industries, petroleum, is the coefficient on dividends for non-mature firms statistically greater than on retentions. Owing to the small number of non-mature companies, this result might reflect in part the large standard errors of the regression coefficients in some industries (e.g. miscellaneous chemicals). Nevertheless, it is reassuring to note that in 9 of 12 industries the estimated coefficients imply that dividends are *relatively* more preferred by the market, for the mature than for the non-mature firms (i.e. that $(D_m - R_m) > (D_n - R_n)$).

Eighteen of the 24 depreciation coefficients (13 of the 15 which are significant at the 5 per cent level) are positive, thus supporting the hypothesis that depreciation contains a component of hidden profits. In 8 of the 12 industries the coefficient for the non-mature companies is greater than for the mature ones as predicted by the life cycle hypothesis. The standard errors are often large, however, so that only 6 statistically significant differences exist. Of these, 4 favour the hypothesis, 2 contradict it. Again the two contradictions occur in relatively progressive industries with high investment opportunities, scientific instruments and drugs.

Although many of the debt coefficients are statistically significant, no clear pattern emerges from an examination of them. Almost as many are positive as are negative and there is no tendency toward a minus one coefficient on this variable.

In sum, the results in Table 8.2 illustrate the importance of the economic age of the firm and its product structure in determining the market's reaction to managerial dividend and retention policies. In 10 of the 12 industries, our estimates suggest the market valued the dividend payments of mature companies significantly higher than their retentions, while the same was true for non-mature firms in only one industry. Similarly, the coefficient for depreciation was larger for non-mature than for mature companies in two-thirds of the industries. The important exceptions to these patterns occur in the technologically progressive scientific instruments, industrial chemicals, and drug industries, where investment opportunities appear sufficiently high to warrant high market valuations of retained profits and/or those hidden in depreciation by the mature firms. Within these progressive industries the distinction between mature and non-mature is obviously less meaningful.

Table 8.2: *Market valuation of dividends and retentions in twelve industry groups*

$$P = aD_m + bR_m + cD_n + dR_n + eDP_m + fDP_n + gDB_m + hDB_n$$

Industry (Sample Size)	D_m		R_m	D_n		R_n	DP_m		DP_n	DB_n	DB_m	$\bar{R}^2$
Food (1365)	18.19 (46.37)[a]	>	5.07 (16.81)[a]	5.78 (0.71)	≈	15.43 (3.89)[a]	-0.50 (1.36)	≈	3.41 (0.52)	-0.13 (3.45)[a]	0.24 (0.46)	0.75
Textiles and Clothing (474)	13.03 (21.25)[a]	>	2.57 (9.25)[a]	17.47 (1.69)	≈	11.06 (3.75)[a]	-1.11 (2.82)[a]	≈	-13.64 (1.84)	0.16 (3.59)[a]	0.15 (0.32)	0.69
Industrial Chemicals (452)	23.04 (23.14)[a]	<	24.91 (25.63)[a]	10.31 (0.93)	≈	8.34 (0.93)	4.38 (3.73)[a]	≈	-2.32 (0.30)	-0.04 (0.41)	1.35 (1.75)	0.86
Drugs (367)	27.11 (14.68)[a]	>	9.48 (3.39)[a]	18.40 (7.00)[a]	≈	23.91 (9.67)[a]	6.04 (1.91)	>	-11.18 (1.73)	-2.27 (6.00)[a]	-0.31 (0.42)	0.66
Miscellaneous Chemicals (488)	19.34 (22.31)[a]	>	8.93 (10.39)[a]	22.27 (1.51)	≈	7.16 (1.12)	-9.18 (8.90)[a]	≈	1.06 (0.06)	0.22 (2.18)[b]	0.35 (0.16)	0.70
Petroleum (573)	11.43 (18.94)[a]	>	5.89 (11.42)[a]	11.03 (2.72)[a]	>	0.69 (0.38)	1.19 (3.41)[a]	≈	2.38 (1.21)	-0.09 (1.79)	0.02 (0.09)	0.69
Stone, Clay and Glass (416)	17.50 (18.71)[a]	>	7.26 (11.91)[a]	13.37 (1.98)[a]	≈	11.27 (1.75)	1.85 (2.03)[a]	<	74.96 (11.18)[a]	0.21 (2.00)[b]	-10.42 (13.15)[a]	0.89
Primary and Fabricated Metals (1027)	11.29 (27.15)[a]	>	3.70 (13.35)[a]	-18.37 (1.18)	<	9.57 (2.03)[a]	0.08 (0.24)	≈	2.10 (0.17)	2.11 (6.32)[a]	1.18 (0.72)	0.64
Mechanical Machinery (1157)	10.32 (12.01)[a]	>	4.38 (7.48)[a]	0.39 (0.23)	<	9.54 (6.65)[a]	3.70 (5.85)[a]	<	22.91 (28.58)[a]	-0.04 (0.36)	-2.79 (14.15)[a]	0.81
Electrical Machinery (881)	14.57 (11.44)[a]	>	3.74 (5.00)[a]	7.27 (5.90)[a]	<	10.39 (13.79)[a]	4.21 (3.31)[a]	<	10.01 (9.47)[a]	-0.06 (0.88)	-0.49 (3.89)	0.57
Transportation (927)	11.52 (22.20)[a]	>	1.60 (6.11)[a]	4.66 (5.49)[a]	≈	3.52 (9.70)[a]	2.73 (5.99)[a]	<	8.47 (12.43)[a]	0.03 (0.62)	-0.15 (1.88)	0.64
Scientific Instruments (343)	1.31 (0.45)	<	11.82 (7.63)[a]	-4.83 (1.46)	<	15.32 (6.67)[a]	28.31 (5.84)[a]	>	9.64 (1.67)	-2.62 (6.60)[a]	-1.07 (1.93)	0.43

[a]Significant at 1% level (2-tail test).
[b]Significant at 5% level (2-tail test).
>or< Hypothesis of equality rejected in favour of indicated inequality (5%, 2-tail test).
≈ Hypothesis of equality could not be rejected (5%, 2-tail test).

V. POLICY IMPLICATIONS

The hypothesis that managers maximize stockholder welfare by equating the marginal return on investment with their cost of capital is hard to accept, given the lower observed yields for mature firms as well as the usually strong preference for dividends over retentions the market exhibited toward these companies. Instead, one must conclude that only young firms or companies operating in technologically progressive industries, with high investment opportunities relative to their internal cash flows, invest at roughly the levels that maximize present values. Managers of mature corporations in technologically unprogressive industries reinvest too large a percentage of their internal funds. Their shareholders would apparently be better off with higher payouts in one form or another.

The efficiency of the economy would be improved if some investment funds were transferred to non-mature firms and industries. Two methods for achieving this transfer will be considered: the first makes greater utilization of the capital market, the second circumvents it.

The capital market's ability to transfer funds could be improved simply by forcing a greater percentage of profit and depreciation flows into the market. A tax could be levied on undistributed corporate profits (and even depreciation), inducing higher dividend pay-outs. Presumably this could be done in such a way as to leave overall taxes on profits unchanged. Investment funds then would have to be raised primarily by new debt and equity issues. Forced to compete with other firms in the capital market, the mature ones would reclaim a smaller share of the total available funds. Competition would induce all to reveal more information about their investment programmes, existing and expected profits, etc., further accelerating the flow of capital away from mature companies, and strengthening the discipline of the market.

An alternative to using the capital market is for the mature companies to transfer funds to non-mature ones directly by buying the latter's equity. Conglomerate mergers, in particular, have been rationalized as a means for shifting capital from old to new technologies (Lintner, 1971 and Williamson, 1970). Some empirical support for this view is provided by Weston and Mansinghka (1971). They compare returns on capital for a sample of companies that engaged heavily in conglomerate mergers with the returns for a random sample of industrials. The conglomerates earned lower returns on capital before they began their acquisition programmes and roughly the same returns after the merger wave of the sixties. These findings are loosely supported in Gort's 1962 investigations of corporate diversification over an earlier period. He found a pattern of resource allocation (through both mergers and internal expansion) from low-growth industries in which firms had high-market shares, to high-growth, low-market share industries.

An interesting variant of the conglomerate merger approach has been suggested by Turner and Williamson (1971). They recommend that merger policy be selectively used to encourage the transfer of capital to young innovative firms without allowing industry concentration levels to increase. One means of accomplishing this would be to require spin-offs of units by conglomerates making new acquisitions (see Williamson, 1970, p. 161). This could also help avoid some of the disadvantages that could result from losses in content, control and incentives as information and commands are transferred within large organizations, as discussed in Section I.

The choice between greater reliance on market or non-market mechanisms to shift capital resources from mature firms raises many classic and fundamental issues in economics: questions of appropriability of information in the firm and the market; of concentration versus deconcentration in the capital market; of markets versus bureaucracies. We cannot resolve these questions here. What we have done is to demonstrate empirically the need for a further discussion of them.

NOTES

1. The life cycle hypothesis is more fully developed by Mueller (1972).
2. Mueller (1972) has shown that if dividends are taxed at a higher rate than capital gains, an equivalent payment can be made through the repurchase of the company's shares. This avoids a tax loss.
3. Categories 2 and 3 are intermediate classes. Some older firms can turn around by shifting into a new technology. A classic example is Xerox, which was a small fifty-year-old photopaper manufacturer when its young entrepreneur-managers happened across the xerography invention. And, even in mature industries there are possibilities of profitable innovations that may spawn new companies.
4. The data on product structures were obtained by first examining Moody's. Where this presented an ambiguous classification, further sources were consulted including annual reports, and *Fortune*, and Dun and Bradstreet employment profiles by SIC class at the establishment and firm level. Firms were dropped chiefly due to mergers between 1968 and 1972 and the inability to determine unambiguously a company's starting date. The list and classification of the 759 firms is available from the authors as a separate appendix.
5. The dependent variable is the increases in actual profits plus depreciation and fixed charges over the normalized profits for the base period. Normalized profits are the predicted profits from a regression of profits on time. Plough-back is actual profit plus depreciation less dividends. New debt is the change in outstanding long-term debt. New equity is the change in outstanding

equity. As in the case of BHMQ, we also tested our model using variants of these definitions (e.g. net rather than gross earnings and retentions) but the results were not altered, in any substantial manner.

6. Since all the variables in equation (2) are flows, we selected a flow-based measure of size (sales) as our deflator. We tested for heteroscedasticity by applying the Goldfeld–Quandt test to the middle cross-section. The homoscedasticity hypothesis was rejected for the undeflated equation and one deflated by sales, but it could not be rejected when the square root of sales was the deflator.

   Friend and Husic (1973) use a simple linear stock measure (assets) as their size deflator. They do not report performing any formal tests for heteroscedasticity. However, they do indicate that experimentation with a non-linear logarithmic assets deflator did not change the results significantly.

   Experimentation on our own sample indicates that one can use either sales or assets, or the square root of these variables, as the size deflator without any qualitative changes in the results. However, our formal tests for heteroscedasticity indicate the square root formulation is the appropriate deflator in the current analysis.

7. The increase in sample size from 498 to 660 over the three periods primarily reflects fewer missing data observations on the Compustat Tape at later points in time. Since the probability of a missing observation in the earlier years is greater for non-mature than mature firms, the later cross-sections provide more meaningful tests of our hypothesis.

8. The failure to allow for differences in investment opportunities limits many prior tests of the impact of managerial control (e.g. Kamerschen, 1968; Larner, 1968; and Monsen, Chiu and Cooley, 1968). For an approach that does attempt to control for such opportunities, *see* Grabowski and Mueller (1972).

9. One of the more ambitious attempts to resolve these paradoxical findings was performed by Friend and Puckett (1964). For a detailed critique of their study, *see* Mueller (1972). The literature on the market response to corporate dividend and retention policies is cited and reviewed in both these papers.

   Recent papers by Brigham and Gordon (1968), and Van Horne and McDonald (1971) also reveal a preference for dividends by the market. Bower and Bower (1969), on the other hand, claim support for the Modigliani–Miller hypothesis after eliminating the highly significant firm effects in their sample. However, their firm dummies undoubtedly capture the age effects stressed in this paper so that their findings are not inconsistent with our life cycle interpretation of these studies.

Part III
Mergers

9 A Theory of Conglomerate Mergers*

Mergers have always been sort of an enigma in the theory of the firm. Surveys of past merger movements have had only partial success in relating the causes of these waves and their size to economic theory (Markham, 1955). Recent increases in merger activity seem to present a further challenge to traditional economic theory, since such a high percentage of these consolidations has been of the conglomerate variety, that is, mergers between firms in unrelated or indirectly related industries (Committee on the Judiciary, 1967).

If firms maximize profit, mergers will take place only when they produce some increase in market power, when they produce a technological or managerial economy of scale, or when the managers of the acquiring firm possess some special insight into the opportunities for profit in the acquired firm which neither its managers nor its stockholders possess.[1] While these 'synergistic' effects and managerial insights are often said to be present in various merger situations, their existence in sufficient strength to warrant the high premiums paid for other firms, often appears implausible when the merger is between firms in seemingly unrelated or loosely related industries. This is especially true when, as frequently happens, the acquired firm is left to operate as an autonomous division of the larger unit, operated by the same management team that controlled it before the merger.

In light of these considerations, proponents of the profit-maximization hypothesis have had to rationalize the post-war merger statistics by arguing either that the industrial community is literally a sea of synergistic merger opportunities, or that a lot of bad decision-making has been going on with respect to mergers (Alberts and Segall, 1966). Neither of these polar positions is likely to leave the student of industrial organization feeling very comfortable.

*This chapter was written with the support of the Brookings Institution under a grant from the Alfred P. Sloan Foundation. Alfred E. Kahn and John E. Tilton made a number of important suggestions which improved the paper, although they are not responsible for any errors that remain. The views presented here are those of the writer and do not necessarily represent those of the other staff members, officers, or trustees of the Brookings Institution. Reprinted from *The Quarterly Journal of Economics*, **83**, November 1969, copyright © John Wiley & Sons, Inc.

This chapter offers an explanation of recent corporate acquisitions based on the hypothesis that firms maximize growth. While this hypothesis can be applied to all types of mergers and corporate investment activities, it is felt to be particularly useful in understanding the seemingly irrational flurry of conglomerate merger activity.

I.   THE GROWTH-MAXIMIZATION HYPOTHESIS

In recent years, a number of writers have put forward the hypothesis that managers maximize, or at least pursue as one of their goals, the growth in physical size of their corporation rather than its profit or stockholder welfare (Baumol, 1959; Galbraith, 1967a; Marris, 1964; Penrose, 1959; Williamson, 1966). In the most detailed development of this hypothesis to date, Robin Marris presents a wealth of behavioural evidence in support of the contention that both the pecuniary and non-pecuniary rewards which managers received are closely tied to the growth rate of their firm (Marris, 1964, ch. 2). Managerial salaries, bonuses, stock options, and promotions all tend to be more closely related to the size or changes in size of the firm than to its profits. Similarly, the prestige and power which managers derive from their occupations are directly related to the size and growth of the company and not to its profitability.

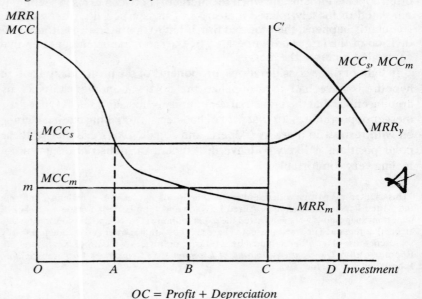

$OC = Profit + Depreciation$

Figure 9.1: The firm investment decision

The impact of managerial pursuit of growth on a mature firm's investment policies is depicted in Figure 9.1. *MCC*, is the familiar marginal cost of capital schedule for a firm which maximizes stockholder welfare. The horizontal stretch of the curve corresponds to the profit and depreciation flows of the firm. Its height above the horizontal axis represents the opportunity costs or rate of time preference of the firm's stockholders, that is, their expected return from investing in the stock of another firm or portfolio of firms of comparable risk. Past the point of its profit and depreciation flow, the firm's cost of capital will exceed i. Since it is impossible for two stocks of equal risk to sell at prices which do not promise the same rate of return to a marginal stockholder (see Section II), the cost of raising capital through new equity issues will equal i plus whatever transaction costs are involved in this form of financing. Increasing contractual debt will also entail additional transaction costs, and, at least after a point, the firm will have to pay an ever larger risk premium to its lenders as the risk of default increases with increasing firm leverage.[2]

MRR_y is the schedule of marginal rates of return on long-run investments[3] for a young firm. The young firm's investment opportunities generally will exceed its internal flow of funds, and its stockholder-welfare-maximizing policy will be to pay no dividends and raise outside capital until its marginal cost equals the firm's marginal return on investment. In Figure 9.1, *OD* investment would be undertaken and *CD* outside capital would be raised.

If managers have the same time preference for growth as stockholders have for income, then *OD* is also the level of investment which will maximize the present value of the firm's growth. For if more investment were undertaken, future profits would be reduced and present growth would be expanded at the expense of future growth. Hence, both the young growth-maximizing and the young stockholder-welfare-maximizing firms will undertake the same investment policies. Both will be dependent on outside sources of capital for part of their investment funds, and both will be forced by this dependence to face the same cost of capital schedule. At this point in the firm's life cycle, managerial and stockholder interests will coincide.[4]

As the firm expands and matures, its profit and depreciation flows will increase and shift *CC'* to the right. While the firm's marginal return on investment schedule also may be expected to shift outward, in most cases it will not shift as rapidly as the flow-of-funds increases, since the firm's opportunities for internal investment will decline in a maturing industry. This will mean that at some point in time the firm's marginal return on investment schedule will intersect MCC_s to the left of *CC'*. To save space, the marginal return schedule for a mature firm (MRR_m) has been drawn in Figure 9.1 in the *relative* position it would have to CC', although both would be far to the right of their positions for a young firm. A stockholder-welfare-maximizing firm having MRR_m would undertake OA in investment, pay out AC in dividends, and raise no additional capital outside of the firm. That is, as the firm's internal investment opportunities decline, it will be in the stockholders' best interests for the firm to begin to repay some of the profit and depreciation flow to the firm so that it can be invested elsewhere. Note that only *long-run* investment and dividend payment policies are depicted in Figure 9.1. We do not mean to imply that the firm will never resort to raising outside capital once it has begun to pay dividends. It may very well borrow in response to short-run changes in investment opportunities and in order to finance lumpy investment projects, such as a major capital expansion programme or a large acquisition.[5] These loans will be quickly repaid, however. What we do argue is that a stockholder-welfare-maximizing firm would not undertake a long-run policy of paying dividends and constantly issuing new equity or increasing its leverage ratio.

The management intent upon maximizing growth will tend to ignore, or at least heavily discount, investment opportunities outside the firm, since these will not contribute to the internal expansion of the firm.[6] The cost of capital schedule for management (m) can be expected to be considerably below that of the stockholders, therefore, for those portions of the two schedules which correspond to the firm's internal funds flows. The height of the managerial curve in this region will depend upon management's sense of obligation to or identification with its stockholders, the outside opportunities of the stockholders, and the extent to which management is constrained to pursue stockholder welfare from the fear of take-over by a dissident group of stockholders or some outside group (Marris, 1964, pp. 29-40).

If the firm experiences diminishing marginal returns on its internal investment opportunities, the marginal return schedule for a mature firm will intersect MCC_s at a point to the left of its intersection with MCC_m. Thus, the mature firm which is run by growth-oriented managers will undertake more internal investment (OB) than a stockholder-welfare-maximizing firm, pay less in dividends (BC), and have a lower rate of return on its marginal investment project.

If managers considered both internal and external investment opportunities, the MRR schedule would tend to flatten out at i, since there would be an almost unlimited range of investment opportunities in the stocks of other firms promising this rate of return. While these investment opportunities will still exist for the growth-oriented firm, they must be internalized if they are to produce growth; hence the outside firms will have to be acquired. The acquisition of firms will entail greater transaction costs than the purchase of some of their stock, since typically a large premium over the stock's market value will have to be paid when the entire firm is acquired, and the costs of assimilating the firm into the parent's organizational unit will have to be incurred. Hence, the flattening out of the *MRR* as greater resort to outside investment opportunities is made will come at a point below *i*, the stockholder's opportunity costs. It should also be noted that this flattening of the *MRR* schedule may result in large disparities in investment and dividend payout policies between firms which have similar opportunities for strictly internal investment, with the differences coming in the percentage of their retentions devoted to internal investment and acquisitions.

In what follows we shall examine firm merger policies assuming that the management evaluates merger opportunities using the present value approach. A growth-maximizing management will then be assumed to calculate the present value of an investment opportunity using a lower discount rate than a stock-holder-welfare maximizer would. As before, this will result in greater investment and lower dividends for the growth maximizer.[7]

II. THE DEMAND AND SUPPLY OF FIRMS WHEN MANAGERS MAXIMIZE STOCKHOLDER WELFARE

If we assume that the managers of a firm engaged in acquiring other companies are perfectly controlled by its stockholders, that they maximize stockholder welfare, and that their expectations are identical to those of the stockholders, then its demand price for other firms will be the discounted expected *increase* in earnings of the acquiring firm following a merger, where the discount rate employed naturally is that of the stockholders. The supply price of a stockholder-welfare-maximizing firm is the present value of the expected earnings stream of the company discounted by the discount rate of its stockholders. If the acquiring firm is referred to as Firm *A*, the firm which is bought as Firm *B*, and the newly combined firm as *C*, and

$$D_A = A\text{'s demand for } B,$$
$$S_B = B\text{'s supply price,}$$
$$\Pi_{Bt}{}^A = \text{Firm } B\text{'s expected profits in period } t \text{ as envisaged by the stockholders of Firm } A,$$
$$K_B = \text{Firm } B\text{'s stockholders' discount rate,}$$

then A will acquire B when

$$D_A \geqslant S_B, \text{ where } D_A = \sum_{t=0}^{\infty} \frac{\Pi_{Ct}^{A} - \Pi_{At}^{A}}{(K_A + 1)^t} \text{ and}$$

$$S_B = \sum_{t=0}^{\infty} \frac{\Pi_{Bt}^{B}}{(1 + K_B)^t}.$$

In a stockholder-welfare-maximizing world, mergers will take place only if (1) both expected earnings streams are the same, and A's owners have a lower discount rate than the sellers of B ($\Pi_{Ct}^{A} - \Pi_{At}^{A} = \Pi_{Bt}^{B}$ for all t, and $K_A > K_B$); or (2) both discount rates are the same, and some synergistic effect is expected to follow the merger so that the increase in the earnings of the newly formed firm exceeds the expected earnings stream of $A+B$ had there been no merger ($K_A = K_B, \Pi_{Bt}^{B} = \Pi_{Bt}^{A}$, and $\Pi_{Ct}^{A} - \Pi_{At}^{A} < \Pi_{Bt}^{B}$ for some t); or (3) no synergistic effect is expected, but the earnings stream for B as envisaged by A's stockholders exceeds that pictured by B's stockholders ($K_A = K_B$, and $\Pi_{Ct}^{A} - \Pi_{At}^{A} = \Pi_{Bt}^{A}$, but $\Pi_{Bt}^{A} > \Pi_{Bt}^{B}$ for some t). The first and third postulates can, we think, be rejected.

We assume that a firm's stockholders are drawn from a common pool of stockholders. Each stockholder maximizes the present value of his income stream, given his particular rate of discount. Because of the ease with which stocks can be turned over, the discount rate of the stockholder who is on the margin of holding a given stock should be the same for all stocks which are traded.[8] This can be demonstrated as follows:

Assume first that the stockholders for both firms envisage the identical earnings streams for both firms A and B, and that the stock of each firm is selling at its present value to its respective marginal stockholder (that is the stockholder of A who is on the margin of selling his stock). If the marginal stockholder of A has a lower discount rate than the marginal holder of B, he will consider B's stock *underpriced*.[9] This will cause him to begin buying shares of B. If he obtains the money to do this by selling shares of A,[10] then, following the transaction, the marginal holder of B will have a lower discount rate than before and the marginal holder of A, a higher one. The arbitration process should continue until the discount rates of the marginal holders of the two stocks are equalled. If we assume that this happens for all pairs of stocks, we can think about a single marginal discount rate for the entire market for stocks.

Because of the ease with which stocks can be traded, even small disequilibria in marginal discount rates can be expected to set in motion equilibrating exchanges of stocks between marginal stockholders.

Certainly one would never expect the disequilibrium to grow so large that all of the shares of B would have to be acquired by the shareholders of A in a single transaction in order to equate the discount rates of the marginal stockholders. Hence, a divergence in stockholder discount rates does not seem to be a plausible cause of mergers in a stockholder-welfare-maximizing world.

An analogous argument can be used to dispose of the third justification for mergers—a divergence in expectations among stockholders. Stockholders can be expected to adjust their portfolios so that the marginal holder of A's stock has the same earnings expectations for firm A as the marginal holder of firm B's stock has for A.

For those who believe that firm managements seek to maximize stockholder welfare, the importance of the existence of synergistic potential as a justification for mergers is now obvious. Certainly many mergers do have the potential of bringing about increases in profit, the most notable example being the horizontal merger which results in an increase in market power for the acquiring firm. But it is hard to discern similar private economies in the union of a television network and a rent-a-car service. It is in the area of conglomerate mergers, therefore, that defenders of profit maximization face their greatest challenge.

Three synergistic effects are most frequently brought forward to justify conglomerate mergers. First, it is said that management is an amorphous substance which can be applied with equal success to totally unrelated lines of business. The stockholders of A and B may desire to see the two companies joined just to have B run by A's management.

The second asserted economy is finance. The giant conglomerate has a large annual cash flow and has access to outside funds at the lowest attainable rates. Hence, it is argued that a small firm can benefit from being absorbed by the larger firm by gaining access to cheaper capital. On closer examination, however, this argument by itself does not hold up as a justification for mergers.

First, consider the case where neither firm has to resort to outside capital. Under these conditions, the costs of capital for both firms will equal the opportunity costs of their stockholders. We have already demonstrated above that any differences in discount rates for the two firms would be eliminated by exchanges of stock between the firms' stockholders.[11] Hence, when both firms are dependent on internal funds for capital, their costs of capital will be equal.

It may be, however, that the smaller firm is dependent in part on outside sources of finance (e.g. perhaps it is a young, fast-growing company). Under these conditions it might have a higher cost of capital. Assume that the cost of outside capital for B is 8 per cent and the cost of internal capital for A is 6 per cent, and that both A's and B's managements have the same expectations regarding B's investment opportunities. A merger will permit investment in B to be pushed until the expected marginal return equals the lower 6 per cent marginal cost of capital of A. Hence, more investment will be undertaken if B is owned by A and more profits will be made.

If we assume, however, that A's management is no more competent than B's, and therefore that the marginal efficiency of investment schedule which they envisage is identical to the one which B's managers picture, then the above situation would justify A's lending to or investing in B, not acquiring it. For example, A might acquire a bond issue of B carrying a yield slightly in excess of 6 per cent, or, if A wishes to share in the risks on B's investments for a higher expected yield, it might purchase some newly issued stock of B at an effective cost of capital to B less than 8 per cent.

The purchase of B's stock or bonds would ordinarily be a cheaper means of supplying it with capital than acquiring the whole company. The typical premium paid by an acquiring firm in a merger is 10–30 per cent above the market price of the acquired firm's stock before the merger (James B. Walker, Jr.). To this must be added the costs of bringing the two firms together, including the managerial costs of assimilating the acquired firm (Penrose, 1959, ch. 8). Finally, by acquiring the entire firm, A loses the flexibility to disengage itself from B quickly and at low cost. All of these costs must be compared with the extremely low transaction costs connected with A's purchase (or later sale) of some of B's stocks or bonds.

The reduction of risk through pooling is the third justification often invoked to justify conglomerate mergers (although it is obviously not unrelated to the second one) (Adelman, 1961). Even when A and B are technically unrelated, the risks surrounding their earnings streams will be reduced when these earnings streams are pooled.

Once again, however, as long as A's management cannot actually improve the performance of B, this argument cannot be used on behalf of A's stockholders to justify the heavy costs of acquisition. The stockholders can achieve the same risk-pooling effect by purchasing some of the stock of both firms, and at a much lower cost than is involved in A's acquiring B. Hence, risk-pooling can be used to defend the diversified portfolio, not the diversified firm.

For the stockholder who invests only a very small amount and cannot thereby acquire a fully diversified portfolio, there is always the mutual fund, which can offer him expert portfolio selection, lower transactions costs, and greater flexibility than the conglomerate firm. Hence, in a stockholder-welfare-maximizing world, risk pooling would take the form of diversified stockholder portfolios and stockholder investments in mutual funds, not the creation of conglomerate firms.

To summarize: If managers and stockholders have the same expectations and discount rates, and managers seek to maximize stockholders' welfare, the only justification for a merger is to achieve some synergistic effect—the many familiar economies in production, distribution, or research and development often cited to justify particular horizontal and vertical combinations. When none of these technological economies can be found, as seems likely in the case of many conglomerate mergers, the only justification for a merger can be to take advantage of managerial economies. For these economies to exist, managerial ability must be a non-specialized proclivity, and the leaders of the acquiring company must be men of much greater talent than those of the corporations they absorb.

III. THE DEMAND AND SUPPLY OF FIRMS WHEN MANAGERS AND STOCKHOLDERS HAVE DIFFERENT EXPECTATIONS

Another possible explanation of mergers consistent with the proposition that managers maximize stockholder welfare (i.e. employ the same discount rate as their stockholders) is that managers' expectations regarding the future earnings of their own corporation and those of other corporations can differ from those of their stockholders. The relevant demand price for a firm is then the price that the acquiring firm's management is willing to pay, based on its expectations of the earnings prospects of the newly combined company.

Two selling prices are possible when management is separated from its stockholders: the management's selling price and the stockholders' selling price. B will be said to have been sold at its management's selling price if its sale takes place via a merger in which A's managers approach B's managers directly; they agree upon a mutually satisfactory price, and then B's managers use their influence and proxy power to persuade their stockholders to approve the merger. A will be said to have purchased B at the stockholders' selling price if its appeal is directly to the stockholders (usually by a tender offer and often over the protest of B's managers). Depending on whether B's management regards its earnings prospects as better or worse than do its stockholders, its selling price will be above or below theirs. Transactions naturally will be expected to take place at the lower of these two prices or, more accurately, at some point between the two supply prices for B.[12]

Even if there are no synergistic possibilities, mergers can take place now because of a divergence in earnings expectations between the managers of A and the sellers of B.

If B is purchased from its stockholders, then A's managers must see an economic potential in B that A's stockholders did not see. For since B will have to be purchased for an average share price a good deal higher than the closing price of B's stock before the acquisition, presumably if A's stockholders (or at least some of them) had seen the same economic potential in B as A's managers do, they would have sold their shares of A and bought shares of B. Since B will be bought at the stockholders' selling price only when this price is less than B's managers' selling price, A's acquisition of B through a stock take-over indicates that the managements of both A and B are more optimistic about the latter firm's future than the stockholders of their respective firms.

When B is bought at its managers' selling price, little can be said other than that A's managers see more in B's prospects than even its own managers do.[13]

Thus, even if no synergistic effects are apparent and the discount rates of the buyers and sellers of a firm are identical, mergers still will take place when the management of the acquiring firm sees opportunities in B which the managers of this firm or its owners and perhaps also the stockholders of A itself do not see in B. This justification is often invoked by defenders of conglomerate mergers. Men who rule the giant conglomerates which have grown principally by merger are described as supermanagement geniuses who see hidden economic potentials in the firms they acquire. While this is a separate characteristic claimed for the managers of conglomerates, it obviously fits in nicely with the one isolated in the previous section—that once the managers of the conglomerate take charge of a new acquisition, they are better at running it than its previous managers were.

IV.   DIFFERENCES IN DISCOUNT RATES AS A CAUSE OF MERGERS

Alternatively, mergers can be explained by the hypothesis that managers maximize the growth rate of their firm, not stockholder welfare. Even if there are no synergistic effects connected with the merger and both managers and stockholders have the same expectations regarding the two firms, mergers will take place when the managers of A have a lower discount rate than the sellers of B.

Consider first the case where the managers of B are its sellers. An often cited instance in which the managers of a firm will have a relatively high discount rate is just before they retire. If a large number of the more important executives in B are reaching retirement age at roughly the same time, they may be willing to help bring about A's acquisition of B in turn for bonuses and stock options in the newly formed C, as a means of capitalizing their 'investment' of time and energy in the acquired firm.

B's managers may have a similarly short time horizon if they are about to be ousted through a take-over bid initiated either by a dissident stockholders' group or by another firm. Since B's managers will have little control over their destinies should the take-over bid be successful, they may be willing to see B merged with yet a third company at a price below their 'normal' selling price, if they can assure for themselves better positions in the newly formed company than they can expect following a successful take-over. Seeking out a new merger partner is becoming an increasingly popular strategy for countering take-over bids (Hayes and Taussig, 1967) and is functionally equivalent to B's managers' increasing their discount rates (lowering their selling price to some third party).

The threat of take-over plays a very important role in Marris' theory of the firm (Marris, 1964, pp. 29–40). This threat will act as a further check on firm managers in their pursuit of their own goals. If they are cautious managers, they will be constrained from being too timid in their pursuit of profit, lest the price of their stock fall to a low enough level to tempt some more aggressive management team to take over their firm and put their assets to better use. It the managers are vigorous pursuers of growth, they will be restrained from a too active pursuit of expansion at the expense of their stockholders' interests, out of fear that the price of their stock will be driven down far enough to lure some other firm to acquire it.[14]

While a firm's management can thus decrease the probability of a take-over raid by pursuing a policy of stockholder-welfare maximization, it cannot avert the possibility entirely. The stock market value of a firm (even at its maximum) will always be less than the discounted present value of the firm to a growth-maximizing management, since the latter's discount rate is below that of the marginal stockholder. Thus, even if the managements of all other firms maximized stockholder welfare, these firms would still be attractive candidates for a take-over raid by a growth-maximizing management. We conclude that a growth-maximizing management will be faced by a seemingly boundless set of merger opportunities, all priced below their present value to the management group.[15] If the management selling price of firm B is the more attractive of the two selling prices, the acquiring company will deal with B's managers. But barring this, they always have the opportunity and *incentive* to purchase B from its stockholders by means of a take-over raid.

Two of the justifications for mergers which we dismissed as invalid in Section II can now be rationalized in terms of the growth-maximization hypothesis. The essence of the difference between growth and stockholder-welfare-maximizing behaviour is the lower cost of capital or discount rate employed by the growth-maximizing managers. Mergers can be rationalized as a means of supplying small firms with the 'cheaper' capital of the large company in a growth-maximizing context. The growth-oriented management will have no inclination to supply a small firm with capital directly by buying its stock or bonds or, more indirectly, by returning the profits to its stockholders and allowing them to supply the capital to the small firm,[16] since neither of these activities contributes to the growth of the company. Only after the two firms have been merged and the small company's investment opportunities have been internalized does it become to the advantage of the acquiring company's management to supply it with the acquiring firm's low-cost capital.

In Section II it was shown that corporate diversification is not an optimal means for pooling risks on behalf of a firm's stockholders. On the other hand, company diversification may be an attractive way to reduce the managers' risks, since their fortunes are tied directly to the corporation itself.

V.   GROWTH MAXIMIZATION IN LIGHT OF RECENT MERGER HISTORY

It is nearly impossible to test rigorously the growth-maximization and stockholder-welfare-maximization hypotheses and discriminate between them (Meyer, 1967), because the key variables needed for such a test are the non-observable expected profit rates and discount rates of the managers and stockholders. Nevertheless, we can survey the post-war merger history and make some judgment as to which of the two hypotheses then seems the more plausible one.

Because of their greater contribution to the acquiring firm's profits, we expect that the growth-maximizing managers will select first those firms which promise some synergistic interaction with their own operations, and turn to firms with no synergistic potential only after the former opportunities have dried up or been blocked. Since all firms are attractive merger partners to a growth-maximizing management, the availability of synergistic merger opportunities should affect the *direction* of a firm's acquisition efforts, but not their magnitude. On the other hand, since mergers can be justified as beneficial to the acquiring firm's stockholders only if some economy of scale or synergistic potential exists, a disappearance of synergistic merger opportunities should result in a decline in merger activity if managers maximize stockholders welfare.

The vigorous enforcement of Section 7 of the Celler-Kefauver Act by the antitrust authorities since it was revised in 1950 seems to have done little to abate the upward trend in merger activity over the period. In 1966 mergers were taking place at roughly nine times the rate that had immediately preceded the war, and at two and a half times the level of the 1946–7 'peak' (Committee on the Judiciary, 1967). Similarly, in terms of total assets of the acquired firms, the increase between 1951 and 1966 was from $201 million to $4,096 million.[17] The chief impact of the new Section 7 appears to have been to substitute conglomerate for horizontal mergers. Over the period conglomerate mergers increased from 51 per cent to 71 per cent of the total, while horizontal mergers declined from 40 per cent to 14 per cent of all mergers.[18] These trends seem to be consistent with the growth-maximization hypothesis.

A similar argument seems to explain the recent trend in the *form* in which acquisitions take place. Because of the reluctance which most corporate managers feel regarding the use of take-overs as a means of acquiring other firms, one expects that their acquisition efforts will focus on those firms whose management selling prices are low relative to their stockholder selling prices. During a prolonged period of intensive merger activity, such as that experienced between 1962 and the present (1968), the selection of firms having low management selling prices will be greatly depleted, as those firms that have retiring management groups or extremely cautious management teams (high management discount rates) are absorbed. Since all firms are attractive buys at their stockholder selling prices, if the desire to grow through acquisitions is to continue to be met during a period of high merger volume, it will have to be satisfied more and more by acquisitions through the stock takeover route. This is precisely what has happened. Between 1962 and 1965 the ratio of stock take-overs to the total number of mergers more than doubled.[19]

If mergers took place only in order to take advantage of economy-of-scale opportunities, one might expect that small or medium-sized firms would enter into mergers to a greater extent than the largest firms. On other a priori grounds, one might expect the percentage of a firm's growth which comes via acquisitions to be independent of its size, so long as the firm was above some minimal size.

In a pond in which all fish seek to devour one another, it is the biggest fish which will be immune to attack and the smallest which will be most digestable. If all firms' managements desire growth, it will be the largest firms which can pursue this goal with the most abandon, confident that few other firms will have the financial resources to attempt to acquire them. Small and medium-sized firms will have to pursue stockholder-welfare-maximizing behavior to a greater extent, in order to try to keep the stock price up and thereby avert take-overs.

The largest firms in the economy generally will also be the most mature and, therefore, are likely to have the lowest internal rates of return. From the discussion of Section I and Figure 9.1, we would predict that these will be the firms which have to make the greatest resort to outside investment opportunities to achieve growth.[20] Hence, John McGowan's finding that the proportion of a firm's growth which stems from mergers is positively related to the size of the firm seems to be consistent with the growth-maximization hypothesis (1965).

With all of this said, it is still possible for the proponent of profits maximization to defend the post-war conglomerate merger boom on the grounds that the acquiring firms' managers *expected* to be able to achieve managerial economies. While to many it may seem implausible that managers with no familiarity with a company's operations or industry could run it or recognize its opportunities for profits better than the firm's own managers or stockholders, no one can say for certain that this is not so. In light of the crucial importance of the existence of these supermanagement capabilities on the part of the acquiring firm's management in conglomerate mergers, it is interesting to note that some of the most aggressive conglomerate merger firms look for companies whose managements are able and willing to continue to run the acquired company after it has been assimilated into the conglomerate's corporate structure (Burch, 1967).

NOTES

1. This proposition is demonstrated in Sections II and III.
2. *See* Duesenberry, (1958). Because interest charges can be deducted from profits before paying corporate taxes, the cost of having some contractual debt outstanding may be less than the stockholders' opportunity costs. The firm can then be regarded as having a target leverage ratio, and the distance OC will represent the profits plus depreciation flow of the firm plus any changes in its bonds outstanding which are required to achieve the target leverage ratio. Raising capital in excess of OC through bond issues will then overlever the firm and result in the rise in the cost of capital depicted in Figure 9.1.
3. We include in long-run investment such as fixed capital equipment, research and development, mergers, and so on.
4. The mature growth-maximizing firm's cost of outside capital may exceed that for the stockholder-welfare-maximizing firm. This will not be the case for the young firm, for this would mean that the growth-maximizing firm would undertake less investment and grow at a slower rate than the stockholder-welfare-maximizing firm. This being the case, it is in the management's best interest to become stockholder-welfare maximizers. Again, we have the conclusion that, for the young firm, managerial and stockholder interests and policies coincide.
5. The necessity to resort to outside capital is increased by stockholder and managerial preferences for a stable dividend payout ratio.

6. Market interest rates will not be completely ignored, of course, since interest earned today can be internally invested to produce growth tomorrow. The further into the future 'tomorrow' is pushed, however, the more the interest rate will be discounted. Hence, market interest rates are likely to affect investment policies only in the short run, and probably will affect only the timing and not the magnitude of investment in the long run.

7. If managers maximized stockholder welfare, stockholders would be indifferent between dividends and retained earnings, *à la* Miller and Modigliani. Many observers have found that stockholders exhibit a seemingly irrational preference for dividends over retentions. Friend and Puckett survey this evidence and attempt to refute it by suggesting various econometric alternatives to previous formulations of the stock price equation. They are only partially successful in their endeavour and are forced to conclude that 'in nongrowth industries as a whole, a somewhat (but only moderately) higher investor valuation may be placed on dividends than on retained earnings within the range of payout experienced, but that the opposite may be true in growth industries'. *See* Friend and Puckett (1964).

This finding is consistent with the behaviour postulated here, if in general non-growth industries are composed of mature firms that do not have to rely heavily on outside capital, while growth industries contain young, capital-hungry firms.

It should be noted that our model differs from that of Miller and Modigliani only insofar as we assume that managers do not maximize stockholder welfare and therefore are willing to see the marginal returns of investment fall below the stockholders' discount rate. *See* Modigliani and Miller (1958).

8. We ignore transactions costs here.

9. The price that a marginal stockholder of A is willing to pay for a share of B will equal

$$\sum_{t=0}^{\infty} \frac{\pi_{Bt}}{(1+K_{At})} \bigg/ E_B$$

where E_B is the number of shares of B outstanding. This is more than the value of the stock to the marginal holder of B (and hence more than the stock's price) if $K_A < K_B$.

10. This assumption is not crucial to the demonstration.

11. Below, under the discussion of risk-pooling, we deal with the argument that the smaller firm's earnings should be discounted by a greater amount because of risk.

12. Since some social disapprobation within the corporate establishment accompanies a take-over of another firm, B will be purchased at its management's selling price when it is equal to or even slightly above the stockholders' selling price. At some differential, A's managers will prefer to incur the disapprobation costs rather than pay the premium of B's management's price over the stockholders' selling price.

13. When B is purchased from its managers, it is, of course, possible that both the managers of A and the stockholders of B see more in this firm than its managers do. Because the stockholders have the final word on any mergers, however, there obviously is a limit to how far below the stockholders' selling price the managers' selling price can be.

14. The curve relating the market value of the firm and its growth rate rises to a peak at the stockholder-welfare-maximizing growth rate and then declines with increasing levels of growth. Hence, a firm may be susceptible to a take-over raid because it is either too timid in its pursuit of growth or too aggressive. (Hayes and Taussig, 1967, pp. 254–9.)

15. The defending management of a firm which is being taken over has a large selection of defensive maneuvers that it can initiate to counter a take-over bid by another firm (Hayes and Taussig, 1967, pp.142–7). Hence, there are additional costs involved in bringing about a successful take-over which raise the effective stockholder selling price above the market value of the firm's outstanding stock. This will tend to make the management's selling price the more attractive one in a number of situations, and limit somewhat the spectrum of attractive merger opportunities.

16. The attractiveness of this alternative cannot be dismissed because of the tax laws, since the profits of a firm can always be returned to its stockholders in the form of capital gains by purchasing its own stock.

17. *See* Committee on the Judiciary (1967), p.5, Table 2. These figures cover only acquisitions for firms with over $10,000,000 in assets and hence should be adjusted for the upward trend in concentration in the economy and for price increases. It seems unlikely, however, that these adjustments would reverse the upward trend.

18. *See* Committee on the Judiciary (1967), p.7, Table 5.

19. This proportion fell somewhat in 1966, when tight money curtailed the flow of cash available for cash tender offers, the more popular form of take-over (Hayes and Taussig, 1967, p. 136).

20. In a stockholder-welfare-maximizing world, these firms would have the highest dividend payout ratios.

10   A Cross-national Comparison of the Determinants and Effects of Mergers*

In this chapter we review the basic results from a cross-national comparison of the determinants and effects of mergers conducted in the late seventies. Separate investigations of each country were conducted by scholars familiar with the data and institutions of their respective country.[1] Each set of authors conducted essentially the same fifteen tests of the determinants and effects of mergers for their country over roughly the same time period. Table 10.1 lists the countries, time periods, and numbers of observations for each country study. The methodology throughout consisted of comparing the statistics calculated for merging firms with those of non-merging control groups. The following abbreviations were employed:

AG   An acquiring firm

MAG   A firm matched to an acquiring firm by industry and size, which did not make significant acquisitions over the sample period

AD   An acquired firm

MAD   An unacquired firm matched by industry and size to an acquired firm

C   Randomly selected non-acquired and acquired firms serving as a control group

MIND   Mean values for the industry from which the acquiring or acquired firms were drawn.

Table 10.1   *Countries participating in the study*

Country	Time Period	Number of Mergers
Belgium	1962–74	39
Federal Republic of Germany	1962–74	55
France	1962–72	62
Netherlands	1962–73	34
Sweden	1962–76	39
United Kingdom	1967–69	290
United States	1962–72	287

*Reprinted from 'The Determinants and Effects of Mergers', Oelgeschlager, Gunn and Hain, 1980.

Table 10.2 summarizes the basic comparisons of the characteristics of the acquiring and acquired firms as reported in each country's study. The inequality signs are meant to indicate statistically significant differences. Thus, $\simeq$ implies no statistically significant difference, $>$ a positive and significant difference, and so forth. The table does not attempt to summarize all of the comparisons of size, profitability, and the other variables presented in the earlier chapters, but instead tries to generalize over the several measures of each characteristic used. In some cases, however, inconsistencies existed from one measure to another. To allow for these, and to indicate possibly weak statistical significance, we have used the symbols $\geq$ and $\leq$. When one of these is used (e.g. $\geq$), one can safely reject the complementary inequality (e.g. $<$), but one should probably reserve judgment as to whether a statistically significant relationship in the implied direction holds.

The first set of comparisons are of the size of the acquiring and acquired firms. These results are quite consistent across all countries. Acquiring firms are larger than randomly selected firms from their industries, larger than the average firm in their industries, and larger than the firms they acquire. In all countries save the United Kingdom and West Germany, the acquired firms are smaller than the average firm in their industries or appear to have been drawn at random from their industries.

In Belgium and the Netherlands the acquiring firms were somewhat less profitable than the control group companies; in France, slightly more so. In the other four countries the two groups appeared to be roughly equal in profitability. In contrast, the acquired firms tended to be either as or less profitable than the control group companies. Thus, the acquiring companies turned out to be as profitable or more profitable than the firms they acquired. No evidence of defensive acquisitions is thus found in any of our countries. In France, West Germany, and the United Kingdom the results are consistent with a 'failing firm' hypothesis, although the hypothesis that the companies were actually failing was not tested.

Dramatic differences in the variability of profits were not observed across the seven countries. Where differences existed between acquiring firms and their control group companies—Belgium, West Germany, and the Netherlands—the acquiring firms had less volatile profits. No clear pattern emerged between the acquired companies and their control samples. In general, bigger firms have less variable profit rates than smaller ones, however, and this was true in our studies. Thus, in four of the seven countries profits were less variable for the acquiring companies than for the companies they acquired. In all countries, the acquiring firms were either as highly levered as or more levered than the control group firms. In France and the United Kingdom the acquired firms also tended to be somewhat more highly levered, but in Belgium the reverse

Table 10.2: *Summary of characteristics of acquiring and acquired firms*

Upper panel

Country	Size			Profitability			Growth		
	AG versus MIND or C	AG, AD	AD versus MIND or C	AG versus MAG or C	AG, AD	AD versus MAD or C	AG versus MAG or C	AG, AD	AD versus MAD or C
Belgium	AG > C	AG > AD	AD ≈ C	AG < C	AG ≈ AD	AD ≤ C	AG > C	AG > AD	AD ≈ C
Federal Republic of Germany									
France	AG > MIND	AG > AD	AD ≥ MAD	AG ≈ MAG	AG ≥ AD	AD < MAD	AG ≈ MAG	AG ≈ AD	AD < MAD
Netherlands[a]	AG > MIND	AG > AD	AD < MIND	AG ≥ MAG	AG ≥ AD	AD ≤ MAD	AG ≈ MAG	AG ≈ AD	AD ≈ MAD
Sweden	AG > C	AG > AD	AD ≈ C	AG ≤ MAG	AG ≈ AD	AD ≈ MAD	AG ≈ MAG	AG ≈ AD	AD ≈ MAD
United Kingdom	AG > C	AG > AD	AD ≥ C	AG ≈ MAG	AG > AD	AD < MAD	AG > MAG	AG > AD	AD ≤ MAD
United States	AG > MIND	AG > AD	AD < MIND	AG ≈ MAG	AG > AD	AD ≈ MAD	AG > MAG	AG > AD	AD ≈ MAD

Lower panel

Country	Profit Variability			Leverage		
	AG versus MAG or C	AG, AD	AD versus MAD or C	AG versus MAG or C	AG, AD	AD versus MAD or C
Belgium	AG ≤ C	AG ≈ AD	AD ≈ C	AG ≈ C	AG ≥ AD	AD < C
Federal Republic of Germany						
France	AG < MAG	AG < AD	AD < MAD	AG > MAG	AG ≈ AD	AD ≈ MAD
Netherlands[a]	AG ≤ MAG	AG ≤ AD	AD ≈ MAD	AG ≈ MAG	AG ≈ AD	AD > MAD
Sweden	AG ≈ MIND	AG ≤ AD	AD ≈ MIND	AG ≈ MIND	AG ≈ AD	AD ≈ MIND
United Kingdom	AG ≈ MAG	AG ≈ AD	AD ≥ MAD	AG > MAG	AG > AD	AD > MAD
United States	AG ≈ MAG	AG ≈ AD	AD ≤ MAD	AG > MAG	AG > AD	AD ≈ MAD

[a] Based on separate calculations for purpose of these comparisons.

AG = acquiring firm.　　MAG = matched AG.　　MIND = matched industry.　　≈ about equal.
AD = acquired firm.　　MAD = matched AD.　　C = control group.　　≥ greater than or equal.
　　　　　　　　　　　　　　　　　　　　　　　　　　　　　　　　　　≤ less than or equal.

occurred. In all cases the acquiring firms were either as highly levered as or more highly levered than the companies they acquired.

A fairly consistent pattern of growth rate differences holds up across all countries. Acquiring firms grow as fast or faster than the size-matched or control group non-acquiring firms. Acquired firms grow as fast as their control group companies, except in the United Kingdom where they grow a bit more slowly and in West Germany where they grow considerably more slowly. Acquiring firms thus are generally faster growing than the companies they acquire. The latter proposition holds for every country but France, where acquiring firms grow at roughly equal rates.

With respect to three characteristics, a consistent pattern has emerged across all countries. Acquiring firms tend to be large, fast growing, highly levered companies relative to the firms they acquire and often relative to randomly selected control group companies. Less consistency exists for the profit variables. Profitability seems to be positively related to size in some countries, while profit variability is inversely related to size, so that a pattern of higher profit levels and lower profit variability of acquiring firms *vis-à-vis* the firms they acquire is discernable. Exceptions to these patterns exist in some countries for some comparisons, but no alternative pattern emerges within any one country.

I. THE DETERMINANTS OF MERGERS

A. Economies of Scale
The first determinants test attempted to see whether merging firms were smaller than randomly selected pairs of companies matched by industry, as might be expected if the companies merged because they were of less than minimum efficient size in some way. The economies of scale motive was consistently rejected (see Table 10.3). Merging companies were on average as big or bigger than randomly selected pairs of companies matched by industry.

B. Risk
Several tests of the riskiness of the acquiring and acquired firms were conducted. The first three tests yielded conflicting results across countries. In West Germany and Sweden there was less variability in pre-merger profits for merging firms than for nonmerging firms; in Belgium, somewhat more. In France, the Netherlands, the United Kindgom, and the United States no significant difference was observed.

Similar ambiguities were observed when comparing the absolute differences in leverage ratios between merging firms to their size-matched pairs and the variability in leverage in the acquiring firm sample.

The acquiring firms were in all countries as highly levered or more highly levered than their size-matched non-acquiring pairs. The same was true for the acquired firms. A greater variability in leverage ratios across the sample of acquired firms was also observed in Belgium, Sweden, and the United Kingdom, while the reverse was never observed. Thus, the leverage ratio does appear to be related in some way to a propensity to merge. The failure of a consistent pattern to emerge for test 2.2, which looks at the absolute spread in leverage ratios between the two merging firms, casts doubt on the hypothesis that a reduction in leverage or a capacity to issue more debt was a cause of the mergers, however. Instead, it would appear that leverage is in some other way related to mergers. If we interpret high leverage as symbolic of aggressive management and a tendency to pursue growth, then it would appear that acquisitions are made by aggressive managers and that the firms they acquire have a wider dispersion of leverages than similar unacquired firms. In France and the United Kingdom, the acquired firms also tended to be more highly levered than the control group firms, however.

C. Economic Disturbances and the Bargain Theory
The economic disturbance theory was supported in Sweden and Holland and rejected in Belgium, the United Kingdom, and the United States. The bargain theory was rejected in every case. Although stock price movements *per se* may lead to some mergers, it is difficult to garner a strong case for this hypothesis from the results presented here. The causes of merger must be sought in the real economic variables that affect company performance and their impacts on stock prices.

II.   THE EFFECTS OF MERGERS

A. Profitability
Tests of the changes in profitability following the merger do not provide a consistent picture across all countries (see Table 10.4). In four countries—Belgium, the Federal Republic of Germany, the United Kindgom, and the United States—the merging firms realized a slightly superior performance based on after tax profits than the size-matched control group companies. In Belgium and the United States the merging firms did not perform better than the average performance of their base industries. Thus, it would appear that in these two countries, the superior performance of the merging companies may reflect a relatively weaker performance by the size-matched control group firms rather than a relative improvement in the merging companies' own performance. In West Germany the merging firms did better than their matched industries

Table 10.3: *Summary of determinants tests*

Country	Test 1 Size	Coefficient of Variation in Profits	Leverage (Mean Abs. Difference)	Test 2, Risk — Leverage (AG Variance)	Test 2, Risk — Leverage (Mean AG)	Test 2, Risk — Leverage (AD Variance)	Test 2, Risk — Leverage (Mean AD)	Test 3 Disturbance Theory High-Low P/E	Test 4 Bargain Theory Mean P/E
Belgium	AG AD > MAG MAD / AG AD > MIND	AG AD > MAG MAD	AG AD ≈ MAG MAD	AG > MIND / AG ≈ MAG	AG ≈ MIND	AD > MIND / AD ≈ MAD	AD ≈ MIND / AD < C	AD < MIND	AD ≥ MIND
Federal Republic of Germany									
France	AG AD > MAG MAD	AG AD ≤ MAG MAD	AG AD ≤ MAG MAD	AG ≈ MAG	AG > MAG	AD ≈ MAD	AD ≈ MAD		AD ≈ MAD
Netherlands	AG AD ≈ MIND	AG AD ≈ MAG MAD	AD AD ≈ MAG MAD	AG ≈ MAG	AG ≈ MAG	AD ≈ MAD	AD ≈ MAD	AD ≈ MAD	AD ≈ MAD
Sweden	AG AD ≈ MIND	AG AD ≤ MAG MAD	AG AD ≈ MAG MAD	AG > MIND	AG ≈ MIND	AD > MIND	AD ≈ MIND	AD > MAD	AD ≈ MAD
United Kingdom	AG AD > MAG MAD	AG AD > MAG MAD	AG AD > MAG MAD	AG ≤ MAG	AG ≈ MAG	AD > MAD	AD ≈ MAD	AD ≈ MAD	AD ≈ MAD
United States	AG AD > MAG MAD	AG AD ≈ MAG MAD	AG AD ≈ MAG MAD	AG > MAG	AG > MAG	AD ≈ MAD	AD ≈ MAD	AD < MAD	AD ≈ MAD

Notes: See Table 10.2.

Table 10.4: *Summary of effects tests*

| Country | Tests 5, 6, 7 | | Tests 8, 9, 10 | Tests 11, 12, 13 | Tests 14, 15 |
	Profitability Pretax	Profitability Posttax	Growth in Size	Rates of Return on a Share of Common Stock	Sharp and Treynor Tests
Belgium		AG AD > MAG MAD / AG AD ≈ MIND	AG AD ≈ MAG MAD / AG AD ≈ MIND	AG ≤ MAG / AG ≥ MIND	
Federal Republic of Germany		AG AD ≈ MAG MAD / AG AD ≥ MIND	AG AD ≈ MAG MAD / AG AD ≈ MIND		
France		AG AD ≤ MAG MAD / AG AD ≤ MIND	AG AD ≈ MAG MAD / AG AD ≈ MIND	AG ≈ MAG	
Netherlands		AG AD < MAG MAD / AG AD < MIND	AG AD < MAG MAD / AG AD < MIND	AG ≈ MAG / AG ≈ MIND	AG ≤ MAG
Sweden	AG AD ≈ MAG MAD / AG AD ≈ MIND	AG AD ≈ MAG MAD / AG AD ≤ MIND	AG AD ≈ MAG MAD / AG AD ≈ MIND	AG ≈ MAG / AG ≈ MIND	AG ≈ MAG
United Kingdom	AG AD > MAG MAD / AG AD > C	AG AD > MAG MAD / AG AD > C	AG AD ≈ MAG MAD / AG AD ≈ C	AG ≤ MAG	
United States	AG AD ≈ MAG MAD / AG AD ≤ MIND	AG AD ≥ MAG MAD / AG AD ≈ MIND	AG AD < MAG MAD / AG AD < MIND	AG ≈ MAG / AG < MIND	AG ≈ MAG[a]

[a]Based on survey of studies in the United States.
Notes: See Table 10.1.

but not much better than the control group firms, suggesting the possibility that it was the larger size of the merging companies rather than the mergers themselves that accounted for the merging companies' superior performance to the matched industries. In the United Kingdom, the merging firms did relatively better than both the size-matched and randomly drawn control group samples. In the United States the differences in profits appeared in only the after-tax figures, suggesting that no improvement in real operating performance occurred as a result of the mergers. Thus, the inference that mergers have led to improved profitability in these four countries emerges with considerable qualification, particularly when one notes that the differences in profitability observed are generally quite small and/or statistically insignificant. Nevertheless, there is some evidence of improved after tax profitability of merging companies in the four countries.

In the other three countries—France, Holland, and Sweden—there was evidence of a relative decline in the profitability of the merging firms following the mergers. As in the first four countries, the differences in sample means were not particularly large, however, and the levels of significance were generally low. No consistent pattern of either improved or deteriorated profitability can therefore be claimed across the seven countries. Mergers would appear to result in a slight improvement here, a slight worsening of performance there. If a generalization is to be drawn, it would have to be that mergers have but modest effects, up or down, on the profitability of the merging firms in the three to five years following merger. Any economic efficiency gains from the mergers would appear to be small, judging from these statistics, as would any market power increases.

B. Growth in Size

Further evidence concerning the efficiency effects of mergers is contained in the growth in size comparisons. If mergers result in an increase in economic efficiency, costs should fall, leading to a fall in prices and an expansion of sales. This occurred in not one single country. In the Netherlands and the United States a slowdown in the growth rates of the merging firms was observed in the post-merger period relative to the change in growth rate performance of the control group companies. In all other countries there was no statistically significant change in growth rates between the merging and control group samples from before and after the mergers. These results clearly suggest that no improvements in economic efficiency took place as a direct result of the mergers, which led to price declines and expansions in sales. It should be noted, however, that in the United Kingdom and the United States, the firms were growing faster in both the pre-and post-merger periods than their size-matched pairs. Tests 8, 9, and 10 merely establish that no relative increase in growth at the time of the merger took place. In the United Kingdom there was no change at all (as in Belgium, West Germany, France, and Sweden); in the United States and Holland there was a relative decline in growth rates.

C.   Rates of Return on a Share of Common Stock

It is possible that the mergers led to either market power or efficiency gains, but that the three to five year periods we had to observe the merging companies following the mergers were too short to reflect these changes in either profitability or growth rates. (Singh, 1971, argued that more than five years are needed before the effects of a company's reorganization become apparent.) The tests of the effects of a merger on the rate of return of an acquiring firm's common shares should get around this problem. Under the usual assumptions made in the finance literature, the capital market is an efficient evaluator of each company's prospects. The current price of a company's common shares would reflect all the information about a company's future performance that is generally available. At the time of the merger, any change in expectations about the future profits of the company as a result of merger should produce a change in the price of the acquiring company's shares. This change in price should in turn lead to a corresponding change in the rate of return from holding an acquiring company's shares.

Evidence of a rise in expectations about the acquiring firm's future at about the time of merger was present in four countries—France, the Netherlands, the United Kingdom, and the United States. In each of these countries, the holders of common shares of the acquiring firms experienced a significantly higher change in the rate of return on these shares between the pre-merger period and the immediate post-merger period than did holders of the common shares of the size-matched control group firms. In each of these four countries, the differences between the two samples' mean values diminished, however, as additional time elapsed following the merger. Three years after the mergers took place, there was no statistically significant difference between the rates of return earned on common shares for the three samples from France, the Netherlands, and the United States. In the United Kingdom the differences had flip-flopped; the non-acquiring, size-matched companies now exhibited a significantly higher rate of return performance than did the acquiring firms. This superior performance by the non-acquiring firms was still in evidence in the United Kingdom after five years had elapsed from the time of the mergers.

Thus, in those cases where mergers appear to have led to an increase in the expected profitability of the merging firms at the time of the mergers, this expectation was eliminated or reversed in the first few years after the mergers took place. It is very difficult to reconcile this pattern of rate of return changes with the hypothesis that future profitability increases resulting from the mergers were expected, but not yet realized in the companies' operating statistics. Some increases in profitability did appear to be expected at the time of merger, but these expectations seemed to sour as more information concerning the mergers became available. In Sweden there was also a deterioration in the performance of the acquiring firms' different control samples as time from the merger elapsed. Here the acquiring companies went from doing as well as the control groups in the year of the merger to doing somewhat worse three years after.

A suggestion that horizontal mergers might, after the passage of a very long period of time, result in profit increases was present in Holland. In the subsample of horizontal mergers, a gradual improvement in the relative performance of the merging companies' common shares was observed. This pattern ran counter to the results for conglomerate mergers in the Netherlands and for the full samples in France and the United States, as just discussed. Separate testing of the horizontal and non-horizontal subsamples in the United Kingdom did not yield this pattern of change either, so these results for the Netherlands must be regarded as an intriguing suggestion that something else may be going on, at least for horizontal mergers. In both Holland and the United States the merging companies did less well against their base industries than they did against the size-matched control group firms, casting further doubt on the hypothesis that future profitability increases were expected. Indeed, in the United States acquiring firms experienced significantly lower increases in returns on common shares than the average firm in their industry in the year of the merger, and in each successively longer post-merger period.

In Belgium the acquiring firms did somewhat better than their base industries and worse than the size-matched control group firms on the basis of changes in rates of return on common shares. This is almost the direct reverse of the results for actual profitability changes in Belgium. Taken together it seems hard to argue that these results suggest significant present or future increases in profitability as a result of the mergers in Belgium.

III.　IMPLICATIONS FOR THE THEORY OF THE FIRM

Having reviewed the basic results of the cross-national comparison, we are now in a position to assess the validity of the leading hypotheses concerning the determinants and effects of mergers. In so doing, we shall also relate our results to those of other studies, where they seem relevant.

A.　Mergers and the Profit Motive

It is difficult to reconcile the bulk of the evidence gathered here with a straightforward, textbook treatment of mergers as attempts to increase profits by improving economic efficiency or increasing market power. The finding that merging firms are as big or bigger than randomly selected firms drawn from the same industries does not sustain an economies of scale motive. The generally neutral or negative effect of mergers on profitability and growth further suggests that mergers have not led to efficiency gains in the countries we studied. A decline in the rate of growth of sales would be expected if mergers increased market power. Such declines were observed in the Netherlands and the United States, but in neither of these countries was there evidence of an increase in operating profits. Thus, if market power did increase, it would appear to be offset on average by efficiency *declines*.

At least two other studies in the United States have detected a slowdown in the internal growth rates of acquiring firms following their acquisitions (Hogarty, 1970a; Lev and Mandelker, 1972). This slowdown is sometimes thought of as a 'shakedown' or 'digestion' effect of the mergers (Lev and Mandelker, 1972; p. 97). By this is implied some reduction in operating efficiency, leading apparently to higher prices or lower quality and thereby a reduction in sales. The possibility of a reduction in sales due to a rise in price to exploit increased market power would be equally consistent with the findings of these other studies, however. Certainly these results do not imply immediate improvements in efficiency and reductions in price following a merger.

The most widely cited study purporting to find an increase in profits resulting from mergers in the United States is by Weston and Mansinghka (1971). They found that a sample of sixty-three conglomerates started the decade 1958–68 with profit levels significantly lower than non-acquiring control group samples but ended it with profit rates equal to the control group firms. Weston and Mansinghka do not allow for the rise in profit rates that would occur simply because the conglomerates acquired companies with higher profit rates than themselves. The tests reported in the present study avoid this shortcoming by projecting the performance of the newly formed firm by the weighted averages of the performances of the merging companies. The Weston–Mansinghka study also stops at a peak year in economic activity just before a recession during which one expected that the highly levered conglomerates would fare poorly (Reid, 1971). A parallel study by Melicher and Rush (1974), which looked at the conglomerates' performance into the downswing of the early 1970s, concluded that the merging firms earned no higher profits than the non-merging control group companies.

The largest single study of mergers prior to the present investigation is undoubtedly Geoffrey Meeks' (1977) investigation of more than 1000 United Kingdom mergers over the post-World War II period. He concluded that these mergers were typified by 'a mild decline in profitability' (p. 25). This conclusion is somewhat more negative than that reached by the authors of the United Kingdom component of the present study. Closer perhaps to the present United Kingdom results, and to the overall results of our cross-national comparison, are the findings of K. Cowling and his colleagues (1979), which are based on a series of detailed case studies. Although they found some evidence of improved economic efficiency, and some evidence of enhanced and exploited market power, the typical merger probably did not result in either.

Any increase in profits that is expected to result in future years from a merger should be reflected as higher returns on the common shares of the acquiring firm at whatever point they are recognized. In the seven country studies, we found no evidence that such future profit increases were expected for as far as three years after the mergers took place. Indeed, one of the most interesting common patterns that emerged, in five of the six countries for which the tests were run, was that the market appeared to revalue the mergers downward in a fairly continuous manner as more and more information about the mergers became available. This same pattern has appeared in several other studies of the United States. Mandelker (1974) investigated some 241 mergers over the period 1941 to 1962 and observed a gradual downward drift in the rate of return performance of the acquiring companies' shares from just before the mergers to forty months afterwards. The same downward drift was observed in a follow-up study by Langetieg (1978). Langetieg pinpointed the beginning of this downward trend more accurately than Mandelker, however. The deterioration in the performance in the acquiring companies' shares begins approximately six months prior to the mergers themselves, at precisely the same time that the shares of the to-be-acquired firms begin to rise rapidly in value. Thus, the acquiring company shares begin to decline at the point when news of the merger appears to reach the market. Dodd and Ruback (1977) examine the stock market's reaction to tender offers. The immediate reaction is favourable. In the month that the tender offer is made, the shares of the successful bidding firms rise by 2.83 per cent. Judging from the performance of the acquired companies' shares, this would also seem to coincide with the market's obtaining news of the merger. Starting six months after the tender offer's first announcement, at roughly the time when the consolidations take place, the returns on the acquiring companies' shares begin to decline, however. This decline continues for the next four and a half years and cumulates to 8.6 per cent, totally wiping out all immediate gains to the bidding companies' shareholders at the time of the offer and in the first few months thereafter. The net cumulative change in the bidding companies' share performance from the month before the bid to five years after is −3.1 per cent.

This general decline in return performance for acquiring companies resembles both our findings for the United States when the acquiring companies were compared to size and industry-matched non-acquiring companies, and the overall pattern of our international comparisons study. Nevertheless, it is difficult to determine how general these findings are. An interesting pattern does seem to emerge for the United States, however. Those studies that have drawn the most positive conclusions about the effects of mergers on the welfare of the acquiring firms' stockholders have based their conclusions on the returns earned up to the mergers or up to a stock market peak (see, in particular, Halpern, 1973; Kummer and Hoffmeister, 1978 and Weston *et al.*, 1972). Those studies that have drawn the most negative conclusions regarding the effects of mergers on the welfare of the acquiring firm's stockholders have extended their analysis beyond the stock market peaks and/or beyond the date that the merger is announced or consummated (see e.g. Hogarty, 1970b; Langetieg, 1978, and Melicher and Rush, 1973).[2]

The study from outside the United States that is most analogous to this literature is Firth's analysis (1979) of 228 successful take-over bids in the United Kingdom. As with the studies of Mandelker, Langetieg and Dodd and Ruback and the general pattern of results reported here, Firth found that the decline in the rate of return performance of the acquiring firm's shares ran from just before the merger is announced to afterwards. Unlike the other studies, however, Firth finds that the adjustment appears to be complete within a few months. Thus, Firth reaches the conclusion that the market is able to evaluate the apparently negative consequences of a merger announcement within a couple of months, a conclusion that does not seem consistent with our United Kingdom results, not to mention those of the other countries. (Kummer and Hoffmeister, 1978, make the same claim, but do not report return results going beyond a single month past the take-over.) Firth's finding that the stockholders of acquiring firms are made worse off as a result of the mergers and, more generally, that the merger's effects are inconsistent with a profit- or stockholder-welfare-maximizing theory of the firm is, however, consistent with the results of our study.

B. Mergers and the Market for Control

One of the most popular explanations for mergers in recent years has been the hypothesis that they replace inefficient management and discipline managers to pursue stockholder-welfare-maximizing policies. Several studies in the United States have found that acquired firms generally (Asquith, 1983, Halpern, 1973; Mandelker, 1974), and take-over targets in particular (Kummer and Hoffmeister, 1978; Smiley, 1976), have significantly worse common share performance in the pre-merger period than the average firm in the market. The latter has also been found by Firth (1979) for the United Kingdom. On the other hand, Langetieg (1978) found that the acquired firms, while performing badly relative to the market, were not performing badly relative to a matched control group; and Dodd and Ruback (1977) found no evidence of negative pre-offer performance among their tender offer firms prior to the bids. Several studies have specifically tested and rejected a failing firm hypothesis (see e.g. Boyle, 1970; and Melicher and Rush, 1974). The existing literature gives an ambiguous answer to this question.

Some evidence suggesting that mergers were a mechanism for eliminating bad management or for rescuing failing firms was noted in our seven country studies. In Belgium, France, West Germany and the United Kingdom the acquired companies had profit rates somewhat lower than the control group samples. In Belgium, the acquiring firms also had lower profits than the matched samples, however, and did not differ significantly in profitability from the companies they acquired. It is thus hard to argue that the stockholders of the acquired companies were being rescued by more competently managed companies. While the acquiring companies in France were somewhat more profitable than the firms they acquired, the two experienced a decline in their profitability relative to the control groups after the mergers. Thus, evidence fully consistent with the market control thesis, in the sense (1) that below average performing companies are (2) acquired by firms performing better than themselves and (3) that the two together show an improvement in performance, can be claimed only for the Federal Republic of Germany and the United Kingdom.

Previous studies of United Kingdom take-overs by Singh (1971) and Kuehn (1975) also obtained results consistent with the market for corporate control hypothesis. But Singh (1971, 1975) found evidence at least as strong of selection on the basis of size (the small disappear) as profitability, suggesting that the market for corporate control might not provide much discipline over managerial pursuit of growth. These earlier studies' conclusion that this market, to the extent that it works at all, does so with considerable slippage and uncertainty would also appear valid for the present study. There is much overlap between the samples of acquired and non-acquired firms before the mergers, and much overlap of the acquiring and non-acquiring samples after the mergers. The relatively poor showing of the acquiring companies' common shares in the post-merger period in the United Kingdom also suggests that any gains from taking over inefficiently run companies in this country were insufficient to offset the premiums that had to be paid to acquire them. Firth (1979) reached an even stronger conclusion. He found the decline in the rate of return performance of the acquiring companies following a merger sufficiently large to more than offset the gains to the acquired companies' stockholders.

The conclusion that mergers increase economic efficiency, as evidenced by profit *and* growth increases, was rejected in every one of our seven countries. This finding, along with the other results just discussed, leads to considerable scepticism about a strong version of the market for control thesis that says that mergers are motivated to and in fact do achieve efficiency gains by displacing inefficient managements. But a weak version of the hypothesis—that a company whose profits and/or share price falls relative to other comparable companies has a greater probability of being acquired—does appear to be valid at least in some countries.

C.   Risk Spreading, Economic Disturbance and Bargain Theories

None of the other theories that have been put forward to explain mergers fared particularly well. The bargain theory was resoundingly rejected and the economic disturbance hypothesis was rejected and accepted an equal number of times. Leverage differences would appear to have something to do with whether or not firms merge, but no systematic pattern emerged across countries. In two countries acquiring firms were more highly levered than non-acquiring firms; in none was the reverse true. In three countries there was a greater variance in leverage ratios across acquired firms; in none was the reverse true. In two countries the acquired companies were more highly levered than non-acquired firms, but in one other country the reverse was true.[3] Thus, it is difficult to conclude that any specific explanation of mergers based on the leverage characteristics of the acquiring and/or acquired firms gets unqualified support. Leverage characteristics do vary systematically with merger activity in some countries, but not to such a degree across all countries to warrant considering these differences as a primary explanation for why mergers take place.

Thus, it does not seem possible to conclude that risk reduction in any broader sense is a major objective behind mergers. None of the (admittedly somewhat crude) tests that we employed suggested that it was. Nor have studies that focused on this objective in the United States, where it would seem most likely to be important if it is anywhere, concluded that risk reduction was a primary motive behind mergers (see e.g. Evans and Archer, 1968; Joehnk and Nielsen, 1974; Lev and

Mandelker, 1972; Mason and Goudzwaard, 1976; Melicher and Rush, 1973; Smith and Schreiner, 1969 and Weston *et al.*, 1972).

IV. CONCLUSIONS

Our cross-national comparisons of merger statistics have produced some consistent patterns across all countries and some inconsistencies requiring further theorizing and/or data. With respect to the determinants tests, none of the hypotheses examined received consistent confirmation across the seven countries. One conclusion one might draw from these results is that Peter Steiner's (1975) 'eclectic' theory of mergers holds; that is, since no single hypothesis explains all mergers, a variety of hypotheses must be assumed to govern. Although the seemingly tautological nature of this hypothesis is somewhat disturbing, it is perhaps the only hypothesis fully warranted by the results reported in this study.

On the effects side, the rather consistent lack of evidence that mergers led to or were expected to lead to significant increases in profits is inconsistent with all the neoclassical theories of mergers. Some form of managerial motive for mergers—as, say, in the pursuit of growth—is left as a sort of residual explanation for why mergers might take place. Certainly these theories would appear to be prime candidates for inclusion in any eclectic set under consideration.

Perhaps the most important findings of our study are the patterns of results we did not observe rather than those we did. At the outset, we expected differences to emerge between the United States and the six European countries, given the much heavier incidence of horizontal merger activity in the European countries. Similarly, we anticipated different results for the United Kingdom and the United States, where the stock market is a highly developed institution, and for the other five countries, where it plays a much smaller role in providing capital and disciplining managers. The failure of important differences to emerge across these countries in a way that can be related to these institutional differences is a significant result with potentially important implications for national and multinational merger policies.

NOTES

1. For the names of the authors and original results *see* Mueller (1980).
2. I believe that this conclusion can be legitimately drawn from Dodd and Ruback's results, too, but it is not the one they themselves draw. For further discussion *see* Mueller (1977).
3. Stevens (1973) also isolated leverage as a sigificant discriminating characteristic between acquired and non-acquired firms for a sample of eighty US companies. He found the acquired firms to have lower leverage ratios, a result found here for Belgium but not the United States.

11 The Effects of Conglomerate Mergers*
A survey of the empirical evidence

I. INTRODUCTION

The United States has experienced three large merger waves within the last century. Each has coincided with a period of strong economic and stock market advance. Each has come to an end along with the collapse of these bull markets and the recessions or depression that followed. The positive relationship between merger activity and stock market and economic advance is one of the well-established if unexplained riddles of this literature (see in particular Beckenstein, 1979; Nelson, 1959, 1966; and Reid, 1968).

The first major merger wave has been described by Stigler as a wave to create monopolies; the second a wave to create oligopolies (1950). The third might be called a wave to create conglomerates. For the distinguishing feature of the mergers occurring in the 1960s was certainly the extent to which these mergers tended to diversify or extend the acquiring companies' product mixes.

Reid, Markham and Steiner have all noted that many of these mergers were not between firms as unrelated in their business activities as the word 'conglomerate' or some of the literature discussing them might imply.[1] Their point is well taken. Nevertheless, a substantial difference does exist between the acquisitions characteristic of this most recent period, and the ones which brought the Standard Oil Company and General Motors together, in terms of both their potential market power advantages, and their potential for plant and production economies, as all observers of the recent wave have admitted. This difference has made it difficult to explain conglomerate mergers in terms of the market power and economic efficiency advantages that have traditionally been put

*This chapter was written while the author was research fellow at the International Institute of Management, Berlin. Thanks are due for the support of this Institute and the helpful comments of John Cable, John Hiller, Thomas Hogarty and Lee Preston. Reprinted from *Journal of Banking and Finance*, 1, December, 1977.

forward as the motives behind mergers. Not surprisingly therefore a new set of hypotheses about the causes (and effects) of mergers has appeared to explain this new form of merger.

This set is so large, however, that it is impossible to cover adequately both the recent theoretical literature on the causes of mergers, and the empirical evidence in support of these hypotheses. Fortunately, the former task has been admirably accomplished by Peter Steiner (1975). Thus, we are free here to focus upon the empirical literature, following a very brief review of the alternative hypotheses (Section II). Following this we review the empirical literature (Section III). Section IV examines the evidence linking mergers to overall concentration changes. The last section draws the policy implications emerging from this review.

Although all Western countries experienced merger waves in the 1960s, and the conglomerate merger has been increasing in popularity in other countries too, it remains the dominant form of merger only within the US, and therefore we shall concentrate most of our attention on the literature concerning this country.

II.   HYPOTHESES

It is convenient in reviewing the hypotheses about mergers to group them into those which predict that mergers generate profits to be shared between the two combining companies, and those claiming that mergers do not necessarily generate extra profits. The former we shall refer to as neoclassical theories of merger, since they are obviously consistent with the profit motive assumption. The latter we shall term managerial theories, since they are all based on the assumption that mergers are means by which managers pursue objectives other than profit or stockholder welfare maximization.

A.   The neoclassical theories
Given the lack of direct productive or technological relationship between the partners in a conglomerate merger, recent theories of this type of merger have often focused on some form of *financial* economy to be gained from the merger. John Lintner has summarized the arguments for five such financial economies (1971), and we follow him over these.[2]

(1) Taxes. Lintner lists the tax exemption of corporate reorganizations, and the use of one firm's tax loss carryovers by its partner as possible stimulants to mergers (p. 107). He notes with respect to the former, however, that 'This "tax free" treatment . . . is not a positive incentive *relative to* continued independent operation.' (*See also* Sherman, 1972.)

(2) Leverage.   Borrowing costs decline with size of firm, and 'Large firms can thus refinance debt of small independent firms at lower

economic cost resulting in a genuine capital gain through merger' (Lintner, 1971, p. 107).

(3) Bankruptcy costs.   Both Levy and Sarnat (1970) and Lewellen (1971) have argued that mergers between companies whose income streams are not perfectly correlated reduces the profitability of bankruptcy and lenders' risk.

(4) Diversification.   More generally, the pooling of imperfectly correlated income streams will produce a superior risk/return asset to the individual streams. Since the advantages of risk-pooling can be achieved by individual stockholder portfolio diversification (Levy and Sarnat, 1970), this argument must be coupled with some restrictions on the stockholder's ability to form his own diversified portfolio (or buy into pre-formed portfolios like mutual funds) to justify mergers.

(5) P/E Magic.   The argument was made that when a conglomerate acquired a firm with a lower *P/E* than its own, the market often evaluated the combined earnings of the two firms at the higher *P/E* of the conglomerate, rather than applying a weighted average of the two *P/E*'s, thus producing an instantaneous capital gain (Lintner, 1971, p. 110; Mead, 1969).

(6) Redeployment of corporate capital.   Oliver Williamson has emphasized the advantages of the *M*-form divisionalized organization for allocating capital (1970, 1975) *see also* Weston, 1970). In this structure the central management moves capital from high average return, low marginal return divisions to those promising the highest marginal returns without undergoing the transactions costs of using the capital market (on these *see also* Sherman, 1972). The conglomerates are prime examples of *M*-form organizations, and redeployment of capital in these ways was one of their stated goals.[3]

(7) Replacement of incompetent managers.   Complementary to the achievement of a more efficient organizational form, conglomerate mergers are often seen as a method for replacing inefficient managements. Dewey's claim that mergers 'are merely a civilized alternative to bankruptcy or the voluntary liquidation that transfers assets from falling to rising firms' (1961, p. 257) has often been cited, and Henry Manne has generalized the argument in constructing a theory of 'the market for corporate control' (1965). In this market, firms compete for control of inefficiently managed companies via the take-over route. Thus, mergers are seen as an economical way of eliminating bad management, reorganizing corporate structures, and improving both allocational- and *X*-efficiency in the corporate sector.

(8) Economic disturbances.   Michael Gort argues that mergers can be explained by the existence of economic disturbances which lead to a discrepancy between the value of a firm's assets placed on it by its

managers or controlling stockholders, and the value placed on them by outsiders (1969). Gort cites three specific types of economic disturbances that are likely to produce accelerated merger activity: rapid growth, technological change and changes in stock market values.

B. The managerial theories

The managerial theories argue that the separation of ownership from control allows managers some discretion to pursue goals other than stockholder welfare maximization. The pursuit of growth, as hypothesized by Robin Marris (1964), seems the most natural managerial goal to be satisfied via mergers (Reid, 1968; Mueller, 1969; Singh 1971). From some of the empirical results has emerged the possibility that managers may be pursuing a speculative or risk-taking motive through mergers. But we shall discuss this hypothesis after reviewing the evidence supporting it.

C. Motives for mergers and merger waves

One of the difficulties with several of the neoclassical motives for mergers is that it is difficult to reconcile them with the occurrence of merger waves in times of economic prosperity and stock market advance. Why should mergers to avoid the transaction costs and taxes involved in bankruptcy reach a feverish pace during a broad, economic expansion when bankruptcies are on the decline? Why is it that the incompetencies of managers become most apparent when profits and stock prices are rising, and are immediately concealed once they begin to plummet? Nor does it seem logical that small firms should feel most compelled to merge with larger ones to obtain capital, at a time when their cash flows are likely to be high, and the demand for new equity issues is favourable.

Gort claims that his economic disturbance theory is consistent with the observed cyclic pattern of merger activity (1969, pp. 624-5). Logically, however, it would seem that valuation discrepancies would be as likely to arise in periods of rapid stock market decline and negative growth, as in periods of advance. Indeed, since stock prices usually fall faster following a boom than they rose during it, one might expect mergers to be counter cyclical under Gort's theory, and conclude, therefore, that the existing evidence runs counter to it.

Gort argues that mergers are more likely in upswings than in downturns, however, because

when security prices are low relative to their mean value over a period of years, managers and long-term investors will tend to consider the shares of their firm undervalued. The stockholders of firms that are potential acquirers, on the other hand, can be expected to resist acquisition prices that are far above those at which the individual investor can purchase securities in the open market on his personal account. Consequently, valuation discrepancies of the type needed for acquisitions to occur will be far more frequent in periods of high than in periods of low security prices (p. 628).

Thus the economic disturbance theory assumes that stockholders and managers base their current valuations of their company's stock on the recent past, but non-holders do not. During an upswing stockholders undervalue their company's earnings' growth, that is, they tend to be bearish relative to non-holders. During a downswing they are again looking backwards and are bullish relative to non-holders. Personally I find this asymmetry in expectations an awkward assumption, but shall not pursue the matter here. For policy purposes, the relevant question is still whether these mergers generate any net efficiency gains.

P/E magic is also compatible with a cyclic-merger pattern. In a buoyant market, the kind of optimistic expectations which are necessary to bring about this magic are most likely to be present. Conversely, when the market breaks, the accompanying switch to pessimism may produce an opposing re-evaluation of P/E's, and a sudden elimination of this possible advantage from mergers. If the merging companies have not achieved real efficiency gains to justify the high P/E's applied to their combined earnings, downward pressure on their stock will be intensified. Note that in this case P/E magic is only consistent with stockholder-welfare maximization in the short run. Only the stockholders who sell out before the market breaks are likely to gain from the mergers.

The managerial theory is also consistent with a cyclical merger pattern. In an upswing corporate profits and cash flows are on the rise. Where ample opportunities for growth via internal expansion are lacking, the only alternatives may be higher dividend payments or growth through merger. Faced with these alternatives, 'it is not surprising that the "expansiveness" of the businessman during periods of prosperity often expresses itself in the merger movement and large business organizations' as Thorp noted in commenting on the 1920s wave.[4]

The constraint upon managerial use of cash flows to achieve goals in conflict with stockholder goals is the threat of take-over (Marris, 1964). But in periods of rising profits and stockmarket values this constraint is likely to weaken as rising returns to stockholders increase their optimism and confidence in their managers. Indeed, the most serious threat of take-over may come from other firms pursuing growth. But, as Singh has shown, growth in size, if it is not at too great of a cost in profits, may offer greater protection from take-over than maximizing profits (1971). Thus, while the desire to grow via mergers may be constant over time, the means and discretion to pursue this goal are likely to be greater with a rising economy and stock market.

But, prosperity may also provide a more conducive environment to consummate mergers in pursuit of some of the above listed neoclassical goals. Thus, a choice between these competing explanations must rest on an examination of their effects. If conglomerate mergers prove to be largely profitable ventures, we shall return to re-examine the set of neoclassical theories to see which is most compatible with the other evidence on their characteristics. If they are not profitable, we shall re-examine the managerial theories.

III.   THE EVIDENCE

A.   Early evidence predating 1960s merger wave

Several good surveys of the evidence on the first two merger waves, as well as the merger history of the late 1940s and 1950s exist, and this literature need not be reviewed here (see in particular Markham, 1955; Nelson, 1959; Reid, 1968 and, most succinctly, Hogarty, 1970a). Most of these studies compare profit rates before and after merger, and are thus somewhat difficult to compare with the more modern approach focusing on stockholder return on equity. Hogarty (1970a) concluded his survey of the early merger history thus:

What can fifty years of research tell us about the profitability of mergers? Undoubtedly the most significant result of this research has been that no one who has undertaken a major empirical study of mergers has concluded that mergers are profitable, that is profitable in the sense of being 'more profitable' than alternative forms of investment. A host of researchers, working at different points of time and utilizing different analytic techniques and data, have but one major difference: whether mergers have a neutral or negative impact on profitability (p. 389).

This conclusion seems fair based on this early evidence. It naturally raises the question of why so many mergers have taken place, and casts some doubt on the maximization of stockholder welfare hypothesis.

B.   The recent evidence—Mergers and profitability

The first study to test for the effects of the conglomerate merger wave of the 1960s was by Weston and Mansinghka (1971). They compared the profitability of a sample of sixty-three conglomerates to that of a randomly selected sample of industrials, and a combined industrial–non-industrial sample. The most interesting comparisons are between the conglomerates and the industrials and are reproduced in Table 11.1. In 1958 the conglomerates, or rather the sixty-three firms that would become conglomerates, had profit rates significantly below the randomly selected sample of industrials. After 1968, the peak year of merger activity, the conglomerates had profit rates roughly equal to those of the industrials.[5] The fourth line of the table gives an indication of how the conglomerates financed their growth. Although their leverage ratios were on average roughly 50 per cent higher than those of the industrials in 1958, they increased to almost double the leverage ratios of the industrials by 1968. Thus, the conglomerates financed their growth in part by an aggressive increase in their leverage ratios. The last line of the table presents the not surprising result that conglomerates grew significantly faster than the industrials during the period of heavy merger activity.

Table 11.1: *Major results from the Weston–Mansinghka study*[a]

	1958			1968		
	Sample Means		*F*-statistic	Sample Means		*F*-statistic
	C	R1		C	R1	
EBIAT/Total Assets	5.8	9.2	9.83*	10.4	8.5	0.44
EBIT/Total Assets	8.7	16.7	17.13*	15.1	15.6	0.02
Net Income/Net Worth	7.6	12.6	10.52*	13.3	12.4	0.81
Debts/Net Worth	95%	56%	8.19*	169%	87%	10.25*
Growth in Total Assets 58–68				22.8%	12.6%	16.25*

[a]Notes: *Significant at 0.01 level.
EBIAT is earnings before interest and preferred dividends, but after taxes.
EBIT is earnings before interest, preferred dividends, and taxes.
For a complete discussion of the variables see Weston and Mansinghka (1971). ·

To explain their results Weston and Mansinghka (1971) put forward a defensive diversification hypothesis:

Analysis of the backgrounds and acquisition histories of the conglomerate firms suggests that they were diversifying defensively to avoid (1) sales and profit instability, (2) adverse growth developments, (3) adverse competitive shifts, (4) technological obsolescence, and (5) increased uncertainties associated with their industries (p. 928).

This hypothesis is also broadly consistent with the findings of Melicher and Rush (1974). They compared the profitability of sixty-one conglomerate firms with the firms they acquired. They found that the conglomerates acquired firms significantly more profitable than themselves. Conglomerates also acquired firms with significantly lower leverage ratios than themselves, suggesting a latent debt or leverage capacity motive (p. 145). These results are in contrast to those from a sample of seventy-one non-conglomerate acquirers, who Melicher and

Rush found acquired firms with roughly the same profitability and leverage ratios as themselves.[6]

Similar findings to Melicher and Rush's were obtained by Boyle (1970). He compared the profitability of firms acquired in horizontal and vertical acquisitions to that of firms acquired by conglomerates. He found that the firms the conglomerates acquired had significantly higher profits than those acquired in horizontal and vertical acquisitions. Boyle specifically tested and rejected the hypothesis that the *acquired* companies were failing at the time of their acquisition, as did Conn (1976).

Weston and Mansinghka (1971) argue their data are consistent with the proposition that the conglomerate firms perform the economic function of preserving the values of ongoing organizations as well as restoring the earning power of the entities (p. 928). This conclusion seems premature. That the profit levels of firms that merge with companies more profitable than themselves rise is no surprise. Whether this activity serves a useful economic function or is simply the result of the arithmetic of averaging depends on whether some additional economies are generated by joining the different sets of companies. If the defensive diversification of the conglomerates through the acquisition of relatively more profitable firms generated real economic efficiencies, the value of the resulting enterprises should exceed the value they would have attained in the absence of these mergers. Here it is particularly important to take into account the much higher leverage ratios the conglomerates developed as part of their acquisition strategies. While diversification reduces a company's risk against a downturn for any single line of activity, increased leverage by increasing fixed interest payments increases a company's risk in the face of a general downturn in economic activity. Thus, while the pre-interest payments profits of the conglomerates may have become more stable as a result of their merger programmes, their post-interest payment profits may have become more volatile over the cycle. Given their heavy reliance on debt, a key performance question about the conglomerates is how they fare over the cycle.

The first suggestion that conglomerate acquisitions did not improve economic efficiency was presented by Reid (1971) in direct response to the Weston–Mansinghka article. Lags in publishing being what they are, Reid was able to base his comment on data extending up through mid-1970, and thus include the initial phase of the collapse of the 1960s bull market, while Weston and Mansinghka's data end in 1968 when the merger wave and the stock market were at their peaks. Reid reported a drop in the average price of the Weston–Mansinghka conglomerates between the end of 1968 and mid-1970 of 56 per cent, compared with a drop in the average price of their industrials of 37 per cent. Perhaps more dramatic and suggesting that the conglomerates had become highly risky due to their heavy levering was the drop in their bond prices of 45.6 per cent over this period compared to a drop in the Dow-Jones Industrial Bond average 7.8 per cent (Reid, 1971, p. 945).

C. The recent evidence—Returns on stocks

Regardless of whether the savings from a merger take the form of a tax gain, avoiding the costs of bankruptcy, diversification economies, superior deployment of capital or for some other reason, these gains should be reflected in the rate of return on the acquiring company's stock, unless the market was capable of fully anticipating the consequences of a merger or series of mergers long before they occurred. Thus, a direct test of the efficiency effects of conglomerate mergers net of the costs (including debt issues, premiums paid, etc.) of consummating them is to examine the returns on acquiring firms' stocks.

Hogarty was one of the first to use rate of return on equity as a performance measure using a sample of forty-three firms engaging in substantial merger activity over 1953–64 (1970b). He specifically avoided choosing conglomerates since his point of comparison was the average firm in the acquiring company's industry. The bulk of the merging firms in his sample performed either no better or worse than the average company in their base industries.

Weston *et al.* (1972) estimate rates of return on equity for a sample of forty-eight of the sixty-three conglomerates in the Weston–Mansinghka sample. Unfortunately they test the performance of the conglomerates against a random sample of fifty mutual funds rather than against the Weston–Mansinghka random samples of operating companies, so the two studies are not directly comparable. They find that the conglomerates outperform the mutual funds over the 1960–9 period on the basis of risk-adjusted rates of return statistics proposed by Sharpe and Treynor and Jensen's measure of portfolio performance.

In addition to their choice of control group, the Weston *et al.* study suffers somewhat from its choice of time period. As noted above, the substantial increase in leverage the conglomerates incurred raises questions about their risk/return performance over the cycle. The period 1960–9 consists mostly of one long upswing, and the very beginning of a sharp drop. Thus, the time period chosen may have been particularly favourable to the aggressively managed conglomerates in a comparison with the conservatively managed mutual funds. This hypothesis is reinforced by the results Weston–Smith–Shrieves report. The average ß for their sample of conglomerates is 1.928, nearly double the ß expected on a fully diversified portfolio.[7] Thus, a one percentage point change in the returns on a diversified portfolio would be accompanied by a nearly two percentage points change for the average conglomerate. In contrast, the average ß for the mutual funds was 0.878 suggesting quite a conservative management. Thus, the conglomerates were characterized by significantly higher market risk than the mutual funds, and were in a far weaker position to ride out the impending storm in 1969.

Melicher and Rush (1973) test the performance of conglomerates against a sample of non-conglomerate firms over a period that does extend through the 'liquidity crisis' of 1970 and into 1971. Their main findings are summarized in Table 11.2. The greater volatility of the conglomerates is again apparent. Their ß values are significantly higher in

Table 11.2 *Main results of Melicher and Rush (1973) (C=conglomerate sample mean; N-C=non-conglomerate sample mean; F=F-statistic)*

Factors		6/66–12/71	6/66–2/69	3/69–12/71
Monthly returns	C	1.008	1.017	0.998
	N-C	1.007	1.011	1.030
	F	0.20	4.50**	11.05*
Standard deviation	C	0.102	0.099	0.105
	N-C	0.094	0.087	0.100
	F	1.95	4.13**	0.59
Beta values	C	1.335	1.522	1.204
	N-C	1.031	1.152	0.952
	F	9.00*	9.89	4.63**
Jensen alpha	C	0.002	0.010	−0.006
	N-C	0.001	0.004	−0.002
	F	0.18	3.75	2.49
Sharpe variability	C	0.045	0.132	−0.041
	N-C	0.047	0.093	0.007
	F	0.03	1.91	4.31**
Treynor volatility	C	0.004	0.009	−0.004
	N-C	0.005	0.008	−0.029
	F	0.80	0.46	1.12

From the equation $R_i - R_f = \alpha_i + \beta_i(R_m - R_f)$, we obtain:

$$\text{Sharpe variability} = \frac{\bar{R}_i - R_f}{\sigma_i},$$

Jensen alpha $= \alpha_i,$

$$\text{Treynor volatility} = \frac{\bar{R}_i - R_f}{\beta_i},$$

where:
R_i = rate of return on equity of firm i,
R_f = risk free rate of return,
R_m = rate of return on the market portfolio.

both subperiods, and their standard deviations in returns are also higher in both subperiods, significantly so in the 6/66 to 2/69 subperiod. This volatility is also evidenced in the first row results presenting the average monthly returns for the two samples. For the period 6/66–2/69 covering the stock market's peak, the rate of return on conglomerate stocks was significantly higher than the average return for the sample of non-conglomerates. For the period 3/69–12/71 including the liquidity crisis and the market's initial phase of decline, the conglomerates earned a significantly lower rate of return than the non-conglomerates. Over the entire five and a half year period the returns on the two stocks were nearly the same. The same conclusions emerge from an examination of the various risk-adjusted measures. All three favour the conglomerates over the first period, two of the three favour the non-conglomerates in the second. Only one of these six comparisons is statistically significant, however, the non-conglomerates had a significantly higher risk-adjusted rate of return than the conglomerates over the 3/69–12/71 using the Sharpe measure. All three statistics are virtually identical for the full period.

D. Risk performance

One of the few questions for which all of the existing evidence and all of the authors' interpretations of their own evidence are in accord is that conglomerate mergers are not an efficient method for reducing risk. The theoretical argument for this proposition is well established (Levy and Sarnat, 1970). Lintner's argument to the contrary assumes that stockholders are limited to fairly small portfolios. But Evans and Archer (1968) have shown that the bulk of the gains from diversification can be achieved with a portfolio of roughly ten stocks, so the following results are not unexpected.

Smith and Schreiner (1969) were the first to study the efficiency of conglomerate diversification directly. Using simulation techniques they compared the portfolio holdings of nineteen conglomerates and eight mutual funds. On average the mutual funds tended to be closer to the efficient portfolio frontier than the conglomerates.

The Weston *et al.* (1972) study was in some ways a direct follow-up to Smith and Schreiner using data on actual conglomerate firm and mutual fund performances. As noted above, the β's for their conglomerates were more than double those of the mutual funds and they in fact reject 'diversification in a risk-reducing sense' as 'the major objective of conglomerate mergers' (p. 362). This conclusion has been further supported by several studies.

Melicher and Rush (1973) did not find β's as high as Weston *et al.* did, but they find conglomerate firm β's to be significantly higher than for their non-conglomerate sample. The same was found by Joehnk and Nielsen (1974). They also tested for a change in β's as a result of mergers using both conglomerate and non-conglomerate firms. They found an insignificant effect on the β's for conglomerate companies making acquisitions. A simlar result was also observed by Lev and Mandelker (1972), although their sample was not limited to conglomerate mergers. Their sample consisted of sixty-nine companies making large acquisitions (more than 10 per cent of their own size) over the period 1952–63. They found no significant difference between the changes in β's for acquiring firms over this period, and the changes in β's for a control group matched by industry, size and time period.[8]

Thus, there is no evidence that conglomerate firms achieved superior risk-spreading performance. Indeed, to the extent their higher β's are a result of their merger activity, the conglomerates became more risky and volatile than a comparable non-conglomerate.

Having rejected 'diversification in a risk-reducing sense' as the objective of conglomerate mergers, Weston, Smith and Schrieves go on to argue that it was the active management of the assets the conglomerates acquired that accounted for their superior performance (p. 362). This hypothesis was directly tested by Mason and Goudzwaard (1976). They compared the performance of twenty-two conglomerates with that of twenty-two portfolios of randomly selected stocks chosen to match the exact industries in which the conglomerates operated. Thus, the comparison was directly of whether the direct management of a portfolio of assets by conglomerate managers achieved significantly better performance than randomly chosen portfolios. It did not. Even after adjusting for the costs of buying and selling stocks, and paying a portfolio manager, the randomly selected portfolios had statistically higher rates of return on assets and accumulated stockholders' wealth over the 1962 to 1967 period. This result is all the more remarkable, because Mason and Goudzwaard end their comparison in 1967, the year Melicher and Rush (1973) found to be the peak performance year for the conglomerates.[9]

E.   Characteristics of the acquired firms

If the benefits to the stockholders of acquiring firms are ambiguous at best, the same cannot be said for the stockholders of the acquired firms. Every study which has examined the latter has found that the stockholders of the acquired firms earn significantly higher rates of return on their shares than other shares are earning, both over the immediate period before the merger and including a reasonable period after the merger is consummated. The results seem robust to type of merger, time period, and the type of compensation the stockholders of the acquired firms accept in return for their shares (see Halpern 1973; Haugen and Udell, 1972; Gort and Hogarty, 1970 and Lorie and Halpern, 1970).

The reason the stockholders of acquired firms fare so well, of course, is that they are paid a substantial premium above the pre-merger price for their shares. Although estimates of the premium paid in a merger vary over a fairly wide range, the minimum average premiums that have been calculated run about 15 per cent (see Gort, 1969; Hayes and Taussig, 1967; Piper and Weiss, 1974 and studies cited in Halpern, 1973, pp. 556-7).

What were the characteristics of these acquired firms, which made their merger partners willing to pay such large premiums for them? As already noted conglomerates acquired firms relatively more profitable than themselves. This characteristic appears to be entirely due to the lower profitability of the conglomerates. Melicher and Rush (1974) compared two samples of sixty-one conglomerate and seventy-one non-conglomerate acquisitions. The firms acquired by the conglomerates differed only in size (being larger) than those acquired by the non-conglomerates. But, since the conglomerate acquirers were less profitable and more highly levered than non-conglomerate acquirers, the firms they acquired were relatively more profitable and less levered than themselves. Both conglomerate and non-conglomerate companies had higher P/E's than the firms they acquired so that P/E magic was listed as a possible motive for both types of acquisitions by Melicher and Rush.

Boyle (1970) compared the profitability of 698 large firms acquired in conglomerate, horizontal and vertical acquisitions between 1948–68. He found that the companies acquired in conglomerate mergers had profit rates somewhat higher than those acquired in horizontal and vertical mergers, and roughly equal to the average over all manufacturing.

Stevens undertook a detailed multivariate discriminate analysis of the financial characteristics of forty firms acquired in 1966 and 40 non-acquired firms matched by size (1973). Of the initial twenty factors investigated six were identified as making independent contributions to explaining whether a sample firm was acquired or not: '(1) leverage, (2) profitability, (3) activity, (4) liquidity, (5) dividend policy and (6) price earnings' (p. 152). In the second phase of the discriminate analysis, only leverage and liquidity held up as significant discriminatory variables. Acquired firms had lower leverage ratios and higher liquidity than their matched non-acquired firms. The profits of acquired and non-acquired firms were the same. Acquired companies had higher dividend payout ratios and lower P/E's, although the differences in sample means were not significant. Additional evidence of P/E magic was obtained by Conn (1973) for pure conglomerate acquisitions over the 48–69 period, and Mead (1969).

Mandelker (1974) found that the 252 acquired firms in his sample earned significantly lower rates of return on equity than other firms over most of the period prior to their acquisition (Table 2, p. 315). He interprets this to imply 'that mergers are a mechanism by which the market replaces incompetent management' (p. 324).

Smiley (1976) has come up with even more dramatic results. He estimates the decline in market value of a taken-over firm up to the date of take-over as from 50 to 60 per cent of its potential maximum, and he estimates the start of this decline as occurring ten years before take-over.

How can the results of Mandelker (1974) and Smiley (1976) indicating significant deterioration in rate of return on equity performance be reconciled with those studies indicating average profitability performance? Perhaps they cannot. The differences may be due simply to differences in samples and time periods covered. Mandelker did not find an inferior rate of return performance for the subsample of 167 acquired firms listed on the NYSE, for example (Table 6, p. 320). Since these are generally larger than the other firms in his sample, it appears that the lower than average performance of acquired firms was most pronounced among the smaller acquired companies.

Mandelker's study covers the period before the conglomerate merger wave, and includes many non-conglomerate acquisitions. Smiley's (1976) study includes the years up through 1968, but is not restricted to conglomerates. The Boyle (1970) study does suggest that a significant fraction of those companies involved in horizontal or vertical acquisitions were losing money or showing profit declines. These firms may be disproportionately represented in the Mandelker and Smiley samples.

Denis Binder (1973) also noted a change in the relative profitability of acquired firms over time. Acquired firms, *which contested acquisitions*, were less profitable than average for the first half of the 1960s but *more* profitable over the 1965–9 period. Mandelker's, but not Smiley's, sample is restricted to firms in the first time period; Melicher and Rush's and Boyle's samples span both periods.

But the two sets of conflicting findings can be reconciled in another way. Those studies, which have concluded that acquired firms are not badly managed, have based their conclusions on profit rate and other accounting data. Those studies, which have concluded they are, have based their conclusions on return on equity data. The picture of an acquired firm emerging from Boyle (1970), Melicher and Rush (1974), Conn (1976) and Stevens (1973) suggests an average (profitability, leverage) to somewhat conservatively (liquidity, dividend payouts) managed company. In a period of sustained stockmarket advance average/conservative financial policies may be under-rewarded by the market *vis-à-vis* more aggressive risk-oriented financial behaviour. Thus, the lower return on equity and *P/E* performance of the acquired firms relative to the companies acquiring them may be explained by the former's more conservative financial policies and the market conditions fostering intensive merger activity.

This interpretation is further supported by the work of Piper and Weiss (1974) and Mingo (1976) on multibank holding company acquisitions. Piper and Weiss found that 'on average the 102 acquisitions [they] studied were breakeven investments that did not result in higher earnings per share for the holding companies in 1967 than would have been achieved in the absence of the acquisitions' (1974, p. 167). Mingo found that the only significant difference between the asset management policies of multibank holding companies and nonholding company banks was that the former held significantly riskier asset portfolios. Both studies concluded that their findings could be rationalized only in terms of a managerial or non-profit-maximizing theory of the firm.

But further work on the characteristics of acquired firms is certainly

F. Premiums and merger success

A few studies have tried to relate the success of a merger, from the point of view of the acquiring firm's stockholders, to various characteristics of the acquiring and acquired firms. The one variable that stands out above all in these analyses is the premium paid over the pre-merger price of the acquired company by its acquirer. The lower this premium is, the greater the likelihood that the acquiring firm's stockholders gain from the acquisition (Gort and Hogarty, 1970; Nielsen and Melicher, 1973; Piper and Weiss, 1974).

Although this result is perhaps not surprising, it does seem inconsistent with those hypotheses which claim that mergers take place to eliminate inefficient managements or to bring about special matchings between the merger partners. If the mergers were to eliminate incompetent managers, the size of the premium would tend to reflect the potential gains to the acquiring firms from replacing the incompetent managers of the firms acquired. There would be no particular reason to expect a merger with a premium of 30 per cent to be more successful than one with 15 per cent. The higher premium in the former would reflect the greater potential gains following the merger, and the higher price the acquirer was forced to pay in a competitive acquisition market.[10] Similarly, under a special matchings thesis, higher premiums would reflect greater latent synergy.

The finding of an inverse relationship between merger success and the size of premium suggests instead that acquired firms do not have special characteristics (e.g. managements of varying qualities), which differ from firm to firm warranting different prices for each firm. Acquired companies would appear to be bundles of assets accurately priced in the market. The payment of a premium for these assets over their market value is on average at best a breakeven investment, and the smaller the premium one pays, the better the chance of doing better than breaking even.

Although Nielsen and Melicher (1973) are not able to relate differences in premiums paid to real or financial (P/E magic) gains *achieved through the merger*, they do find the acquiring firm's cash flow and P/E to be positively related to the size of the premium it is willing to pay. Together these studies of the premiums paid support rather consistently a mangerial-motive thesis about mergers. The higher a firm's cash flow or price/earning ratio, that is, the cheaper capital is to it, the more it is willing to pay to acquire other firms. The amount it is willing to pay does not reflect post-merger gains. Indeed, the more it pays the less likely it is that the merger will be a success.

Unfortunately, the above studies do not deal directly with the conglomerates. One study that did, Haugen and Udell (1972), found that conglomerate acquirers paid significantly higher premiums on average than non-conglomerate acquirers, but it did not relate premium size to acquiring firm profitability.

G. Studies which conclude that mergers improve economic efficiency

The pattern of results that has emerged up to this point seems more consistent with the managerial thesis than with the neoclassical alternative. But before examining this contention specifically, let us pause to consider directly those studies which claim to have rejected the managerial motive hypothesis.

Of the recent studies examined here five have concluded that mergers improve economic efficiency and seem to present evidence directly contradicting a managerial thesis. These are the two papers coauthored by Fred Weston (1971, 1972), and three stemming from the Ph.D. dissertations by Halpern and Mandelker at the University of Chicago (Halpern, 1973; Lev and Mandelker, 1972; Mandelker, 1974). We have already discussed the Weston *et al.* studies in detail and seen that their results, when extended, are quite consistent with the general pattern emerging from the full set of studies, and are not inconsistent with a managerial theory interpretation. We shall focus here, therefore, on the three papers coming out of Chicago.

These studies are based on similar data samples. Halpern uses a sample of seventy-eight mergers between January 1950 and July 1965 'composed of companies for which merging is an infrequent method of growth' (1973, p. 559); Lev and Mandelker have a sample of sixty-nine firms undertaking a single large acquisition between 1952 and 1963; Mandelker has a sample of 241 mergers from November 1941 to August 1962. Thus, none of these studies covers the period of the conglomerate merger wave nor focuses on firms engaged in numerous, conglomerate-type mergers. Nevertheless, each claims that its results contradict some of the hypotheses put forward with respect to the conglomerates, and, since they have not been reviewed before, an examination of their results and claims seems warranted.

Halpern examines the rate of return performance of both partners in a merger up until the date of the merger. He does so by regressing the rate of return of an individual firm on the market return as in the equation presented on the bottom of Table 11.2, and then cumulating the residuals from this equation. He finds that both the larger and the smaller of the two merger partners have positive, average, cumulative residuals up through the date of the merger. But the variances are large, and neither the larger nor the smaller firms involved in these acquisitions have an average cumulative residual as large as the sample standard deviations. An interesting aspect of Halpern's study is that much of the excess returns on the merging companies' stocks is earned in the months preceding *announcement* of the merger. Halpern concludes that 'my results show that the larger company does not give away everything in a merger; the mean adjusted gain to the larger company is positive and the total adjusted gain is divided evenly, on average' (p. 572). This conclusion is stronger than warranted. As noted the positive returns earned by the acquiring firms are not statistically different from zero. In addition, since Halpern's study measures performance only *up to the date* of the merger, it is really a study of the market's *expected* gains from a merger, not of the actual gains.

The latter failing is corrected by Mandelker. He also employs a monthly-residual-approach, but extends his comparisons to up to forty months after the merger takes place. As did Halpern, Mandelker finds a rise in the cumulative residuals of the acquiring firm up to the date of the merger (5.1 per cent). Following the merger there is a drop-off in the cumulative residuals of 1.7 per cent, indicating that the market was somewhat over-optimistic about the merger's success. The cumulative increase in residuals over the entire period remains positive, but the variance is again large and the average residual is not significantly different from zero.

A detailed comparison of the behaviour of the returns on the acquired and acquiring firms' stocks before the merger reveals an important difference. For the acquired companies a significant and steady increase in cumulative residuals occurs over the seven months preceding the merger indicating 'that for some mergers, positive information regarding acquisitions, or any other "good" news correlated with acquisitions, starts leaking out to the market about 7 months before the merger' (p. 314). For the acquiring firms, however, the rise in returns occurs long before the merger takes place, a phenomenon also observed by Ellert (1976). Over the seven months preceding the merger the cumulative residuals for the acquiring firm exhibited a slight decline pointing 'to the possibility that for the stockholders of the acquiring firms, "news" of an acquisition may not be worthwhile news, since no abnormal behaviour is in fact observed during the period $(-7$ to $0)$. The abnormal returns earned long before the merger may have nothing to do with the acquisition *per se*' (p. 321).

In fact, however, it may be the abnormal returns of the acquiring firm long before the merger which are causing the merger, rather than the other way round. The rise in returns on acquiring firms' stocks over the years preceding the merger suggests that these firms were experiencing higher than normal profits and/or P/E's over this period. And it might have been this abnormal prosperity which precipitated the decision to undertake an acquisition. This interpretation is consistent with the Nielsen and Melicher (1973) findings relating high cash flows and P/E's for acquiring firms to the premiums they pay, and the more general phenomenon that merger waves occur in periods of prosperity. If the rise in residuals for the acquiring firms before the merger were the cause of the acquisition, and the *fall* in residuals *following* the merger a result of it, Mandelker's findings would present a more negative view of the successfulness of mergers for the stockholders of the acquiring firms, and would be more in line with the managerial thesis than he is willing to conclude himself.

A closer look at Halpern's results suggests that they *may* follow the same pattern as Mandelker's and be amenable to the same interpretation. Unfortunately, Halpern does not report the monthly residual pattern for the larger and smaller of the two merging firms separately. But he does report these residuals for the two samples combined (1973, p. 567, Table 2). These residuals show a noticeable rise over the period from eighteen to twenty-three months before the merger, and again starting seven months before the merger. If the latter reflected the gains from speculation in the to-be-acquired firm's stock, Halpern's results would conform exactly to Mandelker's. But, it is again hard to believe that the increases in returns being earned between a year and a half and two years before the merger were *caused* by the merger. Instead it is likely that these were higher returns earned by the acquiring firms, and if causality is involved at all it is these returns that caused the merger. Even if the latter conjecture is false, however, it seems unjustified to include as part of the gains *from* mergers, increases in returns on the stocks of acquiring companies earned more than a year and a half before the merger is announced.

The sixty-nine firms making a single large acquisition which Lev and Mandelker study earned higher average returns on their stocks over the five years following the merger than before, as compared with a sample of companies matched by size and industry, but again the difference in sample means was statistically insignificant. Most of the other evidence in their study was also 'largely negative'.

All three of these studies conclude that their findings are inconsistent with the 'allegations' that mergers are not undertaken to improve the welfare of the acquiring firm's stockholders, or lead to real gains in economic efficiency. Halpern and Mandelker argue more specifically that their results suggest that mergers are a means of removing inefficient managements (of acquired companies). If we ignore the question of whether high returns cause firms to become acquirers or the reverse, this is a potentially legitimate interpretation of their findings. For the mergers do appear to have generated gains to the stockholders of the acquired firms. And if they did not do likewise for the stockholders of the acquirers they also did not generate negative returns. So at a minimum the mergers appear to have generated enough efficiency gains to have benefitted unambiguously the stockholders of the acquired firms. But this conclusion still raises some questions about the motives behind the mergers from the point of view of the acquiring firms.

For the mergers are not simply another form of *marginal* investment. The mergers examined in each of these three studies were between firms both of which were large enough to have listed securities. The acquiring firms in the Lev and Mandelker sample grew at roughly double the rate of their matched pairs over the same eleven-year period, as did Weston and Mansinghka's conglomerates compared to their sample of industrials. Why should managers engage in acquisitions or series of acquisitions resulting in such dramatic increases in their company's size and perhaps character when their stockholders obtain no benefits from these changes, if the goal of the managers is to increase their stockholders' welfare? The interpretation of the Halpern, Mandelker and Lev and Mandelker findings these authors themselves give, leaves the managers of the acquiring firms as corporate good samaritans who go about bidding up the prices of badly managed firms and rescuing the stockholders of these firms from their managements, to the benefit of only the stockholders of the acquired firms. The acquiring company managers gain nothing, their stockholders a normal return.

The difficulty in reconciling normal returns to stockholders of acquiring companies, and supranormal returns to stockholders of acquired firms in a neoclassical framework is clearly evidenced in

Mandelker's discussion of why it is that stockholders of *acquired* firms fare so well:

> When a firm is confronted with a tender offer a conflict of interest between management and shareholders may result. Although the stockholders of the acquired firm are likely to profit from the merger more than any other party involved, incumbent management may stand to lose the most, for they may forfeit their controlling position with all of the accompanying benefits (p. 326).

Earlier on the same page he notes that 'Indeed, it is very difficult to acquire a firm if its management resists forcefully,' citing B.F. Goodrich management's successful defeat of a merger bid that would have increased stockholder net worth by 30 per cent. But a take-over fight is but a polar case and the most blatant example of a conflict of interest between managers and stockholders. And just as the existence of a separation between ownership and control can explain why managers reject merger proposals which would result in instantaneous capital gains of 30 per cent and more for their stockholders, it can explain why managers make merger proposals resulting in no gains for their stockholders—and might even be willing to make such proposals if the stockholders suffered a loss. For the same stratagems which allowed B.F. Goodrich's management to resist Northwest Industries' $1 billion tender offer were available to Northwest Industries management should they need them, to ward off unhappy stockholders who felt that was too much to pay for the assets of the Goodrich firm.

Thus, the conclusion that the stockholders of acquiring firms earned a normal return on their companies' acquisition, even if warranted, does not in itself settle the issue as to why the managers of acquiring companies engage in this form of investment. We turn to this issue now.

H.   The evidence as it relates to managerial motives for merger

Gort has noted with respect to earlier mergers that acquiring firms tend to be located in slow-growing sectors and enter fast-growing ones (1966, p. 41). This strategy is consistent with Weston and Mansinghka's defensive diversification hypothesis, as is Gort's finding that *acquired* firms tend to be in R and D intensive industries (1969), and McGowan's that *acquiring* firms are in R and D *unintensive* industries (1971). These tendencies lead to a life cycle view of the firm that is consistent with either a stockholder-welfare-maximization interpretation, as Weston and Mansinghka put forward, or a growth objective (see Grabowski and Mueller, 1975; Mueller, 1972). The conglomerates appear to have been located in industries in which technological maturity and competitive pressures inhibited internal growth.[11] If these firms wanted to grow fast, merger was the only feasible way. The evidence surveyed here indicates that whatever their objective, conglomerate mergers, like their predecessors, did not lead to significant improvements in the risk return performance of the acquiring firms' stocks. Whether it was the objective sought or not, significant increases in growth were achieved via these mergers (Mandelker, 1974; Reid, 1968; Weston and Mansinghka, 1971).

The significantly higher leverage ratios of the conglomerates *before* they undertook their merger activity suggests that they did have more aggressive, expansion-oriented managers than other companies. Singh also found that acquiring firms in the UK had higher leverage (gearing) ratios than non-acquirers, and in addition had higher retention ratios, lower liquidity, and faster growth rates (1971, pp. 160-1). Although Kuehn's results for the UK differ from Singh's in some respects, they are also consistent with the interpretation that acquiring company managers are more aggressive than other managers (1975, ch. 6).

Singh observed that acquired firms earned somewhat lower profits than non-acquired firms, and Kuehn observed both lower profits and valuation ratios for UK companies acquired (1975, ch. 3). Some studies in the US from *before* the conglomerate merger wave have found similar patterns. But, no evidence has been gathered to suggest that acquired firms were to any degree in danger of bankruptcy, however, and the companies the *conglomerates* acquired were earning higher profits than themselves. Lynch has even argued on the basis of case study analysis of twenty-eight conglomerates that they followed a strategy of acquiring 'successful, profitable companies' with 'capable management that can be retained' (1971, pp. 83-5). Indeed, to the extent that a failing-firm or alternative-to-bankruptcy motive for conglomerate mergers emerges at all from this literature, it is the *acquiring* firms that may be trying to improve their positions by *defensively* acquiring companies more profitable than themselves. This is ironic since the usual failing-firm defence of mergers has been couched in terms of rescuing acquired company stockholders from bad managers (e.g. Dewey, 1961; Manne, 1965).

Several of the studies cited found that acquiring firms experienced periods of temporarily higher than normal returns preceding their acquisitions, returns that could not be in any sense 'caused' by the mergers. Nielsen and Melicher's finding that high *P/E*'s and cash flows lead to higher offered premiums on mergers is also consistent with the view that it is 'cheap' internal and external capital which leads to mergers, capital which is cheap in the sense that management does not feel compelled to use it to maximize stockholder welfare. Beckenstein has observed a positive relationship between aggregate merger activity and the cost of external capital, which he interprets as supporting a managerial thesis (1979).

The would-be conglomerates did not have high cash flows and P/E's at the beginning of the 1960s. Nevertheless, the rise in profits and stock market values that occurred during this decade, and the relatively low interest rates prevailing throughout much of it, provided these firms with a more favourable environment to pursue growth through the most attractive avenue available to them: external expansion. The pursuit of this goal subsided at the end of the 1960s, when this environment changed.

Since growth must accompany any significant merger programme, there is no way to establish whether this is the primary objective of these mergers, or auxiliary to some other(s). Space does not allow a review of all possible alternatives (but see Steiner, 1975, ch. 6). One does emerge from this survey, however, and since it has not received much attention in the literature it is worth discussing here.

Both Halpern (1973) and Mandelker (1974) provide evidence that the gains from mergers that do occur often come before the merger takes place or is even announced. This finding has been confirmed by Firth (1976) for the UK and Gagnon *et al.* (1982) for Belgium. Firth found a substantial rise in the stock prices for acquired firms over the twenty-one trading days preceding the announcement of the merger, peaking four days before the announcement (pp. 83-90). No change in the returns to stock on the acquiring firms was noted in this period, however.[12] Gagnon *et al.* found a significant increase in the *volume* of trading in both the acquiring and acquired firms' stocks over the ten *months* preceding a merger's announcement and concluded that information about the merger reached the market during this pre-announcement period.

None of these studies pursues the issue of who it is 'in the market' who has possession of this information about a forthcoming merger that causes an increase in trading volume and a rise, at least for the company to be acquired, in stock price. The most obvious group having access to this information is the management planning the merger. As Manne (1966) has emphasized the access to insider information is one of the important perquisites managers have. And the knowledge that the shares of a to-be-acquired firm will soon rise by 15 per cent or more, is a valuable piece of information. Thus, one possible explanation for why managers engage in mergers that have no benefit to their stockholders is that the mergers provide opportunities for possible gains from insider information.[13] This interpretation also seems easier to accept than that given by Hogarty (1970b) and Gort (1970), that the managers were risk takers maximizing stockholder welfare. For much of the risks arising from a merger fall to the stockholders, and access to insider information gives managers an opportunity to share disproportionately in the gains while avoiding some of the risks.

This interpretation also raises additional questions about studies such as Halpern's (1973) that base their conclusions solely on the gains from mergers on stock price data preceding the merger. To the extent managers do undertake mergers in anticipation of a favourable stock-market reaction to the merger's announcement, an unfavourable reaction might be expected to lead to a cancellation of the merger bid. By focusing on stock market data for only successful bids up to the time of the merger, these studies choose the most favourable time period over which to judge the 'effects' from a merger.

Studies of previous merger waves have concluded that 'promoters profits' played a significant role in explaining the volume of merger activity.[14] The promoters of the conglomerate merger wave were the acquiring firms' managers themselves. The studies surveyed here suggest that someone was profiting on the information about the forthcoming merger, before it became public. Whether this was the managers, and to what extent these profits influenced their decisions, cannot be ascertained. But the hypothesis that speculation of this type may have been a significant factor is certainly consistent with the evidence surveyed here, and the more general phenomenon that merger waves accompany stock market advances.

IV. THE EFFECT OF CONGLOMERATE MERGERS ON CONCENTRATION

A fair concensus exists that conglomerate mergers have not contributed to increases in industry level concentration, at least at a low level of aggregation, and have not had serious anticompetitive effects (FTC, 1972; Goldberg, 1973, 1974; Markham, 1973, ch. 5). But at the same time there appears to be little consensus as to what the effects of mergers have been on overall concentration. Thus, the FTC (1969) concluded:

There can be no doubt that mergers played a key role in increasing the share of manufacturing assets held by [the top 200] companies over the period [1947–1968]. Significantly, whereas industry growth effect played a role about equal in importance to mergers between 1947 and 1960, mergers have been almost exclusively responsible for the increase occurring since 1960 (p. 193).

While Jules Backman (1970) concluded:

Moreover, the growth of large companies is due primarily to internal expansion rather than to mergers. Thus, between 1948 and 1968, the total assets of the 200 largest manufacturing corporations increased by $242.4 billion . . . acquisitions accounted for $50.0 billion or 20.6 percent of this total increase. However, for the 10 largest companies, acquired assets were only 2.8 percent of the asset growth; for the second 10 largest it was (sic) 16.2 percent; and for the 21st to 50th largest, it was (sic) 24.3 percent. Clearly, for the very largest companies mergers have been a minor factor in their growth (p. 122).

Surprisingly, these two sets of conclusions are not as irreconcilable as they appear. These and other similar studies have reached different conclusions because they have been answering different questions. Those studies which have attributed a substantial fraction of firm or overall concentration growth to mergers have been asking the question: What would the growth of large firms or increase in overall concentration have been had there been no mergers?[15]

The most systematic examination of this question is by John McGowan (1965). He found that:

. . . mergers appear to play a substantial role in allowing firms . . . to grow faster than the aggregate growth rate. Furthermore, though there are exceptions, the tendency appears to be that as the firm increases its size its ability to grow faster than the aggregate depends increasingly upon growth by merger . . . as the firm becomes relatively very large its ability just to maintain its position seems heavily dependent upon growth by merger (p. 454).

McGowan concluded that mergers accounted for almost two-thirds of the increase in the 500 firm concentration ratio between 1950 and 1960, and almost three-quarters the increase in the 100 firm ratio (pp. 455-6).

The FTC study quoted above, also tried to answer the same question for the 1960s, although with less sophistication than McGowan, as did Lee Preston (1973). These studies confirm or even strengthen McGowan's conclusions as to the importance of mergers in explaining increases in overall concentration. The FTC's figures indicate an increase in the share of assets held by the largest 200 manufacturing corporations between 1960 and 1968 from 54.1 per cent to 60.9 per cent (1969, pp. 189-93). Over the same period the assets acquired by the largest 200 firms amounted to 10 per cent of total manufacturing assets. Thus, if no mergers had taken place, and other forms of growth were not fully substituted for mergers, overall concentration might have actually fallen over this period. This is in fact what one would expect to have happened. In the absence of mergers overall concentration should rise during periods of contraction due to the greater vulnerability of smaller firms, and fall during upswings, due to new entry and the more rapid growth of smaller companies. This expectation was confirmed over the relatively merger free period of 1929–47 when concentration rates increased substantially during the decline in business activity from 1929 to 1933, and then declined significantly during the economic recovery starting in 1933 and extending through World War II (Scherer (1971, pp. 41-5)). Thus, one would expect overall concentration to have fallen over the sustained economic advance of the 1960s; that it did not is probably attributable to the merger wave.[16] Studies of the impact of mergers on concentration in the UK (Aaronovitch and Sawyer, 1975; Hannah and Kay, 1977) and West Germany (Müller and Hochreiter, 1976) have reached similar conclusions.

Those authors who appear to have reached a different conclusion have in fact been asking the following question: What has been the ratio of assets acquired by the largest firms to their total growth? These studies have generally found this ratio to vary from 10 to 25 per cent depending on the time period and group of firms covered (Backman, 1970; Bock, 1970; Markham, 1973, pp. 114-24; Piccini, 1970; Steiner, 1975, pp. 289-307). That these are different questions, and that the answers obtained are consistent with one another can be most easily seen from the following example. Suppose the economy consisted of 1000 firms of equal size, each growing at 3 per cent per year. In the absence of any mergers, entry or exit, overall concentration would remain unchanged. The 100 largest would always control 10 per cent of assets. Suppose, however, 100 firms begin acquiring 1 per cent of the total assets outstanding each year by acquiring 10 of the other 900 firms per year. This amounts to one acquisition per acquiring firm every 10 years. After 90 years all of the other firms are gone; the 100 largest possess all of the economy's assets. The percentage growth in assets of the top 100 accounted for by mergers would fall from 77 per cent in year one to 25 per cent in year 90. Yet, there would have been no increase in concentration had there not been any mergers. Thus, a falling and eventually relatively small ratio of growth via merger to total growth is consistent with the conclusion that all of the increase in concentration is a result of past mergers. Indeed, a falling ratio of merger to 'internal' growth is inevitable unless the largest firms follow a strategy of acquiring an ever-increasing percentage of the nation's total assets.

Those studies such as Backman (1970), Bock (1970, and earlier, Weston (1953), which adjust overall concentration or firm growth rates by past ratios of acquired to total asset growth, build in the questionable assumption that the acquired firm stopped growing at the time of its acquisition and that all subsequent growth is internal. Thus, over time, the contribution of any given merger to a firm's growth or the change in overall concentration under this procedure tends to zero. The conclusion that mergers are an unimportant source of growth or overall concentration change, which these studies draw, is thus not particularly surprising.

For policy purposes, the relevant question is what the level of concentration would be without any mergers. The answer seems fairly clear—significantly lower.

V.   POLICY IMPLICATIONS

The evidence reviewed in this chapter indicates that mergers result in no net gains to the acquiring firm's stockholders. Those studies which have drawn conclusions to the contrary have based these conclusions on profit and stock price increases occurring in the period of economic and stock market buoyancy, or on returns earned on stocks prior to the merger, and not always directly (or causally) related to the merger. Even then most of the positive results found have not been statistically significant at conventional confidence intervals. These positive results on mergers seem fully offset by those which have concluded on the basis of post-merger results, or data extended beyond the stock market peak, that mergers are breakeven or unprofitable ventures. The results from the relevant studies are summarized in Table 11.3.

This evidence is broadly consistent with the hypothesis that managers pursue corporate growth or other objectives that are not directly related to stockholder welfare and economic efficiency. This hypothesis can explain why managers of acquiring firms undertake mergers providing no benefits for their stockholders; why managers of acquisition targets vigorously resist bids which would greatly enrich their stockholders.

Nevertheless, one might argue that this literature presents no compelling case for government intervention. For there is no evidence that mergers now result in significant anticompetitive effects, and the studies suggesting that mergers are on average failures, are partially offset by those concluding that they are breakeven ventures. If mergers do not make things any better, they also do not make them much worse. Assuming the latter inference is valid, why not let managers pursue whatever goals they choose?

One cost of the pursuit of growth via external expansion, which has been cited in the literature, is that it is likely to come at the expense of more socially productive forms of growth (Reid, 1968; Sichel, 1970). Mergers compete directly with capital investment, R and D and other investment-type expenditures for cash flows and managerial decision-making capacities. While a manager is perhaps indifferent between whether a given rate of expansion is achieved through internal or external growth, society is likely to be better off through the creation of additional assets. Two of the studies discussed here present direct evidence that mergers do come at the expense of internal growth. Hogarty (1970a) found that the post-merger sales of the merging firms were lower than predicted from their pre-merger sales.[17] Lev and Mandelker found that the *internal* growth rates of acquiring firms decreased in the post-merger period, a result they attributed to 'perhaps a "shakedown" or "digestion" effect' (1972, p. 97).

A second cost of mergers is the rise in overall concentration they bring about, as documented in the preceding section, and the reduction in the number of independent economic entities this entails (on the latter see Preston, 1971, p. 21). The usual argument by economists is that increases in industry concentration constitute a potential economic (market power) problem, increases in overall concentration, if anything, a political (power) problem. Up until the 1970s the latter would then be quickly dismissed as unsubstantiated or beyond the bounds of economic analysis. But, I trust, the age of innocence regarding corporate power is now over. Large corporations both have and utilize political power. And it seems reasonable to assume that this power is positively related to company size.[18] A policy curtailing mergers and reversing upward trends in overall concentration would be a first step toward halting, if not reversing, increases in corporate power.

Space precludes a review of all the proposals to constrain merger activity that have been put forward (see Steiner, 1975, ch. 12). The main issues can be illustrated, however, by focusing on the two polar extremes: maintenance of the present policy, or a flat ban on all mergers.

The *economic* rationale underlying the antitrust laws is based on a variant of the invisible hand argument as applied to price competition. If managers maximize profits then the allocation of resources is most efficiently achieved 'through the independently set prices of each firm. Government intervention is warranted only to prevent collusion and other efforts to monopolize. But the invisible hand analogy breaks down when one switches to investment-type activities, and allows for non-profit maximization objectives. Just as there is no proof that competition for sales among firms via advertising results in improved allocational efficiency, there is no proof or evidence that the pursuit of growth via merger leads to anything more than external growth at the expense of internal growth.

Acceptance of this argument would suggest abandoning the invisible hand premise as an underpinning for some parts of antitrust legislation. With respect to mergers this could imply a ban on all mergers, perhaps limited to companies above a given size, and subject to an 'efficiencies defense'. The latter could be written fairly broadly to include explicitly replacement of bad managers (as well as rescue of failing firms), capital transfer efficiencies, and perhaps other efficiency gains put forward in the literature. The major difference between this law and the present one would be in locating the burden of proof. Instead of the government having to prove a substantial lessening of competition, the companies would have to prove likely efficiency gains.

Obviously if anything like the present number of mergers were to take place, such a law could be a tremendous administrative burden. The

Table 11.3 Summary of recent studies of returns from mergers for acquiring firms' stockholders

Author	Sample	Control Group	Time Period	Returns Acquiring Firms	Returns Control Group	Significance Test
Hogarty (1970b)	43 non-conglomerates engaged in heavy merger activity	Firms in acquiring company's base industry	1953–64	−0.01 (one per cent below returns of industry)		$\sigma = 0.11$ (difference from zero insignificant)
Lev and Mandelker (1972)	69 firms making large acquisitions (conglomerate and otherwise)	69 non-merging firms matched by industry and size	1952–63	0.056 (05.6 per cent above return of stock of matched sample)		$Z = 1.40$
Weston, Smith and Shrieves (1972)	48 conglomerates	50 mutual funds	1960–9	Ave. returns 1.262 Sharpe 0.364 Treynor 0.131 α/β 0.097	1.091 0.313 0.054 0.020	$F = 22.83^{**}$ 1.75 6.21^* 6.21^*
Melicher and Rush (1973)	45 conglomerates	45 non-conglomerates base industry as of 1960	6/66–12/71	Ave. returns 1.008 Sharpe 0.045 Treynor 0.004 Jensen α 0.002	1.007 0.047 0.005 0.001	$F = 0.20$ 0.03 0.80 0.18
Halpern (1973)	78 mergers by non-conglomerate firms	market portfolio	1/50–7/65	0.063 (mean cumulative residual of larger firm up to date of merger)		$\sigma = 0.31$ (difference from zero insignificant)
Mandelker (1974)	241 large acquisitions (conglomerate and non-conglomerate)	market portfolio	1941–63	0.0005 (cumulative residual in 7 mos. preceding merger using premerger β).		$t = 0.04$

Table 11.3 *Continued*

Author	Sample	Control Group	Time Period	Returns Acquiring Firms	Returns control Group	Significance Test
				0.0023 (cumulative residual in 20 mos. preceding merger using post-merger β)		t=1.73
				0.0003 (cumulative residual in 20 mos. after the merger using post-merger β)		t=0.033
Haugen and Langetieg (1975)	59 large nonconglomerate mergers	59 matched pairs of firms	1951–68	1>*market index 5<<market index	1>*market index 3<<market index	No significant difference exists in the proportions of success and failures in the two groups
Mason and Goudzwaard (1976)	22 conglomerates	22 matched portfolios	1962–7	0.0746	0.1275 SM portfolio 0.1182 Mutual fund 0.1399 Buy and hold	Z=1.93* Z=1.59 Z=2.33*

[a]Notes: *indicates significant at the 0.05 level,
          **indicates significant at the 0.01 level.

assumption is, based on the surveyed evidence regarding the number of successful mergers occurring, that only a small fraction of the mergers presently undertaken would promise sufficient efficiency gains to be capable of defending on these grounds in court.

It can be argued that such a law would reduce the threat of take-over and thereby increase the scope of managerial discretion and potentially lead to an even more inefficient allocation of resources than under the present law. Smiley (1976) explains the decline in share prices he observes before take-over as evidence of the exercise of managerial discretion, and other studies finding lower returns or profits before merger are consistent with this view. But as noted above, the evidence on this point is in conflict. In addition, Smiley's own results, and the data on returns to acquiring firms, suggests that the gains from replacing incompetent or non-stockholder-welfare maximizing managers have not been all that large. Nevertheless, any effort to curtail the volume of merger activity should, to be consistent, be accompanied by other measures to improve the markets for capital and corporate control. More detailed accounting procedures, less costly procedures for engaging in proxy fights or direct take-overs, and perhaps even measures forcing a greater payout of profits and more reliance on the external capital market.

Some of the evidence surveyed here concerning the greater profitability of the target firms in conglomerate mergers is consistent with the capital redeployment thesis, and also suggests a possible worsening of efficiency from an effective curtailment of merger activity. Here the possibility of internal expansion and diversification should be kept in mind, as well as an 'efficiencies defence' for mergers. The usual argument for mergers over internal expansion is that they allow the firm to achieve the potential efficiency gain faster than if it must expand internally (Williamson, 1968). But, the evidence cited here on profit and return on equity effects indicates that no efficiency gains are realized *or perceived* by the market in the first few years following the merger. Perhaps, this too is a result of the digestion problems Lev and Mandelker suspect are inhibiting post-merger growth. But, whatever the cause, these results imply a small loss, if any, to society from waiting for the benefits from a redeployment of capital to follow internal diversification.[19]

Several writers have pointed out that growth through merger is not the only form of growth, and the conglomerates in particular are not the only or even necessarily the worst abusers of political power (Steiner, 1975, chs. 11, 12; Williamson, 1975, pp. 170–1). Their points are well taken. The reasons for singling out growth through merger, conglomerate or otherwise, for discriminatory treatment are that it is the easiest form of growth to attack, it is a main contributor to increasing overall concentration, and we have good evidence that there will be negligible efficiency losses from such a policy. This policy need not be considered a substitute for or superior to a broad scale attack on existing market power. It is simply a place to start.

VI. CONCLUSION

It has become customary to close a review of the merger literature by observing that the arguments are still in conflict, the main issues still in doubt, and from this draw the prudent conclusion that policy changes should proceed slowly and cautiously. True, the a priori theories of mergers' causes and effects are still in conflict, and will probably always remain so. But the empirical literature, upon which this survey focuses, draws a surprisingly consistent picture. Whatever the stated or unstated goals of managers are, the mergers they have consummated have on average not generated extra profits for the acquiring firms, have not resulted in increased economic efficiency. Admittedly some unresolved riddles remain, but all discussion of serious policy alternatives need not be set aside until these are resolved.

Although a recommendation to proceed cautiously in the face of conflicting evidence seems on the surface reasonable enough, it is in fact a recommendation to accept the neoclassical theories of mergers, stick with the status quo policy on mergers, and accept this policy's underlying premise of an invisible hand guiding the market for control.

We now have almost a century of accumulated evidence as to effects of a *laissez faire* policy toward mergers. Enough time has elapsed and evidence been gathered that one can say that this policy experiment has not been a success. The time has come to try a new experiment. I think we can now legitimately ask managers to prove prior to a merger, that this merger is likely 'to substantially lessen' inefficiency.

NOTES

1. Reid (1968, pp. 74-7), Steiner (1975, pp. 17-22). These two books also present useful surveys of the earlier merger waves and the statistics on each. *See also* Markham (1955, 1973).
2. Lintner actually lists 'dirty pooling' and other accounting gimmicks as one of his five causes, and subsumes bankruptcy costs under leverage. For further discussion of these hypotheses, *see* again Steiner (1975, chs. 2, 4, 5).
3. It should be noted that there are two separate issues involved here concerning M-form efficiency. The first is whether the M-form organization is superior to the U-form for managing a given set of diversified activities.

The second is whether the *M*-form efficiency gains are sufficient to justify the transaction costs of acquiring a large number of *U*-form companies to create a conglomerate *M*-form. The first hypothesis could be valid even if the second is not. It is only the second which is addressed here.

4. Thorp (1931, p. 86) as cited in Reid (1968, p. 67). *See also* Reid's discussion of the 'environment for mergers' and the managerial thesis (chs. 3, 4, 5, 7).

5. Holzmann *et al.* (1975) also found that a sample of twenty-one conglomerates had lower average profitability than a size-matched sample of non-conglomerates for both the 1951–60 and 1961–70 periods, as well as over the entire 1951–70 period. They did not make before and after the merger wave comparisons.

6. Conn (1973, 1976) found no evidence of a difference between the profit rates of acquired and acquiring firms. But while the time periods and samples of Weston–Mansinghka and Melicher–Rush heavily overlap, that of Conn's does not, so his results and theirs are difficult to compare.

7. Brenner and Downes (1979) call into question the W–S–S estimates of β and conglomerate performance as well as those of Melicher and Rush, discussed below, on the basis of the data and statistical tests employed. Unfortunately, their call for new studies employing more refined techniques has yet to be answered, or perhaps even heard.

8. The β's for acquiring firms in Mandelker's study fall significantly following the merger, but this fall seems to begin as much as two years before the merger takes place and does not seem directly related to the mergers, Joehnk and Nielsen (1974) note significant changes in the β's for non-conglomerate firms engaging in a single conglomerate merger over the period 1962–9.

9. Haugen and Langetieg (1975) follow a somewhat similar methodology, although they focus on the risk-reduction effects of fifty-nine large *non-conglomerate* mergers. They find no significant difference in the risk performance of the merging firms, and the matched non-merging portfolios.

10. Even in imperfect competitive markets premium sizes should reflect potential gains, if profitability is the goal, since the acquiring firm's managers and stockholders are then in somewhat of a monopsony situation, and can hold out for a greater share of the net gains.

11. A similar pattern of location for acquiring firms was observed by Kuehn for the UK (1975, pp. 16-24, ch. 4). Given the milder antitrust environment in the UK, however, it was not necessary for these firms to go outside of their industries to achieve growth via mergers.

12. (pp. 142-57) Some rise was noted if the acquiring firm financed the acquisition by a new equity issue, but this was attributed to the arrangement of 'some buying support for their securities' (p. 147). Interestingly enough, the acquiring firm's stock suffered a significant *decline* in value in the thirty trading days *following* the merger's announcement.

13. Some of the rise in the acquired company's stock price may have been brought about through the acquiring firm's 'buying in' before the formal announcement. But Gagnon *et al.* (1982) show that not all of the increase in *volume* of transactions can be explained in this way, and thus probably not all of the change in price. Any change in the volume traded or price of the acquiring firm's stock obviously cannot be explained in this way.

14. For surveys of the early literature on this point, *see* Markham (1955) and Reid (1968, chs. 3, 4, 5).

15. For a similar interpretation of these differences *see* Preston (1971, 1973).
16. This is also consistent with McGowan's conclusion that overall concentration would eventually decline if all mergers were prohibited (1965). *See also* Preston (1973). There are various upward and downward biases in using the percentage of assets acquired as an indication of the importance of mergers, of course, but the figures give one a rough idea. *See* the FTC's discussion of these biases (1969) as well as Bock's (1970).
17. Because of this Hogarty rejects growth in sales as the motive for mergers (1970a, p. 389). His conclusion *ignores* the immediate growth of the acquiring company brought about by the merger. If this is the growth sought, Hogarty's results are not inconsistent with this objective.
18. For a pioneering and largely successful effort to relate political power to *industry* concentration *see* Pittman (1976).
19. Internal expansion is not a viable alternative under Cable's 'information search' variant on the redeployment of capital thesis (1978).

Part IV
The Competitive Process and Capitalist
Performance

12 The Social Costs of Monopoly Power*

In 1954, Arnold Harberger estimated the welfare losses from monopoly for the United States at 0.1 of 1 per cent of GNP. Several studies have appeared since, reconfirming Harberger's early low estimates using different assumptions (e.g. Scherer, 1980; Schwartzman, 1960; Worcester, 1973). These papers have firmly established as part of the conventional wisdom the idea that welfare losses from monopoly are insignificant.

The Harberger position has been, almost from the start, subject to attack, however (e.g. Stigler, 1956). Kamerschen, (1966) followed essentially the Harberger methodology, but assumed an elasticity of demand consistent with monopoly pricing behaviour at the industry level and obtained welfare loss estimates as high as 6 per cent. Posner (1975) made some rough estimates of the social costs of acquiring monopoly power, but, using Harberger's calculations, concluded that the real problem was the social cost imposed by regulation rather than of private market power.

The most sophisticated critique of Harberger's approach has been offered by Abram Bergson (1973). Bergson criticizes the partial equilibrium framework employed by Harberger and all previous studies, and puts forward a general equilibrium model as an alternative. He then produces a series of hypothetical estimates of the welfare losses from monopoly, some of them quite large, for various combinations of the two key parameters in this model, the elasticity of substitution and the difference between monopoly and competitive price. Not surprisingly Bergson's estimates, suggesting as they do that monopoly can be a matter

*This chapter was started during the summer of 1975 when Keith Cowling visited the International Institute of Management and completed during the summer of 1976 when Dennis Mueller participated in the University of Warwick's Summer Workshop. Thanks are extended to both of these institutions for their support. In addition, special thanks are due to Gerald Nelson, who made the welfare loss calculations for the United States and Clive Hicks for making the estimates for the United Kingdom. Keith Cowling and Dennic C. Mueller.

of some consequence, have induced a sharp reaction (see Carson, 1975; Worcester, 1975).[1]

The present paper levels several objections against the Harberger-type approach. It then calculates estimates of the welfare loss from monopoly using procedures derived to meet these objections, and obtains estimates significantly greater than those of previous studies. Although several of the objections we make have been made by other writers, none has systematically adjusted the basic Harberger technique to take them into account. Thus all previous estimates of monopoly welfare losses suffer in varying degrees from the same biases incorporated in Harberger's original estimates.

We do, however, employ a partial equilibrium framework as followed by Harberger and all subsequent empirical studies. Although a general equilibrium framework would be preferable, such an approach requires simplifying assumptions which to our mind are just as restrictive as those needed to justify the partial equilibrium approach. For example, Bergson must assume that social welfare can be captured via a social indifference curve, and further that this indifference curve is the CES variety. The assumption that the elasticity of substitution (σ) is constant further implies, for a disaggregated analysis, that the elasticity of demand for each product (η_i) is the same, since $\eta_i \to \sigma$ as the share of the ith product in total output approaches zero. But the assumption that η_i is the same for all i is the same assumption made by Harberger and most other previous studies. It introduces a basic inconsistency between the observed variations in price/cost margins and the assumed constant elasticities in demand, which the present study seeks to avoid. Given such problems, we have adopted the partial equilibrium framework, with all the necessary assumptions it requires (see Bergson, 1973). We present estimates for both the United States and the United Kingdom based on data gathered at the firm level.

I. THEORETICAL ANALYSIS

We have four substantive criticisms of the Harberger approach:

(1) In the partial equilibrium formula for welfare loss $\frac{1}{2}dpdq$, where dp is the change in price from competition to monopoly and dq is the change in quantity, dp and dq were considered to be independent of each other. Generally low values of dp were *observed* and low values of dq were *assumed*. In Harberger's case he assumed that price elasticities of demand in all industries were unitary. This must inevitably lead to small estimates of welfare loss.

(2) The competitive profit rate was identified with the mean profit

rate and thus automatically incorporated an element of monopoly. In fact the underlying approach was a 'constant degree of monopoly'— one in which distortions in output were associated with deviations of profit rate from the mean, rather than from the competitive return on capital.

(3) The use of industry profit rates introduces an immediate aggregation bias into the calculation by allowing the high monopoly profits of those firms with the most market power to be offset by the losses of other firms in the same industry. Given assumption (1), a further aggregation bias is introduced, which can easily be shown to result in additional downward bias in the estimates.

(4) The entire social loss due to monopoly was assumed to arise from the deviation of monopoly output from competitive levels. To this should be added the social cost of attempts to acquire monopoly positions, existing or potential.

We now seek to justify each of these four criticisms.

A. Interdependence of dp_i and dq_i

Assuming profit-maximizing behaviour we can define the implied price elasticity of demand for a specific firm by observing the mark-up of price on marginal cost:

$$\eta_i = p_i/(p_i - mc_i). \tag{1}$$

For a pure monopolist or perfectly colluding oligopolist η_i is the industry elasticity of demand. In other cases η_i reflects both the industry demand elasticity and the degree of rivals' response to a change in price the ith firm perceives (Cubbin, 1983). Using (1) we shall obtain welfare loss estimates by individual firms from their price/cost margins. These estimates indicate the amount of welfare loss associated with a single firm's decision to set price above marginal cost, given the change in its output implied by η_i.[2] To the extent other firms also charge higher prices, because firm i sets its price above marginal cost, the total welfare loss associated with firm i's market power exceeds the welfare loss we estimate. To the extent that a simultaneous reduction to zero of all price/ cost margins is contemplated, however, η_i overestimates the net effect of the reduction in p_i on the ith firm's output. What the latter effect on output and welfare would be is a matter for general equilibrium analysis and is not the focus here. Rather, we attempt an estimate of the relative importance of the distortions in individual firm outputs, on a firm by firm basis, on the assumption that each does possess some monopoly power, as implied by the price/cost margin it chooses, and uses it.

This approach emphasizing the interdependence of observed price distortions and changes in output contrasts with the methodology of

Harberger (1954), Schwartzman (1960), Worcester (1973) and Bergson (1973), who observe (or, in Bergson's case, assume) $(p_i - mc_i)/p_i$ and then *assume* a value of η_i.[3] Harberger observed generally low values of dp_i and yet chose to assume that $\eta_i = 1$, and therefore that dq_i was also very small. But, it is inconsistent to observe low values of dp_i and infer low elasticities unless one has assumed that the firm or industry cannot price as a monopolist, that is, unless one has already assumed the monopoly problem away.[4] Assuming interdependence we obtain the following definition of welfare loss:

$$dW_i = \frac{1}{2} \frac{dp_i}{p_i} \frac{dq_i}{q_i} p_i q_i, \tag{2}$$

where

$$\frac{dp_i}{p_i} = \frac{1}{\eta_i} \quad \text{and} \quad \frac{dq_i}{q_i} = \eta_i \frac{dp_i}{p_i} = 1,[5]$$

therefore

$$dW_i = \frac{dp_i}{p_i} \frac{p_i q_i}{2} \tag{3}$$

Assuming constant costs we can rewrite (3) in terms of profits:

$$dW_i = \frac{\Pi_i}{p_i q_i} \frac{p_i q_i}{2} = \frac{\Pi_i}{2}. \tag{4}$$

This formulation obviously contrasts sharply with Harberger's:

$$dW_i = \tfrac{1}{2} p_i q_i \, \eta_i t_i^2, \tag{5}$$

where

$$t = dp_i/p_i, \quad \eta_i = 1.$$

It is obvious that if t_i is small the welfare loss is going to be insignificant. If t_i were a price increase due to tariff or tax then it might be assumed to be independent of η_i,[6] and equation (5) would give a reasonable estimate of welfare loss. But where t_i is a firm decision variable, η_i and t_i must be interdependent, and formulae for calculating welfare losses should take this interdependence into account. Interesting here is the Worcester (1975) critique of Bergson for doing essentially this with his hypothetical general equilibrium calculations when Worcester himself followed the Harberger line without demure (Worcester, 1973).[7] In contrast to Harberger and Worcester, Bergson (1973) allowed himself to pick some combinations of t_i and η_i, which implied high values of welfare loss.

Harberger defended his choice of a demand elasticity of 1.0 across all products on the grounds that what was 'envisage[d was] not the substitution of one industry's product against all other products, but rather the substitution of one great aggregate of products (those yielding high rates of return) for another aggregate (those yielding low rates of return)' (p. 79). Thus, the use of $\eta = 1.0$ was an attempt at compensating for the disadvantages of employing a partial equilibrium measure of welfare loss to examine a general equilibrium structural change. But certainly this is a very awkward way of handling the problem which neither answers the criticisms raised by Bergson (1973) against the partial equilibrium approach, nor those we have just presented. For this reason we have chosen to define the partial equilibrium methodology properly and obtain the best estimates we can with this approach, recognizing that it leaves unanswered the issues raised by general equilibrium analysis and the theory of second best regarding the net effect of a simultaneous elimination of all monopoly power. We return to this point below in Subsection E.

B. The Measurement of Monopoly Profits

The obvious measure of monopoly profit is the excess of actual profits over long-run competitive returns. For an economy in equilibrium, the competitive profit rate is the minimum profit rate compatible with long-run survival, after making appropriate allowances for risk. Monopoly profit is thus the difference between actual profits and profits consistent with this minimum rate.

Harberger (1954) and all subsequent studies have based their monopoly profit estimates on the size of the deviation between actual profit rates and the mean rate. To the extent that observed profits contain elements of monopoly rent, the mean profit rate exceeds the minimum rate consistent with long-run survival. The deviations between profit rates above the mean and the mean rate underestimate the level of monopoly returns, and the estimate of monopoly welfare is biased downwards.[8] Indeed, if all firms and industries were in long-run equilibrium, all would earn profits equal to or greater than the minimum and the use of deviations from the mean would minimize the size of the measured monopoly profits.

It is unreasonable to assume that the time periods investigated in Harberger's study, the others which followed, or our own, are long enough or stable enough so that all firms and industries are in equilibrium. The presence of firms earning profits less than the competitive norm creates a methodological problem for a study of monopoly welfare losses. All studies to date have implicitly assumed that a monopolist's costs are the same as those of a firm in competitive equilibrium, and that all welfare loss is from the loss of consumers' surplus from a monopoly price above marginal cost. But, what is the appropriate assumption to make for a firm experiencing losses? It seems unrealistic to assume that its costs are at competitive levels and its prices below them. More reasonable seems the assumption that these firms are in disequilibrium, probably with costs currently above competitive levels.

When calculating monopoly welfare losses, therefore, we simply drop all firms (or industries where relevant) with profits below the competitive return on capital, in effect assuming that they will eventually return to a position where they are earning normal profits or disappear. In either case, they represent no long-run loss to society. (It is possible that some of these losses represent expenditures by firms hoping to secure monopoly positions from other firms in the industry, as discussed below. These losses are then part of the social costs of monopoly. We attempt to account for them in one of our welfare loss formulae.)

Previous studies, to the extent we can ascertain, have followed Harberger and treated deviations in profits below and above the mean symmetrically. That is, an industry whose profit rate was 5 per cent below the mean profit rate was considered to have created as large a welfare loss as an industry whose profits are 5 per cent above the mean.[9] Thus, these studies have not actually estimated welfare loss under monopoly using perfect competition as the standard of comparison, but have effectively compared welfare loss under the present regime with that which would exist were the degree of monopoly equalized across all firms and industries. Under their procedures, a constant degree of monopoly power, however high, would result in no welfare loss. While such an approach has some theoretical support, it raises practical difficulties. How is this elusive concept of a constant degree of monopoly defined and measured? How is such a world created without an omniscient planner or regulator? In addition, monopoly in product markets could be expected to induce distortions in factor markets. Finally, as developed below, the existence of monopoly power in product markets attracts resources to its acquisition and protection, which are part of the social cost of monopoly apart from the distortions in output accompanying it. For these reasons, and because it appears to be most directly in the spirit of the analysis, we have compared monopoly profits to competitive returns, and considered only deviations above the competitive rate when estimating welfare losses.

Following Harberger and other previous studies we have attempted to minimize the transitory component in our estimates by using averages of firm profits over several years.[10] Nevertheless, some of the companies earning profits above competitive levels in our samples are in temporary disequilibrium, and the welfare losses associated with these firms can be expected to disappear over time. Thus, our estimates of monopoly profits are a combination of both long-run monopoly profits and short-run disequilibrium profits. To the extent the time periods we have chosen are representative of the UK and US economies under 'normal' conditions, our calculations are accurate estimates of the annual losses from monopoly, both permanent and transitory, that can be expected in these countries. A further effort to eliminate the transitory monopoly components from the data would require a specification of what is meant by 'permanent' and 'transitory' monopolies. Many economists would take it for granted that in the 'long run' all monopolies are dead and thus monopoly like unemployment is a 'short-run' phenomenon. As with unemployment, the question is how serious is the problem when it exists, and how long does it last. Our paper addresses the first of these questions. A full answer to the second question is clearly beyond the scope of our essentially cross-section analysis.

C. The Aggregation Biases from Using Industry Data

Previous studies of monopoly welfare losses with the exception of Worcester (1973) used industry data at a fairly high level of aggregation. At any point in time some firms in an industry are likely to be earning profits below the competitive level. We have already discussed the methodological issues raised in a study of monopoly welfare losses by firms earning negative economic profits. If our interpretation of these firms as being in short-run disequilibrium is correct, then they should be dropped from an industry before calculating the industry's profit rate. Previous studies which have based their calculations solely on industry data have effectively combined the negative profits of some firms with the positive profits of others in estimating the welfare losses from monopoly. Thus they have implicitly assumed that the monopoly profits earned by the most profitable firms in the industry are somehow offset or mitigated by those experiencing transitory losses. But if there is a monopoly problem in an industry, it is represented by the positive rents earned by those firms with profits above the norm, and the losses of firms that are temporarily unable to compete successfully in no way alleviates the social costs arising from the monopoly positions of the other firms. The present study therefore measures monopoly welfare losses using firm level monopoly profit estimates.

A second aggregation bias is introduced into the estimates of all previous studies other than Kamerschen's (1966) through the assumption of a constant elasticity of demand across all industries. This results in the profit margin's appearance as a squared term in the welfare loss formula. The use of average firm profit margins (including firms with negative profits) implicit in the use of industry data, further biases the welfare loss estimates downwards. The extent of this bias is measured below.

D. Welfare Loss in the Acquisition of Monopoly Power

Tullock (1967) and Posner (1975) have argued that previous studies understate the social costs of monopoly by failing to recognize the costs involved in attempts to gain and retain monopoly power. These costs could take the form of investment in excess production capacity, excessive accumulation of advertising goodwill stocks, and excessive product differentiation through R and D.[11] Efforts to obtain tariff protection, patent protection and other types of preferential government treatment through campaign contributions, lobbying or bribery are parts of the social costs of the existence of monopoly as defined by Tullock and Posner. To the extent that these expenditures enter reported costs in the form of higher payments to factor owners and legitimate business expenses, firm costs in the presence of monopoly exceed costs under perfect competition. Estimates of welfare loss based on those profits remaining *net* of these expenditures *under*estimate the social cost of monopoly in two ways: first, by understating monopoly rents they understate the distortions in output monopoly produces; secondly, by failing to include these additional expenditures as part of the costs of monopoly.

Three adjustments to the usual welfare triangle measure of monopoly welfare loss are made to account for the additional expenditures to redistribute monopoly rents, monopoly power induces. First, advertising is added to monopoly profit in calculating the welfare triangle loss to allow for the understatement of monopoly profit expenditures of this type produce. Second, all of advertising is added to the welfare loss. This takes the extreme view of advertising as merely an instrument for securing market power. To the extent advertising provides useful information to consumers, this measure overstates the cost of monopoly.[12] Thirdly, all of measured, after-tax profits above the competitive cost of capital are used as the estimate of the expenditures incurred by others to obtain control of these monopoly rents. Obviously this estimate is but a first approximation. It is an underestimate, if the firm has incurred expenditures in the acquisition and maintenance of its monopoly position, which are included in current costs. It is an overstatement if actual and potential competitors can successfully collude to avoid these wasteful outlays. This type of argument can always be rebutted, however, by carrying the Tullock/Posner analysis one stage back and positing expenditures of resources to enter the potential competitor's position, and so on. The arguments that after-tax profits underestimate the additional costs associated with monopoly seem at least as reasonable as those suggesting overestimation.

E.   An Objection and Alternative Estimating Technique
The assumption that demand elasticity equals the reciprocal of the price–cost margin, equation (1), can give rise, when price–cost margins are small, to firm level elasticity estimates much greater than existing industry level estimates, and imply large increases in output from the

elimination of monopoly. This has led several observers to criticize the use of the Lerner formula, and the underlying assumption that firms set price as if they possess and utilize market power. Worcester (1969) has made the argument most forcefully.

Serious error . . . arise[s] if the 'monopolist' is only an oligopolist who fears entry, unfavourable publicity, government regulation or a weaker position at the bargaining table should profits be too high, and for such reasons prices at P_0 (Fig. 1) and sells output Q_E in spite of the fact that the marginal revenue is far below zero at that point. [1969, p. 237, note that our Figure 12.1 and Worcester's are drawn to scale.]

The elasticity of demand is lower at P_0 than at P_M, and the expansion in output following a reduction in price to competitive price P_C is obviously much smaller if we assume the 'monopolist' sets price equal to P_0. Thus Worcester's depiction of the problem does meet the objections many have raised against the use of the Lerner formula to estimate demand elasticities. We observe only that if one assumes from the start that 'monopolists' are so constrained in their behaviour that they must set price so low that marginal revenue is negative, it can be no surprise that calculations incorporating this assumption indicate insignificant welfare losses. But any estimates of welfare losses within a partial equilibrium

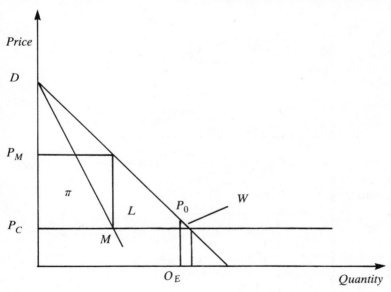

Figure 12.1: π, *Monopoly profit rectangle; L, deadweight loss assuming firm exercises monopoly power; W, Worcester's proposed deadweight loss*

framework, which impose demand elasticities significantly below those implied via the Lerner formula, must implicitly be assuming that firms set price in such an environment, if the data on price–cost margins are accepted at face value.

The latter assumption may not be valid, however, and its abandonment allows a reconciliation of existing profit-margin data with lower demand elasticity figures without also introducing the assumption that monopolists are either irrational or impotent. The preceding section discusses several business outlays that are made to maintain or preserve monopoly positions. Conceptually these are best treated as *investments* out of current profits made to secure future monopoly rents than as current production costs as is done for accounting purposes, and is carried through into the economist's calculations based on accounting data. A rational monopolist will not take these into account in making his short-run pricing decision. We can thus reconcile the monopoly pricing assumption with small demand elasticity estimates by assuming that average costs contain much investment-type expenditure and that marginal production costs are below these.

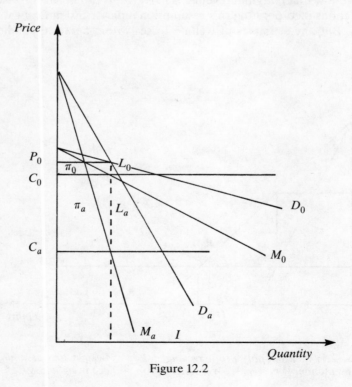

Figure 12.2

In Figure 12.2 let C_0 be observed costs, including investment-type outlays, and P_0 observed price. For such price and cost figures to be consistent with monopoly pricing behaviour the firm's demand schedule would have to be D_0. Price P_0 would be consistent with a much more inelastic demand schedule, D_a say, if actual production costs were at C_a. Note that both profits (π), and the welfare triangle losses (L) are much larger under the more inelastic demand schedule assumption.

Thus, an alternative procedure for calculating the welfare losses from monopoly to the one described above would be to estimate price–cost margins from data on demand elasticities, where now we estimate demand elasticities from data on price–cost margins. We do not pursue these calculations here. First, because we do not have demand elasticity data applicable to firms, and the imposition of any constant η across all firms is obviously *ad hoc*. Secondly, the choice of any η in line with existing industry estimates would lead to welfare loss estimates far greater than those calculated here. The highest of the elasticities used in previous studies has been $\eta = 2.0$. This implies a profit margin of 50 per cent and a welfare triangle loss equal to one-quarter of sales. These estimates exceed those reported here, whenever the firm's profits are *less* than one-half of sales. Since this is true for all our firms, our welfare loss estimates are all smaller than under the alternative procedure.

We believe that reported costs do contain large amounts of investment-type expenditures beyond the advertising we allow for, that production costs are lower therefore, and that individual firm demand elasticities are typically lower than we implicitly estimate. We emphasize, however, that any attempt to take these costs into account, and adjust demand elasticities accordingly, while maintaining the assumption that companies do possess and exercise market power, will lead to larger estimates of welfare loss underlining again the conservative nature of our calculations.

II. EMPIRICAL ESTIMATES

Empirical estimates of the social cost of monopoly power were obtained for both the United States and United Kingdom. We provide two sets of estimates, one based on our assumptions ($\triangle W_{CM}^k$), the other based on Harberger-type assumptions ($\triangle W_H^k$), both measured at the firm level. For each approach we give a range of four estimates defined in Table 12.1.

Thus for $k = 1$ we define two alternative estimates of the welfare triangle, the one ($\triangle W_{CM}^1$) based on interdependence of dp_i and dq_i, the other ($\triangle W_H^1$) based on the Harberger methodology. This latter estimate is included for comparison with previous results especially from the viewpoint of bias due to aggregation. For $k = 2$, the same calculations are performed but in calculating dp_i advertising expenditure (A_i) is deducted from cost. For $k = 3$ we add in advertising expenditure as a social cost, and for $k = 4$ we also add in monopoly profits *after tax* as a further element of social cost. It should be noted at this point that in calculating dp_i the appropriate measure is *before-tax* profit since the price and quantity choice of a monopolist should not be affected by a tax on profits. Thus, in contrast to most previous studies, we use before-tax profits to measure the distortion between price and costs under monopoly (the $\triangle W$'s for $k = 1, 2, 3$). However, it is *after-tax* monopoly profits which provide an inducement to additional expenditures to gain monopoly, and it is these that are added in to obtain our fourth measure of welfare loss.

Table 12.1 *Alternative definitions of social cost*

k	$\triangle W_{CM}^{k}$	$\triangle W_{H}^{k}$
1	$\Pi/2$	$(R/2)\,[\Pi/R]^2$
2	$(\Pi+A)/2$	$(R/2)\,[(\Pi+A)/R]^2$
3	$A+(\Pi+A)/2$	$(R/2)\,[(\Pi+A)/R]^2+A$
4	$\Pi'+A+(\Pi+A)/2$	$(R/2)\,[(\Pi+A)/R]^2+A+\Pi'$

Π, before-tax profit; Π', after-tax profit; A, advertising; R, total revenue.

To estimate monopoly profits an estimate of the return on capital of a firm in a competitive industry is needed. Any estimates based on actual returns earned in existing industries run the danger of including monopoly rents. The stock market might be regarded as coming fairly close to satisfying the free-entry and -exit requirement of a competitive industry, however. The returns on corporate stock will include monopoly rents to the extent that they become capitalized over the period for which the rate is estimated. The use of these returns for the United States is therefore equivalent to assuming that (1) all existing monopoly rents are fully capitalized at the beginning of the period, and (2) changes in monopoly rents over the period are accurately anticipated.

For the United States we use as our estimate of the competitive return on capital the Fisher–Lorie index of returns on a fully diversified portfolio of listed stocks for the same period for which our monopoly profit estimates are made (1963–6). This estimate was 12 per cent which might be compared with the average return on capital earned by the firms in our sample of 14 per cent.

For the United Kingdom we use the pre-tax real cost of capital as calculated by Flemming *et al.* (1976). These estimates avoid the newly capitalized monopoly rent problem mentioned above entirely. For the 1968/9 period they yield an estimate of the cost of capital of 8.15 per cent.[13]

The firms in our samples include companies operating in both intermediate and final goods markets. To justify the addition of triangular-type measures of welfare loss for final and intermediate products, we must assume that the demand schedule for an intermediate product represents a derived demand schedule as in traditional Marshallian analysis. Under this assumption, triangular measures of welfare loss calculated from intermediate product demand schedules fully capture the loss in consumer welfare monopoly distortions in the intermediate markets cause, as Wisecarver (1974) has recently demonstrated. Assuming advertising and other efforts to obtain monopoly power are as wasteful when undertaken in intermediate markets as in final goods markets, the formulae presented in Table 12.1 can be applied for both intermediate and final good producers.

A. US Estimates

The range of welfare loss estimates for the United States are presented in Table 12.2. They refer to the 1963–6 period and the sample comprises the 734 firms on the COMPUSTAT tape with usable information.[14] The firms are ranked according to the size of welfare loss as measured by $\triangle W^4_{CM}$. General Motors leads the list with an annual welfare loss of over $1¾ billion, which alone is over one-quarter of 1 per cent of average GNP during the period, and exceeds Harberger's original welfare loss estimate for the entire economy. Most of the other members of the top twenty are names one also might have expected. One possible exception is AT & T. AT & T's gross profit rate was, in fact, less than our estimate of the cost of capital (≈ 0.12). Its advertising entry on the COMPUSTAT tape (and in this case we did have a COMPUSTAT figure, see appendix) was $¾ billion, and it is AT & T's advertising which leads to the high $\triangle W^4_{CM}$ estimate we have for it. Advertising also weighs heavily in the $\triangle W^4_{CM}$ estimates for Unilever, Proctor and Gamble, Sears Roebuck, Genesco, Colgate–Palmolive, Pan Am and Pacific Tel. At first sight this might seem surprising, particularly with respect to regulated firms like AT & T and Pacific Tel. But, as Posner (1975) has argued, this is precisely what one expects to find in industries with high market power, and, as Posner himself stresses, firms under regulatory constraint can be expected to engage, if anything, in more wasteful dissipation of their monopoly rents than non-regulated firms through expenditures like advertising. It is interesting to note in this regard that six of the forty largest welfare losses are accounted for by regulated firms (three telephone companies and three airlines) in which advertising made up all or most of the losses.

At the bottom of Table 12.2 the losses are summed over the firms with positive profit margins as defined for the $\triangle W^1$ and $\triangle W^2$ measures (see table notes), and then expressed as a proportion of our estimate of the

Table 12.2   Monopoly welfare losses by firm (yearly averages in $ millions): US 1963/6

Company	ΔW_{CM}^1	ΔW_{CM}^2	ΔW_{CM}^3	ΔW_{CM}^4	ΔW_H^1	ΔW_H^2	ΔW_H^3	ΔW_H^4
1. General Motors	1,060.5	1,156.3	1,347.8	1,780.3	123.4	146.2	337.8	770.2
2. AT&T	0.0	257.3	1,025.0	1,025.0	0.0	13.4	781.1	781.1
3. Unilever	0.0	160.0	490.5	490.5	0.0	19.5	350.0	350.0
4. Procter & Gamble	56.7	180.1	427.0	427.0	3.3	33.0	279.9	279.2
5. Dupont	225.1	241.9	275.4	375.3	36.3	41.7	75.2	175.2
6. Ford Motor	160.4	217.5	331.7	331.7	5.2	9.3	123.5	123.5
7. IBM	251.7	264.0	288.7	319.8	36.8	40.5	65.2	96.3
8. Reynolds, R.J.	73.1	138.5	269.3	278.8	10.8	38.5	169.3	178.8
9. Sears Roebuck	36.2	115.0	272.5	272.5	0.5	4.4	162.0	162.0
10. Eastman Kodak	136.3	157.9	201.1	258.5	27.7	36.8	80.0	137.4
11. American Cyanamid Co.	27.6	98.7	240.8	240.8	1.9	23.6	165.8	165.8
12. Genesco, Inc.	0.0	67.5	202.6	202.6	0.0	14.9	150.0	150.0
13. Exxon Corp.	115.6	143.0	197.8	197.8	2.4	3.7	58.5	58.5
14. Colgate-Palmolive Co.	3.9	56.7	160.3	160.3	0.0	7.6	111.8	111.8
15. Chrysler Corp.	39.8	78.4	155.5	155.5	1.1	3.0	80.1	80.1
16. General Electric Co.	83.4	105.2	148.8	148.8	2.6	4.0	47.6	47.6
17. Pan Am Airways	1.1	49.8	147.2	147.2	0.1	7.5	104.9	104.9
18. Pacific Tel. & Tel.	0.0	18.4	138.1	138.1	0.0	0.8	128.5	128.5
19. Gillette Co.	27.8	56.0	112.3	129.2	4.7	18.9	75.3	92.2
20. Minnesota Mining & Mfg.	62.5	77.7	107.1	129.1	8.2	12.6	42.3	64.3
Totals all firms[a]	4,527.1	7,454.9	14,005.4	14,997.6[b]	448.2	897.8	7,448.3	8,440.1[c]
Total/GCP[c]	0.0396	0.0652	0.1227	0.13137	0.0040	0.0079	0.0652	0.0739

[a] The ΔW^1's for all firms having monopoly profits (II) less than zero were set equal to zero. The ΔW^2, ΔW^3, and ΔW^4's for all firms with (II+A)<0 were set equal to zero. The latter was based on the assumption that these firms would not survive in the long run and hence represent no *long-run* welfare loss to society. There are 421 firms with II > 0 and 525 firms with (II+A) > 0 in the sample of 734 firms.

[b] When profits, after deducting taxes and the cost of capital (II'), are less than zero, $\Delta W^4 = \Delta W^3$.

[c] The total welfare loss for all firms by each ΔW measure is first divided by the total sales of the 734 firms in the sample, and then multiplied by the ratio of corporate sales to gross corporate product over all industries (2.873) as given in Laffer (1969)

Gross Corporate Product originating in the 734 firms in the sample. It should be stressed here, again, that the totals do not represent the estimated gains from the simultaneous elimination of all monopoly power. The answer to this question could be obtained only via a general equilibrium analysis. What we estimate via our partial equilibrium analysis is the relative cost of monopoly for each firm, and the column totals present average estimates of these costs for our sample of firms. Note, however, that the *additions* to our cost estimates that occur in moving from the W_{CM}^2 to the W_{CM}^3 and W_{CM}^4 columns do sum across all firms, since these are estimates of the wasted expenditures made in pursuit of monopoly. If we see product market power as a ubiquitous characteristic of the economy, then it might be reasonable to assume that this estimate of monopoly welfare loss could be generalized to the entire economy. To the extent one believes monopoly power is more (e.g. see again Posner, 1975) or less pervasive in other sectors our estimates must be raised or lowered. Assuming the social costs of monopoly are the same across all sectors, we obtain estimates for our preferred model ($\triangle W_{CM}^k$) ranging between 4 and 13 per cent of GCP. Thus, all losses are significant, but the range is considerable depending upon what components of social cost one includes. For the Harberger approach, the range is between 0.4 and 7 per cent. The lowest of these follows the Harberger assumptions most closely, but nevertheless we estimate a welfare loss four times as big as he did. This difference in large part is explained by the aggregation bias incorporated into the industry level estimates.

The extent of this bias can be seen by considering Table 12.3. Its entries are made by assigning each firm to an industry at the appropriate level of aggregation and aggregating over the firms in each industry. Just as negative profit firms were excluded in calculating welfare losses at the firm level, negative profit industries are excluded in calculating welfare losses across industries. For the $\triangle W_{CM}^k$ measures aggregation bias is due simply to the inclusion of losses by some firms in the calculation of each industry's profits. Table 12.3 shows how this bias varies with the level of aggregation and with the choice of measure. Industry estimates are between 78 and 98 per cent of the firm level estimates in aggregate. For the $\triangle W_H^k$ estimates, a further cause of bias is introduced by the squared term, $(\Pi/R)^2$, in the formula. It can be seen from Table 12.3 that for the $\triangle W_H^1$ measures, the two-digit industry estimates aggregate to only 40 per cent of the firm level estimates.[15] Note, however, that the biases are much smaller for the $\triangle W^3$ and $\triangle W^4$ measures and in the case of the $\triangle W_H^3$ measure at the four-digit level the bias goes slightly the other way. This comes about because of the inclusion in the industry estimates of advertising for firms earning less than normal profits. Thus in future work along these lines, when data are limited to industry level observations, the

Table 12.3 *Comparison of firm and industry welfare loss estimates: US 1963/6*

	ΔW^1_{CM}	ΔW^2_{CM}	ΔW^3_{CM}	ΔW^4_{CM}	ΔW^1_H	ΔW^2_H	ΔW^3_H	ΔW^4_H
1. Summation over firms	4,527.1	7,454.9	14,005.4	14,997.6	448.2	897.8	7,448.3	8,440.1
2. Summation over 4-digit industries	3,767.8	6,902.5	13,752.6	14,052.8	276.9	628.8	7,478.9	7,790.2
3. Summation over 3-digit industries	3,619.0	6,680.5	13,355.4	13,512.8	237.4	577.7	7,252.5	7,410.4
4. Summation over 2-digit industries	3,515.2	6,634.5	13,262.7	13,287.9	178.9	485.3	7,113.5	7,148.8
5. (2)/(1)	0.832	0.926	0.982	0.937	0.618	0.700	1.004	0.923
6. (3)/(1)	0.799	0.896	0.954	0.901	0.530	0.643	0.974	0.878
7. (4)/(1)	0.776	0.890	0.947	0.886	0.399	0.541	0.955	0.847

Table 12.4   *Monopoly welfare losses by firm (£ million): UK 1968/9*

Company	ΔW_{CM}^1	ΔW_{CM}^2	ΔW_{CM}^3	ΔW_{CM}^4	ΔW_H^1	ΔW_H^2	ΔW_H^3	ΔW_H^4
1. British Petroleum	74.1	74.4	75.1	82.7	5.1	5.1	5.8	13.4
2. Shell Transport & Trading	49.4	50.8	53.6	53.6	2.2	2.3	5.1	5.1
3. British American Tobacco	26.8	27.0	27.5	49.1	1.0	1.1	1.6	23.1
4. Unilever	2.8	11.3	28.2	29.0	0.0	0.2	17.2	18.0
5. I.C.I.	17.6	18.8	21.1	27.9	0.5	0.5	2.9	9.6
6. Rank Xerox	13.9	14.0	14.2	27.5	3.4	3.4	3.5	16.9
7. IBM (UK)	11.1	11.2	11.3	21.9	2.2	2.2	2.4	12.9
8. Great Universal Stores	9.6	10.0	11.0	21.6	0.5	0.5	1.5	12.1
9. Beecham	6.2	8.9	14.3	20.4	0.6	1.3	6.7	12.8
10. Imperial Group	2.8	8.6	20.1	20.1	0.0	0.1	11.7	11.7
11. Marks & Spencer	9.8	9.8	9.8	18.6	0.6	0.6	0.6	9.5
12. Ford	7.2	7.8	8.8	16.6	0.2	0.2	1.3	9.1
13. F. W. Woolworth	7.3	7.4	7.8	15.9	0.3	0.4	0.7	8.9
14. J. Lyon	0.0	0.7	2.8	14.2	0.0	0.0	2.1	13.4
15. Burmah	5.3	5.5	5.9	13.9	0.2	0.3	0.7	8.7
16. Distillers	5.6	6.1	7.1	13.4	0.2	0.2	1.2	7.5
17. Rank Organization	11.5	11.7	12.1	12.5	1.2	1.2	1.7	2.1
18. Thorn	5.6	6.1	7.1	12.5	0.3	0.3	1.4	6.7
19. Cadbury Schweppes	1.8	5.0	11.4	12.3	0.0	0.3	6.7	7.6
20. Reckitt & Colman	2.9	4.7	8.3	10.4	0.1	0.3	3.9	6.0
Totals all firms (102)	385.8	435.0	537.4	719.3	21.4	24.2	118.8	304.4
Total ÷ GCP	0.0386	0.0436	0.0539	0.0720	0.0021	0.0024	0.0119	0.0305

No. of firms with II>0=82.
No. of firms with II+A>0=86.

$\triangle W^3$ and $\triangle W^4$ measures have an additional advantage over the other two measures.

B. UK Estimates

These have been calculated on the same basis as the US estimates but since no convenient computer tape was available we contented ourselves with an analysis of the top 103 firms in the United Kingdom for the periods 1968/9 and 1970/4.[16] Over the periods in question these firms were responsible for roughly one-third of the GNP and were therefore proportionally more important than the 734 firms sample from the COMPUSTAT tape for the United States. The time periods used have been dictated by the availability of data. The basic source has been EXTEL cards but advertising expenditure was estimated by aggregating up from the brand level, using estimates of press and TV advertising contained in MEAL. We can therefore expect that our advertising expenditure figures will be biased down by the amount of non-media advertising, as is true also for the United States. Table 12.4 gives the results for 1968/9, with firms again being ranked by $\triangle W^4_{CM}$. The two major oil companies, BP and Shell, dominate the table. The social cost associated with BP alone is roughly a quarter of 1 per cent of GNP. The other members of the Top Ten are industry leaders plus British–American Tobacco. Two interesting features of the Top Twenty are the high ranking of Rank Xerox despite its size (explained presumably by its UK patent rights) and, in contrast to the United States, the low ranking of motor-car manufacturers (absent from the Top Twenty in 1970/4). We have computed estimates of welfare loss for the 1970/4 period, but we have not reported these results here. It is well known that the early seventies was a period of very rapid inflation in the United Kingdom and this undoubtedly raises problems such as how to account for stock appreciation and the revaluation of capital adequately. Despite these problems, it is somewhat reassuring to note that the 1970–4 results look very much like the 1968/9 results except that the oil companies become even more dominant.[17]

The aggregate estimates of welfare loss for $\triangle W^k_{CM}$ range between 3.9 and 7.2 per cent of GCP for the 1968/9 period. The estimate for $\triangle W^1_{CM}$ is almost identical with that for the United States but in each of the other cases the value for the United Kingdom is well below that for the United States. The obvious and important difference between the two sets of results is the apparent greater expenditure on advertising in the United States. Taking direct account of advertising quadruples the welfare loss estimate for the United States but in the case of the United Kingdom welfare loss goes up only about 40 per cent (compare $\triangle W^1_{CM}$ with $\triangle W^3_{CM}$).[18] Using the Harberger approach estimates of welfare loss vary between 0.2 and 3 per cent of GCP for the United Kingdom in the same 1968/9 period.

Again, we must conclude that our evidence suggests significant welfare loss due to monopoly power. One other point is also brought out particularly by the UK results (e.g. in the case of the oil companies) and that is the international distribution of these social costs. Monopoly power held by UK companies in foreign markets may be advantageous to the UK economy whilst being disadvantageous in the global sense. Thus the issue is a distributional one and adds an international dimension to the distributional issues already implicit in our analysis. In any national evaluation of the social costs imposed by the actions of a particular company, the international distribution of these costs would presumably gain some prominence.

III. IMPLICATIONS AND CONCLUSIONS

Previous studies of the social costs of monopoly have generally (and often unconsciously) assumed that 'monopolies' set prices as if they did not possess market power, that the only important distortions in output are brought about through the deviations in one firm's market power from the average level of market power, that the losses of some firms (perhaps incurred in unsuccessful attempts to obtain monopoly power) legitimately offset the monopoly rents of others, and that all of the expenditures made in the creation and preservation of monopoly positions are part of the normal costs which would exist in a world without monopolies. With the problem so defined, it is not surprising that most of these studies have found the welfare losses from monopoly to be small.

Since we know from general equilibrium analysis that monopoly allocation distortions may be offsetting, the conclusion that partial equilibrium analysis yields small welfare loss estimates has seemed all the more impressive. Yet each of the studies that has come up with low estimates has done so in large part because it has made assumptions (e.g. demand elasticities equal to 1.0, monopoly profits are deviations from mean profits) that can be rationalized only as *ad hoc* attempts to answer the general equilibrium question. In contrast, the present study defines a procedure for estimating the costs of monopoly that is consistent with a partial equilibrium analysis that assumes market power does (or may) exist. Our results reveal that the costs of monopoly power, calculated on an individual firm basis, are on average large. The conclusion that 'even' a partial equilibrium analysis of monopoly indicates that its costs are insignificant no longer seems warranted.

This conclusion has potentially important policy implications.

Antitrust policy consists typically not of a frontal attack on all existing market power, but of selective assaults on the most flagrant offenders. Our partial equilibrium estimates of monopoly welfare losses indicate the most significant contributors to these losses. The tops of our lists of the largest welfare losses by firm are logical starting points for intensified enforcement of antitrust policy. Our figures and supporting analysis further demonstrate that 'the monopoly problem' is broader than traditionally suggested. A large part of this problem lies not in the height of monopoly prices and profits *per se*, but in the resources wasted in their creation and protection. These costs of monopoly should be considered when selecting targets for antitrust enforcement.

One might argue that the high profits of some firms reflect economies of scale advantages, and, therefore, these firms should not be the victims of antitrust policy. This argument points to some form of regulatory or public enterprise solution to the monopoly problem. With respect to this type of policy, our estimates of the losses from monopoly represent a still further understatement of their potential magnitude. If a policy were adopted forcing the most efficient size or organizational structure upon the entire industry, the welfare loss under the existing structure would have to be calculated using the profit margin of the most efficient *firm and the output of the entire industry*, rather than the profit margins of the individual firms and their outputs.

These considerations suggest the difficulty in estimating the social gains from the elimination of all monopoly power, since one almost has to know what form of policy is to be used (antitrust, regulation), and what the underlying cause of monopoly power is, before answering this question. Nevertheless, this has been the question that has traditionally been asked in studies of monopoly welfare losses, and the reader who has persisted to this point can justifiably ask what light our figures cast on this question. By their very nature partial equilibrium calculations cannot give very *precise* estimates of these gains, but they may establish orders of magnitude. As stressed above, we regard the Harberger-type calculations based on uniform demand elasticities of 1.0 as essentially efforts to solve the general equilibrium problem inherent in this question. As such, we regard them as the most conservative estimates of what the elimination of all monopoly would produce. Thus, we would expect the elimination of all monopoly to yield gains at least as large as the 7 and 3 per cent of gross corporate product we estimate for the United States and United Kingdom, respectively, using $\triangle W_H^4$. To the extent that firms sell differentiated products, and operate in separate markets, that is, to the extent that they have and utilize market power, these gains are pushed in the direction of our $\triangle W_{CM}^4$ estimates of 13 and 7 per cent. Further upward pressure on these estimates is created by considering some of the other factors ignored in our calculations. We have already emphasized that reported profits understate true profits to the extent that firms compete for monopoly power by investing in excess plant capacity, advertising, patent lawyers, and so on. But much of the competition for *control* over monopoly rents may take place within the firm itself among the factor owners. Such competition will lead to an understatement of actual monopoly rents both through the inflation of costs that wasteful competition among factors owners brings about, and through the inclusion of part of the winning factor owners' shares of monopoly rents as reported costs. A large literature now exists on the variety of objectives managers have and the ways in which these objectives are satisfied through their discretionary control over company revenues. To the extent that managerial control over firm revenues is the reward for competing against other factor groups and potential managers successfully, reported profits understate the true profitability. By ignoring these possibilities we have erred in being conservative when estimating the social cost of monopoly. It is our reasoned guess that these additional costs would at least equal the 'washing out' effect of the simultaneous elimination of all monopoly power on our partial equilibrium estimates and, therefore, that these latter figures are, if anything, underestimates of the true social costs of monopoly.

In this respect, it is useful to note an alternative, aggregative approach to the question. Phillips, in an appendix to Baran and Sweezy (1966), isolated several categories of expenditure dependent on the existence of 'Monopoly Capitalism' (e.g. advertising, corporate profits, lawyers' fees). Their sum came to over 50 per cent of US GNP. Although the assumptions upon which these calculations were made are rather extreme, they do suggest both an alternative method of analysis and the potential magnitude of the problem. Here too it should be noted that our approach has been essentially micro-orientated and neoclassical in that we have taken the returns on corporate stocks as our cost of capital. From a more aggregative view it could be argued that profits are not required at all to generate the savings required to sustain a given rate of growth, since alternative macro policies are available. From this perspective, all profits are excess profits and our estimates of social cost are too conservative. Still further weight would be added against the position that monopoly power is unimportant if the link with the distribution of political power were considered.

Of course, any public policy has its own sets of costs and inefficiencies. For Tullock–Posner reasons a concerted effort to apply or strengthen the antitrust laws induces large, defensive expenditures on the part of business. Price and profit regulation leads to efforts to change, influence, or circumvent the application of the rules. The public enterprise solution raises the same sort of problems, with members of the bureaucracy participating in the competition for monopoly rents. Thus it might be that any alternative for dealing with existing monopoly power would involve higher costs than the monopolies themselves create. The present study does not answer this question. What it does do is dispel the notion that it need not even be asked, since the costs of monopoly within the present environment are necessarily small. The question of what the costs and benefits from alternative antimonopoly policies are still seems worth asking.

APPENDIX
DATA: DEFINITIONS AND SOURCES

United States

All data on individual firms with one exception were taken from the COMPUSTAT tape of 1969, and all definitions conform therefore to those given in the COMPUSTAT manual. The numbers in brackets { } refer to the variable numbers assigned on the COMPUSTAT annual industrial file.

The competitive return on capital used in calculating monopoly profits was 0.1197, the geometric mean of the monthly Fisher–Lorie index of returns on the market portfolio between January 1963 and December 1967. The firm's capital was measured as Total Assets/Liabilities and Net Worth less Intangibles (goodwill, patents, etc.). The latter were deducted on the grounds that they largely represent capitalized monopoly rents (see Kamerschen, 1966; Stigler, 1956). Thus, the firm's opportunity cost of capital was estimated as:

$$CC = 0.1197\,(DATA\,\{6\} - DATA\,\{33\}).$$

Two estimates of monopoly profits were formed to compute the triangle-type measures. The first is gross profit flow (net income+interest expense+income taxes) less the cost of capital (CC).

$$\Pi = DATA\,\{18\} + DATA\,\{15\} + DATA\,\{16\} - CC.$$

The second is the first plus advertising ($A = DATA\,\{45\}$). For roughly 85% of the sample firms the COMPUSTAT entry for advertising was missing, however. The product of the firm's sales ($DATA\,\{12\}$) and the industry advertising to sales ratio for the firm's industry as given in *Advertising Age* (7 June 1965, pp. 101–3) was substituted for this entry in these cases.

To calculate the $\triangle W^4$ measures, income taxes (*DATA* {16}) were subtracted from II to obtain II'.

United Kingdom

All the data on individual firms with the exception of advertising has its origin in the data tabulations of the Exchange Telegraph Statistics Service (EXTEL). Most of the relevant data in a summarized form was available in various issues of *The Times Review of Industry and Technology*. In the case of advertising the firm data had to be estimated via a process of aggregating estimates of press and TV advertising of the various products produced by each firm. These data were extracted from various issues of *MEAL* (*Advertisers' Annual Analysis of Media Expenditure*) and, in the case of 1968, from the *Statistical Review of Press and TV Advertising* (Legion Publishing Company). *Who Owns Whom* was used in the process of aggregation.

Each firm's capital was measured as total tangible assets less current liabilities (excluding bank loans, overdrafts and future tax). Profit was measured before interest and tax and then adjusted for the estimated cost of capital (taken from Flemming *et al.*, 1976).

NOTES

1. In addition to the points Bergson (1973) raises in his own defence, we have serious objections to the arguments made by Carson (1975) and Worcester (1975). Some of these are presented below in our critique of previous studies.
2. We need here an assumption of perfect competition everywhere else, of course. We shall ignore problems of the second best, along with the general equilibrium issue more generally, throughout the paper.
3. The Harberger and Schwartzman estimates are at the industry level.
4. This position is questioned by Wenders (1967) and others who attempt to show how implausible the implied η_i's are. However, their calculations are erroneous because they fail to recognize that (a) the degree of collusion is a variable—we need not assume perfect joint profit maximization and (b) that entry is conditional on the same variables (plus others) that determine $(p_i - mc_i)/p_i$, for example η, the degree of concentration and, for differentiated products, advertising also.
5. This is true so long as the firm is in equilibrium, i.e. that the firms' expectations about the behaviour of rivals are actually borne out. If this were not the case then the elasticity on which the pricing decision was made would not correspond to the elasticity implied by the change in output. We assume firm equilibrium in our calculations.
6. But not necessarily so. Taxes and tariffs may be applied according to elasticity expectations.
7. Worcester (1975) also offers some empirical support. His collection of industry price elasticities is either irrelevant (including many agricultural

products and few manufacturing ones) or suspect (no allowance having been made in the studies quoted for quality change over time), and is certainly not comprehensive.

8. Worcester (1973) makes some allowance for this bias by using 90% of the median profit rate, but this adjustment is obviously rather *ad hoc*.

9. One might believe that the losses by firms earning profits below the norm represent a form of *factor surplus loss* which must be added to the consumer surplus loss to obtain the full losses from monopoly. But, as Worcester (1973) has shown, these factor-surplus losses, if properly measured, are *an alternative way* of estimating the consumer surplus losses and should be used *instead of* the consumer surplus measure, rather than in addition to it, if used at all.

10. Harberger chose five years of 'normal' business activity in the 1920s for his original study of the United States. Following his lead we have chosen four years in the 1960s for the US estimates falling between a recession and the Vietnam War boom. The results reported below for the United Kingdom are for only two years, 1968/9. The UK results for 1970/4 indicate that averaging profits over five years does not change the nature of the outcome.

11. *See* Spence (1977). It is interesting to note that this type of activity generally dominates the entry-limiting pricing response. Entry-limiting pricing can be thought of as having extra capacity because of potential entry and actually using it to produce output. Thus the profits associated with restricting output are lost. From this viewpoint we cannot accept Posner's position that the elimination of entry regulation would eliminate waste. As the probability of entry increases so would the optimal degree of excess capacity. Monopoly pricing would be maintained but social waste would still occur.

12. There will always be an inherent bias in the information provided given the interests of the agent doing the advertising so the argument for advertising as a provider of information should not be taken too seriously. Even if we base our welfare measures on post-advertising preferences it is still possible to demonstrate that monopolies (and *a fortiori* oligopolies) invest in too much advertising (*see* Dixit and Norman, 1978).

13. It may be argued that because of inflation we are undervaluing land or capital. This would not be a serious problem for the United States since our data follow a period of quite modest price increases. Given that inflation in the United Kingdom in 1968/9 was substantial, although very much less than in the seventies, we have corrected our data at the company level. Using data from Walker (1974), we multiplied the profit figure derived from the company accounts by the ratio of the average rate of return at replacement cost to the average rate of return at historical cost and subtracted from this the estimated book value of assets times the cost of capital. The ratio of rates of return used was 9.4:13.4 in 1968 and 8.2:12.4 in 1969. We should in fact be using the ratio of the rate of return at replacement cost to the rate of return at book value but the latter rate was not available on a comparable basis (*see* Walker, 1974, Table 3). This means that our measure of excess profits and therefore of welfare loss will tend to be biased down, given that (a) asset revaluations generally take place at merger, when acquired assets are given a current market valuation, and (b) revaluations, of land and buildings especially, do take place periodically, their frequency being related to the rate of inflation. The cost of capital measure used was the forward-looking, pre-tax measure which was estimated at 8.15% for the period 1968/9 (Flemming *et al.*, 1976).

14. The COMPUSTAT tape contains data on a sample of large firms, mostly in manufacturing, listed on US stock exchanges. The data definitions used in making the estimates are discussed in the appendix.
15. Worcester (1973) plays down the extent of the bias by focusing on the *absolute* differences between the measures. Given that the absolute values of losses are small using $\triangle W_H^1$, even very large relative biases result in small absolute distortions, as one would expect. For additional evidence on the importance of aggregation bias in previous studies, *see* Siegfried and Tiemann (1974).
16. The top 100 varies somewhat over time.
17. Indeed, comparing the results for the two periods indicates the large extent to which oil companies have benefited from the recent 'oil crisis'. However, this inference has to be qualified by the problems raised for the measurement of profit by stock appreciation during a period of rapid inflation of oil prices.
18. This does not of course mean that advertising implies no additional social costs, since profit margins and the level of excess profits may both be partly determined by advertising in so far as elasticities of demand and entry barriers are influenced by the level of advertising in monopolistic industries. We should also note that in some cases our direct adjustment for advertising is very significant (e.g. Unilever, Imperial Group and Beecham Group).

13 The Persistence of Profits Above the Norm*

In an efficient market economy, profits above or below the norm should quickly disappear. Although uncertainty, innovations and changes in tastes can lead to gains or losses for given firms or industries, the flow of resources into activities earning excess profits and the flow of resources from activities earning less-than-normal profits should bring all returns back to competitive levels. If this process is relatively quick, the appearance of gains and losses has the useful function of signalling the direction of movement required to satisfy consumer demand. If the process is slow, however, the persistence of positions of excess profits (or losses) indicates only the occurrence of a continual misallocation of resources.

Despite the importance of persistent excess profits in evaluating the efficiency of a market system, this question has received relatively little empirical attention. The most notable exception is the work of Yale Brozen (1970, 1971a,b). Brozen has attacked the widely held position that high profits are associated with high concentration and entry barriers by arguing that the above-average returns other studies have found are a disequilibrium phenomenon (see also McEnally, 1976; Winn and Leabo, 1974). There are several problems with Brozen's position. There must almost certainly be some tendency for relatively high profits to fall and low profits to rise. But can we expect high profits to fall to competitive levels, and how long must we wait? On these questions Brozen presents little direct evidence, and the evidence he does present has been contested (Wenders, 1971a,b).

I. FOCUS AND HYPOTHESES

The main difference between the present study and previous examinations of the question is the use of profit rate data for individual

*Helpful suggestions for improving this chapter were received from John Cable, Henry Grabowski, and William Shepherd. Valuable assistance in making the empirical computations was provided by Gerald Nelson and Jonathan Palfrey. Reprinted from *Economica*, **44**, November 1977.

firms. Most previous studies have based their conclusions on industry aggregates. This was natural in Brozen's work, since the focus of his attack was the *industry* concentration–profit relationship. But, once the persistence of excess profits issue is separated from the role of concentration in creating profits, there is no compelling reason to focus on industry data. The existence of a firm with profits continually above average presents the same potential allocational inefficiencies as are thought to exist when industry profits remain high.

In addition, there are several reasons why data on individual firms may be preferable. The traditional focus on industry data in industrial organization stems from an implicit assumption that all products are homogeneous, so that definitions of the market, barriers to entering the market and concentration within the market, all have unambiguous meanings. In such a world, the appearance of profits above competitive rates of return is a good indication that prices are above marginal costs, and their disappearance is a good indication of expanding output and falling prices. When important product differentiation exists, however, all of this is changed. The definitions of markets, concentration levels and entry barriers all become arbitrary. More importantly, a decline in profits within an industry, however defined, can no longer be assumed to have necessarily come about from an expansion in output and fall in price, and therefore can no longer be regarded as direct evidence of an improvement in social welfare. In the extreme, the higher-than-normal profits of those firms which have, for example, successfully differentiated their products may simply be 'averaged out' against the losses of other firms unsuccessfully trying to differentiate theirs. We thus prefer to test for the persistence of above-normal profits at the firm level, and a good case could be made for an even finer breakdown if data were available.

Brozen offers as his justification for industry profit data, Bain's reason, that individual firm accounting differences will average out over an industry. But equally, if specific accounting entries are subject to important variations, it is as reasonable to assume that firms in the same industry adopt similar conventions as to assume that differences of this type average out *within* an industry. Finally, industry data have their own empirical difficulties. Most firms operate in a large number of industries, and the classification of all the profits of any single firm as arising from one of its activities is arbitrary and raises unknown biases of its own. This criticism has been raised by MacAvoy *et al.* (1971) specifically regarding Brozen's tests for the persistence of above-normal profits. Thus, on purely empirical grounds there seems to be as much to defend firm level estimates as to criticize them.

The two alternative hypotheses to be tested in this chapter can now be briefly stated. The competitive environment hypothesis is that entry and exit in each product area are sufficiently free to bring profits quickly into line with competitive rates of return. Regardless of its initial profit level, each firm's return on capital should tend towards the competitive rate over time (with appropriate allowance for risk), and this convergence should be fairly rapid. Stated another way, the profits of a firm at any two points in time should be independent of one another, given a reasonable separation of the two points of time.

The alternative hypothesis is that profits earned in one period, whether from luck or skill, provide the resources to maintain profits into the future. Some companies erect entry barriers through increased product differentiation, others via scarce natural resources or land sites. Some obtain legal protection for their positions (e.g. patents, tariffs, licences) by purchasing the services of scientists and technicians, lawyers or lobbyists, or more directly by contributions to politicians and public officials themselves. The means vary, but the ends are the same, the preservation of an existing monopoly rent. The alternative to the competitive market hypothesis is that the profits of all firms do not quickly converge on the competitive rate of return, instead, the probability that a firm has a given profit rate at any point in time is directly related to its past profits, even extending the time span far into the past.

II.   THE MODELS AND RESULTS

The hypotheses were tested using data on US firms from the COMPUSTAT tape. This is a useful source since Standard and Poors attempt to record the data in a comparable manner across both companies and years. Since observations were missing at the end and beginning of the period, we had to choose between longer series of data with fewer firms, and shorter series with more companies. We settled on a 472-firm sample with twenty-four years of data.

The main variable in the analysis is the rate of return on capital defined as net income before taxes divided by total assets.[1] Before-tax profits were used to avoid the instabilities changes in taxes sometimes introduce. However, all of the models were also tested using an after-tax definition of profits, and the same qualitative results were obtained, with the only important difference being that the oil companies ranked much higher using an after-tax definition of profits.

It should be noted that the use of total gross assets as a measure of capital stock significantly biases the result in favour of the competitive environment hypothesis. Many of the monopoly rents a firm earns can be expected to be capitalized over time into gross capital lowering the measured rate of return on this measure of capital stock. The results reported below are all the more striking when this bias is kept in mind.

If profits above and below the norm are transitory phenomena, the probability of a firm having a given profit rate at any point in time should be independent of its previous profit rate, for a period of time taken sufficiently far back. To test this hypothesis, the 472 firms in the sample were divided into 8 groups of 59 firms, each based on their initial profit rates; that is the 59 firms with the highest profit rates in 1949 were placed in group 1, the 59 firms with the next highest profit rates were placed in group 2, and so on. Each firm was then assigned a rank from 1 to 8 in the same way for each of the other 23 years in the sample. We then computed the probabilities that a firm initially in any group i would in period t be in group j. These were defined as the number of firms initially in group i which are in group j in period t divided by the size of the group (59). Thus for each year we have 64 probability estimates:

$$P_{ij}, i=1,8 \text{ and } j=1,8.$$

The competitive environment hypothesis is then that the probability that any given firm is eventually a member of group j is independent of the identity of its initial group. All P_{ij} are, with the elapse of enough time, the same (0.125). (The hypothesis here is identical to that put forward by Prais, 1955, with regard to social mobility.)

To test this hypothesis, we regressed each of the P_{ij} on the reciprocal of time for the twenty-four years of observations available:

$$P_{ijt} = \alpha_{ij} + \beta_{ij}/t + u_{ijt}. \tag{1}$$

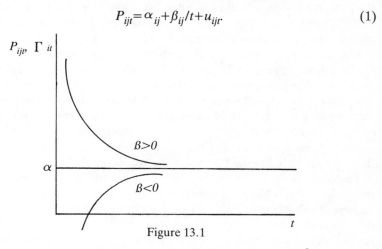

Figure 13.1

These equations take the form as depicted in Figure 13.1.[2] For the P_{ii} equations we expect $\beta_{ii} > 0$, that is, the probability that any firm is in the same profit group as initially is high after only a few years elapse but drops steadily approaching 0.125. For all P_{ij} ($i \neq j$), the β_{ij} should be negative.

The probability that a given firm moves to any other profit group should rise over time approaching 0.125. There are thus two parts to the competitive environment hypothesis. The α_{ij} for all equations should be the same (0.125), and the convergence on these α_{ij}s should be fairly rapid, that is, the ß should be small in absolute value.

The alternative hypothesis is that the probability that a firm moves to a high-profit group is higher, the higher its initial profit group. All equations do not have the same intercept terms, and the intercepts are related in a predictable way to initial profit levels. In addition, the convergence on these asymptotic probability values will be slow.

The basic fit of the equations was quite good. All of the eight equations for the P_{ii} had positive ß as predicted, and t-values above 9.80. All but one of the other equations had negative ß, and most of these were significant. In all, 54 of the 64 equations estimated had significant ß's.

The hypothesis that all probabilities converge on the same value did not fare well, however: 43 of the 64 α_{ij} were significantly different from 0.125, see Table 13.1. This result resembles those found in most social mobility studies, and indicates less than full social mobility. Of particular interest are the first and last rows. The first gives the asymptotic probabilities that a firm starting in the highest profit group is eventually in each of the eight different groups. The probability that it stays in the highest group is 0.34, the highest value in the table, and significantly greater than 0.125 (t=18.92). The probability in the limit that a firm from the first group moves to the second group is also significantly greater than 0.125. The probability estimates that a firm from the first group moves to any one of the bottom five groups are all significantly less than 0.125.

The last row in Table 13.1 presents the limit estimates of P_{ij} for firms starting in the lowest profit group. The pattern is the reverse of that just discussed. The probability that a firm starting at the bottom moves to the top profit group is only 0.04. The probability that its projected rank is in the bottom group is 0.19. Note that, as one would expect from the *non-*competitive environment hypothesis, the probability that a firm starting in the highest group *can* stay there is much greater than the probability that a firm starting in the bottom group must stay there.

The columns in Table 13.1 indicate the probabilities of movement to a particular group. They tell a similar story as above. Movement into the highest or lowest profit groups is much more probable for firms starting in the adjacent groups.

One mildly surprising result is that the four α_{ii} in the middle of the distribution (α_{33}, α_{44}, α_{55}, α_{66}) are all less than 0.125, while the α_{ii} on the extremes are all above 0.125. Thus, movement out of one's initial group is much more likely if one starts towards the centre of the distribution than if one starts towards the tails. This is precisely the

Table 13.1 *Long-run probability lines on intergroup mobility. (Each entry gives the projected probability that a firm which started in the ith profit class in 1949 would eventually be in the jth class, i.e. the α_{ij}.)*

| | | | | | j | | | |
i	(1)	(2)	(3)	(4)	(5)	(6)	(7)	(8)
(1)	0.34**	0.17**	0.12	0.10*	0.06**	0.06**	0.07**	0.08**
(2)	0.21**	0.13	0.20**	0.14	0.10**	0.08**	0.06**	0.08**
(3)	0.14*	0.19**	0.08*	0.13	0.15*	0.12	0.11	0.09
(4)	0.08**	0.14	0.14	0.09	0.19**	0.18**	0.12	0.07**
(5)	0.08**	0.13	0.15**	0.17**	0.08	0.14	0.14	0.11
(6)	0.07**	0.09**	0.13	0.14	0.11	0.07*	0.21**	0.19**
(7)	0.04**	0.07**	0.08**	0.13	0.15**	0.20**	0.13	0.20**
(8)	0.04**	0.08**	0.10**	0.11	0.15*	0.15*	0.17*	0.19**

*Significantly different from 0.125, two-tailed test, 0.05 confidence level.
**Significantly different from 0.125, two-tailed test, 0.01 confidence level.

opposite of what one would expect if higher/lower-than-normal profits were a temporary, disequilibrium phenomenon. Indeed, one might argue that the competitive environment hypothesis would predict *lower* probabilities of remaining in the same profit group for firms lying further from the mean. That the reverse has been observed indicates strong rejection of the competitive environment hypothesis.

With the exception of the P_{ii} equations, the ß were small in absolute value indicating a fairly rapid convergence on the α_{ij}, the limit values for the probability estimates. The $ß_{ii}$ were all around 0.8, however. Thus, twenty years after the starting point, the probability that a firm was in the same profit group as the one in which it began was four percentage points above its limit value. The probability that a firm in the highest profit group in 1949 was still in the highest profit group in 1969 was nearly 0.38.

The competitive environment hypothesis can also be tested using the individual ranks of the firms, their actual profits and normalized profits. This was done with similar results in each case, so that only the last of these are presented here.

If deviations from the competitive rate of return are transitory, the profits of any firm i at time t should equal the competitive rate of return (perhaps adjusted for risk) plus a random error term.

$$\Pi_{it} = \bar{\Pi}_t + \mu_{it}. \tag{2}$$

Subtracting the competitive return from both sides of (2) and dividing through by it gives

$$\frac{\Pi_{it} - \bar{\Pi}_t}{\bar{\Pi}_t} = \frac{\mu_{it}}{\bar{\Pi}_t}. \qquad (3)$$

The expected value of this variable should be zero. To test this hypothesis, the normalized profit rate for each firm was formed by taking the deviation of its profit rate in any year, from the mean profit rate for that year over the entire sample of 472 firms:

$$\Gamma_{it} = \frac{\Pi_{it} - \bar{\Pi}_t}{\bar{\Pi}_t}, \qquad (4)$$

Where

$$\bar{\Pi}_t = \sum_{i=1}^{472} \Pi_{it}/472$$

This normalized profit rate was then used as a dependent variable in a regression similar to those run above:

$$\Gamma_{it} = \alpha_i + \beta_i/t + u_{it}.$$

The competitive environment hypothesis is that each firm's profit rate should regress on to the mean, the α_i should equal zero and be independent of the initial profit position of the firm. Table 13.2 summarizes the results for these equations. If the hypothesis that projected profit rates are independent of initial profits is correct, the same percentages of firms should have α_i above (or below) zero in the highest profit groups, defined as above, as in the lowest. Columns (4) and (5) in Table 13.2 present the percentages of firms in each of the eight groups of fifty-nine firms having α_i significantly greater than or less than zero. The percentage of firms with projected normalized profits above zero is over 50 per cent for the highest profit group, and falls steadily as one moves down the list of initial profit rank groups. Roughly the reverse pattern is observed for the negative α.

Column (6) presents the mean α for each group. These fall steadily from 0.46 to −0.24. The average projected profit rate at time $t=\infty$ for firms in the highest profit group is 46 per cent above the mean; the average projected profits of those in the lowest group are 24 per cent below the mean. The average projected profits are significantly greater than zero for the top two groups, less than zero for the bottom three. The hypothesis that a firm's subsequent profits are independent of its initial profits is again rejected.

Columns (2) and (3) present the percentages of significant β for each group. There is a greater tendency for profits to fall for firms in the highest profit groups ($\beta>0$), and a greater tendency for them to rise in the lower groups. As such, this pattern is consistent with what one would expect under the competitive environment hypothesis. Its rejection comes about because a significant number of firms on both ends of the distribution do not exhibit systematic changes in profits (significant β), and those that do do not fall or rise by enough to substantiate the hypothesis.

Table 13.2   *Regression results for normalized profits* ($\Gamma_{it} = \alpha_i = \beta_i/t + u_{it}$)

Sample	Beta*+	Beta*−	Alpha*+	Alpha*−	Mean α	*t*-value
(1)	(2)	(3)	(4)	(5)	(6)	(7)
1	0.49	0.05	0.54	0.19	0.46	4.36
2	0.53	0.08	0.42	0.24	0.19	2.65
3	0.34	0.10	0.42	0.44	0.05	0.87
4	0.34	0.12	0.25	0.54	−0.01	−0.20
5	0.14	0.15	0.25	0.46	−0.05	−1.01
6	0.05	0.31	0.22	0.54	−0.17	−2.77
7	0.03	0.32	0.12	0.68	−0.23	−4.59
8	0.02	0.54	0.12	0.56	−0.24	−4.94

*Percentages of regression coefficients significant at 0.05 level, two-tailed test. Each subsample has 59 observations.

To the extent that firms are earning monopoly rents, the average profit rate for the sample exceeds the competitive rate of return. Evidence that this may be so is provided by the results for the bottom three groups in Table 13.2. The projected, mean, long-run profit rates for firms in these groups are 17, 23 and 24 per cent below the sample average, respectively. If we assume that no firm can survive in the long run without earning a competitive rate of return on capital, then these results suggest that the average rate of return on capital for the sample is as much as 24 per cent below the mean. The projected average profits of the highest profit group would then be 70 per cent higher than the competitive rate of return on capital, making the rejection of the competitive environment hypothesis even more convincing.

A substantial fraction of the regressions summarized in Table 13.2 were plagued by autocorrelation. Although autocorrelation leaves the regression coefficients unbiased, and thus should not affect the tests based on the mean α in each group, it does affect the estimates of the standard errors of the regression coefficients and can lead to an overestimate of the number of significant regression coefficients. To correct for this the Durbin procedure was applied to the equation

(Johnston, 1960, pp. 192–9). These results are summarized in Table 13.3 using the same format as Table 13.2. Although the coefficients of the independent variables remain exact estimates of the true parameters in the original structural equation under the Durbin procedure, the intercepts are equal to only $(1-r)$ times their true values, where r is the regression coefficient from the autoregressive equation run on the residuals. To compute the projected, long-run normalized profits from the equations estimated using the Durbin procedure, the $\hat{\alpha}_i$ were divided by $(1-r)$. These adjusted αs were used to compute the statistics presented in columns (6) and (7). Application of the Durbin procedure eliminated autocorrelation in all but a handful of cases. As might be expected, its use led to greater variability in the estimates across the groups. Nevertheless, the same pattern of results emerges from Table 13.3 as was observed in Table 13.2. The competitive environment hypothesis is still safely rejected.[3]

Table 13.3   *Regression results for normalized profits after applying Durbin procedure*

Sample	Beta*+	Beta*−	Alpha*+	Alpha*−	Mean Adjusted** $\hat{\alpha}$	t-value
(1)	(2)	(3)	(4)	(5)	(6)	(7)
1	0.69	0.25	0.44	0.15	0.37	2.91
2	0.56	0.37	0.31	0.10	0.22	3.16
3	0.58	0.29	0.29	0.24	−0.15	−0.49
4	0.59	0.31	0.15	0.31	0.10	0.90
5	0.63	0.31	0.10	0.34	−0.03	−0.26
6	0.62	0.37	0.10	0.37	−0.21	−3.20
7	0.46	0.51	0.08	0.47	−0.21	−3.35
8	0.36	0.51	0.12	0.44	−0.13	−1.19

*Percentages of regression coefficients significant at 0.05 level, two-tailed test. Each subsample has 59 observations.
**Equal to $\alpha/(1-r)$.

III.   ALTERNATIVE EXPLANATIONS AND HYPOTHESES

In this section we discuss several possible objections or alternative explanations for our results which might be raised.

A.   Risk

It might be argued that the persistently higher profits that some of the firms earned are warranted by the substantially higher risks involved in their activities. To check if this is true, we formed a subsample of the firms in the top two groups, which had projected normalized profits at $t=\infty$

significantly greater than zero. If risk does explain higher-than-normal profits, these fifty-nine companies should be inherently riskier than the others in the sample. The mean variance in profits for these fifty-nine firms was not significantly different from that of the other firms, however (t=0.21).

Following the logic of the capital asset-pricing model, we also tested to see if there was a higher covariance between the profits of the stable, high profit firms and the mean of the sample than for the other firms. The average ß for the fifty-nine stable profit firms from a regression of their profits on the sample mean was 1.19. The average for the other firms was 0.97. The difference was insignificant ($t=0.20$).[4] Further investigation indicated that a much higher percentage of the 118 firms in the top two groups had ß significantly greater than 1.0 than for the rest of the sample (0.46 versus 0.23). Within the top two groups, however, a much smaller percentage of the fifty-nine firms with projected normal profits above zero had ß significantly greater than 1.0 (0.32) than of those with $\alpha \leq 0$ (0.59). Thus, the permanently higher-than-normal profits of these fifty-nine firms cannot be rationalized on the basis of their greater risk as evidenced by either a variance or covariance measure of risk.

One might argue that the risks involved in these firms' activities were higher *ex ante* than in other activities, but I see no way to test this hypothesis and separate it from the barriers to entry hypothesis. Many firms did lose money trying to compete with Gillette, Kellogg, Maytag, General Motors and so on, and many more firms may have been deterred from trying to compete owing to their fear of losing money. Thus, the risks born *by these other firms* may indeed have been high. But that is, I believe, what is meant by a barrier to entry.

B. The choice of sample or time period

The sample is drawn from the population of largest companies in the United States, the group in which persistent monopoly profits should reside if they are present at all. The sample includes all of the companies for which the relevant data were available, and it contains enough familiar names to suggest that the results are not due to data oddities. The nature of the tests does preclude taking into account the disappearance of firms from the sample. But this is unlikely to affect the results. It would do so only if a disproportionately large percentage of firms from the highest profit groups disappeared with lower-than-average profit levels, an unlikely event.

The argument that the choice of time period biases the results also cannot be sustained. The competitive environment hypothesis postulates that *all* above-normal profits are disequilibrium phenomena. All time periods are atypical, therefore, with respect to *which* firms have profits above or below the norm. If the starting point for our series, the year 1949, was in some sense more atypical than others, then the hypothesis that profits quickly return to normal levels would have been favoured. Indeed. this hypothesis has already been considerably favoured by basing the initial rankings on profit data for a single year. It might further be argued that the period of time for the investigation was too short to allow profit levels to return to their equilibrium values. The tests were formulated to avoid this criticism, however. The competitive environment hypothesis has been rejected not on the basis of the profit levels (probabilities) actually *obtained* after twenty-four years, but on the basis of the profit levels and probabilities *projected* at $t=\infty$. For this type of criticism to have validity one must argue that twenty-four years is too short even to project the eventual equilibrium values of these variables. Even if valid, it would seem hard to combine this criticism with an argument that profits above or below the norm are a *temporary* disequilibrium phenomenon.

C.   Superior talent

Now let us return to the hypothesis that firms with continually high profits possess superior managerial talent. First, it should be noted that, even if true, this hypothesis is inconsistent with the competitive environment hypothesis, at least in its most general form. The same is true of patent rights, locational advantages and other possible causes of above-normal returns. The persistence of above-normal profits for sustained periods is consistent with a special talents rationale only for traditional entrepreneurial firms, therefore, where the innovator-entrepreneur has the residual claim to profits and where, by definition, no market exists for his services. The number of entrepreneurial firms of this type in a sample of companies listed on the major stock exchanges, as the present one is, must be very small. Nevertheless, nearly half of those firms in the first two groups which had projected normalized profits greater than zero could be classified as owner-controlled.[5] This is a far higher percentage than is found in other samples of this type, or in the remainder of the present sample. Many of these companies are controlled by outsiders, however, and an examination of the remainder suggests that an 'innovator-entrepreneur' hypothesis is unlikely to explain much of the higher profits these firms earned. But a full resolution of this possibility would require detailed case studies of each company.

The appearance of a disproportionate number of owner-controlled firms in the subsample of high, long-run projected profits companies can be explained in another way. The managers of a company reporting continually high profits can be expected to come under pressure to pay increasing percentages of these out as dividends. When the managers are in control of the firm, they can be expected to avoid these pressures by diverting some profits into expenditures which satisfy their own personal goals, as has been extensively discussed in the literature. Of particular importance here is the pursuit of growth through diversification and merger. A firm with high monopoly profits which engages in substantial diversification and merger activity may exhibit a fall in profits towards the average. But this will provide no information about whether the rents it earns on the products it monopolizes have been dissipated. It is well known that a large amount of diversification and merger activity took place in the United States during the 1950s and 1960s. Yet the sample used above made no adjustments for the likely tendency of this activity, and the managerial pursuit of other goals, to drive above-normal profits towards the mean. That a stable relationship between high profits would hold up over time in spite of ignoring these potentially offsetting factors is all the more remarkable.

D. Possible extensions

The results presented here are consistent with some of the recent findings of Shepherd (1975). Shepherd has found firm profit rates to be related to market shares, and has argued that high market shares are relatively stable over time. That firms with high profit rates have high market shares is, perhaps, not surprising. Indeed, the direct linkage between profit rates and market shares is one of the most important theoretical underpinnings of the industrial organization literature (see Cowling and Waterson, 1976). And if profit levels are stable over time one probably can expect market shares to be. An obvious follow-up to the present study would be to relate the persistence of above-normal profits to market share indexes, pricing strategies and various measures of entry barriers. But caution must be exercised in formulating and testing such hypotheses; for the set of strategies available to a firm for preserving a dominant position may be so large and varied that no simple set of identifiable variables can capture it well. The underlying hypothesis, that the positions of above-normal monopoly profits can and will be sustained over time by whatever means available, would still be valid. It is this latter hypothesis that has been tested and supported in this paper.

NOTES

1. COMPUSTAT defines net income as 'income after all operating and non-operating income and expense and minority interest, but before preferred and common dividends. It is stated after extraordinary items which are not net of applicable taxes'. To this is added all income taxes imposed by Federal and

State governments to form the numerator. The denominator is 'total assets [which] represent current assets plus net plant plus other non-current assets (including intangible assets, deferred items, and investments and advances)'.

2. A difficulty is raised in using these equations in that the P_{ij} should fall between 0 and 1.0. We defined the first year as $t=1$, so the α_{ii} and β_{ii} for each equation should sum to 1, and the α_{ij} and β_{ij} to 0. We did not constrain the coefficients in this way, but the unconstrained estimates were in fact quite close to these values. The next set of regressions is free of this problem.

3. Fourteen of the equations using transition probabilities had Durbin–Watson statistics indicating autocorrelation, and another twelve had DWs falling in the indeterminate interval. Application of the above procedure to these equations left the pattern of results and general conclusions unchanged.

4. The variances of the two samples were not significantly different indicating the appropriateness of a simple t-test.

5. These classifications were based on those made by Palmer (1973b), McEachern (1975) and data published in *Value Line*, 1971. A table listing the fifty-nine firms with projected normalized profit significantly greater than zero is available from the author on request.

14   The Corporation, Competition, and the Invisible Hand*

I.   INTRODUCTION

Few would disagree that Adam Smith's invisible-hand theorem is the heart of the economist's *Weltanschauung*. Ask whether trade barriers should be lowered, the spread of multinational corporations restrained, oil prices deregulated, cartels dissolved, or more fundamentally whether a market-based capitalist system is economically superior to a state-run socialist system, and economists almost certainly will begin to answer the question by trying to apply the theorem.

Every student knows that the theorem depends on the assumption of atomistic competition, which in turn assumes that the system is decentralized and that no competitor is large relatively to others. There is another crucial assumption, however, that is often ignored and usually underemphasized, namely that all competition is price competition. In reality one of the most distinctive features of capitalism—one that is most often raised in lay discussions of its merits and demerits—is the prevalence of other forms of competition, such as competition in research, development, and advertising; competition to obtain and hold monopoly; and competition for corporate growth. These various forms of 'non-price' competition, we shall aim to show, are not clearly analogous with the theory of price competition: more non-price competition, rather than less, is not necessarily *Pareto optimal*.

Self-evidently, the production side of a market economy is decentralized only to a limited degree, that is to the level of a decision-making unit composed of more than one human. Such a unit—playing neuron to the invisible hand—is typically called a 'firm'. It is in fact a team. Rather than remaining small, firms are in practice composed of any number of individuals from a handful to half a million. Some firms in large market economies contain more members than the entire working

*Reprinted from *Journal of Economic Literature*, **18**, March 1980.
Robin Marris and Dennis C. Mueller.

populations of a small market economy. Since rich and successful nations include both large and small economies, there is no obvious connection, either way, between the prevalence of giant corporations and economic performance. Neoclassical theory makes no prediction that large economies should contain more large firms than small economies do, nor indeed any other significant prediction concerning the size distribution of business firms.

The foregoing is just one example of significant phenomena that are not addressed in the prevailing neoclassical theory of the firm. Another is the phenomenon of so-called 'conglomerate' growth, sometimes occurring through chains of mergers, sometimes through internal diversification;[1] also (less frequently) by a mixture of both strategies. More generally, the neoclassical theory has no full explanation of why firms grow at all, nor why it is that the typical pattern of the growth rates of firms seems to lead inexorably towards persistently increasing aggregate business concentration.[2] The absence of evidence that the development of giant firms creates clear benefits for society (John R. Carter, 1977; S. J. Prais, 1976) or for stockholders (Carter, 1977; Michael Gort, 1969; Douglas Kuehn, 1975; Robert G. Morgan, 1977; Mueller, 1977) is a related puzzle for the neoclassical observer.

Clearly, a market economy is not a simple problem-solving machine. It is what cyberneticists have called a self-organizing system, a system that can and does modify its own structure and programming in the course of and as a result of its own operations. Economic theory has traditionally ignored self-organizing processes and has traditionally concentrated attention on the behaviour of systems with given structures. Intuitively, however, it seems likely that the economic welfare of the citizens of the modern state is as likely to be affected at least as much, if not more so, by the way economic structure develops as by the performance of the system within a given structure. This consideration leads to a third concept of efficiency—which might be called 'adaptive efficiency'—to be added to two existing concepts of allocative efficiency and what is now (following Harvey Leibenstein, 1966, 1969, 1975, 1976) called X-efficiency.

Self-organizing systems are not easy to analyse. There may have been a good case in the early history of our discipline for conducting analysis *as if* self-organizing forces were of secondary importance. This case, however, is surely well overdue for reconsideration. Thus Oliver Williamson has written:

It is . . . widely agreed that if mechanism B, not mechanism A is thought to be generating the phenomena of interest, the intellectually respectable thing to do is to build theory B. The heavy emphasis on the development of mathematical economics in the past thirty years, however, has often favored theory A constructions. (1975, p. 249).

In the field of industrial organization, a typical 'Theory A' model (in Oliver Williamson's sense) will assume that firms are small and more or less the same size (or at least that their size distribution is not, as it is in reality, heavily skewed) and also that firms do not grow. But with such a theory it is impossible to make any prediction concerning the expected path of business concentration, or to say anything interesting about the dynamic implications of monopoly.

The proposition that monopoly results in some degree of *static* (allocational) welfare losses is widely accepted. However, Arnold Harberger presented some estimates a quarter of a century ago to suggest that the welfare loss due to monopoly was quite small (1954). Although these estimates have been challenged from time to time,[3] the belief that monopoly pricing does not result in a significant static welfare loss is a firmly established part of the economist's credo.

This moderate view of monopoly is reinforced by the widespread belief that competition to become a monopoly has largely beneficial effects. One of the early, and still most persuasive, proponents of this position was Joseph Schumpeter (1934). Schumpeter described economic development as taking place through the implementation of new products, production processes, and organizational techniques. The entrepreneurial role is the introduction of these innovations, and the incentive for doing so is the profits or rents of monopoly the innovators receive. But, as Schumpeter described it, the monopoly rents an innovator receives are short lived. Each innovation is soon imitated, and then replaced by yet another innovation. The monopoly an innovator obtains gives him but a brief respite from 'the perennial gale of creative destruction' taking place in a free-enterprise economy; monopoly rents give him only the means to pursue new innovations. Any firm that merely attempted to maintain and enjoy a present position of monopoly would be doomed to extinction under the forces of dynamic competition Schumpeter described.

The Schumpeterian view of the dynamics of the competitive process is quite compatible with that of Frank Knight (1921). Knight's quasi-static approach emphasized the role of uncertainty in the creation of profit. The entrepreneurial role is to make decisions under uncertainty and assume responsibility for the consequences of these decisions. To make good decisions in the face of uncertainty requires good information, and so the entrepreneurial role becomes one of gathering, evaluating, and utilizing information. The competitive process selects those entrepreneurs and firms capable of making correct decisions under uncertainty for survival (Armen Alchian, 1950). As in the Schumpeterian theory, profits appear as a transitory disequilibrium quasi-rent in Knight's theory. With the gathering of information, uncertainty disappears. Entry into information gathering is free, and so the existence of uncertainty is short, and so too the existence of uncertainty related profits. The micro-history of a market economy is one of the continual appearance and erosion of economic profits. This picture of 'competition as a dynamic process' comes as close to being an invisible hand theorem for non-price competition as exists in the literature to date (e.g. Clark, 1961; Kirzner, 1973).

In the following pages we challenge both this rather sanguine view of the normative properties of the competitive process and the positive predictions of the micro-theory of the firm upon which it rests in part. In doing so, we focus explicitly on the behavioural characteristics of the firm (the corporation) and the methods by which it competes. We deal first with the general behavioural characteristics of the modern corporation; then with various dynamic aspects of corporate competition (growth, merger, etc., including macro consequences); then with the static welfare effects of competition for R and D and monopoly; finally we attempt some normative conclusions.

II. THE CORPORATION

A. The Neoclassical Theory of the Firm

Kenneth Arrow has pointed out that in classical, as against neoclassical, economics there was no theory of the firm: constant returns to scale implicitly pervaded all activities, and cost-determined prices were independent of institutions (1971). Alfred Marshall—the first edition of whose *Principles* was published in 1890—was perhaps the first economist to recognize the significance of industrial organization for economic theory. No industry in his system could sustain equilibrium under conditions of constant or increasing scale economies within firms, and he therefore badly needed an assumption to guarantee decreasing returns. This he obtained by observing that in England (he rather ignored the US where the sociology was already different) the sons of successful entrepreneurs, having been raised in luxury and coddled by nursemaids, lacked what today would be called achievement-orientation. Family businesses, therefore, like trees in a forest, tended to wither and die. Joint stock companies (at least in the first edition) were not a successful alternative in practice. But as we all know, while these predictions were in process of publication, the United States entered her first great wave of trust formation and concentration; while in the UK the commencement of a process of persistently increasing aggregate business concentration was only ten years later (Prais, 1976).

Nevertheless, the theory of monopolistic competition as developed in the 1930s accepted and formalized the presumption of decreasing returns as limiting the expansion of firms, and based on it, in fact, the influential excess-capacity theorem. The justification for 'the bend in the U' was usually provided in no more than a few words on the problems of coordination within top management (see e.g. Nicholas Kaldor, 1935; Marris, 1972b; E. A. G. Robinson, 1931). After World War II, a revival of interest in the formal properties of purely-competitive systems relegated the theory of the firm, as such, to a diminishing role, often pedagogically confined to courses on industrial organization expected to be taken by those graduate students who might have difficulty with courses in more advanced theory. The result, in our view was a considerable spread of a form of short-sightedness, which might be called, 'paradigmatic myopia'.[4] In Thomas Kuhn's (1962) as well as in Plato's conception, a 'paradigm' is not synonymous with a 'model': it is a perfect example by which everything is judged. Propositions that cannot be related to the exemplar are not so much denied, as ignored, which has certainly been the fate of heterodox propositions in industrial organization. Yet, three new lines of development in the theory of the firm have recently begun to converge to a possible situation that could redress the balance. We discuss in Subsections B, C, and D each line of development in turn. In Subsections E, F, and G, we explore further implications of the third line, which is concerned with the growth of firms.

B. Internal Organization Approach

Ronald Coase's celebrated article addressed to the question 'why do firms exist?' may be regarded as the father of this school (1937). Another considerable, though partly tangential, influence has been that of Herbert Simon. Although most of the field has continued to pursue optimizing models, Simon's emphasis on human attributes in organizational settings has been a key factor in the general background (1957a, 1959). Thus, the significance of Coase's original question lay in the paradox that if prices are efficient transmitters of information (Friedrich A. Hayek, 1945), no subunit should contain more than one member. The answer implied in Coase's analysis is that, considered as information systems, markets are inherently costly and imperfect. Administrative integration of information exchange, despite other disadvantages, could reduce such costs. Hence firms existed wherever the costs of market exchange of relevant information exceeded the inefficiencies of centralization.

The revival of this type of inquiry dates from an article by Joseph Monsen and Anthony Downs (1965) who, although they made no reference to Coase, adopted a similar *a priori* approach, but with a different conclusion about the benefits. Whatever the reasons for the existence of firms, Monsen and Downs found considerable dysfunctional potentialities within the process of internal information exchange: large corporate bureaucracies, with ownership separated from control, were plagued by information bias, by risk aversion, by expense preference, and also by satisficing, rather than optimizing, behaviour on the part of the managers. Hence (implied Monsen and Downs) the modern corporate system was socially dysfunctional.

Some years later, Alchian and Harold Demsetz (1972), ignoring Monsen and Downs but referring to Coase, reached diametrically the opposite conclusion. On account of informational and other functional inseparabilities, firms were needed to exploit the advantages of team work. In teams, however, the incentive for individuals to contribute their best performance is inadequately internalized, the greater part of the benefit of marginal performance falling to the group as a whole; in other words, the benefit is a public good. Thus—to borrow another terminology—Monsen and Downs could be said to have defined 'not-shirking' as a public good to the team. Lacking adequate individual incentive, teams therefore required central monitors to control actual or potential shirkers. But if the central monitor consists of humans who are themselves team members, the benefit of their performance is also a public good. Hence it is desirable to adopt institutional forms here the full benefit of monitoring belongs to the monitor(s). Since managers are the chief monitors in the corporate team, they would appear to be the logical recipients of the residual of the profits of the corporation. As we shall see, other 'managerial' approaches to the corporation do effectively assume that managers exercise a claim on a significant share of the residual. Alchian and Demsetz, however, assumed that the monitor-managers are indeed monitored, but not by individual stockholders as had been traditionally posited in the neoclassical theory, for stockholder monitoring would also be a public good activity plagued by free-rider problems. Managers were monitored by potential take-over raiders. Because take-over raiders can capitalize (i.e. internalize) the benefit of take-over, the incentive to undertake or at least to threaten, take-over raids was assumed adequate as a permanent, effective monitor on management. Thus, the argument implied that although society does have options among organizational forms, the joint-stock corporation, when selected, is efficient. The general legal regime of capitalism selected efficient mechanisms.[5]

Oliver Williamson, having made his mark (see below) in the managerial (static) field, later became convinced that the key to the understanding of the economic role and performance of firms lay in the study of internal organization. Two books, *Corporate Control and Business Behavior* (1970) and *Markets and Hierarchies* (1975) together with the various outputs of a symposium on internal organization, which he organized in 1974, bear witness to his continuing contribution to the field.

The main feature of the new approach is to treat markets on the one hand, and administrative organizations—or 'hierarchies'—on the other, as alternative modes of production. In comparing the typical performance of each mode in various capacities it is necessary to take account, in the case of markets, of transactional frictions whose effects have in the past often been underappreciated and, in the case of hierarchies, of the elementary attributes of human nature, especially the opportunism that necessarily occurs within the daily life of bureaucracies. Hierarchical bureaucracies are also, like markets, subject to internal inertia and other forces that are analogous to transactional frictions. Thus the study of internal organization parallels the study of the structures of markets. 'Organizational failures', like market failures, are not necessarily self correcting, and society does not always select efficient mechanisms.

The totality of the resulting (and still developing body of theory could be summarized as follows. The reasons why society may adopt hierarchies are various: functional inseparabilities (Alchian and Demsetz, 1972); the nature of the employment relation (Simon, 1957a, b; Joseph E. Stiglitz, 1975; Williamson, 1975); uncertainty concerning one's own abilities or others' perceptions of them (James Mirrlees, 1976); or informational economies of scale (Robert Wilson, 1975). In so doing, society experiences various dysfunctions—in communication, in information management, and in monitoring. 'Control loss' includes both communications errors and monitoring ineffectiveness. The pathology of control loss produces the symptom of proliferating monitors.

Mirrlees concludes that hierarchies with optimal incentive systems are subject to weak diseconomies of scale, which may become negligible among the largest organizations (1976). Wilson concludes that, at least at the technical level, there are inherent informational economies, rather than diseconomies of scale (1975).

The theorem of weak diseconomies of scale originates in the mathematics of pyramids as first set out by Herbert Simon in a model of executive compensation (1957b) and later developed in alternative forms by Williamson (1967) and Marris (1972a). All organizational control involves message exchange between human brains; the brain, however, has evolved in such a way that its remarkable capacities for access to memory have been bought at the price of a considerable restriction in short-term processing capacity. The brain is therefore easily saturated with incoming information of a certain type, namely information coming directly or indirectly from other brains. Unlike computers, humans cannot simultaneously monitor many channels. The bureaucratic pyramid attempts to solve the problem by restricting the number of other individuals with whom any one individual must maintain contact. This restriction is called the span of control. The number of stages into which the control system is thus subdivided, or 'levels' in a hierarchy, can be seen as the length of a chain of command.

It then turns out that the length of the chain of command to a given level is equal to the logarithm of the number of individuals at that level divided by the logarithm of the span of control (assuming for simplicity that the latter is constant). Hence, if the number of people at a given level, say the 'lowest' level (i.e. level furthest from the control centre) is taken as a measure of the size of the organization, the fundamental theorem is that the length of the chain of command varies directly (in fact is a fixed proportion of) the log of the organization's size. But if communication errors are passed on in a first-order Markov chain and are uncorrelated with previous errors or with the messages to which they relate, cumulative error increases only linearly with the length of the chain of command. This combination of a linear law with a semi-log law creates a condition where the first derivative of aggregate error with respect to size is positive, but the second derivative is negative—a law of diminishing marginal inefficiency.

Williamson, however, pointed out that errors are likely to multiply, that is, are not only unlikely to be independent of the messages to which they relate, but to be positively correlated with them (1970). Hence, the error process is likely to be explosive, an effect that he believed would usually offset the damping implied above. But it could also be argued (see e.g. Joseph L. Bower, 1970, 1974; Guillermo Calvo and Stanislaw Wellisz, 1978) that corporations can design effective monitoring and incentive systems to make errors partially self correcting, so that errors may be negatively rather than positively correlated with the messages to which they relate.

Monitoring, however, has its own costs: because the subjects are opportunistic human beings, they may well reduce, rather than improve, their performance if they feel over-monitored. As Leibenstein has written (1975, p. 598):

The (hierarchial) structure facilitates the basic function of the organization which is to receive, evaluate, and translate signals from the outside in order to induce performance from the inside. But in the process of carrying out these functions, a number of *distortions* can arise: first, the individuals receiving signals can always to some degree determine their response; second, there are simultaneously 'cooperative-conflict' considerations and influences that may contribute distortions.

Were it not for such considerations, one could simply represent monitoring as implying a decrease in the span of control: then because a reduced span of control also implies a longer chain of command, it might appear that there exists an optimum span of control. Could one therefore investigate the theory of returns to scale on the assumption that for each given size, the span had been optimized? It turns out, however, that the answer is rather unexpected. If the firm can find a method of increasing monitoring (as represented in span of control), which is effective at least up to the point where errors are on average self correcting (Leibenstein's argument implies of course that this is by no means inevitable), it can be proved that, provided the organization can pass a critical size, it has always the power to create conditions where there are constant or increasing returns to scale for any further expansion. As this is widely underappreciated, we will set out the proof.

Let X_L represent a message received at level L, purporting to be a message from $L+1$. If the message is not correctly received or is misinterpreted, there is an error $(X_L - X_{L+1})$. Let the possible correlation between the error and the message most generally be expressed by a regression equation,

$$X_L - X_{L+1} = (\beta - 1)X_{L+1} + \mu_L$$
$$X_L = \beta X_{L+1} + \mu_L \tag{1}$$

Williamson implicitly assumed that β would be greater than one (1970). With effective monitoring, however, β could be less than one.

The resulting Markov chain has the equations:

$$\sigma^2_{X(L)} = \sigma^2_\mu (1 - \beta^{2L})/(1 - \beta^2)$$
$$\text{for } \beta \neq 1 \tag{2a}$$

$$\sigma^2_{X(L)} = \sigma^2_\mu \cdot L$$
$$\text{for } \beta = 1 \tag{2b}$$

where $\sigma^2_{X(L)}$ represents the variance of the cumulative noise delivered to each individual at L, assuming σ^2_μ constant through levels. If N is the number of members at the end of the chain (a measure of organization size) and S is the span of control, with n and s representing their respective logarithms to the base 10, we obtain the following formula for the error variance received at the end of the chain in an organization of size N, this being an appropriate measure of average control loss, or 'efficiency' of the whole organization,

$$\sigma^2_{X(N)} = \sigma^2_\mu (1 - \beta^{2n/s})/(1 - \beta^2) \tag{3}$$

By appropriate differentiation we can obtain the elasticity, e_n, of σ^2_X with respect to lower case n:

$$e_n = \frac{(\beta^{-2}-1)}{(\beta^{-2n/s}-1)}$$

for $\beta \neq 1$ (4a)

$$e_n = 1$$

for $\beta = 1$ (4b)

Because e_n is a measure of unit inefficiency, the critical conditions for increasing or decreasing returns to scale are indicated by the sign of this elasticity, that is, increasing returns implies $e_n < 0$, not $e_n < 1$. If, however, e_n is not only positive, but always increasing with n, not only are there decreasing returns but the effect is explosive. If e_n is positive, but decreasing with n, there are decreasing returns, but the effect is damped. If $e_n = 0$, there are constant returns.

Inspection shows that the explosive case is impossible. If β is greater than 1, as n increases, e_n declines asymptotically to $(1-\beta^{-2})$. Once this limit has been reached, if the organization can obtain other kinds of scale economies, with elasticity of effect greater than $(1-\beta^{-2})$, it can obtain constant or even increasing returns to scale for further expansion. Alternatively, if by reducing the span of control β can be made less than 1.0, e_n declines asymptotically to *zero* as n increases. Thus, despite the initial penalty, it is again the case that provided the organization can get big enough, it can be guaranteed at least constant returns to further expansion. Mirrlees's more elaborate treatment reaches similar but less definite conclusions (1976). We believe our simpler result, however, to be rather general.

It has the unusual feature that the sharpest (informational) decreasing returns occur in the earliest phase of expansion, that is, in precisely the phase at which other positive scale economies are most likely to occur. It has often been noticed that young 'dynamic' organizations, however successful for other reasons, often appear to be rather badly managed. By contrast, large, stable organizations, though rather 'bureaucratic' (monitored) seem surprisingly efficient especially at the operating level.

The upshot is that there is a very strong case, in general analysis of the capitalist process, for adopting the assumption of constant internal returns to scale. It seems to follow that there is nothing in the self-organizing structure of the capitalist system to prevent it progressing smoothly towards the limit of one large corporation, although no doubt before that point entering into increasing partnership with the government. Or, given the extremely skewed size distribution that presently exists, the co-existence of giant corporations with a large number of small firms (with high birth and death rates) might continue, but with increasing concentration at the top.

C. The Managerial (Static) Approach

In 1959 William Baumol published *Business Behavior, Value and Growth*, and in 1964 Oliver Williamson published *The Economics of Discretionary Behavior*. In these works firms were assumed to be in more or less the same kind of market environment and to have production constraints as in the usual model of monopolistic competition, but their managers were now endowed with explicit utility functions containing arguments consisting either of things that stood proxy for familiar operating objectives, such as sales (Baumol), or of things directly pertaining to their own living standards, such as emoluments or 'expenses'—the latter being perks, subordinates, etc. (Williamson). Such utility functions were the maximized subject to a minimum profit constraint, leading to a number of partial equlibrium results that were easily relevant to typical paradigmatic problems. Alternatively, profits can be added to the arguments of the utility function and an appropriate utility-maximizing solution obtained.

Williamson made ingenious use of case studies to show that, in adversity, firms reduced expense in a manner that was inconsistent with the hypothesis that they had previously been maximizing profits. Typical comparative static results are that with the utility argument defined as sales, and sales a function of advertising, the firm expands advertising, and hence sales, until the minimum profit is reached. Any increase in the level of the minimum profit constraint will, therefore, reduce advertising. In Williamson, when a continuous utility function is assumed, because expense is untaxed, an increase in the rate of tax lowers the marginal cost of expense in terms of profits, but will not necessarily lead to an increase in expense on account of the presence of an income effect as well as a substitution effect.

In 1963 Richard Cyert and James March published *A Behavioral Theory of the Firm*. This was an explicit attempt to incorporate Herbert Simon's satisficing concepts simultaneously into the theories of internal organizational behaviour and into the behaviour of oligopolistic markets. In particular these applications were believed to display much greater predictive power than traditional models. In a celebrated application (1963, p. 129), Cyert and March showed that the pricing of products in department stores could be predicted to the nearest penny. Other applications were published in Cyert and Kalman J. Cohen (1965) (to duopoly) and in G.P. Clarkson (1962) (to portfolio selection).

Richard Nelson and Sidney Winter have incorporated the satisficing assumption into an 'evolutionary' model of the firm with which they have succeeded fairly well in simulating the growth pattern of the economy, of firms, and the intra-industry size distribution of firms (1974, 1977, 1978). Baumol and Maco Stewart (1971) tried to repeat some of the Cyert and March experiments, however, and concluded that although 'satisficing' models were instructive, there was some question as to whether they represented a testable theory.

In 1972, Richard Cyert and Charles Hedrick published in this journal results of a survey to ascertain to what extent the 'new' theories of the firm, and especially non-maximizing theories, were replacing neoclassical theory. For this purpose they selected all the relevant articles published in three American journals (*AER, JPE* and *QJE*) during 1970 and 1971, classifying the articles according to the type of model used. They concluded that there was evidence of unease with the neoclassical system, but no displacement.

Our view is that although the force of the argument for satisficing is unmistakable, theories of the firm that have so far been developed based directly on the satisficing approach have displayed a tendency to contain too many detailed and specific assumptions to make them easily generalizable for application to broad problems. To satisfice, as to maximize, it is necessary to specify not only a structure of behaviour, but also a structure of constraints. Some of the more profound issues of current concern are open ended and raise questions (such as the choice of markets or hierarchies), which transcend the question of whether, once a structure is selected, the humans within it satisfice or maximize.

D. Managerial (Growth) Models

In these models the rate of change (usually the proportionate rate of change) of the size of the firm replaces other proxies for utility objectives such as absolute size or absolute expense. The utility function then contains two arguments, the growth rate of the firm and some appropriately normalized measure of its stock-market value. The function can be either smooth or lexicographic. In the latter case a minimum stock-market value is the first priority, and growth is maximized subject to a stock-market value constraint. In early versions (Marris, 1963, 1964) the level of the constraint was exogenous, but in later versions, (Marris, 1972b; John H. Williamson, 1966; G. K. Yarrow, 1973, 1976) it is more plausibly endogenous. In the endogenous case, the minimum, safe stockmarket valuation is assumed to be some fraction of the maximum value that could be placed on the firm by a management pursuing valuation-maximizing policies. In either case, the firm is said to be 'classical' if the weight given to the growth rate in the utility function is negligible and the firm's prime objective is to maximize through stock-market value stockholder welfare. This does not mean that a no-growth policy is inevitable, but rather that the sole criterion for choice of growth rate is that of stock-market value. When the utility function displays a positive preference for growth, the firm is said to be 'managerial'. Unlike the 'classical' label, managerialism is a matter of degree, depending on how much utility weight is given to growth *per se*, relative to the competing claims of stock-market valuation.

Both the static and growth variants of the managerial model assume that managers are capable of exercising a claim on a significant share of firm profits, thus reducing the present value of the firm's stock. Baumol (1959) and Oliver Williamson (1964) postulated a minimum profit constraint on management's discretionary use of corporate profits. Marris (1963, 1964) was the first to hypothesize that managers were constrained by the threat of take-over. If stock-market value falls sufficiently so that a take-over raid becomes likely,[6] management job security is threatened. Thus, in the managerial utility function: growth rate is proxy for income, power, prestige and accompanying managerial gains from growth;[7] and stock-market value is proxy for job security.

Henry G. Manne (1965, 1966), Alchian and Demetz (1972), and Jensen and Meckling (1976) and to some extent Williamson (1970, 1975) have used the threat of take-over to argue that capitalism selects optimal organizational structures. The internal-organization and managerial approaches are thus linked through their reliance on the take-over mechanism to constrain managers. They differ, however, in their views as to how effective this constraint is. Marris had emphasized that take-over raiders were in practice frequently other managerial organizations, or alternatively 'traditional' wheeler-dealers lacking the resources of top management (1963, 1964, p. 32, 1968). The take-over market was highly imperfect. Take-over threats created some incentive for what is now called X-efficiency, but would not necessarily threaten all policies, such as growth, that would tend to be favoured by managers, since such policies were also included in the utility functions of many potential raiders. Indeed, the pursuit of growth may be self-reinforcing; the more managers pursue this objective, the more other managers feel they must conform. Ajit Singh presents evidence suggesting that large size may offer greater protection from take-over than high profitability (1971). All empirical work to date supports Marris's original contention of considerable slack in the take-over mechanism.[8] Consequently, rather than deviant managerial behaviour being driven out by stockholder-welfare-maximizing behaviour, the so-called 'deviant' behaviour has more likely driven out the other.

Growth models, unlike managerial-static models, required the development of a new type of transformation function to specify the constraint against which utility was to be maximized. They required, that is to say, a body of theory to indicate the tradeoff between growth rate and stock-market value—a 'valuation curve' with the (normalized) *level* of stock-market value on one axis and the expected growth rate of the size of the firm on the other. Such transformation relationships were provided by presuming that the firm could, at a certain cost in marketing expenditures, etc., shift outward the demand curves for its products progressively through time at rates that varied directly with the (normalized) level of marketing expenditure incurred (Robert M. Solow, 1971). Marris, however, strongly emphasized growth achieved by progressive diversification (1963, 1964, ch. 4, 1972b,, 1979).[9] The transformation relationship was then 'closed' by specifying the relationships involved between the maximum supply of finance (needed to purchase new assets for growth) that a firm can obtain in a given period relative to that period's operating surplus (John Lintner, 1971; Marris, 1964, ch. 5, 1971, ch. 1; Solow, 1971; J.H. Williamson, 1966). The relationships were also embellished by taking account of the costs of administrative inefficiencies caused by rapid growth in size ('dynamic' diseconomies of scale, not to be confused with static phenomena) as suggested by E.T. Penrose (1959) and elaborated, in the context, by Marris (1964, ch. 3) and H. Uzawa (1969). All these effects and relationships combined to determine the path of dividends that could be expected from a given growth rate: faster growth needed more resources—in demand-expansion expenditures, diversification effort, administrative costs, and new asset formation—for internal purposes, less for current dividends. Hence, these relationships created a tradeoff between current and future dividends. This tradeoff, with an appropriate theory of stock-market values, could determine the tradeoff between growth and valuation, that is, the valuation curve referred to above. These curves were found to have an inverted-U appearance, thus, the maximum would indicate the optimum growth rate for the 'classical' (stockholder-welfare-maximizing) firm. 'Managerial' firms would choose some growth rate to the right of the maximum.

The models are quite complex because a considerable number of substantial theoretical ingredients are involved in the final construction of the valuation curve. For this reason alone they do not appear to have been very well understood. Edith Penrose's book, *The Theory of the Growth of the Firm* published in 1959, first drew attention to the growth of firms over long periods and to the internal administrative forces that enhance and restrain the process. In 1962 William Baumol published a note in the AER, which compared a policy of maximizing discounted profits over time with a policy of maximizing discounted sales over time, but this model only exhibited a part of the system of relationships described above. Marris would claim that his article (1963), followed by the book of 1964, represented the first comprehensive model in the class. The subsequent literature includes J.H. Williamson (1966); Marris (1971, 1972b); Lintner (1971); Solow (1971); G.M. Heal and Aubrey Silbertson (1972); Yarrow (1973, 1976); Alfred S. Eichner (1976); J.B. Herendeen (1979) and A. Silberston (1979). The article by Yarrow is a good analytical survey of both static and growth-oriented managerial theories of the firm in general (1976). Silberston reports a long-range empirical study (1979). H. Odagiri, in a recent book, both surveys and develops the field (1981), as well as provides a comprehensive integration of the theory of the growth of the firm, the growth of the economy, monetary theory, and stock-market values; it is referred to again in Subsection F below.

Lintner, by assuming only 'classical' motivation (1971), developed a general theory of stock-market behaviour, which, given the utility functions of investors and the expected growth rates of firms, would predict all stock prices. Solow's is the only rigorous model to produce an explicit simultaneous solution (admittedly restricted to a single-product firm under monopolistic competition) for product price, marketing expenditure, growth rate, and also absolute size. He then showed that the system could in principle reallocate capital so that the aggregate market value of all listed stocks was maximized at each point of time; in other words, the capital market maximized the welfare of the stockholding class. The model, therefore, represents a neoclassical response to the criticism that the prevailing paradigm ignored the growth of firms, while at the same time preserving the normative properties of the neoclassical model.[10]

In the years that followed their publication, the managerial-growth models have been widely misunderstood as 'non-profit-maximizing' models, this being due to the absence of a familiar appellation for 'stockholder-welfare-maximizing'. The models are maximizing models; they maximize managerial utility. Whether profits are sacrificed in the process depends on how profits are defined: some reported profits will be sacrificed if growth-fostering expenditures, which are akin to investment, are reported as operating costs. If operating profits are defined gross of all growth-fostering expenditures, the managerial-growth models imply that management should always aim to maximize operating profits (J.H. Williamson, 1966). It should operate as efficiently as possible and satisfy all of the marginal conditions of the static neoclassical theory of the firm so that there may be maximum resources for growth for a given stock-market value. Consequently, contrary to what frequently has been asserted, for example, Monsen and Downs (1965), the managerial corporation has no more and no less incentive to be X-efficient than any other; nor does evidence supporting the assumptions of neoclassical price theory contradict the managerial theory as Fritz Machlup suggested (1967). The managerial (growth) and neoclassical theories of the firm differ only in how the short-run maximized profits of the firm are divided between the managers' pursuit of growth and the stockholders. Some economists (e.g. Solow, 1968, 1971) have inferred that the difference is not, therefore, important. We contend that such an inference is naive: we can show that managerial motivation is a crucial influence on the adaptive efficiency of the economic system and thence on economic welfare.

E.   The Life Cycle Hypothesis

All the foregoing growth models assume steady state growth: once the policy variables have been set the firm grows at a constant exponential rate, with constant profit rate and retention ratio and (hence with equal growth rates of profits and assets) until something, either the policy variables or the environment, changes. Mueller's life cycle theory posited a non steady state firm growth pattern (1972). He hypothesized the existence of 'young' firms (not necessarily young in terms of time measured from their foundation, but at least young in terms of time since some events, for example a technological or commercial breakthrough that had rejuvenated them) that had 'taken off' into a process of fast, accelerating growth associated with good profitability. The valuation curve presented no negative tradeoff between growth and stock-market value because at this stage the return on retained profits was better than could be obtained elsewhere. The interests of managers and stockholders converged to maximum feasible growth. Later, as the exceptional circumstances fade, the optimum growth rate for stockholders gradually declines and may finally become negative. During this phase, which may be very long if not indefinite, conflict between managerial and stockholder interests emerges, and it is presumed the managerial interests prevail.

The life cycle/growth hypothesis seems capable of explaining a number of otherwise anomalous facts of corporate capitalism. First note that the hypothesis does not necessarily predict that the fastest growing firms in the economy are the ones for which the managerial/stockholder conflict is most severe. The fast-growing firms could be young firms with high growth and profit potential. The most extreme managerial/stockholder conflict may arise for firms that are hardly growing at all and have only modest opportunities for profit. The stockholders of these firms could benefit from winding up the company and selling off the remaining physical assets, while management for obvious reasons would not. The life cycle hypothesis can also explain why the stockholders of some companies exhibit a seemingly irrational (from the point of view of neoclassical capital theory) preference for dividends over retentions and why some firms earn such low rates of return on ploughed back capital (as found, for example, by Baumol *et al.*, 1970). In both cases we would expect the firms in question to be mature, managerial firms.[11]

The life cycle/growth hypothesis also appears capable of explaining one of neoclassical theory's most enigmatic investments—the corporate merger (Mueller, 1969). Mergers are an obvious way to avoid the slowdown in growth that product maturity brings. Assuming that acquiring firms can operate their acquisitions at roughly the same efficiency levels as the acquired firms previously experienced, growth through merger can be accomplished at only the transaction costs of consummating the merger, including the premium paid to the acquired firm's stockholders. A process of continuous growth through successive mergers can safely be pursued by a mature firm provided only that in this process the firm does not depress the value of its own stock so far as to invite, in return, a raid against itself (Marris, 1964, ch. 1.).

Numerous explanations of mergers have been put forward based on the assumption that managers maximize stockholder welfare.[12] Increases in market power and/or efficiency, most notably the redeployment of capital (J. Fred Weston, 1970; O.E. Williamson, 1970) and the replacement of bad managers (Manne, 1965), have been posited. Although each of these explanations is undoubtedly valid in some cases, none seems capable of explaining the pattern of merger activity that has been observed. For example, mergers in the US have generally followed a wave pattern corresponding to stock-market activity. There is no obvious reason why the redeployment of capital, the replacement of managers, or other synergies should increase dramatically in attractiveness as the health of the economy and the stock market improves. The constraints on the pursuit of growth through merger in the managerial model are the threat of take-over and the amount of resources to consummate mergers. Both of these will be eased in a buoyant economy as cash flows, price–earnings (P/E) ratios, and rates of return on stockholder shares rise. The managerial theory does predict a procyclical merger wave pattern.

The strongest prediction of the neoclassical theory is, of course, that mergers increase the welfare of the stockholders. This hypothesis has not been confirmed for (1) the early merger history of the US where the predominant form of merger was horizontal, (2) recent US conglomerate mergers, or (3) recent European mergers of a largely horizontal nature.[13] By contrast, the managerial prediction that mergers will take place when firms have the resources and discretion to consummate them, whether they are profitable or not, and even when the share performance of the acquiring firms may suffer, seems as consistent with the evidence as any.

F.   Corporate Growth and Macroeconomic Growth

From time to time attempts have been made to relate the microeconomic theory of corporate competition (including the micro theory of the growth of firm) to macroeconomic theories of economic growth and other general-equilibrium problems, such as the general level of stock-market values (e.g. Luigi L. Pasinetti, 1962; Marris, 1964, ch. 7; Kaldor, 1966; or Marris, 1972b). Although this work had implications for non-price competition, its theoretical development did not appear to us adequate for survey at present. At a very late stage in the preparation of this chapter, however, there was made available to us the manuscript of a major work by H. Odagiri (1981), currently in the process of publication, which we believe to be of such relevance that, although we cannot do it justice, we should make some brief attempt to summarize. Odagiri, using basically a neoclassical style of analysis, develops a mathematical two-sector economy, one sector of which is essentially 'corporate' and the other essentially 'neoclassical'. By a rather powerful extension of an earlier theorem of Pasinetti (1962), he shows that corporate-sector behaviour completely dominates the macroequilibrium equations of growth. In this sector, management prefers growth, to some degree, and is restrained by take-overs. The potentiality of take-overs, however, is in turn restricted by transactions costs. Assuming that management at all times maximizes utility and that shareholders to some degree (a behavioural variable) treat capital gains as income—and save and invest accordingly—and assuming that the supply and demand for funds to the stock market is always in equilibrium, Odagiri is able to determine an equilibrium, long-run, full-employment growth rate for the whole economy. This growth rate is derived from technical progress, but the latter is partly endogenous because it depends partly on the effort devoted by firms in general to R and D.

The greater the effective growth-preference of the average corporate management, the faster the rate of technical progress and the faster the equilibrium or actual growth rate of the whole economy. The effective growth-preference of management will depend in turn on a number of factors; sociological (e.g. social forces that emphasize sales volume as a factor in managerial prestige), mobility (e.g. if managers cannot easily move between firms they are more likely to attempt to satisfy their ambitions by pressing the growth of their existing firm), and the transactions costs of take-overs; if the latter are relatively high, take-overs are less potent and management growth-preference is more effective. From the foregoing it follows that sociological pressure against profits and in favour of 'size', social restrictions on the inter-firm mobility of top managers, or substantial imperfections in the capital market all tend to increase, rather than decrease, the equilibrium and actual growth rate of an economy. The author then rather effectively applies this theory to an explanation of the fast recent economic growth of Japan compared to the United States. He could have added that some of the factors (e.g. the imperfect capital market and weaker inter-firm executive mobility) have also been present in two other fast-growing economies, namely those of France and Germany. By contrast, the UK, where the capital-market is highly organized and take-over activity has been even more intense than in the US, is as slow-growing an economy as that of the United States.

By orthodox standards, these are amazingly paradoxical conclusions. We demonstrate below that because R and D has additional social costs as well as benefits, we cannot prove that competition to intensify such activity is *Pareto optimal*. Nor can one make normative judgments about macro growth *per se* given its various external costs (e.g. negative environmental phenomena) and given the absence of a commonly accepted social discount rate. Nevertheless, it remains a rather startling proposition that in the event faster growth were a social objective, discouraging managerial mobility and reducing the efficiency of the take-over market might help achieve it. But, there must be some theorem that the same results could be achieved more cheaply by less second-best measures.

G. Corporate Growth and Business Concentration

The theory of the size distribution of firms has generated a substantial if not enormous literature, which includes the names of Marx, Marshall (1890), Robert Gibrat (1931), Irma Adelman (1958), P.E. Hart and S. Prais (1956), Prais (1976), Herbert Simon and Charles P. Bonini (1958), Simon and Yuji Ijiri (1964, 1967) and Ijiri and Simon (1971). Marris has claimed to discern a division between two schools, one that might be called 'Stochastic', and the other, for want of a better word, 'Empiricist' (1979). The Empirical school tends to explain waves of concentration by particular historical chains of cause and effect and also tends to base theories of aggregate concentration on models based on industry-level concentration. The 'Stochastic' school, as the name implies, while by no means necessarily implying that the growth of a firm in a particular period is a totally chance phenomenon, always includes some significant chance elements. In the view of this school, the *process* of concentration, as originally suggested by Gibrat (1931) is therefore necessarily to some degree Markov-like. Until recently, however, there had been no published attempts at marriage between specific theories of the firm, on the one hand, and stochastic-concentration theories on the other, although Joseph Steindl's *Random Processes and the Growth of Firms* (1965) was an important transitional step, and Marris made pre-nuptial gestures (1972b). Recently, however, with the publication of Nelson and Winter (1978) and Marris (1979), the position has considerably changed.

Nelson and Winter postulate an oligopolistic industry, which is price-taking; that is, firms sell all their capacity output at the ruling price. If, however, the resulting price yields high profits, they undertake investment, which defines their growth and the development of capital concentration in the industry. The progress of costs in individual firms, however, is governed by partly-stochastic internal processes, associated with R and D, so that the profit-experience, and hence the growth of individual firms, is partly stochastic. Assumptions are made concerning the nature of these internal stochastic processes that have the effect of generating serial correlation in growth rates and/or growth rates correlated with size and/or heteroscedastic disturbances—all phenomena that have been discussed or empirically observed (Edwin Mansfield, 1962; Yuji Ijiri and Herbert Simon, 1971; Ajit Singh and Geoffrey Whittington, 1975; Steindl, 1965). Simulation is then used to investigate intra-industry concentration processes.

Thus Nelson and Winter have integrated the microeconomic theory of oligopoly with the theory of microeconomic concentration. Marris developed a parallel integration of the theory of conglomerate growth with the theory of macroeconomic concentration (1979). For simplicity he assumed that a firm's growth is only internally financed. There are then seven equations (g_i=growth rate of firm i):

$$d_i = \hat{p}_i - a_i g_i - g_i \qquad\qquad a_i > 0 \qquad\qquad (5)$$
$$v_i = d_i(b_1 + b_2 g_i) \qquad\qquad b_1, b_2 > 0 \qquad\qquad (6)$$
$$\hat{p}_i = \bar{p} e_i \qquad\qquad\qquad e_i > 0 \qquad\qquad (7)$$
$$K_i = e_i/(1 + a_i) \qquad\qquad\qquad\qquad (8)$$
$$K_i = \gamma x_i + \mu_i \qquad\qquad\qquad\qquad (9)$$
$$v_i \geq b_1 d_i \qquad\qquad\qquad\qquad (10)$$

Maximizing g_i subject to (10),

$$\text{Max } g_i = \bar{p}(\gamma\, x_i + \mu_i) - b_1/b_2 \qquad\qquad (11)$$

Equation (5) states that the dividend per dollar of assets (d) of firm i is equal to operating profits per dollar of assets ($\hat{p}$), less expenditures on growth promotion per dollar of assets ($a_i g_i$), less retained profits per dollar of assets, which with no external financing has to be equal to g_i itself, where a_i is a coefficient reflecting the costs of growth (e.g. a_i would be relatively small in a young firm, then become larger with maturity).[14] Equation (6) states that the stock market value, per dollar of assets (v) depends on the dividend and the expected growth rate of the dividend, which in steady state is equal to the growth rate of the firm. The coefficients b_1 and b_2 reflect the stock market environment. b_1 is the P/E ratio if i has zero expected growth rate, and $b_1 d_i$ is the corresponding stock market value. Equation (7) states that firm i's operating return is equal to the average profit rate, $\hat{p}$, of all other firms multiplied by a coefficient, e_i, reflecting the particular circumstances of i (e.g. e_i is high if i is young, etc.). Equation (8) defines a composite variable K_i. Equation (9) states that this composite variable is related to the log of the size of the firm, measured by assets (x_i) via a coefficient, γ and a disturbance term μ_i. The prior assumption is that γ is positive for young firms, negative for middle-aged firms, and zero for mature firms. Equation (10) states that the firm's utility function is such that it will not permit the stock-market value to fall below the value that would be placed on the firm by a classically motivated raider. Equation (11) gives the result of combining the equations and maximizing the growth rate subject to this constraint.

The foregoing is a complete theory for precisely determining the expected growth rate of a managerial firm subject to a disturbance term.

Although the managerial theory tells us something about the characteristics of acquiring firms in mergers (e.g. limited internal growth opportunities), it says nothing about the characteristics of the companies they acquire. All that can safely be said is that they are firms that for one reason or another have become cheap on the stock exchange relative to their underlying assets or earning power (Kuehn, 1975; Smiley, 1976). Although the cheaper firms tend to be the ones taken, we do not at present have a clear idea of what makes them cheap.[15] Furthermore, given that a number of firms are at a particular time cheap, we do not know which ones will be taken over and which survive. In the long run, say a period of 20 years, given typical aggregate take-over rates, the chances of *any* firm surviving are quite low—only a little better than 50 per cent. In principle we should be able to estimate the probability distribution of the size relationships between acquired and acquiring firms. Some attempts have been made on this estimate by John J. McGowan (1965). Below we assume that this probability distribution exists and resort to simulation to estimate the consequences.

In effect it is not difficult to show (see Marris, 1979, pp. 116–35) that if there exists a reasonably stable transition matrix defining the probabilities that firms in given size classes will take over a given number of firms in various other size classes, in a given period, the time path of merger-related aggregate business concentration is determinate and predictable. More precisely, this result obtains when supported by some additional assumptions concerning the pattern of new entry (which in practice takes place mainly into the smallest size classes (Ijiri and Simon, 1971; Marris, 1979, p. 137; McGowan, 1965) and also concerning the interaction of individual firms and their individual capacities or propensities for internal growth (Pitts, 1976). Simulation has shown (Marris, 1979, pp. 136–41) that under these conditions, given a plausible distribution of the elements of the above-described transition matrix, concentration due to merger will increase progressively through time.

Even if all mergers were prohibited, however, a population of firms governed by a partly-stochastic internal-growth model of the type described above will also tend—through a Markov chain—to display persistently increasing concentration. The effects of merger and the effects of (stochastically-disturbed) internal growth can be combined into a general model of the total concentration process. The implications of this model are so important, and so little understood by general economists, that we again feel it necessary to set out the relevant equations in full.

In a population of constant size, as might be expected from the interplay of new entry against 'exits' of firms acquired in mergers, it is accepted that the variance of the logs of the sizes of firms (logs being used because of the skew distribution) is a satisfactory measure of aggregate concentration that in these circumstances moves in step with other familiar measures. If this measure is signified by σ_x^2 and the annual increase in this measure caused by mergers is signified by m, then the equations below precisely describe the path of concentration that will be followed if individual firms are governed by an internal-growth model of the type summarized above in equation (11). (The coefficient γ is now interpreted as reflecting the average degree of 'youth' or 'senility' of the population [of firms] or more precisely the overall correlation between the sizes of firms and their capacities to grow).

$$\sigma_{xt}^2 = (\bar{p}^2 \sigma_\mu^2 + m) \cdot \frac{1 - (1 + \gamma \bar{p})^{2t}}{1 - (1 + \gamma \bar{p})^2} \tag{12}$$

and

$$\frac{d\sigma_{xt}^2}{dt} = (\bar{p}^2 \sigma_\mu^2 + m)(1 + \gamma \bar{p})^{2(t-1)} \qquad \text{for } \gamma \neq 0 \tag{13}$$

$$\sigma_{xt}^2 = (\bar{p}^2 \sigma_\mu^2 + m)t, \tag{14}$$

and

$$\frac{d\sigma_{xt}^2}{dt} = \bar{p}^2 \sigma_\mu^2 + m, \qquad \text{for } \gamma = 0 \tag{15}$$

The foregoing assumes all firms are equal in size at time 0. When $\gamma = 0$, the model develops a lognormal distribution whose mean natural size grows at a constant exponential rate equal to $(\bar{p} - b_1/b_2)$, this being the predicted macroeconomic growth rate (with investment equal to aggregate retained profits) in a private sector with only internal financing. Given the assumptions concerning the μ_i as set out above, the variance of this distribution grows linearly at the rate given by equations (14) and (15); these are the equations of increasing concentration given by Gibrat's Law (1931) to which much attention has been paid in subsequent research. Deviations from the assumptions, such as heteroscedastic disturbances, will produce more complex patterns, but the distribution will nevertheless continue to display extreme skewness, which becomes much more symmetrical under a logarithmic transformation. Ijiri and Simon used simulation to analyse elegantly the effects of serially correlated growth rates (1971). They were deceived however by erroneous data into believing that aggregate concentration in the US has for some time been stable, which, of course, it has not.

Empirically, aggregate size distributions of business firms are always extremely skewed but amenable to much greater symmetry under the semilog transformation, as predicted above, a result that has no easy interpretation in the Marshallian neoclassical system. Sometimes these distributions appear lognormal; sometimes, they seem to deviate in various ways from lognormality. The latter results can be ascribed either to non-fulfillment of the assumptions concerning disturbances or to $\gamma \neq 0$.

When γ is less than zero, it is not the case, as might be supposed, that concentration tends to decline. Rather it increases asymptotically to a limit as time approaches infinity. When γ is greater than zero, concentration does, as expected, explode. Simulations described in Marris suggest that either the linear case or the slightly damped case may have been at work in the US data since the end of World War II (1979). In Europe there is some evidence of the explosive case (Prais, 1976).

The general conclusion is that the legal and institutional permissions of capitalism imply a self-organizing process leading to persistently increasing concentration in the absence of special legal restrictions on conglomerate growth or in the absence of specific fiscal handicaps imposed on larger firms (some theoretical possibilities in the latter regard are explored in Marris (1979)). To the extent that the evolution of the size distribution of firms is the outcome of stochastic growth in a Gibratian world, this evolution is without normative implications. To the extent that the process of increasing concentration is enhanced by managerial pursuit of growth through internal expansion, macroeconomic growth may be increased, and with it social welfare. But, if managerial pursuit of growth is by socially unproductive investments (e.g. in merger activity), increasing aggregate concentration may imply declining social welfare.

III.   COMPETITION FOR MONOPOLY

A.   The Implications of Non-price Competition

The invisible hand doctrine teaches that price competition leads to a *Pareto optimal* allocation of resources through costless movements along demand and cost schedules. If price competition induces an individual to switch from A to B, then knowledge that he considers himself better off following the switch suffices to ensure that society is better off, since the process of price competition itself is assumed to consume no resources. There is only a reallocation of simple production resources.

As noted in the introduction, however, many observers consider the salient modes of competition to be investments that *shift* demand and cost schedules. These do use up resources. Knowledge that an individual has been induced to switch from B to A because of investments that improve the quality of A or expenditures to provide more information about A does not suffice to prove that society is made better off. The question is whether the net benefits consumers obtain from such a switch exceed the investment costs of bringing the switch about.

Within the last few years, a number of papers have appeared examining the major modes of non-price competition: invention, innovation, information gathering, and dissemination. Some conclude that these activities are best undertaken by a monopoly; others are indecisive. They agree, however, that free entry and exit into non-price-competitive activities do not generally produce a *Pareto optimal* utilization of resources. Although several of these contributions have received considerable individual attention, the extent to which they fit together and reinforce one another has not been appreciated generally. Section III attempts to mitigate this latter deficiency. We begin by reviewing the question of the optimal investment in inventive activity.

B.   The Optimal Investment in Inventive Activity

Consider an invention that reduces costs. The invention's potential social benefits are the discounted present value of the additional consumer's surplus (V) generated by using the new, lower, cost function. If all firms have access to the invention once it exists, no firm has an incentive to undertake the investment necessary to create it. To induce this investment, some form of monopoly of its benefits must exist. To ensure that all inventions costing less than V are made, the inventor must be able to capture the full additional consumer's surplus generated by the invention. One way for this to occur is for the invention to be made by or sold to a perfect price-discriminating monopolist. The inventor then secures the full potential benefits from the invention, and any invention that costs less than V is undertaken. If the purchaser of the invention is not either the consumer of the product or a perfect price discriminator, the realized benefits may be less than this, and some potentially beneficial inventions will not be undertaken (see Yoram Barzel, 1971, and William D. Nordhaus, 1969).

The potential profits an inventor can earn, in the limit V, should lead to competition to produce the invention and secure the monopoly of it. But any expenditure above the minimum necessary to produce the invention is an unnecessary duplication of effort. Thus, with full knowledge of the benefits and costs of an invention, the optimal investment in cost-reducing invention occurs only if each invention is undertaken by a single inventor or firm, and sold either to a perfect price-discriminating monopolist or to the government, which freely licenses the invention.[16]

This conclusion relies on the assumption that the full benefits and costs of invention are known. This assumption eliminates the uncertainties surrounding the invention process and makes the process resemble oil-well digging when the depth, location and size of the pool are known. In such a world, the optimal investment is to dig one hole and is made whenever the value of the oil pool exceeds the cost of the digging. But the typical analogy is between invention and oil-well digging where the position and size of the pools are not known. Here the introduction of competition can lead to the discovery of additional pools.

Richard Nelson has presented the most persuasive case for competition among inventors (1961). As Nelson notes, each additional inventor is not only a potential duplicator of another's effort, but also potentially a discoverer of a different invention. With large numbers of potential inventions, and alternative paths to these, additional inventors (firms) increase the number of paths taken, and thereby the number of and speed at which inventions are introduced. But, as Nelson recognizes, the desirability of parallel R and D efforts in a world of uncertainty is not in itself sufficient to demonstrate the superiority of competitive market structures over either monopolized markets or central planning. Hypothetically, the most exhaustive non-duplicative R and D effort could be achieved by a single organization, which gathered information on all possible inventive paths and made sure that all potentially beneficial paths were followed, and no path followed twice. While in practice such an organizational structure might prove to be less than some form of competitive or oligopolistic private market structure, the latter's greater efficiency has not yet been demonstrated theoretically and must rest upon empirical support. Here, Nelson's example of the government's successful employment of competing laboratories to develop the atom bomb during World World II, which he uses to support his case for parallel R and D efforts, seems equally convincing as a demonstration of the potential flexibility and feasibility of centralized non-market solutions to the optimal invention problem.[17] Thus, on a theoretical level, the argument that invention is most efficiently undertaken by a single firm or organizational unit acting as a first-degree price discriminator seems to stand on as solid ground as the argument for competition among inventors.[18]

C. The Social Benefits from a New Product

Any competition to introduce the same new product obviously results in the same wasteful duplication of effort as competition to introduce the same cost-reducing invention. Thus, the arguments of the previous section carry over here. Let us consider, therefore, competition to introduce different new products.

Several papers have appeared recently demonstrating that the introduction of new products under monopolistic competition in general does not result in an equilibrium in which the socially optimal product mix is offered (A.K. Dixit and Joseph Stiglitz, 1977; R. W. Koenker and M.K. Perry, 1981; Kelvin Lancaster, 1975; Michael Spence, 1976a). In a world of product differentiation and monopolistic competition the introduction of a new product generates additional consumer's surplus for the new product, but reduces the consumer's surplus achieved on the displaced product(s). If changes in profits and changes in consumer's surplus were always one for one, as they would be in the case of perfect price discrimination, the introduction of profitable new products under conditions of monopolistic competition would yield a socially optimal product mix. But changes in profits and net changes in consumer's surplus need not go hand in hand. When they do not, knowledge that it is profitable to introduce a new product does not tell us whether additional net consumer's surplus has been created. Monopolistic competition avoids goods with high ratios of consumer's surplus to obtainable profits (i.e. goods with inelastic demand schedules) and avoids goods with high ratios of fixed to variable costs (Dixit and Stiglitz, 1977; Spence, 1976a, b). The number of products emerging under new product rivalry and monopolistic competition can exceed or fall short of the social optimum.

Similar arguments apply to advertising. Much has been written about whether advertising informs consumers about actual attributes of products or *persuades* them about imaginary ones. Most observers undoubtedly regard the former activity as socially more useful than the latter. Yet in either case, competition via advertising could result in a net reduction in social welfare. Just as we do not know whether the mix of products offered in equilibrium under monopolistic competition is socially optimal, we cannot say whether a change in that mix is an improvement. Changes in the equilibrium mix under monopolistic competition brought about by informative advertising could raise or lower social welfare.[19]

D. Monopoly Rent Seeking and Social Welfare

Invention, innovation, and information gathering are classic 'natural monopoly' activities involving heavy up-front investments and low if not zero marginal costs of use and dissemination. The socially optimal institutional arrangement for undertaking these activities is for society to compensate the inventor or information gatherer fully and then make the results freely available to all (Nordhaus, 1969). No feasible, first-best institutional structure appears capable of achieving this outcome, however. The second-best alternative of granting a limited property right to the monopoly rents from invention and prior information is typically followed.

When property rights to rent-generating assets exist, however, an additional form of wasteful competition arises. Further expenditures by the monopolist to maintain its position and by others to gain control of it can be expected. This point has been made by Gordon Tullock (1967) and Richard Posner (1975) in criticism of the traditional approach to 'the monopoly problem'. Since their point is novel, and we believe not generally understood and/or accepted, we elaborate on it.[20] It is useful to distinguish between competition for monopoly among *firms* and competition for monopoly within firms among *factor owners*. This distinction is further explored in Subsection E and F.

E. Competition for Monopoly Among Firms

Consider a world of clearly defined products in which each product is sold by a firm or firms with some market power. Firms vie for the right to sell a given product and earn the potential monopoly rents associated with it. The right to sell a product may be a legal privilege granted by the government or the right accompanying the successful displacement of other firms in a non-regulated market. The monopoly rents won by this competition accrue to the factor owners of each successful firm. In the limit we could assume that no change in the set of products ever took place and all competition was over the property rights to the monopoly rents attached to each individual product. Any investment to change the ownership of a product would then always represent a loss to society. The increase in monopoly rents received by those gaining control of a monopoly would always equal the loss in monopoly rents by those giving up control *less the cost of bringing about the transfer*.

Legal monopolies include tariff-protected industries, 'natural' monopolies protected by the government (e.g. electricity, gas, transportation, radio), and fair trade restrictions on price or other forms of competition. Competition for control of these monopolies usually takes the form of expenditures to influence government policies. Lobbying, campaign contributions, and bribes are examples of these. Some of these, for example bribes, are direct transfers and result in no waste in resources. To the extent obtaining a legal monopoly requires an expenditure of time and resources by the competing firms' managers, lawyers, accountants and lobbyists, this competition wastes resources. And, to the expenditures of the competing firms must be added the resources spent by government representatives and bureaucrats monitoring and controlling this competition.

In non-regulated markets, firms compete directly for monopoly rents within the product markets. Virtually all forms of non-price competition are attempts to differentiate products and create or transfer the monopoly rents accompanying product differentiation. Market research, product design, packaging, public relations and some fraction of the legal services of corporations may constitute expenditures to maintain or obtain monopoly rents. Chief among these are probably advertising and R and D. Several investigators have found that these activities can lead to entry barriers which raise average returns (e.g. William S. Comanor and Thomas A. Wilson, 1967). These returns will induce large expenditures, by those within the industry and potential entrants, to transfer control over these rents. High monopoly rents may be the cause of heavy advertising and R and D, as well as the reverse. Studies showing low (often negative) *marginal* returns on advertising suggest that this form of non-price competition results, from the point of view of the competitors themselves, in inefficiency—a competing away of the monopoly rents existing within the industries (Jean-Jacques Lambin, 1969; Kristian Palda, 1964; Richard Schmalensee, 1972). And there is some evidence that the same sort of self-destructive competition occurs for R and D in some R and D intensive industries (Grabowski and Mueller, 1978). Unlike the outcome of price competition, any erosion of monopoly rents that comes from non-price competition to redistribute these rents is a loss to both society and the companies involved.

Jensen and Meckling have noted that the separation or ownership from control gives managers extra incentive to undertake risky investments (1976). Competition for monopoly via advertising, R and D, and product differentiation are precisely the kinds of 'risky' investments that are likely to be stimulated. Should an R and D programme be successful in coming up with an important invention, the managers can use their 'insider's position' to secure large speculative gains, and these may not be limited to the securities of their own company.

Jack Hirshleifer has observed that an inventor can profit from his invention by buying long claims on the profits of firms that will rise following the invention's introduction (e.g. complements) and selling short claims against firms whose profits (π) will fall (1971). In the limit an inventor could capture all of the changes in asset values brought about by the invention if he can accurately anticipate them. Thus, while ΔW, the net social benefits from inventing new product, n, assuming perfect price discrimination, is the *difference* in the profits it brings about as in (16),

$$\Delta W = \pi_n + \sum_{i=1}^{n-1} \Delta\pi_i,$$ (16)

the private benefits (PB) to its inventor could conceivably equal the *sum of their absolute values*.

$$PB = \sum_{i=1}^{n} |\Delta\pi_i|.$$ (17)

This can occur because the inventor actually possesses two assets of value: the invention itself (or say the patent to it) and prior knowledge of it. The first allows him to claim some or all of the monopoly rents resulting from the direct implementation of the invention. Prior information of the invention allows him to speculate on all of the purely redistributive changes in asset values, which may result from the invention's introduction. Since both of these returns are direct consequences of the invention, both can induce expenditures to come up with the invention, and could, in theory, lead to total expenditures to invent a product far in excess of its net social benefits.[21]

Another explanation for why corporate managers undertake acquisitions yielding negligible benefits for their own stockholders, but producing large gains to the stockholders of the companies they acquire, is that the acquiring company managers are in an excellent position to 'speculate' on the substantial price rise of the acquired firm's shares their merger offer brings about. It is more than just a curiosity that large increases in trading volume and much of the rise in the acquired firm's share price accompanying its acquisition occur *before* the acquisition is announced.[22]

The more general point is that offsetting changes in asset values, however irrelevant to our notions of social welfare, are of great interest to the parties involved and can lead to investment in information gathering to anticipate these changes. Prior information about future prices of Monet paintings, rare stamps, and antique furniture can yield high returns without affecting the production of these goods. But, prior information has social value only when it does affect *and improve* the allocation of resources. Estimates of the resources devoted to gathering, processing and disseminating information by Marc U. Porat run to over 25 per cent of GNP (1975). The information provided via the daily racing form, stock market reports and assessments, surveys of economic trends, as well as more formal market research and R and D activities can have both private and social value. To the extent it leads to pure redistributions of wealth, this information has no (or at least an ambiguous) net social value and is likely to be an *over-investment* of resources.

F. Competition for Monopoly among Factor Owners

Consider next competition for monopoly rents among the firm's factor owners. Assume a given population of firms, each with a given degree of monopoly power. Competition among factor owners determines which owner(s) receive the monopoly rents.

The theories discussed in Section II, especially Subsection C, imply that a substantial part of the potential profits of the firm are probably appropriated by the managers. John P. Palmer's study (1973a) showing lower *reported* profits for management-controlled firms in high market power industries than for owner-controlled companies further implies that managers do appropriate part of the rents, which accompany market Power. The literature on the managerial theory of the firm, static or growth, suggests that the reward for succeeding in the competitive struggle to reach the top comes precisely through the power to control these monopoly rents. The various theories differ only in their assumptions regarding the uses to which these revenues are diverted by managers in pursuit of their self interest.

Competition among managers for control of a corporation's monopoly rents may take the form of extra hours of work, skill development and investment in education. Tibor Scitovsky has noted the surprisingly large *reduction* in the amount of leisure enjoyed by managerial and professional groups since the turn of the century (1976); a pattern not followed by other groups. This development may reflect competition among managers and professionals for the monopoly rents available to them in the occupations they have chosen, and further, the possible expansion of these rents over time. The decline of the entrepreneurial firm relative to the corporation may have carried with it a shift in the competition for monopoly rents away from the struggle for market control among existing and new firms to a struggle for control of existing market power among present and new managers. The rise of the take-over raid as a means of displacing managers would be further evidence of the shift toward displacement of managers in existing firms by other managers, rather than the displacement of one firm by another as the means for transferring control over monopoly. Take-overs require an investment in time and resources by the take-over raider—gathering information, soliciting proxies, the inevitable lawyers' fees. These are, from the point of view of society, wasted to the extent that they simply transfer control of a given monopoly rent from one group to another.

The same type of competition may occur among individuals outside of the firm. In medicine, for example, high entry barriers present opportunities for high monopoly rents via the practice of price discrimination.[23] The ability to price discriminate depends on the ability to offer a special service (differentiated product), however, and has resulted in an elaborate licensing system and competition among doctors to obtain qualification within the special areas. These expenditures may have in large part simply redistributed the potential rents inherent in the industry among the competing physicians. Similar licensing schemes, pricing practices and competition characterize other professions with similar results likely.

The argument is not that all expenditures on skill development and education represent social waste, any more than that all R and D or advertising does. Some of the additional training and education doctors receive undoubtedly does improve the quality of the services they perform, just as some of the education and skills managers acquire in their competitive struggle for control of the corporation may lead to improvements in efficiency or product quality. But a surgeon may be able to earn a large increase in income by winning patients from another surgeon and securing the monopoly rents the other was earning, on the basis of only a small advantage in skill. A manager who is skillful at obtaining monopoly rents is equally valuable to his company regardless of whether the rents arise from real improvements in product quality or corporate efficiency, or from transfers of control over existing monopolies.

The bulk of competition for monopoly rents involves expenditures that enter into company costs. R and D, advertising, legal services and other forms of inter-firm competitive expenditures all are reported as costs by firms. Managerial effort, to the extent that it is compensated by higher managerial salaries, and on-the-job, company-financed consumption also become a part of reported costs.

From this discussion, it should be obvious that the profits firms report *net* of most of their expenditures to expand and secure monopoly positions are a bad understatement of the extent of their market power. Studies such as Arnold Harberger's (1954) and David Schwartzman's

(1960), which base their estimates of monopoly welfare loss on the levels of *reported* industry profits most certainly underestimate the extent of these losses.[24] Nor do levels of industry or firm profits provide a good indication of the magnitude of resources wasted in zero-sum efforts to redistribute monopoly rents. To measure these one must examine the expenditures by firms and individuals directly.[25]

G.   Summary on Competition for Monopoly

Under the invisible hand theorem, *Pareto* optimality emerges as a beneficial side-effect of the pursuit of profit through a process of costless price competition. In Schumpeter's description of the competitive process, the monopoly profits from one innovation become the means for developing another and monopoly profits are sustained over time only by the successive introduction of new innovations, thereby offsetting the 'perennial gale of destruction' that imitation of an innovation brings (1934, 1950). But, the introduction of a new innovation is not the only way to preserve a monopoly rent, nor necessarily the cheapest. The monopoly rents of one period can be extended into the next by investments in patent lawyers, lobbyists, bribes to government officials, campaign contributions, and myriad other expenditures of questionable social merit.[26] To induce the benefits from non-price competition, property rights to the resulting rents must be granted. But then, additional outlays to predict, create, maintain and transfer ownership of these property rights are induced. Our welfare criterion, the *Pareto* principle, ignores distributional considerations, however. Since part of these investments are to achieve pure redistributions, non-price competition must produce some waste, and the more competition of this form there is, the more waste there will be. The possibility thus arises that the total cost of investments in non-price competition exceed the benefits. There simply is no analogue to the invisible hand theorem for non-price competition.

IV.   CONCLUSIONS

If one were to give an honours student in economics *Capitalism, Socialism and Democracy* to read, and then ask for an essay on the 'Schumpeterian hypothesis', the student would probably write something about capitalism's efficiency relative to socialism in the era of the large corporation. If one asked a graduate student in industrial organization to write about the 'Schumpeterian hypothesis', the student would write something about whether firms with market power or large absolute size undertake more innovative activity than other companies. This latter hypothesis, a conjecture presented in a few lines (1950, pp. 87–8), has been the one to draw the profession's attention. Schumpeter's 'other' hypothesis has usually been ignored.

It is ironic that Schumpeter should have written a book almost condoning if not advocating a shift from capitalism to socialism (1950). The view of capitalism as a dynamic process of competition for and erosion of monopoly profits has never been expressed better than by Schumpeter in *The Theory of Economic Development* (1934). Schumpeter formulated this roseate view of capitalism at the turn of the century, and by mid-century he had abandoned it. The development of the large corporation had changed the nature of capitalism. The entrepreneur-innovator was no longer the source of new innovations; the innovation process was now routinized and centralized in the large corporation. It could easily be taken over by central government without serious loss in dynamic efficiency. One of the outstanding features of Schumpeter's work, in the context of this essay, is that it clearly recognized the importance of examining the organizational structure and efficiency of the corporation along with the nature and efficiency of the competitive process.

John Kenneth Galbraith has also placed the corporation on centre stage in his analysis (1967a). His focus is also chiefly on non-price forms of competition. Essentially the same evolutionary view of capitalism is contained in the *New Industrial State* as is in *Capitalism, Socialism and Democracy*. Invention and innovation take place within the corporate R and D laboratory, and these laboratories along with corporate advertising and marketing departments dictate consumer demand. Galbraith does not go so far as Schumpeter in predicting the absorption of the corporate sector by government, but argues instead for a partnership between government and business.

The views of mid-twentieth-century capitalism of Schumpeter and Galbraith are also surprisingly close to those of Baran and Sweezy (1966). The parallels are surprising because Baran and Sweezy are, of course, Marxist in both their objectives and methodology. Many of the expenditures treated here as wasted under competition for monopoly rents appear in their essay as 'selling costs', whose purpose is to absorb the rising surplus monopoly capitalism produces and avoid ever impending stagnation by stimulating demand (1966, pp. 108–11). Like Galbraith, Baran and Sweezy emphasize the importance of separation of ownership from control and the discretion it gives managers to use the internal cash flows of the corporation (1966, ch. 2). Since their book was written at the time the managerial discretion theories were first appearing, they make no direct use of them. But, the hypothesis that managers *over*-invest in product differentiation, advertising and other growth-producing activities as developed by Marris (1964) is an implicit part of their thesis, as the Marris growth-maximization hypothesis is explicitly incorporated into Galbraith's theory (1967a).

In the present paper we have tried to show that a large literature has now evolved within the formal bounds of the discipline that is as much at odds with the implications of the invisible hand theorem as was the previous 'heterodox', institutionalist, or Marxist literature. The new literature is rigorous, amenable to empirical testing and, we would argue, more consistent with empirical evidence than the neoclassical model, where the two differ in their predictions. It thus meets the criteria of positive economics. Where it differs from the traditional theory most fundamentally is in its normative implications. There either are none, or they are negative. Managerial pursuit of self interest need not lead to maximum present values of investment streams; too much may be retained, too much reinvested. Non-price competition need not produce greater social benefits than costs. Too much may be invested to secure the redistributive gains of monopoly power.

The major alternatives in industrial policy in the United States today would appear to be: (1) preservation of the present form of managerial capitalism with its heavy emphasis on growth through merger and non-price competition among the few; (2) further movement along the road to democratic socialism or a government–business partnership as predicted by Schumpeter, Galbraith and Baran and Sweezy; (3) a reverse shift to an industrial structure more reminiscent of that first described by Schumpeter, through the breakup of large corporations and possible restrictions on mergers and on some forms of non-price competition such as advertising. The choice from among these is not obvious and cannot be left to the evolutionary process of corporate capitalism on the grounds that whatever organizational and industrial structure emerges must be assumed most efficient simply because it is the one the process 'selected'. The choice must reflect an understanding of the nature of the corporation and of its actual modes of competition.

We do not think this is a weak conclusion. In relation to the neoclassical paradigm it is very aggressive. Taking a broader view, however, as Marris discussed in (1974), it may be clear to most people that a system of some hundreds of competing planned economies (i.e. giant corporations) operating in close partnership with government will be both more X-efficient and offer more personal liberty than a system that had literally converged into a Soviet-type system. We share this belief. Where most observers will differ is over how the giant corporation–government partnership and some more 'old fashioned', decentralized industrial structure compare. Those who support a given scenario are entitled to their ethical preference, but they are almost certainly wrong if they claim to be able to prove that the overall efficiency of their favoured system—defined as ability to pursue successfully their political, social and economic goals—would necessarily bè superior to any other.

NOTES

1. It has been found that firms specialize to some degree in growing by the one means or by the other. Robert A. Pitts has usefully classified the two types, 'Internal Growth Diversified' and 'Acquisition Growth Diversified', and reported that each type tends to adopt internal arrangements best suited to its speciality (1976). Alternatively, where this adaptation is not the case, performance is weak. *See also* J. Hassid (1977).
2. Since around the turn of the century, the 200 largest US manufacturing enterprises (of course, a changing group) have increased their share of total manufacturing assets on average by about one-half of a percentage point per annum, now holding from 58 to 63 per cent, depending on the data source. The most official series, provided by the Federal Trade Commission, unfortunately underwent a major break in the period 1971–3, which had the effect of causing an apparent drop in concentration (David W. Penn, 1976). After the 1973 break the top-200 share, as newly defined, has resumed its upward climb, averaging +0.4 of one percentage point per annum for 1973–8. In the old series, from 1950–70, the trend increase was +0.6 of a per cent. From 1910 to 1950, using the best available and appropriately adjusted series (Marris, 1979), the figure was about 0.45. Thus the trend for the 1970s, while less than for the 1950s and 1960s, is not significantly lower than for the whole half century. In more recent years, concentration has greatly increased in the financial sector and during the whole post-war period has moderately increased in the distributive sector. By contrast, since 1950, the median value of the four-firm concentration ratio in individual US industries has not significantly changed. The theoretical relationship between 'industrial' (micro) concentration and 'business' or macroconcentration is further discussed in Marris (1979). Lawrence G. Goldberg (1974) and others have shown that mergers do not necessarily increase average industrial concentration ratios. Marris emphasizes that macroconcentration is much smaller in terms of employment than in terms of assets and that heavy macroconcentration in assets is consistent with the permanent coexistence of a very large pool of very small firms (1979). In developed market economies other than the United States, the recent rate of increase of aggregate concentration seems to have been faster. For the United Kingdom, *see* Prais (1976); for Germany, *see* Jürgen Müller and Rolf Hochreiter (1976).
3. *See* George Stigler (1956); David R. Kamerschen (1966); Keith Cowling and Mueller (1978).
4. The dictionary defines paradigmatic as exemplary. Our expression is intended to describe shortsightedness caused by excessive loyalty to a false example.
5. For further development of this line of argument, *see* Michael C. Jensen and William H. Meckling (1976).

6. For evidence *see* Kuehn (1975); Singh (1971, 1975); and Robert Smiley (1976).
7. For arguments and evidence up to 1964, *see* Marris (1964, ch. 2). For a bibliography of subsequent debate on the implications of executive compensation data, *see* David H. Ciscel (1974).
8. *See* again, Kuehn (1975), Singh (1971, 1975), Smiley (1976).
9. Marris specified successive diversification into new activities as the sales from existing activities successively took off, accelerated, and saturated. This concept seems fairly well supported by the empirical evidence on diversification. *See* Adrian Wood (1971) and Hassid (1977).
10. For debate *see* Solow (1967a, 1967b, 1968), John Kenneth Galbraith (1967b), and Marris (1968; 1971, pp. 26–36).
11. For further discussion of the relevant empirical literature and a first successful testing of the hypothesis, *see* Mueller (1972) and Henry Grabowski and Mueller (1975).
12. For a survey, *see* Peter O. Steiner (1975).
13. For surveys of the early US experience, *see* Jesse W. Markham (1955) and Thomas F. Hogarty (1970a); of recent US experience, Mueller (1977); and for Europe, Geoffrey Meeks (1977) and Mueller (1980, ch. 2).
14. The coefficient *a* also reflects the 'product environment' of the firm and will tend to be large when for one reason or another demand expansion is difficult. However, given the several means of growth open to the firm—including diversification and merger—it is essential to avoid identifying this concept of an 'environment' with the more narrowly defined characteristics of the product markets in which the firm happens to be involved at a particular time. Thus, *a* includes *inter alia* the costs and potentialities of diversification, as has repeatedly been emphasized (Marris, 1963, 1964, 1971).
15. The notion that they are cheap because they are failing does not appear to be generally true. *See* Stanley E. Boyle (1970), Donald L. Stevens (1973), Ronald W. Melicher and David F. Rush (1974), and Mueller (1980, ch. 2).
16. Barzel develops these arguments in detail (1971). Much of his focus is on the *timing* of inventions rather than the amount of inventive activity. Here competition to be first is also inefficient leading to inventions introduced *too soon* rather than too much investment.
17. Nordhaus presented a model of the invention process, which allowed for both the possibilities of beneficial spillovers from multiple R and D efforts, as well as wasteful duplication (1969, ch. 3). In principle, one can solve for the optimal number of firms in an industry to internalize the spillover effects from invention, a number smaller than the competitive solution, but not necessarily one.
18. It should be noted that the controversy over the relative incentives to invent for monopolistic and competitive industries launched by Arrow (1962) is a separate issue. Arrow recognizes and emphasizes the non-optimality of a competitive solution to the invention problem. His discussion of invention incentives *assumes* a monopolist-inventor and asks the question whether he invests more in invention (given full knowledge of the benefits of the invention) if he sells to a monopolist or to a competitive industry. Thus, Arrow's proof is based entirely on differences in static monopoly rents earned after the invention, as are the counter proofs by Harold Demsetz (1969) and Morton I. Kamien and Nancy L. Schwartz (1970). The *dynamic* competition

for invention question is not addressed in this debate.

19. S. C. Salop (1978). A number of papers have appeared recently challenging the efficiency of the market system in providing information about relative scarcities via the price system and in providing proper incentives for gathering information. These papers are briefly summarized and the relevant literature cited in Sanford J. Grossman and Stiglitz (1976).

20. A mushrooming literature now exists here, too. Part of it is captured in J. M. Buchanan *et al.* (1980).

21. Of course, the uncertainties and spillovers from inventive activity tend to offset the potential for over-investment, which the speculative value of information does provide (Arrow, 1962; Hirshleifer, 1971, pp. 570–2).

22. *See* e.g. Paul J. Halpern (1973), Gershon Mandelker (1974), Michael A. Firth (1976), J. M. Gagnon *et al.* (1982).

23. *See* Erwin Blackstone's case study of pricing in the specialist fields of medicine for support for the arguments in this paragraph (1974).

24. While Posner correctly criticizes Harberger for underestimating the welfare losses from monopoly by basing his calculations on reported profits, Posner then goes on to make the *ad hoc* assumption that prices in manufacturing and mining are 2 per cent above the competitive level, and from this calculates a welfare loss for this sector of 0.6 per cent of GNP (1975, p. 819). But advertising alone exceeds 2 per cent of GNP, and R and D runs about the same. While not all of these expenditures are 'wasted', they make up but a small part of the set delineated by Posner (1975) and Tullock (1967), and expanded on here.

25. Here the discussion in Paul A. Baran and Paul M. Sweezy of how to measure 'socially necessary costs' of production could serve as a good introduction to the problem (1966, pp. 131–41). In the appendix to their book, Joseph Phillips tried to remove the 'Waste in the Business Process' from the national product statistics following the implications of the Baran and Sweezy critique. His estimates will seem excessive to all but the most devout of Marxists. What is interesting about his calculations from the point of view of the present paper, however, is how closely they follow the implications of the recent literature reviewed here and how similar his methodology is to that employed by non-Marxists Nordhaus and Tobin (1973).

26. The possibility of extending a monopoly rent from one period to the next by reinvesting part of it makes possible the prolongation and intensification of the unequal distribution of rents accompanying an initial distribution of monopoly power. On this and other points touched upon in this paragraph *see* Victor P. Goldberg (1974).

REFERENCES

Aaronovitch, S. and Sawyer, M.C., 'Mergers, growth and concentration', *Oxford Economic Papers*, March 1975, **27**, pp. 136–55.

Adams, Walter and Dirlam, Joel B., 'Steel imports and vertical oligopoly power', *American Economic Review*, September 1964, **54**, pp. 626–55.

Adams, Walter and Dirlam, Joel B., 'Steel imports and vertical oligopoly power: reply', *American Economic Review*, March 1966, **56**, pp. 160–8.

Adams, Walter and Dirlam, Joel B., 'Big steel, invention, and innovation', *Quarterly Journal of Economics*, May 1966, **80**, pp. 167–89.

Adams, Walter and Dirlam, Joel B., 'Big steel, invention, and innovation: reply', *Quarterly Journal of Economics*, August 1967, **81**, pp. 475–82.

Adelman, Irma, 'A stochastic analysis of the size distribution of firms', *Journal of American Statistical Association*, December 1958, **53**, pp. 893–904.

Adelman, Morris A., 'The Antimerger Act, 1950–60', *American Economic Review*, May 1961, **51**, pp. 236–44.

Alberts, William W. and Segall, Joel E., eds., *The Corporate Merger*, Chicago: Chicago University Press, 1966.

Alchian, Armen A., 'Uncertainty, evolution, and economic theory', *Journal of Political Economy*, June 1950, **58**, pp. 211–21.

Alchian, Armen A., 'The basis of some recent advances in the theory of management of the firm', *Journal of Industrial Economics*, November 1965, **13**, pp. 30–41.

Alchian, Armen A., 'Information costs, pricing, and resource unemployment', in Phelps, Edmund S., *Microeconomic Foundations of Employment and Inflation Theory*, New York: Norton, 1970.

Alchian, Armen A. and Demsetz, Harold, 'Production, information costs, and economic organization', *American Economic Review*, December 1972, **62**, pp. 777–95.

Amacher, R.C., Tollison, R.D. and Willett, T.D., 'Risk avoidance and political advertising', in *The Economic Approach to Public Policy*, Ithaca: Cornell University Press, 1976, pp. 405–33.

Amihud, Yakov and Lev, Baruch, 'Risk reduction as a managerial motive for conglomerate mergers', *Bell Journal of Economics*, Autumn 1981, **12**, pp. 605–17.

Anderson, W.H.L., *Corporate Finance and Fixed Investment*, Cambridge, Mass.: Harvard University Press, 1964.

Anderson, W.H.L., 'Business fixed investment: a marriage of fact and fancy', in *Determinants of Business Investment Behavior*, New York: National Bureau of Economic Research, 1967, pp. 413–25.

Arrow, Kenneth J., 'Economic welfare and the allocation of resources for invention', in *The Rate and Direction of Inventive Activity*. Princeton: Princeton University Press, 1962, pp. 609–25.

Arrow, Kenneth J., 'The firm in general equilibrium theory', in Marris and Wood (1971), pp. 68–110.

Arrow, Kenneth J., *The Limits of Organization*, New York: Norton, 1974.

Arrow, Kenneth J. and Hahn, Frank H., *General Competitive Analysis*, San Francisco: Holden-Day, 1971.

Asquith, O., 'Merger bids, uncertainty and stockholder returns', *Journal of Financial Economics*, April 1983, **11**, pp. 51–83.

Averch, Harvey and Johnson, L.L., 'Behaviour of the firm under regulatory constraint', *American Economic Review*, December 1962, **52**, pp. 1052–69.

Backman, J., 'Conglomerate mergers and competition', *St John's Law Review*, Spring 1970, special edition **44**, pp. 90–132.

Baldwin, William L., 'The motives of managers, environmental restraints, and the theory of managerial enterprise', *Quarterly Journal of Economics*, May 1964, **78**, pp. 236–58.

Baran, P. and Sweezy, P., *Monopoly Capital*, New York: Monthly Review Press, 1966.

Barzel, Yoram, 'Investment, scale and growth', *Journal of Political Economy*, March/April 1971, **79**, pp. 214–31.

Baumol, William J., *Business Behavior, Value and Growth*, New York: MacMillan, 1959, rev. edn. 1967.

Baumol, William J., 'On the theory of expansion of the firm', *American Economic Review*, December 1962, **52**, pp. 1078–87.

Baumol, William J., Heim, P., Malkiel, B.G. and Quandt, R.E., 'Earnings retention, new capital and the growth of the firm', *Review of Economics and Statistics*, November 1970, **52**, pp. 345–55.

Baumol, William J., Heim, P., Malkiel, B.G. and Quandt, R.E., 'Efficiency of corporate investment: reply', *Review of Economics and Statistics*, February 1973, **55**, pp. 128–31.

Baumol, William J. and Stewart, Maco, 'On the behavioral theory of the firm', in Marris and Wood (1971), pp. 118–43.

Beckenstein, A.R., 'Merger activity and merger theories: an empirical investigation', *Antitrust Bulletin*, Spring 1979, **24**, pp. 105–28.

Becker, Gary S. and Stigler, George J., 'Law enforcement, malfeasance, and the compensation of enforcers', *Journal of Legal Studies*, January 1974, **3**, pp. 1–18.

Bell, R., Edwards, D.V. and Wagner, R.H., eds., *Political Power*, New York: Free Press, 1969.

Bergson, A., 'On monopoly welfare losses', *American Economic Review*, December 1973, **63**, pp. 853–70.

Berle, Adolf A. and Means, Gardner C., *The Modern Corporation and Private Property*, New York: Commerce Clearing House, 1932; rev. edn. New York: Harcourt, Brace, Jovanovich, 1968.

Binder, D., 'An Empirical Study of Contested Tender Offers: 1960–1969', S.J.D. thesis, Law School, University of Michigan, 1973.

Blackstone, Erwin A., 'A misallocation of medical resources: the problem of excessive surgery', *Public Policy*, Summer 1974, **22**(3), pp. 329–52.

Blau, P.M., *Exchange and Power in Social Life*, New York: John Wiley & Sons, Inc., 1964.

Bock, B., 'Statistical games and the "200 largest industrials", 1954 and 1968', New York: National Industrial Conference Board, 1970.

Bodenhöfer, Hans-Joachim, 'The mobility of labor and the theory of human capital', *Journal of Human Resources*, Fall 1967, **2**, pp. 431–48.

Boudreaux, K.J., Chiu, J.S. and Monsen, R.J., 'A Note on the Controversy Regarding Ownership and Performance', mimeo, 1970.

Bower, Joseph L., *Managing the Resource Allocation Process: A Study of Corporate Planning and Investment*, Boston: Harvard University, Graduate School of Business Administration, 1970.

Bower, Joseph L., 'On the amoral organization', in Marris (1974), pp. 178–214.

Bower, R.S. and Bower, D.H., 'Risk and the valuation of common stock', *Journal of Political Economy*, May/June 1969, **77**, pp. 347–62.

Bowles, S., Gordon, D.M. and Weisskopf, T.E., *Beyond the Wasteland*, Anchor/Doubleday, 1983.

Boyle, Stanley E., 'Pre-merger growth and profit characteristics of large conglomerate mergers in the United States, 1948–68', *St. John's Law Review*, Spring 1970, special edition **44**, pp. 152–70.

Bradley, K. and Gelb, A., *Worker Capitalism: The New Industrial Relations*, Cambridge, Mass.: Massachusetts Institute of Technology Press, 1983.

Bradley, K. and Gelb, A., *Cooperative Industrial Relations: The Mandragon Experience*, Cambridge, Mass.: Massachusetts Institute of Technology Press, 1983.

Brainard, W.C., Shoven, J.B. and Weiss, L., 'The financial valuation of the return on capital', *Brookings Papers on Economic Activity*, 1980, **2**, pp. 453–502.

Brenner, Menachem and Downes, David H., 'A critical evaluation of the measurement of conglomerate performance using the capital asset pricing model', *Review of Economics and Statistics*, May 1979, **61**, pp. 292–96.

Brigham, E.F. and Gordon, M.J., 'Leverage, dividend policy, and the cost of capital', *Journal of Finance*, March 1968, **23**, pp. 85–105.

Brittain, J.A., *Corporate Dividend Policy*, Washington: The Brookings Institution, 1966.

Bronfenbrenner, Martin, 'A reformulation of naive profit theory', *Southern Economic Journal*, April 1960, **27**, pp. 300–9.

Brozen, Yale, 'The antitrust task force deconcentration recommendation', *Journal of Law and Economics*, October 1970, **13**, pp. 279–92.

Brozen, Yale, 'Bain's concentration and rates of return revisited', *Journal of Law and Economics*, October 1971a, **14**, pp. 351–69.

Brozen, Yale, 'Concentration and structural and market disequilibria', *Antitrust Bulletin*, 1971b, **16**, pp. 241–48.

Buchanan, James M. and Tullock, Gordon G., *The Calculus of Consent*, Ann Arbor: University of Michigan Press, 1962.

Buchanan, James M., Tollison, Robert D. and Tullock, Gordon, eds., *Towards a Theory of the Rent-Seeking Society*, College Station: Texas A&M Press, 1980.

Burch, Gilbert, 'The perils of the multi-market corporation', *Fortune*, February 1967, **75**.

Burns, A.F., *Production Trends in the United States Since 1870*, New York: National Bureau of Economic Research, 1934.

Business Week, 'What puts the whiz in Litton's fast growth', April 16th, 1966.

Business Week, 'The new industrial relations', May 11th, 1981, pp. 59–68.

Business Week, 'A work revolution in U.S. industry', May 16th, 1983, pp. 58–64.

Buttrick, J., 'The inside contracting system', *Journal of Economic History*, Summer 1952, **12**, pp. 205–21.

Cable, J., 'A search theory of diversifying merger', *Recherches Economiques de Louvain*, 1978, **42**, pp. 225–42.

Calvo, Guillermo A. and Wellisz, Stanislaw, 'Supervision, loss of control, and the optimum size of the firm', *Journal of Political Economy*, October 1978, **86**, pp. 943–52.

Carson, R., 'On monopoly welfare losses; comment', *American Economic Review*, December 1975, **65**, pp. 1008–14.

Carter, John R., 'In search of synergy: a structure–performance test', *Review of Economics and Statistics*, August 1977, **59**, pp. 279–89.

Cartwright, D., 'Influence, leadership and control', in James G. March, ed., *Handbook of Organizations*, Chicago: Rand-McNally, 1965.

Chandler, Alfred D., *Strategy and Structure*, Cambridge, Mass.: Massachusetts Institute of Technology Press, 1962.

Chandler, Alfred D., Jr., *The Visible Hand*, Cambridge, Mass.: Belknap Press, 1977.

Cheung, Steven N.S., 'Transaction costs, risk aversion and the choice of contractual arrangements', *Journal of Law and Economics*, April 1969, **12**, pp. 23–42.

Ciscel, David H., 'The determinants of executive compensation', *Southern Economic Journal*, April 1974, **40**, pp. 613–17 .

Clark, John M., *Competition as a Dynamic Process*, Washington, DC: Brookings Institution, 1961.

Clark, K.B., 'Unionization and productivity: micro-econometric evidence', *Quarterly Journal of Economics*, December 1980, **95**, pp. 613–39.

Clarkson, Geoffrey P., *Portfolio Selection: A Simulation of Trust Investment*, Englewood Cliffs, NJ: Prentice-Hall, 1962.

Clendewin, J. and Van Cleave, M., 'Growth and common stock values', *Journal of Finance*, September 1954, **9**, pp. 365–76.

Coase, Ronald H., 'The nature of the firm', *Economica*, November 1937, **4**, pp. 386–405; reprinted in *Readings in Price Theory*, Homewood, Ill.: Irwin, 1952, pp. 331–51.

Coase, Ronald H., 'The problem of social cost', *Journal of Law and Economics*, October 1960, **3**, pp. 1–44.

Comanor, William S., 'Research and technical change in the pharmaceutical industry', *Review of Economics and Statistics*, May 1965, **47**, pp. 182–90.

Comanor, William S., 'Racial discrimination in American industry', *Economica*, November 1973, **40**, pp. 363–78.

Comanor, William S. and Leibenstein, Harvey, 'Allocative efficiency, X-efficiency and the measurement of welfare losses', *Economica*, August 1969, **36**, pp. 304–9.

Comanor, William S. and Scherer, F.M., 'Patent statistics as a measure of technical change', *Journal of Political Economy*, May–June 1969, **77**, pp. 393–8.

Comanor, William S. and Wilson, Thomas A., 'Advertising, market structure and performance', *Review of Economics and Statistics*, November 1967, **49**, pp. 423–40.

Committee on the Judiciary, Antitrust Subcommittee, 'Celler–Kefauver Act: Sixteen years of Enforcement', Washington, 1967, p. 7, Table 5.

Commons, J.R., *Legal Foundations of Capitalism*, New York: Macmillan, 1924.

Conn, R.L., 'Performance of conglomerate firms: comment', *Journal of Finance*, June 1973, **28**, pp. 154–9.

Conn, R.L., 'The failing firm/industry doctrines in conglomerate mergers', *Journal of Industrial Economics*, March 1976, **24**, pp. 181–7.

Cowling, Keith and Mueller, Dennis C., 'The social costs of monopoly power', *Economic Journal*, December 1978, **88**, pp. 727–48.

Cowling, Keith and Mueller, Dennis C., 'The social costs of monopoly power revisited', *Economic Journal*, September 1981, **91**, pp. 721–5.

Cowling, K., Stoneman, P., Cubbin, J., Cable, J., Hall, G., Domberger, S. and Dutton, P., *Mergers and Economic Performance*, Cambridge: Cambridge University Press, 1979.

Cowling, K. and Waterson, M., 'Price–cost margins and market structure', *Economica*, August 1976, **43**, pp. 267–74.

Cragg, J.G., 'On the relative small sample properties of several structural equation estimators', *Econometrica*, January 1967, **35**, pp. 89–110.

Crew, M.A., Jones-Lee, M.W. and Rowley, C.K., 'X-theory versus management discretion theory', *Southern Economic Journal*, October 1971, **38**, pp. 173–84.

Crozier, M., *The Bureaucratic Phenomenon*, Chicago: University of

Chicago Press, 1964.

Cubbin, John, 'Apparent collusion and conjectural variations in differential oligopoly', *International Journal of Industrial Organisation*, June 1983, **1**, pp. 155–63.

Cyert, Richard, M. and Cohen, Kalman, J., *Theory of the Firm: Resource Allocation in a Market Economy*, Englewood Cliffs, NJ: Prentice-Hall, 1965.

Cyert, Richard, M. and Hedrick, Charles L., 'The theory of the firm: past, present and future; an interpretation', *Journal of Economic Literature*, June 1972, **10**, pp. 398–412.

Cyert, Richard M. and March, James G., *A Behavioral Theory of the Firm*, Englewood Cliffs, NJ: Prentice-Hall, 1963.

Dahl, R.A., 'The concept of power', *Behavioral Science*, 1957, **2**, pp. 201–15, reprinted in Bell, Edwards and Wagner (1969), pp 79–93.

De Alessi, Louis, 'Property rights, transaction costs and X-efficiency: an essay in economic theory', *American Economic Review*, March 1983, **73**, pp. 64–81.

Demsetz, Harold, 'Information and efficiency: another viewpoint', *Journal of Law and Economics*, April 1969, **12**, pp. 1–22.

Dewey, Donald, 'Mergers and cartels: some reservations about policy', *American Economic Review*, May 1961, **51**, pp. 255–62.

Dhrymes, P.J. and Kurz, M., 'Investment, dividend and external finance behavior of firms', in *Determinants of Investment Behavior*, Princeton: National Bureau of Economic Research, 1967, pp. 427–67.

Dixit, Avinash and Norman, Victor, 'Advertising and welfare', *Bell Journal of Economics*, Spring, 1978, **9**, pp. 1–17.

Dixit, A.K. and Stiglitz, Joseph E., 'Monopolistic competition and optimum product quality', *American Economic Review*, June 1977, **67**, pp. 297–308.

Dodd, Peter and Ruback, Richard, 'Tender offers and stockholder returns: an empirical analysis', *Journal of Financial Economics*, December 1977, **5**, pp. 351–74.

Doeringer, Peter B. and Piore, Michael J., *Internal Labor Markets and Manpower Analysis*, Lexington: Lexington Heath, 1971.

Downs, A., *An Economic Theory of Democracy*, New York: Harper and Row, 1957.

Downs, A., *Inside Bureaucracy*, Boston: Little, Brown & Company, 1967.

Duesenberry, James S., *Business Cycles and Economic Growth*, New York: McGraw-Hill Book Company, 1958, pp. 87–97.

Durand, David, 'The cost of capital, corporation finance and the theory of investment: comment', *American Economic Review*, September 1959, **49**, pp. 639–54.

Edwards, Franklin R. and Heggestad, Arnold, 'Uncertainty, market structure and performance in banking', *Quarterly Journal of Economics*, August 1973, **87**, pp. 455–73.

Eichner, Alfred S., *The Megacorp and Oligopoly: Micro Foundations of*

Macro Dynamics, Cambridge and New York: Cambridge University Press, 1976.

Eisner, R., 'A permanent income theory for investment: some empirical explorations', *American Economic Review*, June 1967, **57**, pp. 363–90.

Eisner, R. and Nadiri, M.I., 'Investment behavior and neo-classical theory', *Review of Economics and Statistics*, August 1968, **50**, pp. 369–82.

Ellert, J.C., 'Mergers, antitrust law enforcement and stockholder returns', *Journal of Finance*, May 1976, **31**, pp. 715–32.

Elliott, J.W., 'Theories of corporate investment behavior: revisited', *American Economic Review*, March 1973, **63**, pp. 195–207.

Enos, John L., 'Invention and innovation in the petroleum refining industry', in National Bureau of Economic Research, *The Rate and Direction of Economic Research*, Princeton: Princeton University Press, 1962, pp. 299–321.

Evans, J.L. and Archer, S.H., 'Diversification and the reduction of dispersion: an empirical analysis', *Journal of Finance*, December 1968, **23**, pp. 29–40.

Fama, Eugene F., 'Agency problems and the theory of the firm', *Journal of Political Economy*, April 1980, **88**, pp. 288–307.

Federal Trade Commission, *Economic Report on Corporate Mergers*, Washington DC: US Government Printing Office, 1969.

Federal Trade Commission, *Economic Report on Conglomerate Merger Performance, An Empirical Analysis of Nine Corporations*, Washington, DC: US Government Printing Office, 1972.

Firth, Michael A., *Share Prices and Mergers*, Westmead, England: Saxon House, 1976.

Firth, Michael, 'The profitability of takeovers and mergers', *Economic Journal*, June 1979, **89**, pp. 316–28.

Firth, Michael, 'Takeovers, shareholder returns and the theory of the firm', *Quarterly Journal of Economics*, March 1980, **94**, pp. 315–47.

Fisher, I.W. and Hall, G.R., 'Risk and corporate rates of return', *Quarterly Journal of Economics*, February 1969, **83**, pp. 79–92.

FitzRoy, F.R. and Mueller, D.C., 'Cooperation and contract in contractual organizations,', *Quarterly Review of Economics and Business*, 1985.

FitzRoy, F.R. and Wilson, N., 'Towards a New Industrial Relations: Work Organization and Worker Participation', mimeo, International Institute of Management, Berlin, 1984.

Fizaine, Francoise, 'Analyse statistique de la croissance des entreprises selon l'âge et la taille', *Revue d'Economie Politique*, July/August 1968, **78**, pp. 606–20.

Flemming, J.S., Price, L.D.D. and Byers, S.A., 'The cost of capital, finance and investment', *Bank of England Quarterly Bulletin*, June 1976, **16**, pp. 193–205.

Fox, A., *Beyond Contract: Work, Power and Trust Relations*, London: Faber and Faber, 1974.

Freeman, C., 'Research and development in electronic capital goods', *National Institute of Economic Review*, November 1965, **34**, p. 64.

Freeman, R.B. and Medoff, J.L., 'The two faces of unionism', *Public Interest*, Fall 1979, pp. 69–93.

Friend, I. and Blume, M., 'Measurement of portfolio performance under uncertainty', *American Economic Review*, September 1970, **60**, pp. 561–75.

Friend, I. and Husic, F., 'Efficiency of corporate investment', *Review of Economics and Statistics*, February 1973, **55**, pp. 122–7.

Friend, Irwin and Puckett, Marshall, 'Dividends and stock prices', *American Economic Review*, September 1964, **54**, pp. 656–82.

Gagnon, J.M., Brehain, P., Brouquet, C. and Guerra, F., 'Stock market behavior of merging firms: the Belgian experience', *European Economic Review*, February 1982, **17**, pp. 187–211.

Galbraith, John K., *American Capitalism*, Boston: Houghton Mifflin, 1952.

Galbraith, John K., *The New Industrial State*, Boston: Houghton Mifflin, 1967a.

Galbraith, John K., 'A review of a review', *Public Interest*, Fall 1967b, **9**, pp. 109–18.

Galbraith, John K., *The Great Crash, 1929*, Boston: Houghton Mifflin, 1961, third edn., 1972.

Gallaway, Lowell E., 'Age and labor mobility patterns', *Southern Economic Journal*, October 1969, **36**, pp. 171–80.

Gibrat, Robert, *Les inegalities economiques*, Paris: Receuil Sirey, 1931.

Goldberg, Lawrence G., 'The effect of conglomerate mergers on competition', *Journal of Law and Economics*, April 1973, **16**, pp. 137–58.

Goldberg, Lawrence G., 'Conglomerate mergers and concentration ratios', *Review of Economics and Statistics*, August 1974, **56**, pp. 303–9.

Goldberg, Victor P., 'Institutional change and the quasi-invisible hand', *Journal of Law and Economics*, October 1974, **17**, pp. 461–92.

Goldfeld, S.M. and Quandt, R.E., 'Some tests of homoscedasticity', *Journal of American Statistical Association*, June 1965, **60**, pp. 539–47.

Gordon, D.M., Edwards, R. and Reich, M., *Segmented Work, Divided Workers*, Cambridge: Cambridge University Press, 1982.

Gordon, M.J., 'Dividends, earnings and stock prices', *Review of Economic Statistics*, May 1959, **41**, pp. 99–105,

Gordon, R.J., 'Why U.S. wage and employment behavior differs from that in Britain and Japan', *Economic Journal*, March 1982, **92**, pp. 13–44.

Gort, M., *Diversification and Integration in American Industry*, Princeton: National Bureau of Economic Research, 1962.

Gort, M., 'Diversification, mergers and profits', in W. Alberts and J. Segall, eds., *The Corporate Merger*, Chicago: University of Chicago Press, 1966.

Gort, M., 'An economic disturbance theory of mergers', *Quarterly*

Journal of Economics, November 1969, **83**, pp. 624–42.

Gort, M. and Hogarty, T.F., 'New evidence on mergers', *Journal of Law and Economics*, April 1970, **13**, pp. 167–84.

Grabowski, Henry G., 'The determinants of industrial research and development', *Journal of Political Economy*, March-April 1968, **76**, pp. 292–306.

Grabowski, Henry G. and Mueller, Dennis C., 'Imitative advertising in the cigarette industry', *Antitrust Bulletin*, Summer 1971, **16**, pp. 257–92.

Grabowski, Henry G. and Mueller, Dennis C., 'Managerial and stockholder welfare models of firm expenditures', *Review of Economics and Statistics*, February 1972, **54**, pp. 9–24.

Grabowski, Henry G. and Mueller, Dennis C., 'Life-cycle effects on corporate returns on retentions', *Review of Economics and Statistics*, November 1975, **57**, pp. 400–9.

Grabowski, Henry G. and Mueller, Dennis C., 'Industrial research and development, intangible capital stock, and firm profit rates', *Bell Journal of Economics*, Autumn 1978, **9**, pp. 328–43.

Graham, Benjamin and Dodd, O.L., *Security Analysis*, 3rd edn., New York: McGraw-Hill, 1951.

Grossman, Sanford J. and Stiglitz, Joseph E., 'Information and competitive price systems', *American Economic Review*, May 1976, **66**, pp. 246–53.

Haggerty, P.E., 'Innovation and the private enterprise system in the United States', in National Academy of Engineering, *The Process of Technological Innovation*, Washington: National Academy of Sciences, 1969.

Hall, R.E., 'Comment' in Brainard *et. al.*, 1980.

Hall, R.L. and Hitch, D.J., 'Price theory and business behavior', *Oxford Economic Papers*, 1939, **2**, pp. 12–45.

Halpern, Paul J., 'Empirical estimates of the amount and distribution of gains to companies in mergers', *Journal of Business*, October 1973, **46**, pp. 554–75.

Hamberg, Daniel, 'Invention in the industrial research laboratory', *Journal of Political Economy*, April 1963, **71**, pp. 95–115.

Hannah, L. and Kay, J.A., *Concentration in Modern Industry*, London: Macmillan, 1977.

Harberger, Arnold C., 'Monopoly and resource allocation', *American Economic Review*, May 1954, **44**, pp. 77–87.

Hart, P.E. and Prais, S.J., 'The analysis of business concentration: a statistical approach', *Journal of the Royal Statistical Society*, 1956, **119**, pp. 150–81.

Hassid, J., 'Diversification and the firm's rate of growth', *Manchester School of Economic and Social Studies*, March 1977, **45**, pp. 16–28.

Haugen, R.A. and Langetieg, T.C., 'An empirical test for synergism in merger', *Journal of Finance*, September 1975, **30**, pp. 1003–14.

Haugen, R.A. and Udell, J.G., 'Rates of return to stockholders of acquired companies', *Journal of Financial and Quantitative Analysis*, January 1972, **7**, pp. 1387–98.

Hayek, Friedrich A., 'The use of knowledge in society', *American Economic Review*, September 1945, **35**, pp. 519–30.

Hayes, Samuel L., III and Taussig, Russell A., 'Tactics of cash takeover bids', *Harvard Business Review*, March/April 1967, **45**, pp. 135–48.

Heal, G.M. and Silberston, Aubrey, 'Alternative managerial objectives: an explanatory note', *Oxford Economic Papers*, July 1972, **24**, pp. 137–50.

Herendeen, J.B., 'Alternative models of corporate enterprise in growth maximization and value maximization', *Quarterly Review of Economics and Business*, Winter 1979, **19**, pp. 57–75.

Hiller, J.R., 'Long-run profit maximization: an empirical test', *Kyklos*, 1978, **31**, pp. 475–90.

Hirschman, Albert O., *Exit, Voice and Loyalty*, Cambridge, Mass.: Harvard University Press, 1970.

Hirshleifer, Jack, 'The private and social value of information and the reward to inventive activity', *American Economic Review*, September 1971, **61**, pp. 561–74.

Hogarty, T.F., 'Profits from mergers: the evidence of fifty years', *St John's Law Review*, Spring 1970a, special edition **44**, pp. 378–91.

Hogarty, T.F., 'The profitability of corporate mergers', *Journal of Business*, July 1970b, **43**, pp. 317–27.

Holzmann, O.J., Copeland, R.M. and Hayya, J., 'Income measures of conglomerate performance', *Quarterly Review of Economics and Business*, Autumn 1975, **15**, pp. 67–78.

Ijiri, Yuji and Simon, Herbert A., 'Effects of mergers and acquisitions on business firm concentration', *Journal of Political Economy*, March/April 1971, **79**, pp. 314–22.

Jensen, Michael C. and Meckling, William H., 'The theory of the firm: managerial behavior, agency costs and ownership structure', *Journal of Financial Economics*, October 1976, **3**, pp. 305–60.

Jensen, M.C. and Ruback, R.S., 'The market for corporate control', *Journal of Financial Economics*, April 1983, **11**, pp. 5–50.

Jewkes, John, *et al.*, *The Sources of Invention*, New York, 1959.

Joehnk, M.D., and Nielsen, J.F., 'The effects of conglomerate merger activity on systematic risk', *Journal of Financial and Quantitative Analysis*, March 1974, **9**, pp. 215–25.

Johnson, H.G., *The Theory of Income Distribution*, London: Grey Mills, 1973.

Johnston, J., *Statistical Cost Analysis*, New York: McGraw-Hill, 1960.

Jorgenson, D.W. and Siebert, C.D., 'A comparison of alternative theories of corporate investment bahavior', *American Economic Review*, September 1968, **58**, pp. 681–712.

Jorgenson, D.W. and Siebert, C.D., 'Optimal capital accumulation and corporate investment behavior', *Journal of Political Economy*, December 1968, **76**, pp. 1123-69.

Kahn, Alfred E., *The Economics of Regulation*, Vol. 1, New York: Wiley, 1970.

Kaldor, Nicholas, 'Market imperfection and excess capacity', *Economica, N.S.*, February 1935, **2**, pp. 33–50.

Kaldor, Nicholas, 'Marginal productivity and the macro-economic theories of distribution: comment on Samuelson and Modigliani', *Review of Economic Studies*, October 1966, **33**, pp. 309–19.

Kamerschen, David R., 'An estimation of the welfare losses from monopoly in the American economy', *Western Economic Journal*, Summer 1966, **4**, pp. 221–36.

Kamerschen, David R., 'The influence of ownership and control on profit rates', *American Economic Review*, June 1968, **58**, pp. 432–47.

Kamerschen, David R., 'A theory of conglomerate mergers: comment', *Quarterly Journal of Economics*, November 1970, **84**, pp. 668–73.

Kamien, Morton I. and Schwartz, Nancy L., 'Market structure, elasticity of demand and incentive to invent', *Journal of Law and Economics*, April 1970, **13**, pp. 241–52.

Kirzner, Israel M., *Competition and Entrepreneurship*, Chicago: University of Chicago Press, 1973.

Klein, B., Crawford, R.C. and Alchian, A.A., 'Vertical integration, appropriable rents and the competitive contracting process', *Journal of Law and Economics*, October 1978, **21**, pp. 297–326.

Knight, Frank H., *Risk, Uncertainty, and Profit*, New York: Harper and Row, 1965, first edn., 1921.

Koenker, R.W. and Perry, M.K., 'Product differentiation, monopolistic competition, and public policy', *Bell Journal of Economics*, Spring 1981, **12**, pp. 217–31.

Kuehn, Douglas, *Takeovers and the Theory of the Firm: An Empirical Analysis of the United Kingdom, 1957–1969*, London: Macmillan, 1975.

Kuh, Edwin, *Capital Stock Growth: A Micro-Economic Approach*, Amsterdam: North Holland, 1963.

Kuh, E. and Meyer, J.R., *The Investment Decision*, Cambridge, Mass.: Harvard University Press, 1957.

Kuhn, Thomas S., *The Structure of Scientific Revolutions*, Chicago: Chicago University Press, 1962.

Kummer, Donald R. and Hoffmeister, J. Ronald, 'Valuation consequences of cash tender offers', *Journal of Finance*, May 1978, **33**, pp. 505–16.

Laffer, A.B., 'Vertical integration by corporations, 1929–65', *Review of Economics and Statistics*, February 1969, **51**, pp. 91–3.

Lambin, Jean-Jacques, 'Measuring the profitability of advertising: an empirical study', *Journal of Industrial Economics*, April 1969, **17**, pp. 86–103.

Lancaster, Kelvin, 'Socially optimal product differentiation', *American Economic Review*, September 1975, **65**, pp. 567–85.

Langetieg, T.C., 'An application of a three-factor performance index to measure stockholder gains from merger', *Journal of Financial Economics*, December 1978, **6**, pp. 365–84.

Larner, Robert J., 'Ownership and control in the 200 largest nonfinancial corporations, 1929 and 1963', *American Economic Review*, September 1966, **56**, pp. 777–87.

Larner, Robert J., 'Separation of Ownership and Control and Its Implications for the Behavior of the Firm', Ph.D. dissertation, University of Wisconsin, Madison, 1968.

Leibenstein, Harvey, 'Allocative efficiency vs. "X-efficiency"', *American Economic Review*, June 1966, **56**, pp. 392–415.

Leibenstein, Harvey, 'Organizational or frictional equilibria, X-efficiency, and the rate of innovation', *Quarterly Journal of Economics*, November 1969, **83**, pp. 600–23.

Leibenstein, Harvey, 'Aspects of the X-efficiency theory of the firm', *Bell Journal of Economics*, Autumn 1975, **6**, pp. 580–606.

Leibenstein, Harvey, *Beyond Economic Man: A New Foundation for Microeconomics*, Cambridge, Mass.: Harvard University Press, 1976.

Lev, B., and Mandelker, G., 'The microeconomic consequences of corporate mergers', *Journal of Business*, January 1972, **45**, pp. 85–104.

Levy, H. and Sarnat, M., 'Diversification, portfolio analysis and the uneasy case for conglomerate mergers', *Journal of Finance*, September 1970, **25**, pp. 795–802.

Lewellen, Wilbur G., *Executive Compensation in Large Industrial Corporations*, New York: Columbia University Press, 1968.

Lewellen, Wilbur G., 'A pure financial rationale for the conglomerate merger', *Journal of Finance*, May 1971, **26**, pp. 521–37.

Lewellen, Wilbur G. and Huntsman, Blaine, 'Managerial pay and corporate performance, *American Economic Review*, September 1970, **60**, pp. 710–20.

Lilienthal, D.E., *Big Business: A New Era*, New York, Harper & Row, 1952.

Lintner, John, 'Distribution of income of corporations among dividends, retained earnings and taxes', *American Economic Review*, May 1956, **46**, pp. 97–113.

Lintner, John, 'Expectations, mergers and equilibrium in purely competitive securities markets', *American Economic Review*, May 1971, **61**, pp. 101–11.

Lintner, John, 'Optimum or maximum corporate growth under uncertainty', in Marris and Wood (1971), pp. 172–241.

Littlechild, Stephen, 'Misleading calculations of the social costs of monopoly power', *Economic Journal*, June 1981, **91**, pp. 348–63.

Lorie, J.H. and Halpern, P., 'Conglomerates: the rhetoric and the evidence', *Journal of Law and Economics*, April 1970, **13**, pp. 149–66.

Lynch, H.H., 'Financial Performance of Conglomerates', Boston: Harvard Business School, 1971.

MacAvoy, Paul W., McKie, James W. and Preston, Lee E., 'High and stable concentration levels, profitability and public policy: a response',

Journal of Law and Economics, October 1971, **14**, pp. 493–9.

Machlup, Fritz, *The Economics of Sellers' Competition*, Baltimore: Johns Hopkins Press, 1952.

Machlup, Fritz, 'Theories of the firm: marginalist, behavioral, managerial', *American Economic Review*, March 1967, **57**, pp. 1–33.

Maddala, G.S. and Knight, P.T., 'International diffusion of technical change—a case study of the oxygen steel making process', *Economic Journal*, September 1967, **77**, pp. 531–58.

Malmgren, Harold B., 'Information, expectations, and the theory of the firm', *Quarterly Journal of Economics*, August 1961, **75**, pp. 399–421.

Mandelker, Gershon, 'Risk and return: the case of merging firms', *Journal of Financial Economics*, December 1974, **1**, pp. 303–35.

Manne, Henry G., 'Mergers and the market for corporate control', *Journal of Political Economy*, April 1965, **73**, pp. 110–20.

Manne, Henry G., *Insider Trading and the Stock Market*, New York: Free Press, 1966.

Mansfield, Edwin, 'Entry, Gibrat's law, innovation, and the growth of firms', *American Economic Review*, December 1962, **52**, pp. 1023–51.

Mansfield, Edwin, *The Economics of Technological Change*, New York: Norton, 1968.

Mansfield, Edwin, *Industrial Research and Technological Innovation*, New York: W.W. Norton and Company, Inc., 1968.

Marglin, S.A., 'What do bosses do? The origins and functions of hierarchy in capitalist production', *Review of Radical Political Economics*, Summer 1974, **6**, pp. 33–60.

Markham, Jesse W. 'An alternative approach to the concept of workable competition', *American Economic Review*, June 1950, **40**, pp. 349–61.

Markham, Jesse W., 'Survey of the Evidence and Findings on Mergers, Business Concentration and Price Policy', New York: National Bureau of Economic Research, 1955, pp. 141–82.

Markham, Jesse W., *Conglomerate Enterprise and Public Policy*, Boston: Harvard Business School, 1973.

Markowitz, H., *Portfolio Selection: Efficient Diversification of Investments*, New York: John Wiley and Sons, Inc., 1959.

Marris, Robin, 'A model of the "managerial" enterprise', *Quarterly Journal of Economics*, May 1963, **77**, pp. 185–209.

Marris, Robin, *The Economic Theory of Managerial Capitalism*, Glencoe: Free Press, 1964.

Marris, Robin, 'Galbraith, Solow, and the truth about corporations', *Public Interest*, Spring 1968, **11**, pp. 37–46.

Marris, Robin, 'An introduction to theories of corporate growth', in Marris and Wood (1971), pp. 1–37.

Marris, Robin, 'Review of Wilbur G. Lewellen, *The Ownership Income of Management*', *Journal of Economic Literature*, June 1972a, **10**, pp. 491–93.

Marris, Robin, 'Why economics needs a theory of the firm', *Economic Journal*, March 1972b, **83**, pp. 321–52.

Marris, Robin, ed., *The Corporate Society*, London: Macmillan; and New York: Wiley, Halsted Press, 1974.

Marris, Robin, *Theory and Future of the Corporate Economy and Society*, Amsterdam: North Holland, 1979.

Marris, Robin and Wood, Adrian, eds., *The Corporate Economy: Growth, Competition and Innovative Potential*, Cambridge, Mass.: Harvard University Press, 1971.

Marshall, Alfred, *Principles of Economics*, 1st edn., London, 1980; 8th edn., New York: Macmillan, 1920.

Marx, Karl, *Capital*, New York: Kerr, 1906.

Mason, R.H. and Goudzwaard, M.B., 'Performance of conglomerate firms: a portfolio approach', *Journal of Finance*, March 1976, **31**, pp. 39–48.

Masson, R.L., 'Executive motivations, earnings and consequent equity performance', *Journal of Political Economy*, November/December 1971, **79**, pp. 1278–92.

McAdams, Alan K., 'Big steel, invention, and innovation reconsidered', *Quarterly Journal of Economics*, August 1967, **81**, pp. 457–74.

McCain, Roger A., 'Competition, information, redundance: X-efficiency and the cybernetics of the firm', *Kyklos*, 1975, **28**, pp. 286–308.

McCallum, J., 'Inflation and social consensus in the seventies', *Economic Journal*, December 1983, **93**, pp. 784–805.

McDonald, John, 'Why Evans Products Co. had a bad year', *Fortune*, May 1967, pp. 139–44.

McEachern, William A., *Managerial Control and Performance*, Lexington, Mass.: Heath, 1975.

McEnally, R.W., 'Competition and dispersion in rates of return: a note', *Journal of Industrial Economics*, 1976, **25**, pp. 69–75.

McGowan, J.J., 'The effect of alternative antimerger policies on the size distribution of firms', *Yale Economic Essays*, Fall 1965, **5**, pp. 423–74.

McGowan, J.J., 'International comparisons of merger activity', *Journal of Law and Economics*, April 1971, **14**, pp. 233–50.

Mead, W.J., 'Instantaneous merger profit as conglomerate merger motive', *Western Economic Journal*, December 1969, **7**, pp. 295–306.

Meeks, Geoffrey, *Disappointing Marriage: A Study of the Gains from Merger*, Cambridge: Cambridge University Press, 1977.

Melicher, R.W. and Rush, D.F., 'The performance of conglomerate firms: recent risk and return experience', *Journal of Finance*, May 1973, **28**, pp. 381–8.

Melicher, R.M. and Rush, D.F., 'Evidence on the acquisition-related performance of conglomerate firms', *Journal of Finance*, March 1974, **29**, pp. 141–9.

Meyer, John R., 'An experiment in the measurement of business motivation', *Review of Economics and Statistics*, August 1967, **49**, pp. 304–18.

Meyer, J.R. and Glauber, R.R., *Investment Decisions, Economic*

Forecasting, and Public Policy, Cambridge, Mass.: Harvard University Press, 1964.

Mills, C.W., *The Power Elite*, New York: Oxford University Press, 1956.

Mingo, J.J., 'Managerial motives, market structures and the performance of holding company banks', *Economic Inquiry*, September 1976, **14**, pp. 411–24.

Mirrlees, James A., 'The optimal structure of incentives and authority within an organization', *Bell Journal of Economics*, Spring 1976, **7**, pp. 105–31.

Modigliani, Franco and Miller, Merton H., 'The cost of capital, corporation finance and the theory of investment', *American Economic Review*, June 1958, **48**, pp. 261–97.

Monsen, R. Joseph, Chiu, J.S. and Cooley, D.E., 'The effect of separation of ownership and control on the performance of the large firm', *Quarterly Journal of Economics*, August 1968, **82**, pp. 435–51.

Monsen, R. Joseph, Jr and Downs, Anthony, 'A theory of large managerial firms', *Journal of Political Economy*, June 1965, **73**, pp. 221–36.

Morgan, Robert G., 'Merger motives: conglomerates versus congenerics', *Nebraska Journal of Economics and Business*, Winter 1977, **16**, pp. 47–54.

Morrissey, Fred P., 'Current aspects of the cost of capital to utilities', *Public Utilities Fortnightly*, August 14th, 1958, **62**, pp. 217–27.

Mueller, Dennis C., 'Patents, research and development, and the measurement of inventive activity', *Journal of Industrial Economics*, November 1966, **15**, pp. 26–37.

Mueller, D.C., 'The firm decision process: an econometric investigation', *Quarterly Journal of Economics*, February 1967, **81**, pp. 58–87.

Mueller, Dennis C., 'A theory of conglomerate mergers', *Quarterly Journal of Economics*, November 1969, **83**, pp. 643–59.

Mueller, D.C., 'A theory of conglomerate mergers: reply', to Kamerschen (1970), *Quarterly Journal of Economics*, November 1970, **84**, pp. 674–9.

Mueller, D.C., 'A life cycle theory of the firm', *Journal of Industrial Economics*, July 1972, **20**, pp. 199–219.

Mueller, D.C. 'Information, mobility and profit', *Kyklos*, 1976, **29**, pp. 419–48.

Mueller, Dennis C., 'The effects of conglomerate mergers: a survey of the empirical evidence', *Journal of Banking and Finance*, December 1977, **1**, pp. 315–47.

Mueller, Dennis C., ed., *The Determinants and Effects of Mergers: An International Comparison*, Cambridge, Mass.: Oelgeschlager, Gunn, and Hain, 1980.

Mueller, D.C., 'The case against conglomerate mergers', in R.D. Blair and R.F. Lanzillotti, eds., *The Conglomerate Corporation*, Cambridge, Mass.: Oelgeschlager, Gunn and Hain, 1981, pp. 71–95.

Mueller, D.C., 'Further reflections on the invisible hand theorem', in P.

Wiles and G. Routh, *Economics in Disarray*, Oxford: Basil Blackwell, 1984, pp.159–83.

Mueller, D.C. and Tilton, John E., 'Research and development costs as a barrier to entry', *Canadian Journal of Economics*, November 1969, **2**, pp. 570–9.

Müller, Jürgen and Hochreiter, Rolf, *Stand und Entwicklungstendenzen der Bundesrepublik*, Göttingen: Schwartz, 1976.

Nelson, R.L., *Merger Movements in American Industry, 1895–1956*, Princeton: Princeton University Press, 1959.

Nelson, R.L., 'Business cycle factors in the choice between internal and external growth', in W. Alberts and J. Segall, eds., *The Corporate Merger*, Chicago: University of Chicago Press, 1966.

Nelson, R.R., 'The economics of invention: a survey of the literature', *Journal of Business*, April 1959, **32**, pp. 101–27.

Nelson, Richard R., 'The simple economics of basic scientific research', *Journal of Political Economy*, June 1959, **67**, pp. 297–306.

Nelson, Richard R., 'Uncertainty, prediction, and competitive equilibrium', *Quarterly Journal of Economics*, February 1961, **75**, pp. 41–62.

Nelson, Richard R., 'Uncertainty, learning and the economics of parallel research and development efforts', *Review of Economic Statistics*, November 1961, **43**, pp. 351–69.

Nelson, Richard R. and Winter, Sidney G., 'Neoclassical vs. evolutionary theories of economic growth: critique and prospects', *Economic Journal*, December 1974, **84**, pp. 886–905.

Nelson, Richard R. and Winter, Sidney G., 'Simulation of Schumpeterian competition', *American Economic Review*, February 1977, **67**, pp. 271–6.

Nelson, Richard R. and Winter, Sidney G., 'Forces generating and limiting concentration under Schumpeterian competition', *Bell Journal of Economics*, Autumn 1978, **9**, pp. 524–48.

Nelson, Richard R., Peck, Merton J. and Kalachek, Edward D., *Technology, Economic Growth, and Public Policy*, Washington: Brookings Institution, 1967.

Nerlove, Marc, 'Factors affecting differences among rates of return on investments in individual common stocks', *Review of Economics and Statistics*, August 1968, **50**, pp. 312–31.

Nielsen, J.F. and Melicher, R.W., 'A financial analysis of acquisition and merger premiums', *Journal of Financial and Quantitative Analysis*, March 1973, **8**, pp. 139–48.

Niskanen, W.W., Jr, *Bureaucracy and Representative Government*, Chicago: Aldine-Atherton, 1971.

Nordhaus, William B., *Invention, Growth, and Welfare: A Theoretical Treatment of Technological Change*, Cambridge, Mass.: MIT Press, 1969.

Nordhaus, William B. and Tobin, James, 'Is growth obsolete?' in Milton Moss, ed., *The Measurement of Economic and Social Performance*,

New York: NBER; distributed by Columbia University Press, 1973, pp. 509–32.

Nutzinger, H.G., 'The firm as a social institution: the failure of the contractarian viewpoint', *Economic Analysis*, 1976, **10**, pp. 217–37.

Odagiri, H., *The Theory of Growth in a Corporate Economy: An Inquiry into Management Preference, R&D and Economic Growth*, Cambridge: Cambridge University Press, 1981.

Okun, A.M., *Prices and Quantities*, Washington: Brookings Institution, 1981.

Olson, M.J., *The Logic of Collective Action*, Cambridge, Mass.: Harvard University Press, 1965.

Ouchi, W.G., *Theory Z*, Reading, Mass.: Addison-Wesley, 1981.

Palda, Kristian S., *The Measurement of Cumulative Advertising Effects*, Englewood Cliffs, NJ: Prentice-Hall, 1964.

Palmer, John P., 'The profit-performance effects of the separation of ownership from control in large U.S. industrial corporations', *Bell Journal of Economics and Management Science*, Spring 1973a, **4**, pp. 293–303.

Palmer, John P., (Unpublished appendix to) 'The profit-performance effects of the separation of ownership from control in large U.S. industrial corporations', *Bell Journal of Economics and Management Science*, 1973b, **3**, pp. 293–303.

Parsons, T., 'On the concept of political power', *American Philosophical Society*, 1963, **107**, pp. 232–62, reprinted in Bell, Edwards and Wagner (1969), pp. 251–84.

Pasinetti, Luigi L., 'Rate of profit and income distribution in relation to the rate of economic growth', *Review of Economic Studies*, October 1962, **29**, pp. 267–79.

Pauly, M., 'The economics of moral hazard', *The American Economic Review*, June 1968, **58**, pp. 531–7.

Penn, David W., 'Aggregate concentration: a statistical note', *Antitrust Bulletin*, Spring 1976, **21**, pp. 91–8.

Penrose, Edith, *The Theory of the Growth of the Firm*, Oxford: Blackwell, 1959.

Phelps, Edmund S., *Microeconomic Foundations of Employment and Inflation Theory*, New York: Norton, 1970.

Piccini, R., 'Mergers, diversification, and the growth of large firms: 1948–1965', *St John's Law Review*, Spring 1970, special edn. **44**, pp. 171–92.

Piper, T.F. and Weiss, S.J., 'The profitability of multibank holding company acquisitions', *Journal of Finance*, March 1974, **29**, pp. 163–74.

Pittman, R., 'The effects of industry concentration and regulation on contributions in three 1972 U.S. Senate campaigns', *Public Choice*, Fall 1976, **27**, pp. 71–80.

Pitts, Robert A., 'Diversification strategies and organizational policies of large diversified firms', *Journal of Economics and Business*, Spring/Summer 1976, **28**, pp. 181–8.

Porat, Marc U., *The Information Economy*, Institute for Communication Research, Stanford University, 1975.

Posner, Richard A., 'The social cost of monopoly and regulation', *Journal of Political Economy*, August 1975, **83**, pp. 807–27.

Prais, S.J., 'Measuring social mobility', *Journal of the Royal Statistical Society*, 1955, **A118**, pp. 56–66.

Prais, S.J., *The Evolution of Giant Firms in Britain: A Study of the Growth of Concentration in Manufacturing Industry in Britain, 1909–70*, Cambridge and New York: Cambridge University Press, 1976.

Preston, L.E., *The Industry and Enterprise Structure of the U.S. Economy*, New York: General Learning Press, 1971.

Preston, L.E., 'Giant firms, large mergers and concentration: patterns and policy alternatives, 1954–1968', *Industrial Organization Review*, 1973, **1**, pp. 35–46.

Racette, G.A., 'Earnings retention, new capital and growth of the firms: a comment', *Review of Economics and Statistics*, February 1973, **55**, pp. 127–8.

Radice, H.K., 'Control type, profitability and growth in large firms: an empirical study', *Economic Journal*, September 1971, **81**, pp. 547–62.

Reich, R.B., *The Next American Frontier*, New York: Random House, 1983.

Reid, S.R., 'Mergers, managers and the economy', New York: McGraw-Hill, 1968.

Reid, S.R., 'A reply to the Weston/Mansinghka criticisms dealing with conglomerate mergers', *Journal of Finance*, September 1971, **26**, pp. 937–46.

Ricardo, David, *The Principles of Political Economy and Taxation*, London: Dent, 1911.

Robinson, Edward A.G., *The Structure of Competitive Industry*, London: Nisbet, 1931.

Robinson, Joan, *The Economics of Imperfect Competition*, London: Macmillan, 1933.

Rourke, F.E., *Secrecy and Publicity*, Baltimore: Johns Hopkins Press, 1961.

Rourke, F.E., *Bureaucracy, Politics and Public Policy*, Boston: Little, Brown & Company, 1969.

Rukeyser, William S., 'Litton down to earth', *Fortune*, April 1968.

Russell, B., *Power*, New York: Norton, 1938.

Salop, S.C., 'Second-Best Policies in Imperfect Competition: How Improved Information May Lower Welfare', University of Warwick, Department of Economics, Economic Research Paper, No. 124, 1978.

Scherer, F.M., 'Firm size, market structure, opportunity and the output of patented inventions', *American Economic Review*, December 1965, **45**, pp. 1097–125.

Scherer, F.M., *Industrial Market Structure and Economic Performance*, Chicago: Rand McNally, 1971, second edn. 1980.

Schmalensee, Richard, *The Economics of Advertising*, Amsterdam:

North Holland, 1972.

Schmookler, J., *Invention and Economic Growth*, Cambridge, Mass.: Harvard University Press, 1966.

Schumpeter, Joseph A., *The Theory of Economic Development*, Cambridge, Mass.: Harvard University Press, 1934.

Schumpeter, Joseph A., *Capitalism, Socialism and Democracy*, third edn., New York: Harper & Row, 1950.

Schwartzman, David, 'The burden of monopoly', *Journal of Political Economy*, December 1960, **68**, pp. 627–30.

Scitovsky, Tibor, *The Joyless Economy*, New York: Oxford University Press, 1976.

Sharpe, William F., 'Capital asset prices: a theory of market equilibrium under conditions of risk', *Journal of Finance*, September 1964, **19**, pp. 425–42.

Shepherd, William G., *The Treatment of Market Power*, New York: Columbia University Press, 1975.

Sherman, R., 'How tax policy induces conglomerate mergers', *National Tax Journal*, December 1972, **25**, pp. 521–9.

Sichel, W., 'Conglomerateness: size and monopoly control', *St John's Law Review*, Spring 1970, special edn. **44**, pp. 354–77.

Siegfried, J.J. and Tiemann, T.K., 'The welfare cost of monopoly: an inter-industry analysis', *Economic Inquiry*, June 1974, **12**, pp. 190–202.

Silberston, A., 'Factors Affecting the Growth of Firms—Theory and Practice', Paper Presented at Meeting of UK Association of University Teachers of Economics, Exeter University, 1979.

Simon, Herbert A., 'A comparison of organization theories', *Review of Economic Studies*, 1952, **20**, pp. 40–8.

Simon, H.A., 'Notes on the observation and measurement of power', *Journal of Politics*, 1953, **15**, pp. 500–16, reprinted in Bell, Edwards and Wagner (1969), pp. 69–78.

Simon, H.A., *Models of Man: Social and Rational*, New York: John Wiley & Sons, Inc., 1957a.

Simon, Herbert A., 'The compensation of executives', *Sociometry*, March 1957b, **20**, pp. 32–5.

Simon, Herbert A., 'Theories of decision making in economics and behavioral science,', *American Economic Review*, June 1959, **49**, pp. 253–83.

Simon, Herbert A. and Bonini, Charles P., 'The size distribution of business firms', *American Economic Review*, September 1958, **48**, pp. 607–17.

Simon, Herbert A. and Ijiri, Yuji, 'Business firm growth and size', *American Economic Review*, March 1964, **54**, pp. 77–89.

Simon, Herbert A. and Ijiri, Yuhi, 'A model of business firm growth', *Econometrica*, April 1967, **35**, pp. 348–55.

Singh, Ajit, *Take-overs: Their Relevance to the Stock Market and the Theory of the Firm*, Cambridge: Cambridge University Press, 1971.

Singh, Ajit, 'Take-overs, "natural selection" and the theory of the firm',

Economic Journal, September 1975, **85**, pp. 497–515.

Singh, Ajit and Whittington, Geoffrey, 'The size growth of firms', *Review of Economic Study*, January 1975, **42**, pp. 15–26.

Slesinger, Reuben E., 'Steel imports and vertical oligopoly power: comment', *American Economic Review*, March 1966, **56**, pp. 152–5.

Smiley, Robert, 'Tender offers, transactions costs and the theory of the firm', *Review of Economics and Statistics*, February 1976, **58**, pp. 22–32.

Smith, Adam, *The Wealth of Nations*, New York: Random House, 1937.

Smith, Keith V. and Schreiner, John C., 'A portfolio analysis of conglomerate diversification', *Journal of Finance*, June 1969, **24**, pp. 413–27.

Smith, Richard A., *Corporations in Crisis*, Garden City, New York: Doubleday, 1963.

Solow, Robert M., 'The new industrial state or son of affluence', *Public Interest*, Fall 1967a, **9**, pp. 100–8.

Solow, Robert M., 'A rejoinder', *Public Interest*, Fall 1967b, **9**, pp. 118–9.

Solow, Robert M., 'The truth further refined: a comment on Marris', *Public Interest*, Spring 1968, **11**, pp. 47–52.

Solow, R.M., 'Some implications of alternative criteria for the firm', in R. Marris and A. Woods, ed., *The Corporate Economy*, Cambridge, Mass.: Harvard University Press, 1971, pp. 318–43.

Spence, Michael, 'Job market signalling', *Quarterly Journal of Economics*, August 1973, **87**, pp. 355–79.

Spence, Michael, 'Product differentiation and welfare', *American Economic Review*, May 1976a, **66**, pp. 407–14.

Spence, Michael, 'Product selection, fixed costs, and monopolistic competition', *Review of Economic Studies*, June 1976b, **43**, pp. 217–35.

Spence, M., 'Entry, capacity, investment and oligopolistic pricing', *Bell Journal of Economics*, Autumn 1977, **8**, pp. 534–44.

Steindl, Joseph, *Random Processes and the Growth of Firms: A Study of the Pareto Law*, New York: Hofner, 1965.

Steiner, Peter O., *Mergers: Motives, Effects, Policies*, Ann Arbor: University of Michigan Press, 1975.

Stevens, D.L., 'Financial characteristics of merged firms: a multivariate analysis', *Journal of Financial and Quantitative Analysis*, March 1973, **8**, pp. 149–58.

Stigler, G.J., 'Monopoly and oligopoly by merger', *American Economic Review*, May 1950, **40**, pp. 23–34.

Stigler, George J., 'The statistics of monopoly and merger', *Journal of Political Economy*, February 1956, **64**, pp. 33–40.

Stigler, George J., 'The economies of information', *Journal of Political Economy*, June 1961, **69**, pp. 213–25.

Stigler, George J., *Capital Rates of Return in Manufacturing*, Princeton: Princeton University Press, 1963.

Stigler, G.J., 'Imperfections in the capital market', *Journal of Political*

Economy, June 1967, **75**, pp. 287–92.

Stigler, George J. and Friedland, Clair, 'The literature of economics: the case of Berle and Means', *Journal of Law and Economics*, June 1983, **26**, pp. 237–68.

Stiglitz, Joseph E., 'Incentives, risk and information: notes toward a theory of hierarchy', *Bell Journal of Economics*, Autumn 1975, **6**, pp. 552–79.

Stone, K., 'The origins of job structures in the steel industry', *Review of Radical Political Economy*, Summer 1974, **6**, pp. 113–73.

Taylor, M., *Anarchy and Cooperation*, London: John Wiley & Sons, Inc., 1976.

Thorp, W.L., 'The persistence of the merger movement', *American Economic Review*, March 1931, **21**, pp. 77–89.

Thurow, L.G., *Generating Inequality*, New York: Basic Books, 1975.

Tullock, Gordon, 'The welfare costs of tariffs, monopolies, and theft', *Western Economic Journal*, June 1967, **5**, pp. 291–303.

Turner, D.F. and Williamson, O.E., 'Market structure in relation to technical and organizational innovation', in J.B. Heath, ed., *Proceedings of the International Conference on Monopolies, Mergers and Restrictive Practices*, London: HMSO, 1971, pp. 127–44.

US Department of Commerce, Office of Technical Services, *Patterns and Problems of Technical Innovation in American Industry*, Report to NSF by Arthur D. Little, Inc., September 1963, p. 150.

Uzawa, H., 'Time preference and the Penrose effect in a two-class model of economic growth', *Journal of Political Economy*, July/August 1969, **77**, Part II, pp. 628–52.

Van Horne, J.C. and McDonald, J.G., 'Dividend policy and new equity financing', *Journal of Finance*, May 1971, **26**, pp. 507–19.

Vanek, Jaroslav, *The General Theory of Labor-Managed Market Economies*, Ithaca: Cornell University Press, 1970.

Villard, Henry H., 'Competition, oligopoly, and research', *Journal of Political Economy*, December 1958, **66**, pp. 491–7.

Wagner, R.H., 'The concept of power and the study of politics', in Bell, Edwards and Wagner (1969), pp. 3–12.

Walker, J.L., 'Estimating companies' rate of return on capital employed', *Economic Trends*, November 1974, pp. 20–9.

Walker, James B., Jr, *Financing the Acquisition*, Financial Management Series, No. 114.

Weber, M., *The Theory of Social and Economic Organization*, T. Parsons, ed., New York: Free Press, 1947.

Weiner, J.B., 'What makes a "best managed" company', *Dun's Review of Modern Industry*, December 1963, **82**, pp. 40–8.

Wenders, J.T., 'Entry and monopoly pricing', *Journal of Political Economy*, October 1967, **75**, pp. 755–60.

Wenders, John T., 'Profits and antitrust policy: the question of disequilibrium', *Antitrust Bulletin*, Summer 1971a, **16**, pp. 249–56.

Wenders, John T., 'Deconcentration reconsidered', *Journal of Law and*

Economics, October 1971b, **14**, pp. 485–8.

Weston, J. Fred, 'A generalized uncertainty theory of profit', *American Economic Review*, March 1950, **40**, pp. 40–60.

Weston, J.F., *The Role of Mergers in the Growth of Large Firms*, Berkeley: University of California Press, 1953.

Weston, J. Fred, 'The nature and significance of conglomerate firms', *St John's Law Review*, Spring 1970, special edn., **44**, pp. 66–80.

Weston, J. Fred and Mansinghka, S. K., 'Tests of the efficiency performance of conglomerate firms', *Journal of Finance*, September 1971, **26**, pp. 919–36.

Weston, J.F., Smith, K.V. and Shrieves, R.E., 'Conglomerate performance using the capital asset pricing model', *Review of Economics and Statistics*, November 1972, **54**, pp. 357–63.

Whittington, G., 'The profitability of retained earnings', *Review of Economics and Statistics*, May 1972, **54**, pp. 152–60.

Williamson, John, 'Profit, growth and sales maximization', *Economica*, February 1966, **33**, pp. 1–16.

Williamson, Oliver E., 'Managerial discretion and business behavior', *American Economic Review*, December 1963, **53**, pp. 1032–57.

Williamson, Oliver E., *The Economics of Discretionary Behavior: Managerial Objectives in a Theory of the Firm*, Englewood Cliffs, NJ: Prentice-Hall, 1964.

Williamson, Oliver E., 'Hierarchical control and optimum firm size', *Journal of Political Economy*, April 1967, **75**, pp. 123–38.

Williamson, O.E., 'Economies as an antitrust defense: the welfare tradeoffs', *American Economic Review*, March 1968, **58**, pp. 18–36.

Williamson, O.E., 'Allocative efficiency and the limits of antitrust', *American Economic Review*, May 1969, **59**, pp. 105–18.

Williamson, Oliver E., *Corporate Control and Business Behavior: An Inquiry into the Effects of Organization Form on Enterprise Behavior*, Englewood Cliffs, NJ: Prentice-Hall, 1970.

Williamson, Oliver E., *Markets and Hierarchies: Analysis and Antitrust Implications*, New York: Free Press, 1975.

Williamson, Oliver E., 'Transaction cost economics: the governance of contractual relations', *Journal of Law and Economics*, October 1979, **22**, pp. 233–62.

Williamson, Oliver E., 'The organization of work: a comparative institutional assessment', *Journal of Economic Behavior and Organization*, March 1980, **1**, pp. 5–38.

Williamson, Oliver E., 'The modern corporation: origins, evolution, and attributes', *Journal of Economic Literature*, December 1981, **19**, pp. 1537–68.

Williamson, Oliver E., 'Organization form, residual claimants, and corporate control', *Journal of Law and Economics*, June 1983, **26**, pp. 351–66.

Williamson, Oliver E., 'The economics of governance: framework and implications', *Journal of Theoretical Economics*, March 1984, **140**, pp. 195–223.

Williamson, Oliver E., Wachter, M.L. and Harris, J., 'Understanding the employment relation: the analysis of idiosyncratic exchange', *Bell Journal of Economics*, Spring 1975, **6**, pp. 250–78.

Wilson, Robert, 'Informational economies of scale', *Bell Journal of Economics*, Spring 1975, **6**, pp. 184–95.

Winn, D.N. and Leabo, D.A., 'Rates of return, concentration and growth-question of disequilibrium', *Journal of Law and Economics*, April 1974, **17**, pp. 97–115.

Winter, Sidney G., 'Satisficing, selection, and the innovating remnant', *Quarterly Journal of Economics*, May 1971, **85**, pp. 237–61.

Wisecarver, D., 'The social costs of input-market distortions', *American Economic Review*, June 1974, **64**, pp. 359–72.

Wood, Adrian, 'Economic analysis of the corporate economy: a survey and critique', in Marris and Wood (1971), pp. 37–68.

Worcester, Dean A., Jr, 'A reconsideration of the theory of rent', *American Economic Review*, June 1946, **36**, pp. 258–77.

Worcester, D.A., Jr, 'Innovations in the calculations of welfare loss to monopoly', *Western Economic Journal*, September 1969, **7**, pp. 234–43.

Worcester, D.A., Jr, 'New estimates of the welfare loss to monopoly: U.S. 1956–69', *Southern Economic Journal*, October 1973, **40**, pp. 234–46.

Worcester, D.A., Jr, 'On monopoly welfare losses: comment', *American Economic Review*, December 1975, **65**, pp. 1015–23.

Yarrow, G.K., 'Managerial utility maximization under uncertainty', *Economica, N.S.*, May 1973, **40**, pp. 155–73.

Yarrow, G.K., 'On the predictions of managerial theories of the firm', *Journal of Industrial Economics*, June 1976, **24**, pp. 267–79.

Index